TOWARDS A SOCIAL INVESTMENT WELFARE STATE?

Ideas, policies and challenges

Edited by Nathalie Morel, Bruno Palier and Joakim Palme

This book has been published with the support of the European research project RECWOWE (Reconciling Work and Welfare in Europe), 2006–2011, co-funded by the European Commission, under the 6th Framework Programme for Research – Socio-economic Sciences and Humanities (contract nr 028339-2) in the Directorate-General for Research. The information and views set out in this book are those of the authors and do not necessarily reflect the official opinion of the European Union. Neither the European Union institutions and bodies nor any person acting on their behalf may be held responsible for the use which may be made of the information contained therein.

First published in Great Britain in 2012 by

The Policy Press   Tel +44 (0)117 331 4054
University of Bristol   Fax +44 (0)117 331 4093
Fourth Floor   e-mail tpp-info@bristol.ac.uk
Beacon House   www.policypress.co.uk
Queen's Road
Bristol BS8 1QU, UK

North American office:
The Policy Press   t: +1 773 702 7700
c/o The University of Chicago Press   f: +1 773-702-9756
1427 East 60th Street   e:sales@press.uchicago.edu
Chicago, IL 60637, USA   www.press.uchicago.edu

© The Policy Press 2012

British Library Cataloguing in Publication Data
A catalogue record for this book is available from the British Library.

Library of Congress Cataloging-in-Publication Data
A catalog record for this book has been requested.

ISBN 978 1 84742 925 4 paperback

Cover pictures and design by Elke Schröter.
Printed and bound in Great Britain by TJ International, Padstow
The Policy Press uses environmentally responsible print partners

Contents

Part IV Meeting the challenges ahead?

List of tables

List of figures

List of acronyms

ABM	*Arbeitsbeschaffungsmaßnahmen*
ALMP	active labour market policy
CDA	*Christen-Democratisch Appèl* (Christian Democratic Appeal in the Netherlands)
CEE	Central and Eastern Europe
CES	*Contrats emploi-solidarité*
CSD	UN Commission on Sustainable Development
CSU	*Christlich-Soziale Union in Bayern* (The Christian Social Union in Bavaria)
DL	discretionary learning
ECEC	early childhood education and care
EEA	European Environment Agency
EES	European Employment Strategy
EMU	European Monetary Union
ESF	European Social Fund
EU	European Union
EU-ETS	European Union Emissions Trading Scheme
FPD	*Freie Demokratische Partei* (Free Democratic Party in Germany)
FPÖ	*Freiheitliche Partei Österreichs* (The Freedom Party of Austria)
GDP	gross domestic product
GDR	German Democratic Republic
IALS	International Adult Literacy Survey
ICT	information and communication technology
IMF	International Monetary Fund
KIS	knowledge intensive services
MP	Member of Parliament
OECD	Organisation for Economic Co-operation and Development
ÖVP	*Österreichische Volkspartei* (The Austrian People's Party)
PES	public employment services
PIL	*Programmes d'insertion locale*
PLMP	passive labour market policy
PSOE	*Partido Socialista Obrero Español* (The Spanish Socialist Workers' Party)
PvdA	*Partij van de Arbeid* (Dutch Labour Party)
RMI	*Revenu minimum d'insertion*
RSA	*Revenu de solidarité active*
SI	social investment

SPD	*Sozialdemokratische Partei Deutschlands* (The Social Democratic Party of Germany)
TUC	*Travaux d'utilité publique*
UN	United Nations
UNESCO	United Nations Educational, Scientific and Cultural Organization
VVD	*Volkspartij voor Vrijheid en Democratie* (People's Party for Freedom and Democracy in the Netherlands)
WSSD	World Summit for Sustainable Development
WTO	World Trade Organization

Notes on contributors

The editors

Nathalie Morel is research associate at the Centre d'etudes européennes at Sciences Po, France. She has also worked as a post-doctoral researcher at the Institute for Futures Studies in Sweden. Her main research interest is comparative European social policy, with a special focus on child-care and elderly-care policies.

Bruno Palier is CNRS research director at Sciences Po, Centre d'études européennes. He is studying welfare reforms in Europe. He was the scientific coordinator of the European Network of excellence RECWOWE. He has published numerous articles on welfare reforms in France and in Europe and various books on welfare state reforms.

Joakim Palme is professor at the Department of Government, Uppsala University, and director of the Institute for Futures Studies in Stockholm. He has published a number of comparative studies on welfare state institutions, and the sources and consequences of cross-national variations in these institutions. His research interests also include the European Social Model, tensions between population changes and public policy, and social policy in a development context.

The contributors

Giuliano Bonoli is professor of social policy at the Swiss graduate school for public administration (IDHEAP) at the University of Lausanne. He has been involved in several national and international research projects on various aspects of social policy. His work has focused on pension reform, labour market and family polices, and the politics of welfare state transformation. He has published some 40 articles and chapters, as well as a few books.

Caroline de la Porte is associate professor at the Political Science department at the University of Southern Denmark. She is affiliated to the Centre for Welfare State Research and is coordinator of the department's 'Euro-politics' network. Her research interests are EU and national social policy reform, new modes of governance, the open method of coordination, and reforms in Central and Eastern European countries.

Patrick Diamond is Gwilym Gibbon Fellow at Nuffield College, Oxford, a visiting fellow in the Department of Politics at the University of Oxford, and a senior fellow of Policy Network. He is the former head of policy planning in 10 Downing Street and senior policy adviser to the Prime Minister.

Anton Hemerijck is dean of the Faculty of Social Sciences of the Free University of Amsterdam. He was the director of the Netherlands' Scientific Council for the Government Policy from 2001 to 2009. In 2012, Oxford University Press will publish his latest monograph, *Changing Welfare States*.

Kerstin Jacobsson is professor of sociology at Södertörn University, Sweden. Her research interests are soft forms of governance in the European Union, the Europeanisation of labour market policy, and social movements and social mobilisation in Central and Eastern Europe.

Jane Jenson was awarded the Canada Research Chair in Citizenship and Governance in 2001 at the Université de Montréal, where she is professor of political science. She is also member of the Successful Societies Programme of the Canadian Institute for Advanced Research. Her research interests include social policy and social citizenship in Canada and the European Union. She has published numerous books and articles, most recently in *Global Social Policy*, *Social Politics* and *Comparative European Politics*.

Roger Liddle is chair of Policy Network and a Labour member of the UK House of Lords. From 2009 to 2010 he chaired the UK government's New Industry, New Jobs, Universities and Skills advisory panel. He is a former economic adviser to European Commission President Jose Manuel Barroso and was Tony Blair's Europe adviser from 1997 to 2004.

Thomas Lindh is professor of labour economics at Linnaeus University in Växjö, and is also affiliated to the Institute for Futures Studies in Stockholm. His research has focused on age structure effects on the macroeconomy and intergenerational transfers. Currently he coordinates European research cooperation around National Transfer Accounts, an international project to map transfers across generations within the National Accounts framework.

Edward Lorenz received his BS from MIT, MA from UC Berkeley and PhD from the University of Cambridge. He is currently professor of economics at the University of Nice-Sophia Antipolis and assigned professor at the University of Aalborg. His research focuses on the comparative analysis of national innovation systems and the development of empirical indicators of organisational innovation and change.

Bengt-Åke Lundvall is professor in economics at the Department of Business Studies at Aalborg University in Denmark and at the International MPA programme at Sciences Po, Paris. His research is on innovation systems and the learning economy. He gives policy advice to governments and international organisations and he coordinates the global academic network Globelics.

Kimberly J. Morgan received her PhD from Princeton University and is associate professor of political science and international affairs at George Washington University. She is the author of two books, *Working Mothers and the Welfare State* (2006) and *The Delegated Welfare State: Medicare, Markets, and the Governance of American Social Policy* (2011). She is currently co-editing the *Oxford Handbook of the American Welfare State*.

Moira Nelson is *Oberassistentin* at the University of Berne, where she conducts research and teaches courses on comparative politics. Previous work has been published in *Comparative Education*, *Comparative Political Studies*, the *European Journal of Political Research* and the *Journal of European Social Policy*. Areas of interest include political parties, the welfare state and education policy.

Rita Nikolai is currently working as an assistant professor (*Juniorprofessur*) for the System-related School Research at the Humboldt-University Berlin in Germany. Her research interests include comparative education, especially school policy, educational governance, school autonomy and the relation between education and welfare policy in international comparison.

Lena Sommestad is professor of economic history and former Swedish minister for the environment (2002–6). She is currently affiliated to the Swedish Institute for Futures Studies. She has devoted most of her research to comparative studies on the history of work, industrial development, social policy and demography. Her assignments include membership of the Swedish Welfare Commmission, 1999–2001.

John D. Stephens is Lenski Professor, Political Science Department; Director, Center for European Studies, University of North Carolina, Chapel Hill. His main interests are comparative social policy and political economy. He is the author or co-author of four books including *Capitalist Development and Democracy* (with Evelyne Huber and Dietrich Rueschemeyer, 1992) and *Development and Crisis of the Welfare State* (with Evelyne Huber, 2001) and numerous journal articles.

Acknowledgements

This book is the outcome of a project which started in May 2009 with the organisation of a conference in Stockholm on the future of social investment. It was part of the Institute for Futures Studies' activities in connection with the Swedish EU presidency in the second half of 2009, and an attempt to contribute to the discussion of the post-Lisbon Agenda. The conference brought together scholars and policy makers from around Europe as well as from North America. Support for this conference was provided by the Nordic Centre of Excellence NordWel and we also benefited from the participation of the Policy Network and the Fondation Terra Nova. In 2010, NordWel, the Institute for Futures Studies, Sciences Po and the European Network of Excellence Recwowe provided support for two subsequent seminars, one in Stockholm in March and one in Paris in December, which allowed us to pursue the academic discussion around the social investment approach. We gratefully acknowledge the contributions of all those who in various ways contributed to the conference and the seminars. Jakob Larsson and Helena Rantanikunen deserve special thanks for their help with the organisation of the different events. The involvement of the Institute for Futures Studies has in all phases been facilitated by grant 2007-1037 from the Bank of Sweden Tercentenary Foundation. Special thanks are also due to Scott Bradford for doing the index, to Elsa Tirén for checking all the references and to Elke Schröter for designing the book cover for us.

Above all, we would like to express our deepest appreciation to the team of contributors whose amazing enthusiasm and strong commitment have carried this project forward in a very stimulating way!

The Editors

ONE

Beyond the welfare state as we knew it?

Nathalie Morel, Bruno Palier and Joakim Palme

The twentieth century may be called the century of the welfare state. It saw the emergence, expansion and maturation of the welfare state as we know it. Some have claimed that these developments represent a 'growth to limits' (Flora, 1986) and in a way this communicates a vision that we, at the turn of the century, were about to see the end of history, or at least the end of the welfare state evolution. However, we have learnt from the first decade of the twenty-first century that, not only does the welfare state appear to be here to stay, it is also subject to continued reform. This started already in the late 1990s, when various attempts were made to redefine the principles, goals and instruments of the welfare state to adapt it to the new socioeconomic context of the post-industrial era. Central to this new thinking is the emphasis that is placed on developing policies that aim at 'preparing' rather than 'repairing'. These ideas have been developed most notably in OECD (1996), Giddens (1998), Esping-Andersen et al. (2002) and Rodrigues (2003). While different terms and labels have been used (such as 'social development', 'the developmental welfare state', 'the social investment state', 'the enabling state' and 'inclusive liberalism'), all these analyses point towards a similar policy logic based on what can be labelled 'social investment'.

The social investment perspective is intended to sustain a different economy than that after 1945 – the knowledge-based economy. In this new economy, knowledge is considered as the driver of productivity and economic growth. The knowledge-based economy thus rests on a skilled and flexible labour force, which can easily adapt to the constantly changing needs of the economy but also be the motor of these changes. The social investment perspective also aims at modernising the post-war welfare state so as to better address the new social risks and needs structure of contemporary societies, such as single parenthood, the need to reconcile work and family life, lack of continuous careers, more precarious forms of contracts and possessing low or obsolete skills (Bonoli, 2005).

Consequently, the social investment approach rests on policies that both invest in human capital development (early childhood education and care, education and lifelong training) and that help to make efficient use of human capital (through policies supporting women's and lone parents' employment, through active labour market policies, but also through specific forms of labour market regulation and social protection institutions that promote flexible security), while fostering greater social inclusion (notably by facilitating access to the labour market for groups that have traditionally been excluded). Crucial to this new approach is the idea that social policies should be seen as a productive factor, essential to economic development and to employment growth. This represents a fundamental break from the neoliberal view of social policy as a cost and a hindrance to economic and employment growth.

This social investment perspective has underpinned the Lisbon Agenda, which the European Union adopted in 2000 with the aim of making Europe 'the most dynamic and competitive knowledge-based economy in the world, capable of sustainable economic growth with more and better jobs and greater social cohesion, and respect for the environment'. While this way of viewing social policies as a productive factor is novel at the EU level – and beyond that also at OECD level as the chapters by Hemerijck and by Jenson emphasise – this perspective has its roots as far back as the 1930s, in the ideas developed by Alva and Gunnar Myrdal in Sweden. However, the productive social policy approach promoted by the Myrdals did not impose itself as a paradigm outside of Sweden. Instead, Keynesian macroeconomic policies and social policy came to dominate, which meant that some of the productive aspects of social policy were cast aside. In the wake of the 1973 economic crisis, Keynesianism was thought to have demonstrated the limits of a demand-side approach. Neoliberals put forth a new supply-side economic paradigm, which involved a new view of social policy as a wasteful cost and as hampering economic growth. The turn since the late 1990s towards a social investment perspective, based on a new understanding of social policy as a productive factor, may well be the sign of the emergence of a new paradigm, in the way that Hall (1993) has defined the concept.[1]

In the first section of this chapter, we start by tracing the different approaches to social policy as they have developed over time, starting with the early origins of the social investment perspective in the Myrdals' 'productive social policy' approach put forward in Sweden in the 1930s, before turning to a brief analysis of the Keynesian and neoliberal eras of social policy. We then take a closer look at what has been going on since the late 1990s and suggest that the social investment perspective may represent an emerging social and economic policy paradigm.

In the second section, we review the different critiques that have been levelled at the social investment perspective. We then suggest that some of these critiques may be linked to some of the tensions and ambiguities embedded in the social investment perspective, which in part is a result of the different intellectual sources behind it.

In the third section we present the aims and focus of the book, which is to assess the achievements, shortcomings and potentials of social investment policies, to question whether the 'social investment' strategy is able to regenerate the welfare state, promote social inclusion, create more and better jobs, and help address the challenges posed by the economic crisis, globalisation, ageing and climate change. The final section presents the book's structure and contents.

The long road towards a social investment strategy

The early origins of the social investment perspective

The early origins of the social investment perspective can be traced back to the early years of the social-democratic Swedish welfare state. Against the background of the Great Depression and a severe fertility crisis, Alva and Gunnar Myrdal, two prominent Swedish social-democrats, developed a new conception of social policy oriented towards the efficient organisation of production and reproduction, and which viewed social policy as an investment rather than a cost. They developed their ideas in a number of reports and books, and most famously in their 1934 book *Kris i Befolkningsfrågan* (Crisis in the population question). Here they used the demographic argument to overcome the Conservatives' reticence towards the development of a more ambitious social policy. Turning around the Conservatives' concern with both the quantity and quality of the population, they put forward the argument that the decline in fertility was due to socioeconomic hardship brought about by industrialisation and fast urbanisation: children were no longer seen as extra labour on the farm, but as an extra cost for households and an extra burden in overcrowded housing. Policies were therefore needed to provide economic support to families – both through cash transfers and through policies supporting a dual breadwinner model – and to improve housing standards in order to promote fertility. But increasing fertility was not an aim in itself. More important than the 'quantity' of the population was its 'quality'. Here the Myrdals addressed the Conservatives' eugenic preoccupations with the quality of the

3

Swedish population by arguing that the 'quality of children' was not biologically determined, but linked to socioeconomic factors and to education (Appelqvist, 2007). Thus was it necessary to put in place a wide array of policies that would invest in the nation's human capital such as the development of quality day care, education, health care, economic support to families and policies to support women's labour force participation.

While the Myrdals addressed the demographic concerns of the time, their argument was also, in a period of deep economic crisis, very much linked to a concern with economic growth and productivity: without a healthy and educated population that also reproduced itself, the productivity of the economy could not be sustained. Social policy was presented not simply as a means for the provision of individual security and redistribution, but also for the efficient organisation of production. This new understanding of the role of social policy was encapsulated under the term 'productive social policy' which Gunnar Myrdal coined. As underlined by Andersson (2005), this concept indicates that the productive effects of resources devoted to social policy can be compared to the productive effects of resources devoted to productive activities as conventionally understood in classical economics. As such it constitutes in itself a critique of classical economics in which the productive effects of social policy cannot be measured or quantified. This new understanding of the interaction between social policy and economic growth became a guiding principle for Swedish social democracy from the 1930s onwards. While the emphasis was on developing policies to support human capital formation, the preservation of human capital through active labour market policies but also through unemployment compensation was regarded as equally important. Guaranteeing income security in particular was seen as a vital element in helping to overcome workers' fear of change and thus of economic restructuration.

As Esping-Andersen has argued, through this 'productive social policy' approach, Swedish social democracy succeeded in reconciling the dual goals of equality and efficiency which had hitherto been understood as conflicting goals:

> Equality was not promulgated as merely compatible with efficiency. It became, indeed, a precondition for its optimization: more equally distributed purchasing power is a precondition for macroeconomic performance; family policy is an investment in future human capital; the equalization of resources, such as health or education, is the foundation for optimal labor productivity; solidaristic

wage policy and active manpower programs spur industrial modernization; income security helps overcome workers' natural resistance to rationalization; and preventive social policy diminishes human waste and economic costs. (Esping-Andersen, 1992: 38)

What is particularly interesting is the way this 'productive social policy' perspective seemed to be able to resolve the tension between individual security and social solidarity on the one hand, and the collective interest of economic efficiency and individual productive participation on the other, that is to say the Marshallian dichotomy between rights and responsibilities (Andersson, 2005: 3). For Andersson, the concept of 'productive social policy' can thus be interpreted as an economic discursive defence of solidarity and individual security, advocating social rights with reference to their effects on economic efficiency (ibid, p. 4).

This productivist approach was in some respects similar to the Keynesian understanding of economic growth and social policy. As such, the rise of Keynesianism across the developed countries in the 1930–1940s provided an extra impetus for the productive social policy approach in Sweden. In other countries, however, Keynesian countercyclical demand-side macroeconomics came to dominate, with policies that were more oriented towards 'passive' social policies to promote and sustain demand in the here and now than towards human capital development and investments in the future.

The Keynesian era

As Hemerijck reminds us in Chapter Two, Keynesianism rose to prominence in the wake of the Great Depression and came to dominate macroeconomic policies across the developed world until the late 1970s. Keynesian economic theory offered a new understanding of the causes of slow growth and unemployment, linking them to problems of insufficient demand and of the natural tendency towards cyclical fluctuations of unfettered capitalism.

Keynes saw government intervention in the economy in the form of monetary and fiscal policy as necessary for the stability of the economy. Public spending in particular could function as an important regulator which could be used to stimulate the economy at a time of a slump or to dampen growth if it happened too quickly. In this respect, spending on welfare policy was seen as a particularly useful economic tool, helping to balance the economy in periods of recession.

Social policy thus had a positive economic role to play in that it could function in a countercyclical way by maintaining workers' wages in times of recession and therefore prop up demand and stimulate growth. Furthermore, Keynes argued, similarly to the Myrdals, that reducing income inequalities and investing in health and education were essential ingredients in boosting economic growth, which in turn provided the means for further expansion of social rights. For Keynes, far from being polar opposites, open markets and organised solidarity prospered together. Welfare state construction and expansion, together with significant declines in income inequalities, came to be viewed as essential ingredients in any strategy to boost economic growth (see Chapter Two).

While Keynesianism shared with the Myrdals' productive social policy approach a belief in the mutually reinforcing qualities of social policy and economic growth, and of equality and efficiency, the two approaches also differ on a number of points.

For one thing, the kind of welfare state development that Keynesianism promoted was, as Hemerijck (Chapter Two) reminds us, 'as much progressive in design, based on organized labour support and class compromise, as it was conservative in intent'. Unlike the Myrdals' emphasis on supporting female labour market participation and gender equality, and on promoting children's wellbeing and social rights, Keynesian employment and social policies very much supported the traditional family and the male breadwinner model in which men's employment opportunities were in focus, along with men's social rights. While women and children also benefited from social benefits, this was through their link to a male breadwinner (see also Chapter Three).

Keynesianism is also founded on a different notion of time than that associated with the productive social policy approach. In the latter approach, social policy was more explicitly conceptualised as an *investment*, which would yield returns not just in the present (propping up demand) but also in the future (notably through investment in the education and health of young children, and through investment in human capital more generally). In the Keynesian perspective, on the contrary, as Jenson reminds us (Chapter Three), 'the here-and-now was the most important timeframe and social citizenship focused on inequalities, inequities and challenges of the present that would be addressed in the present. The countercyclical economic instruments obviously supported such a notion of time.' The social policies developed under the Keynesian epoch were thus mainly 'passive' social policies to promote and sustain demand, notably through the development of cash-transfer programmes in the form of social insurances.

There are exceptions to this passive approach, though. In Sweden in the 1950s, the active labour market policy approach formulated as part of the Rehn-Meidner model appears to be a parallel track inspired by Schumpeter as much as by the Myrdal legacy. Following Schumpeter, the Rehn-Meidner model was actually designed to reinforce the destructive forces of capitalism in order to promote the establishment of new and more wealth-creating structures but, following the Myrdals, the model also provided the policy instruments for equipping the workers of the old structures with skills and other resources that would enable them not only to access but also to gain from the new structures.

The neoliberal era

Following the economic crisis of 1974 and Keynesian economic theory's incapacity to explain and respond to the simultaneous rise in both unemployment and inflation, Keynesian economic policies came under severe attack from proponents of neoliberal macroeconomic theory, ultimately leading to a paradigmatic shift from Keynesianism to monetarism (Hall, 1993). The new neoliberal paradigm placed the emphasis on budgetary rigour, wage restraint, monetarism and corporate competitiveness (Jobert, 1994). In this macroeconomic thinking, social expenditures no longer played a central role in ensuring economic growth. In fact, social policies became portrayed as a cost rather than a stimulator of economic growth or a promoter of political and social stability. The Keynesian notion that there was no tradeoff between social security and economic growth, or between equality and efficiency, was rejected. For neoliberals, inequalities were inherent in markets and in fact necessary to motivate economic actors.

For neoclassical economists, high unemployment and low growth were the consequences of labour market rigidities. Unemployment was thus interpreted as a microeconomic problem of market distortions linked to strong job protection, high minimum wages and generous unemployment insurance, rather than as a macroeconomic problem of insufficient demand (cf. OECD, 1994, 1997). Generous social policy was held responsible for poor job-search motivation and for creating a culture of dependency (see also Chapter Two). The understanding of the causes of unemployment and slow growth, and thus the remedies put forward, therefore shifted from a demand-side to a supply-side approach.

Such a view was accompanied by a growing demand for the role of the state to be rolled back, since it was perceived as too costly and inefficient, and for a reallocation of social responsibilities towards other social actors, such as the market, the family or community associations (see Chapter Three).

While social policies were not dismantled as such, a new orientation towards *activation* was given to social policy. Less emphasis was placed on providing income security and more focus was placed on providing incentives (in a more or less coercive fashion) to return to the labour market.

Finally, as underlined by Jenson (see Chapter Three), unlike Keynesian social policy, which argued for the use of public spending to alleviate poverty and inequalities and to support demand in the here and now, the neoliberal perspective was much more oriented towards the future: the argument against public spending and public deficits was made in the name of future generations whose wellbeing should not be mortgaged; and the argument in favour of policies to curb wage increases, diminish job protection and to increase corporate profit margins was made in the name of the jobs this would create in the future. As famously coined by former German Chancellor Helmut Schmidt: 'today's profits will be tomorrow's investments, which will create the jobs for the day after tomorrow'.

The social investment perspective on the policy agenda

Starting in the late 1990s, new ideas concerning the role and shape of social policy and its role in relation to the economy began to emerge (Jenson and Saint Martin, 2003; Perkins et al., 2004; see also Chapters Two and Three in this volume).

While there is no unified theory and no single intellectual source behind these new ideas, and while different labels have been used (such as 'social development', 'the developmental welfare state', 'the social investment state', 'the enabling state', 'inclusive liberalism' or, the term we have chosen here, the 'social investment perspective'), these different conceptions have in common the fact that they stress the productive potential of social policy and thus provide a new economic rationale for social policy provision.

These ideas developed partly as a critique of neoliberalism, but in some ways they also build on the neoliberal critique of the traditional post-war welfare state. Above all, the ideas put forward are based on an understanding that social policies need to respond to a radically changed economic and social order.

The increasing polarisation and poverty rates, including in-work poverty, which appeared – especially in those countries that had gone furthest in implementing neoliberal policies – and the growing problem and cost of social exclusion, gave rise to a critique of neoliberal social prescriptions.

At the same time, the traditional post-war male-breadwinner welfare state came under increasing criticism, not least from social policy analysts who argued that the 'old' welfare state was ill-equipped to deal with the transition to post-industrialism, the social and demographic transformations of families and society, and the resulting emergence of new social risks. In this respect, the conservative welfare regimes of continental Europe have been especially singled out, both for their failure in responding to changing social risks and needs, and for their seeming inability to create jobs. Likewise, the financial sustainability of these welfare states, and their capacity not to mortgage the wellbeing of future generations, has been severely questioned (Esping-Andersen, 1996, 1999; Scharpf and Schmidt, 2000; Esping-Andersen et al., 2002).

Traditional forms of 'passive' social policy intervention of the post-war welfare state have moreover come to be presented as out of kilter with the needs of the new economy, often described as the 'knowledge economy'. It is argued that to succeed in this 'knowledge economy' it is necessary to have a highly skilled and educated workforce, who can quickly adapt to the constantly changing needs of the economy, and who is also the motor of this change thanks to its creative and innovative potential. In this thinking, unemployment is linked to a lack of adequate skills to fill today's jobs, and this lack of adequate skills and education is also expected to stymie future economic growth and employment creation, unless the necessary investments are made to foster human capital development (OECD, 1997; EU, 2000, 2009).

These different criticisms have led to calls for a modernisation of welfare systems in order to address the issue of growing poverty and social exclusion, to better respond to the new needs and new social risk structures of contemporary society, to make welfare systems sustainable, and to make them 'productive' in the sense that they should promote and support employment and economic growth. Central to this modernisation of welfare systems is the idea that social policy should aim at 'preparing' the population to prevent certain social and economic risks associated with changing employment conditions and family patterns, and to minimise the intergenerational transfer of poverty, rather than at 'repairing' through passive income maintenance schemes after the risk has occurred.

As such, social expenditure should be rechannelled from passive to active social policies. In this sense, the social investment perspective shares with neoliberalism the notion that social spending should be directed towards activating people in order to allow individuals and families to maintain responsibility for their wellbeing via market incomes, rather than towards passive benefits (see Chapter Three). However, while the social investment perspective retains the focus on activation that neoliberalism instituted, there is a shift away from the idea that 'any jobs' are good and that social benefits should be scaled back so as to 'make work pay'. Instead, the idea is that social policy should help to 'make work pay' through positive economic incentives (by improving net income for those who work, first of all at the bottom end of the wage distribution), and that it should assist in promoting the creation of 'quality jobs'.

Therefore, where Keynesian and neoliberal macroeconomic policy share in common a purely quantitative understanding of work and labour (Keynesians aim at creating demand for jobs in general while neoliberal economists aim at increasing the supply of labour in general), the social investment perspective focuses more attention on the processes through which labour is transformed (through upskilling and learning).

While the social investment perspective maintains a belief in the efficacy of the market system (Perkins et al., 2004: 2), it qualifies in important respects the neoliberal belief that unfettered markets are necessarily the most appropriate and efficient organising principle in all circumstances. The social investment perspective acknowledges the importance of market failures and the need for government intervention and direction of market forces in order to improve both economic and social outcomes. As underlined by Jenson (Chapter Three), contrary to neoliberalism, the social investment perspective is based on a more positive theory of the state. While the state is still portrayed as a dynamic entrepreneur, it is expected to have the public interest in mind (Giddens, 1998). Furthermore, the state is assigned a key role in fostering the development of human capital (through investments in education and training) and in providing the necessary services and benefits to help make efficient use of human capital (policies providing support for labour market participation, particularly among categories such as lone parents and young parents, for example, day care services) and to avoid human capital depletion (provision of in-work benefits, rather than social assistance or allowances, as well as support for job training and job searches (in addition to unemployment insurance)).

While the social investment perspective displays some continuity with the social thinking of neoliberalism, it nonetheless breaks away from the neoliberal paradigm on a number of key points. Most importantly, social investment proponents have renewed with the Keynesian idea that it is possible to reconcile efficiency with equity, or growth with social inclusion.

The policies put forward for achieving this differ from the Keynesian epoch in a number of ways, however, the focus being more on the life cycle and on the future than on equality of outcomes in the present. Indeed, one of the main aims of the social investment approach is to minimise the *intergenerational* transfer of poverty (Chapter Three), but also to promote the intergenerational transmission of knowledge. While the policies put forward focus on promoting equal opportunity in the present (by facilitating access to education and training and to the labour market), this is expected to produce benefits in the future in terms of a reduction in the intergenerational transfer of poverty and inequalities, but also in terms of economic and employment growth. Indeed, not only are social policy and economic growth seen as mutually reinforcing, social policy is in fact seen as a *precondition* for economic growth.

By emphasising the economic benefits for society of new forms of social policy that invest in human capital, the social investment perspective renews the concept of 'productive social policy' put forward by the Myrdals in Sweden in the 1930s. In fact, the European Commission has been using that concept of 'productive social policy' since 1997, when the Dutch EU presidency staged a high-level conference entitled 'Social Policy as Productive Factor' which set the scene for the EU's new *Social policy agenda* (see Chapter Two). The economic arguments in favour of considering social policy as a productive factor have since then been put forward most notably in a report for the Employment and Social Affairs DG entitled 'Costs of non-social policy: towards an economic framework of quality social policies – and the costs of not having them' (Fouarge, 2003).

Social investment as a new policy paradigm?

In order to highlight the main differences between the Keynesian and neoliberal paradigms and the social investment perspective, we summarise in Table 1.1 the key characteristics of each approach according to four dimensions that have been identified in the literature as characterising policy paradigms: (1) the diagnosis of the problems (understanding of the causes of unemployment and relation between social policy and the economy); (2) the values and principles pursued; (3) the norms for public action; and (4) the instruments used (cf. Jobert and Muller, 1987; Hall, 1993; Mandin and Palier, 2004).

Table 1.1: Paradigms, principles and policies summarised and compared

	Keynesian paradigm	Neoliberal paradigm	Social investment perspective
Diagnosis on unemployment	Unemployment and slow growth due to insufficient demand	Unemployment and inflation due to constrained supply because of labour market rigidities (excessively high labour costs, too much labour regulation, social benefits acting as work disincentives)	Unemployment linked to lack of adequate skills to fill today's jobs and to create the jobs of tomorrow.
Social policy and the economy	Positive economic role of social policy: development of social insurances to prop up demand and stimulate growth	Negative economic role of public social expenditure: the welfare state as a cost and as the cause of slow growth and inflation	Positive economic role of new forms of social policy: social policies that invest in human capital to increase employability and employment levels; to support labour market fluidity (flex-security); to prepare for the 'knowledge-based' economy **Social policy as a precondition for economic growth and job creation**
Key values and principles	• Social equality • Jobs for all (men) • Decommodification	• Individual responsibility • Any jobs • Activation	• Social inclusion • Quality jobs • Capabilities approach: Equality of opportunity; 'Prepare rather than repair'

Key norms for public action	• Big state • Central economic planning • Welfare state development	• Lean state • Deregulation • Dismantling of the welfare state	• Empowering state • Investment • Recasting of the welfare state
Key instruments	• Policies to support demand • Development of social insurance schemes for income maintenance • Development of the public sector • Unemployment compensation	• Monetarist economic policies to fight inflation • Deregulation of the labour market • Privatisation of social and health services, development of capitalisation to finance pension schemes • Activation and workfare	• Human capital investment policies to increase competitiveness and job creation • Development of social services and policies to support the labour market: early childhood education and care; higher education and life-long training; active labour market policies; policies to support women's employment • Flex-security

As this brief account of the different periods of welfare state development shows, perspectives on the link between social policy and the economy have varied substantially over time, reflecting different dominating policy paradigms. While there is generally a wide consensus on describing the post-war period until the mid-1970s as that of Keynesianism (cf. Hall, 1989) and the period since the mid-1970s as that of neoliberalism (cf. Jobert, 1994), it is not yet clear whether the social investment perspective that has been put forward since the late 1990s can be considered as forming a new policy paradigm.

While there is certainly a shared new set of ideas that have spread across the international community (at the level of international organisations such as the OECD, UNICEF, EU, World Bank – cf. Mahon, 2008; Jenson, 2010 and Chapter Three) and that have been circulated through an international epistemic community and integrated in the discourses and practices of most European governments, and while there seems to be a certain convergence on the understanding of the nature of the problems these new ideas and policies are meant to be addressing, it is not yet entirely clear that there is a shared belief in the failure of neoliberalism as an economic paradigm to address the economic and social challenges of the early twenty-first century.

As we have seen, whereas neoliberalism is fundamentally at odds with Keynesianism with respect to macroeconomic theory, the social investment perspective shows more continuity with neoliberalism, even if it does depart from neoliberal economic and political theory on some key points.

The severe economic crisis that broke out in 2008 may, however, provide the necessary trigger for a more profound questioning of present macroeconomic policies, and thus open the way for a paradigmatic change in which the social investment perspective could serve as the new reference. In Chapter Fourteen we will discuss what we believe to be still missing from the social investment perspective to become a new policy paradigm, and the conditions under which it could become the new paradigm for the twenty-first century.

In the meantime we prefer to talk about social investment as an 'emerging paradigm', and choose to use the expression 'social investment perspective' or 'social investment strategy' in the book to designate the new ideas and policies that have been promoted since the late 1990s.

The critiques of the social investment perspective

While a fairly wide consensus around the social investment perspective seems to have been established at the international level and in some European countries, this approach has also attracted critiques from different academics. As we shall see, some of these critiques relate to problems linked to the implementation of the social investment strategy, but some of the critiques also hit more at the core of the social investment perspective itself.

A first set of critiques relates to the socioeconomic consequences of the social investment strategy's focus on the future. Briefly stated, the argument is that the focus on investing for future returns by rechannelling expenditure from 'passive' social security benefits (not least unemployment benefits) to activation and spending in the fields of family-oriented services and education has meant not only that today's poor have been left aside, but more critically that such a rechannelling has increased poverty in many countries as social spending has become less adequate in relieving poverty and as its redistributive profile has become less 'pro-poor' (and is more oriented towards 'work-rich' rather than 'work-poor' families) (Cantillon, 2010).

A second critique, to some extent linked to the one just outlined, has to do with the strong emphasis on activation that characterises the social investment perspective and which has both offered a justification for cutting back on benefits that previously allowed certain groups to remain outside the labour market (such as lone parents or people on long-term sickness leave) and also meant that the issue of the quality of work has been sidelined in favour of 'any jobs'. As Bonoli shows (Chapter Seven), active labour market policies have represented more of a continuation of neoliberal 'workfare' policies than a shift towards upskilling and the development of 'more and *better* jobs'.

A third critique concerns the way the social inclusion or social cohesion aspect seems to have been paid lip service in the actual implementation of the strategy, not least at the EU level, despite the Lisbon Strategy's stated dual objectives of enhancing both economic and social cohesion, between and within member countries. Indeed, the policy instruments appear to have been underdeveloped in strategic terms, as well as in terms of resource allocation (cf. Kap and Palme, 2009; Lundvall and Lorenz, Chapter 13).

A more fundamental critique has been put forward by feminists and gender theorists, who have highlighted the kind of instrumentalisation of gender equality policies, and especially policies for reconciling work and family life, that the social investment strategy has given rise to. Indeed, several commentators have noted how the focus on increasing women's employment levels has been motivated by economic objectives (to raise the number of tax payers and thus ensure the sustainability of the new political economy) rather than by a real concern with women's aspirations. Stratigaki (2004), for example, has shown, based on a content analysis of EU documents, how the concept of 'reconciliation of working and family life' which was introduced to encourage gender equality in the labour market gradually shifted in meaning from an objective with feminist potential (sharing family responsibilities between women and men) to a market-oriented objective (encouraging flexible forms of employment) as it became incorporated in the European Employment Strategy of the 1990s – the European Employment Strategy being a central pillar of the Lisbon Strategy, itself very much based on the social investment perspective (cf. Chapters Two and Five). Jenson has also highlighted some of the ambiguities linked to this strategy's focus on the future: while it addresses the needs of children, including girls, the focus on the future means that the situation of women today is not really addressed, other than in their reproductive capacity. Indeed, demographic concerns and the need to encourage fertility have underpinned the discourse around reconciliation policies. The policies pursued to raise female employment levels while enabling them to have children have therefore not had gender equality as their prime objective, despite gender equality having been a central element in the social investment discourse (Jenson, 2009).

This gender critique feeds into an even broader concern with the way social goals and the social citizenship rights perspective that underpins the social investment approach have been harnessed to an economic agenda. Not only has gender equality been instrumentalised in favour of economic objectives, but also children have become instrumentalised as 'citizen-workers' of the future rather than as 'citizen-children' of the present, that is, as 'becomings' rather than as 'beings' with social rights in their own right, as (non-productive) children (Lister, 2003). It would seem as though conventional redistributive arguments based on conceptions of need, altruism, equality and social rights no longer provide a sufficient rationale for the welfare state. Instead, the social or humanitarian rationale for social policy has been replaced by an economic rationale. As Midgley and Tang have pointed out: 'the social investment perspective challenges the tenets of neoliberal thinking about economic growth and social policy not by defensively claiming that the abolition of state welfare will cause suffering and social harm, or by appealing to a humanitarian concern for those in need'. Instead, 'it makes the argument that retrenchments in social welfare will impede economic development. Its central premise, which is based on the need to integrate economic and social policy, posits that social expenditures in the form of social investments do not detract from but contribute positively to economic development' (Midgley and Tang, 2001: 246).

In some ways, one could argue that just as the Myrdals had used some of the Conservatives' concerns with low fertility and slow growth to argue their case for an expansion of social policy in Sweden, so have social investment proponents framed their arguments in ways that can respond to neoliberals' critique of social spending as wasteful and a source of dependency in order to get their ideas across. However that might be, this may in fact be one of the social investment perspective's weakest points as it allows for much ambiguity and tensions in the goals actually assigned to the policies implemented in its name.

These tensions and ambiguities may, however, also stem from the differing intellectual and political sources and influences that have shaped this perspective. Indeed, while the social investment perspective rests on a number of common themes both at the ideational level and in terms of the policy instruments put forward, different aspects are given different emphasis by different thinkers and policy makers.

Tracing some of the ambiguities and tensions in the social investment perspective

At the ideational level, sources of inspiration for the social investment perspective can be found in the works of economists as diverse as Gary Becker and James Heckman with their work on human capital, and Amartya Sen and his capabilities approach.

Likewise, arguments for a recasting of the welfare state along the lines of a social investment strategy have been made by social-democratic academics and policy makers such as Gøsta Esping-Andersen or Frank Vandenbroucke, as well as by Third Way intellectuals such as Anthony Giddens.

While their respective analyses share some common understandings of some of the shortcomings and inadequacies of the post-war welfare state with respect to the new social risks structure of contemporary societies and the requirements of the new knowledge-based economy, and while they do display some common policy orientations, they also diverge on a number of key issues.

At the core of this divergence lies a different understanding of the role and meanings of social citizenship in the knowledge-based economy. This different understanding revolves around five key points.

First, there is a different understanding of what constitutes productive and unproductive social expenditure. In the Third Way perspective, spending on unemployment benefits for instance is considered as an unproductive social expenditure, whereas in the social-democratic perspective, such benefits can be seen as a means of protecting the human capital of working adults and of preventing the unemployed from being caught up in a spiral of debt and poverty.

Second, and linked to the first point, there is a different understanding of what constitutes positive and negative incentives – and perhaps beyond that a different understanding of human nature. Generous benefits, according to Giddens, increase the risks of 'moral hazard' and of fraud. This theory according to which a generous welfare state generates fraud and social dependency constitutes one of the most significant points of cleavage between Giddens and other European (social-democratic) social reformers (Jobert, 2002). Esping-Andersen et al. (2002), for instance, argue that generous unemployment benefits limit the risk of falling into poverty and are more favourable to a quick return into employment as long as they are coupled to an adequate activation policy.

Accordingly, this leads to a divergence in the weight that is placed on rights and duties respectively. For Giddens, the recasting of the welfare state is very much about reinforcing the duties side of social citizenship, whereas the social-democratic perspective emphasises the productive effects of the rights side of social citizenship (which was central to the Myrdals' approach).

Likewise, the notion of 'equality' is viewed very differently. While equality is seen as a central ingredient for the pursuit of economic efficiency and reducing inequality is presented as an explicit aim of the social investment strategy in the thinking of Esping-Andersen et al. and of Vandenbroucke (Vandenbroucke and Vleminckx, 2011), Giddens considers the quest for equality to be the historical mistake of the old Left (Jobert, 2002; see also Blair and Schröder, 2000). Giddens explicitly shares with neoliberal thinkers the notion that inequalities are a necessary ingredient for the dynamism of the economy. The emphasis for Giddens then is on promoting equality of opportunity, and on pursuing the goal of 'social justice'.

Finally, the role assigned to social policy differs. Conceived to act as a 'springboard' for change in the Third Way approach (with the 'spring' coming from both investments in human capital and the strong (negative) incentives towards activation), in the social-democratic variant social policy is expected to provide people with both the necessary capabilities and incentives *and* with the necessary security to accompany the changing needs of the economy (cf. Andersson, 2007).

Thus for Giddens and the Third Way, welfare state restructuring is about going from 'passive' social policies to 'active' social policies, whereas in the social-democratic approach put forward by Esping-Andersen et al. and Vandenbroucke, the new welfare state architecture must rest on *both* an 'investment strategy' and a 'protection strategy' (cf. Vandenbroucke and Vleminckx, 2011), what Hemerijck calls combining social protection and social promotion (see Chapter Two). In fact, Esping-Andersen explicitly takes a stance against the Third Way approach, stating that:

> The Third way may be criticized for its unduly selective appropriation of social democratic policy. First, it has the tendency to believe that activation may substitute for conventional income maintenance guarantees. This may be regarded as naïve optimism, but, worse, it may also be counterproductive ... [T]he minimization of poverty and income security is a precondition for an effective social investment strategy. Second, ... a truly effective and sustainable social investment strategy must be biased towards preventative policy. (Esping-Andersen, 2002: 5, quoted in Vandenbroucke and Vleminckx, 2011: 4)

The social investment perspective thus covers under the same umbrella a 'social democratic' approach, inspired by the example of the Nordic welfare states, and a 'Third Way' approach which represents an 'anglo-liberal' view of social policy. The resulting ambiguity of this perspective is perhaps what has enabled its broad adoption at the EU level, as part of the Lisbon Strategy. As Jenson (2010: 73) has highlighted, policy communities have been able to appeal to one version or the other, or even combine the two.

Aims and focus of the book

The aims of this book are to analyse the content and coherence of the ideas put forward in this new perspective, but also to assess how far the social investment strategy has actually come in terms of the policies effectively implemented.

While there are a growing number of publications dealing with the social investment perspective (under different labels), these publications have mainly been of two types. A first set of more normative publications has sought to promote social investment and a new architecture for the welfare state, highlighting the positive, win–win aspects of this strategy (Giddens, 1998; Esping-Andersen et al., 2002; Rodrigues, 2003). A second set of publications has been concerned with analysing the ideas and policy logic behind the social investment strategy, as well as its diffusion (Jenson and St Martin, 2003; Perkins et al., 2004; Jenson, 2010). However, there is to date no extensive analysis of the actual contents and implementation of social investment policies and of their successes, tensions, contradictions or failures. Likewise, the conditions for success or the obstacles in implementing a social investment strategy are largely understudied.

This book therefore seeks to contribute to filling these gaps by offering an empirically informed assessment of social investment policies, analysing their successes and failures, contradictions, tensions and synergies, and looking at the factors that facilitate or impede the implementation of social investment policies.

Our geographical focus

Since we consider the social investment perspective as an emerging paradigm, we adopt a broad lens in the first few chapters in the book so as to provide a qualitative and quantitative mapping of the development of social investment ideas and policies across the OECD countries.

However, we then narrow our focal length to the European context, not only because this is where we find the most developed welfare states, but also because there have been some explicit objectives set by the European Union, most notably through the Lisbon Agenda, that are very much inspired by the social investment perspective. Indeed, as Hemerijck reminds us, the Lisbon Strategy represented an attempt to relaunch the idea of the positive complementarities between equity and efficiency in the knowledge-based economy by way of investing in people and developing an active and dynamic welfare state. In addition to the aim of raising employment rates throughout Europe, the Lisbon Agenda placed human capital, research, innovation and development at the centre of European social and economic policy. This broadened the notion of social policy as a productive factor beyond its traditional emphasis on social protection, to include social promotion and improving the quality of training and education. There is thus a strong political relevance in assessing the achievements and failures of the policies promoted in the European countries, not least now that a new strategy (EU2020) is being put into place.

European countries also represent by and large an instance of 'most comparable cases'. Detailed examination of some European countries, as provided in Part III of this book, allows for a more precise analysis of the institutional, political and ideational causes of divergence in the absorption and implementation of this emerging social investment paradigm.

The analytical task of this book

The analytical task of this book is thus not only to uncover the policy logic behind this emerging social investment paradigm, but also to analyse the policies that have effectively been implemented in Europe: to what extent has the social investment perspective shaped policy making at the European and national level? What are the different varieties of social investment policies? What have been the driving forces or barriers for the adoption and implementation of such policies in different countries? What have been the achievements and failures of this strategy?

The book also addresses the social investment perspective's potential in responding to some of the current and future challenges that welfare states are facing, such as population ageing; the global financial crisis; the impact of migration, integration and identity on social citizenship and cohesion; and environmental concerns and the threats of climate change.

Presentation of the book structure and contents

The book is divided into four parts. The first part is devoted to the analysis of the ideas carried by the social investment perspective. The second part seeks to map the progress of the social investment policies throughout the most advanced and richest market economies and more specifically in Europe. The third part presents some detailed analyses and assessment of specific social investment policies. Finally, the last part provides various points of view on the future challenges that the social investment approach needs to meet in order to become a fully fledged social policy paradigm for Europe. In the following, we summarise the purpose and contents of the four parts and remaining 13 chapters of the book.

The first part of the book develops a historical perspective on social and economic policies, identifying three time periods each dominated by an overarching paradigm (a Keynesian policy paradigm, a neoliberal policy paradigm, and what we analyse in this book as the emerging social investment paradigm). It presents the ideas behind the social investment perspective, the way these ideas have spread and the kind of policy content associated to these ideas.

In Chapter Two, Anton Hemerijck analyses the three distinct phases of welfare state reconfiguration: the era of welfare state expansion and class compromise, starting at the end of World War II; the period of welfare retrenchment and neoliberalism, which took shape in the wake of the oil shocks of the mid- to late 1970s, and the more recent epoch since the mid-1990s in which social investment policy prescriptions took root. He provides us with an understanding of each period as marked by distinctive social policy repertoires, anchored in hegemonic economic theories, designed to respond to both the socioeconomic and the political contexts and challenges of the day. Importantly, this chapter analyses the economic thinking that can be associated to the social investment perspective.

In Chapter Three, Jane Jenson documents the characteristics of the social investment perspective in comparison to two other policy paradigms: those of Keynesianism and neoliberalism. In order to map the ideal-typical characteristics of social citizenship under the influence of a social investment perspective, the chapter uses the heuristic of the citizenship regime, an analytic grid that makes visible the intersecting dimensions of social citizenship (rights and duties; access and governance; and the responsibility mix).

While the first part of the book traces the development of the ideas behind the social investment paradigm, **the second part** offers an empirical analysis of the development of the policies that underpin the social investment perspective. The two chapters of this section provide us with a measure of the extent to which these policies have actually developed and in which countries. These chapters open up for an analysis of the differences between welfare regimes in pursuing a social investment strategy, while also highlighting some intra-regime variations.

In Chapter Four, Rita Nikolai traces the development of welfare state change in the established OECD member states and provides a quantitative mapping of the development of social investment policies in 21 advanced OECD countries from the mid-1980s up to 2007. The analysis takes into account expenditures for families, active labour market policies, education, old age and passive labour market policies. The chapter distinguishes between investment and compensatory social spending as a tool to identify social investment states, and shows a great diversity in the combinations of these types of expenditure, underlining that in the majority of welfare systems social investment-related expenditures have not expanded. Nikolai underlines that amongst social expenditures, it is those devoted to old age that have increased over the last 25 years, while spending on education has decreased. Moreover, amongst the various routes to social investment, she identifies two main ways: a Nordic one, which combines traditional social protection with social investment; and an Anglo-Saxon one, which tends to substitute traditional compensatory spending with new investments in human capital.

In Chapter Five, Caroline de la Porte and Kerstin Jacobsson deliver a more qualitative mapping of the social investment policies in the European Union through an analysis of the national implementation of the European Employment Strategy (EES). The chapter assesses the progress made thus far as well as the remaining challenges in a number of selected member states from different welfare state configurations, with the main focus on the changes in labour market policy. In terms of the employment policies implemented in Europe since the late 1990s, de la Porte and Jacobsson see much more 'recommodification' than social investment. The chapter shows how the impact of the EES is mediated by institutional legacies, economic and financial situations and political priorities and agendas in the member states. It is argued that the contradictory pressures for social and economic reform from the EU pose a strong challenge for all member states, but in particular for the new member states which have been pursuing a reform path with at best a very modest investment content.

The chapters in **the third part** of the book look at the forms taken by social investment policies in different national settings and try to account for the differences observed. These chapters also provide an assessment of how successful social investment policies are in achieving the stated aims of promoting growth, more and better jobs, and in reconciling economic and social aims (efficiency and equity). In doing so, this section also highlights the tensions, contradictions and limits of social investment policies as they have developed so far, as well as the obstacles faced by certain countries. In particular, attention is drawn to the fact that the way institutions are shaped and the way they interact contributes to providing more or less favourable preconditions and outcomes for a social investment strategy. The different chapters also underline how important it is that equality, not least gender equality, becomes an essential element of the social investment strategy: the analyses show that it is both a precondition for its success and an expected outcome.

In Chapter Six, Kimberly Morgan analyses the development of child care and work–family reconciliation policies in three groups of countries: (1) countries where early childhood education and care policies are well-developed (Sweden and France); (2) path-shifting countries who in the past decade or so have broken from decades of entrenched immobility on child care and leave time policy (Germany, the Netherlands and the UK); (3) countries which so far have not developed any such policies (Austria, Italy and Spain). The chapter characterises the nature of the recent changes that have taken place, compares these reforms to the social investment ideals that are commonly articulated, and then probes the political forces driving these reforms. It shows that the policies that have been implemented have not always been designed in the most gender egalitarian way, and that gender equality and the quality of child care have often been sacrificed in the name of labour market participation.

In Chapter Seven, Giuliano Bonoli examines the different types of active labour market policies (ALMPs) that have been in use in Europe since the 1950s from the perspective of social investment. He argues that ALMP is too broad a category to be used without further specification, and develops a typology of four different types of ALMPs: incentive reinforcement, employment assistance, occupation and human capital investment. These are discussed and examined through ALMP expenditure profiles and policy trajectories in Denmark, Italy, Germany, France, Sweden and the UK. The chapter shows that the orientation of ALMP changes over time, and follows the overall economic and labour market context. It identifies three periods: the 1950s and 1960s, when labour shortage prompts countries to develop ALMP systems geared towards retraining jobless people so that they can be available for industry again; from the mid-1970s to the mid-1990s, when ALMPs tend to become alternatives to market employment and the mid-1990s to the late 2000s, when the main orientation of policy is activation, that is, a mix of negative and positive incentives for jobless people to enter mostly low-skill employment in the service sector. He concludes that social investment oriented programmes have a stronger representation in the earliest phase, while the later phase is more ambivalent in relation to this perspective.

In Chapter Eight, Moira Nelson and John Stephens test the ability of the social investment strategy to produce employment and particularly employment in high-quality jobs. In order to do so, they examine the impact of social investment (in skill) policies on employment in 17 OECD countries. They find that short-term unemployment replacement rates, active labour market policy, day care spending, sick pay, education spending and educational attainment are very strongly related to employment levels, and that all of these policies – with the exception of sick pay – are very strongly related to employment levels in knowledge intensive services. Second, on the question whether social investment policies and high levels of human capital are related to the production of not just more jobs but good jobs, they do find strong, albeit preliminary, evidence affirming a positive relationship between social investment policies, human capital and quality employment.

In Chapter Nine, Bengt-Åke Lundvall and Edward Lorenz characterise the new economic context as a 'globalising learning economy' in which global competition increases the need to constantly develop and renew skills and competences. They show that the firms in which constant learning and autonomy are organised are the best equipped for this new economic context. They document that people work and learn quite differently in different parts of Europe. In Southern Europe jobs are simple or Taylorist, while jobs in the Nordic countries are characterised by more access to learning and to discretion in pursuing tasks. Such differences seem to reflect the type of policies implemented. The chapter argues that open and egalitarian education and training systems and labour markets characterised by labour market flexicurity constitute institutional settings that best support the learning economy.

The fourth part of the book analyses the main challenges which European welfare states are facing today (demographic ageing, economic crisis, climate change) and the social investment strategy's capacity to respond to them, as well as the conditions under which it can do so. In particular, these contributions warn against short-sighted policies that may result from the current economic crisis and emphasise the importance of taking, instead, a long-term perspective and investing in well-informed productive social policy.

In Chapter Ten, Thomas Lindh analyses the demographic challenge that all European countries have to face, and asks whether the social investment strategy is able to cope with the challenges of ageing populations. The chapter argues that social investment in human capital must be the main route to maintain the sustainability of the welfare states that have made it possible for the population to live ever longer in the first place. It applies a broad definition of how human capital is created which, besides education, also includes fertility, family policies, child care and migration as crucial inputs. European welfare states are at different stages in their ageing processes and the institutions for intergenerational transfers differ considerably. The chapter argues that policy strategies must be formed according to these differences. Productive social policies have to be designed to fit current demographic structures, taking into account their consequences for future demographics and the repercussions the population structure has on both economics and the sustainability of welfare systems. This requires long-term perspectives as well as an integrated view of the policy system. To make this discussion concrete, the late-twentieth-century experience of Sweden is used as an illustration.

In Chapter Eleven, Patrick Diamond and Roger Liddle examine the chances and relevance of the social investment perspective with respect to the consequences of five interlocking social crises the EU countries face in the aftermath of the global financial crisis: rising unemployment and the social consequences of the global financial crash; growing divergence throughout the EU; the long-term crisis of winners and losers that originates in economic globalisation; the structural trends of demography and rising life expectancy that bear down on the welfare state; and the impact of migration, integration and identity on social citizenship and cohesion. They ask whether the social investment paradigm can survive in the wake of the global financial crisis and the consequent rush to fiscal austerity and budgetary consolidation. They underline that there are many obstacles to reform, as reallocating resources from passive income distribution to investment in children and younger families appears to contravene politically significant vested interests. The global recession may also reinforce policies that are about safeguarding existing jobs and welfare entitlements, rather than investing in the future. They claim that the task for national governments and the EU is to facilitate the functional recalibration of the social investment approach, making it not only more financially sustainable, but able to cope more efficiently with the great social challenges of the age. The chapter concludes by setting out common principles by which such recalibration can be brought about across the EU.

In Chapter Twelve, Lena Sommestad tests the idea of connecting climate policies and the social investment approach in order to elaborate a European model for sustainable development. The chapter argues that the success of EU climate policies will be strongly dependent on social policy design. EU climate policies have hitherto been largely unrelated to social policy. EU climate strategies have been designed in favour of liberalised energy markets, market-related policy instruments and limited state intervention. But these neoliberal EU climate policies are viewed with growing discontent. Problems identified include volatile energy prices, lack of investment in low-carbon energy and 'fuel poverty'. The chapter argues that income redistribution and appropriate employment policies to reskill the labour force in order to respond to the needs of a low-carbon economy are crucial elements for successful climate change mitigation. The chapter then discusses the likelihood for a policy shift in the EU towards a paradigm for sustainable development. From the point of view of social investment, a shift to a new EU policy framework based on the concept of sustainability could bring important advantages. In contrast to neoliberalism, the paradigm for sustainable development combines concerns for environment and global social justice with classic European social policy topics such as social equity, citizenship and prevention (social sustainability). By providing a coherent approach to climate policy and social policy, the paradigm for sustainable development has potential to strengthen the social investment approach and improve social policy design in support of climate change mitigation.

In Chapter Thirteen, Bengt-Åke Lundvall and Edward Lorenz ask whether the various European economic, environmental and social strategies implemented from the Lisbon Strategy to the Agenda EU2020 have carried the social investment ideas and objectives in the past, and are likely to do so in the future. The new strategy EU2020 aims at re-establishing smart, green and inclusive growth in Europe. In this chapter, this new strategy is compared with the Lisbon Strategy and assessed critically. The chapter compares the two strategies in terms of context and content and discusses the consequences of the mid-term revision of the original Lisbon Strategy. It analyses whether and how the Lisbon Strategy contributed to employment, social cohesion and knowledge-based economic growth. The Lisbon Strategy (especially in its revised version) appears to have served as scaffolding for the Economic and Monetary Union. The chapter concludes that Europe needs a new vision as well as a more ambitious strategy than the one offered in EU2020.

In our conclusion, we summarise what we have learnt from the contributions to the book. We discuss how far the social investment approach has come in terms of an emerging paradigm, and the necessity to more clearly distinguish its ideas from the previous neoliberal paradigm. We then ask questions around the achievements of this perspective, and conclude that the few cases of implementation confirm the possible successes, the main problem being the lack of real social investment policies in Europe. In order to identify the driving forces and constraints for future reforms, we examine the politics and political economy of the approach. We end by exploring the EU dimension for the challenges and prospects of the social investment approach.

Note

[1] In Peter Hall's now classic formulation, a policy paradigm is 'a framework of ideas and standards that specifies not only the goals of policy and kind of instruments that can be used to attain them, but also the very nature of the problems they are meant to be addressing' (Hall, 1993: 279).

References

Andersson, J. (2005) 'Investment or Cost? The Role of the Metaphor of Productive Social Policies in Welfare State Formation in Europe and the US 1850-2000', paper presented at the World Congress in Historical Sciences, Sydney, July 2005.

Andersson, J. (2007) 'Solidarity or competition? Creating the European knowledge society', in L. Magnusson and B. Stråth (eds) *European Solidarities. Tensions and Contentions of a Concept*. Brussels: P.I.E. Peter Lang.

Appelqvist, Ö. (2007) 'L'argument démographique dans la genèse de l'État providence suédois', *Vingtième Siècle. Revue d'histoire*, 95, 15–28.

Blair, T. and Schröder, G. (2000) 'Europe: the third way/die Neue Mitte', in B. Hombach (ed.) *The Politics of the New Centre*. Oxford: Blackwell, pp. 157–77.

Bonoli, G. (2005) 'The politics of the new social policies. Providing coverage against new social risks in mature welfare states', *Policy and Politics*, 33 (3), 431–49.

Cantillon, B. (2010) 'Disambiguating Lisbon. Growth, employment and social inclusion in the Investment State', CSB Working Paper No. 10/07.

Esping-Andersen, G. (1992) 'The making of a social democratic welfare state', in M. Misgeld and K. Åmark (eds) *Creating Social Democracy. A Century of the Social Democratic Labor Party in Sweden*. Pennsylvania: The Pennsylvania State University Press.

Esping-Andersen, G. (ed.) (1996) *Welfare States in Transition. National Adaptations in Global Economies*. Thousand Oaks, CA: Sage.

Esping-Andersen, G. (1999) *Social Foundations of Post-Industrial Economies*. Oxford: Oxford University Press.

Esping-Andersen, G., Gallie, D., Hemerijck, A. and Myles, J. (2002) *Why we Need a New Welfare State*. Oxford: Oxford University Press.

Fouarge, D. (2003) 'Costs of non-social policy: towards an economic framework of quality social policies – and the costs of not having them', Report for the Employment and Social Affairs DG, European Commission.

Giddens, A. (1998) *The Third Way: The Renewal of Social Democracy.* Cambridge: Polity Press.

Hall, P. (ed.) (1989) *The Political Power of Economic Ideas. Keynesianism across Nations.* Princeton, NJ: Princeton University Press.

Hall, P. (1993) 'Policy paradigm, social learning and the state', *Comparative Politics,* 25 (3), 275–96.

Jenson, J. (2009) 'Lost in translation: The social investment perspective and gender equality', *Social Politics,* 16 (4), 446–83.

Jenson, J. (2010) 'Diffusing ideas for after-neoliberalism: The social investment perspective in Europe and Latin America', *Global Social Policy,* 10 (1), 59–84.

Jenson, J. and Saint Martin, D. (2003) 'New routes to social cohesion? Citizenship and the social investment state', *Canadian Journal of Sociology,* 28 (1), 77–99.

Jobert, B. (1994) *Le Tournant Néo-Libéral en Europe.* Paris: L'Harmattan.

Jobert, B. (2002) 'Une troisième voie très britannique. Giddens et l'Etat-providence', *Revue Française de Sociologie,* 43 (2), 407–22.

Jobert, B. and Muller, P. (1987) *L'État en Action.* Paris: PUF.

Kap, H. and Palme, J. (2009) 'Analysis of the economic and social situation in Europe – challenges for social inclusion ahead', Background paper for the keynote speech at the 8th European Roundtable on Poverty and Social Exclusion, 15–16 October 2009, Stockholmsmässan, organised by the Swedish Presidency of the European Union.

Lister, R. (2003) 'Investing in the citizen-workers of the future: transformations in citizenship and the state under New Labour', *Social Policy and Administration,* 37 (5), 427–43.

Mahon, R. (2008) 'Babies and bosses: Gendering the OECD's social policy discourse', in R. Mahon and S. McBride (eds) *The OECD and Transnational Governance.* Vancouver: University of British Columbia Press, pp. 260–75.

Mandin, L. and Palier, B. (2004) 'L'Europe et les politiques sociales. Vers une harmonisation cognitive des réponses nationales', in Y. Surel, and C. Lequesne (eds) *L'Intégration Européenne. Entre Emergence Institutionnelle et Recomposition de l'Etat.* Paris: Presses de Sciences Po.

Midgley, J. and Tang, K.-L. (2001) 'Social policy, economic growth and developmental welfare', *International Journal of Social Welfare,* 10, 244–52.

Myrdal, A. and Myrdal, G. (1934) *Kris i Befolkningsfrågan.* Stockholm: Albert Bonniers Förlag.

OECD (1994) *The OECD Jobs Study. Facts, Analysis, Strategies.* Paris: OECD.

OECD (1996) *Beyond 2000: The New Social Policy Agenda.* Paris: OECD.

OECD (1997) *The OECD Jobs Strategy. Making Work Pay. Taxation, Benefits, Employment and Unemployment*. Paris: OECD.

Perkins, D., Nelms, L. and Smyth, P. (2004) 'Beyond neo-liberalism: the social investment state?', Social Policy Working Paper No. 3, Centre for Public Policy University of Melbourne.

Rodrigues, M. (ed.) (2003) *The New Knowledge Economy In Europe. A Strategy for International Competitiveness and Social Cohesion.* Northampton: Edward Elgar.

Scharpf, F. and Schmidt, V. (eds) (2000) *Welfare and Work in the Open Economy*, vol. 2: *Diverse Responses to Common Challenges.* Oxford: Oxford University Press.

Stratigaki, M. (2004) 'The Cooptation of Gender Concepts in EU Policies: The Case of "Reconciliation of Work and Family"', *Social Politics*, 11 (1), 30–56.

Vandenbroucke, F. and Vleminckx, K. (2011) 'Disappointing poverty trends: is the social investment state to blame? An exercise in soul-searching for policy-makers', CSB Working Paper No. 11/01.

Part I

Towards a new social policy paradigm

Two or three waves of welfare state transformation?

Anton Hemerijck

Introduction

Most comparative welfare state researchers divide the post-war era into two periods: a phase of construction and expansion, from 1945 to the mid-1970s; and one of consolidation and retrenchment, from the mid-1970s to the early years of the twenty-first century (Pierson, 2002). I wish to put forward an alternative periodisation by subdividing the post-war period until the early twenty-first century into three distinct phases of welfare state reconfiguration. These are: (1) the era of welfare state expansion and class compromise, starting at the end of World War II; (2) the period of welfare retrenchment and neoliberalism, which took shape in the wake of the oil shocks of the mid- to late-1970s; and (3) the more recent epoch since the mid-1990s in which social investment policy prescriptions took root. Each phase of welfare state development can be conceptualised as promoted by distinct policy expert advocacy, designed to effectively respond to impending socioeconomic challenges and to achieve shared policy objectives, supported by fairly robust political compromises. It should immediately be emphasised that no single country welfare transformation experience maps neatly onto the suggested three-stage developmental sequence. This applies all the more so to the social investment perspective. As Morel, Palier and Palme underline in Chapter One, the social investment perspective is an emerging, rather than a settle, paradigm. To date the social investment perspective has not been fully accepted as a hegemonic new welfare state paradigm on a par with Keynesian welfare state expansion and neoliberal social retrenchment. Moreover, its overall historical fate very much lies in the evolution of the precarious aftermath of the 2007–10 global financial crisis.

Moments of fundamental policy change are often associated with successive waves of economic adjustment. Especially deep economic crises provide important political windows for policy redirection.

At such junctures, social policy redirection was often guided by economic and social policy analysis innovation, better able to respond to the predicament of the day. In the first phase after 1945, economic security transformed from 'charity' into a 'right' for which potentially every citizen was eligible. Keynesian economic theory, the brainchild of the 1930s, provided the intellectual ammunition for the post-war construction and expansion of the modern welfare state, based on demand stabilisation through income-transfer social insurance provision with male-breadwinner full employment as the prime objective. In the second phase, the aftermath of the oil crises of the 1970s revealed the practical limitations of Keynesianism in fighting stagflation. In its wake a new economic policy consensus took root, inspired by neoclassical economics, favouring price stability, budgetary discipline, flexible labour markets and retrenched welfare commitments.

In the absence of a deep economic crisis on a par with the Great Depression of the 1930s or the Great Stagflation of the 1970s, the social investment turn is far more difficult to delineate than either the post-war era of Keynesian welfare expansion or the neoliberal epoch of retrenchment. Whereas in the two preceding periods, economic turmoil critically influenced the realm of politics and, subsequently, the direction of welfare state adaptation to new social and economic realities, the social investment rise to prominence was primarily political, triggered by growing disenchantment with neoliberal policy prescriptions. The global economic meltdown in the autumn of 2008 changes all this. The first crisis of twenty-first-century capitalism will be a stress test for the welfare state, and by implication for the social investment turn. Will the social investment perspective carry the day, or revert to marginality? To the extent that the crisis will go down in history as the crisis of the economics of neoliberalism, the social investment perspective is likely to gain in intellectual strength and coherence. It remains, however, to be seen to what extent calls for a social investment strategy will be sustained once the calls for an 'exit strategy' of deficit and debt reduction grow louder. Moreover, in spite of the precipitous downfall of the neoliberal efficient market hypothesis, two long decades of loss of faith in public action will not make it easier to accelerate welfare state renewal along social investment lines in the aftermath of the 2007–10 crisis.

The intellectual reception, collective expression and political acceptance of any novel set of social and economic ideas are coloured by many factors, ranging from power resources, political ideology, critical events like economic and political crises, state structures and institutional capacities to enact social policy innovation, and processes of political coalition formation and interest intermediation. In this chapter, special attention will be given to the intellectual properties of social and economic policy analysis behind long-run welfare state change. It should, however, not be forgotten that the policy objectives of Keynesian full employment, universal coverage, neoliberal labour market flexibility and lean states, and social investment dual earner family servicing and human capital enhancement, as Jane Jenson argues in the next chapter, are based on a normative image of a social contract, with important claims on equity and fairness, the work ethic, gender and family roles, intergenerational fairness, and collective and individual responsibility (see also Jenson and Saint-Martin, 2003). In the next three sections the emphasis is on ideas of social and economic analysis, more narrowly understood. I describe how policy expertise gained acceptance over three successive waves of welfare state reconfiguration, this against the background of socioeconomic change and processes of social mobilisation and institutional building. The final section reflects on the implications of the current crisis for the future of social investment.

Universal social insurance and the stability imperative

The post-war European welfare state represents an unprecedented historical achievement. As Fritz Scharpf puts it, never before in history 'has democratic politics been so effectively used to promote civil liberty, economic growth, social solidarity and public well-being' (Scharpf, 2003: 5). Almost all Western European countries launched sweeping social reforms in the 1940s and 1950s. Basic systems of universal social security were developed that included effective systems to combat poverty, and high-quality provision of health care, housing and education to encourage equality of opportunity. A full range of income transfer programmes – unemployment insurance, workers' compensation, disability benefits, old age pensions, survivors' benefits, children's allowances and social assistance, financed largely out of progressive taxation and/or social contributions from workers and employers, were introduced to protect citizens from the social risks associated with modern industrialism.

Modern social security has its roots in late nineteenth and early twentieth century poverty relief and social insurance legislation, but the experience of the Great Depression and World War II were pivotal in shaping European welfare states after 1945. After the Liberation, Western Europe was in dire need of a new social contract. A profound consensus emerged around the need for social and economic reconstruction, which triggered a sequence of social policy innovation that lasted until the 1970s. Justified in terms of nation building, the hegemony of reform-oriented social democracy in the Scandinavian countries, and the predominance of Christian democracy with its organic conceptualisation of social order in Austria, Germany, the Netherlands and Belgium, provided propitious ideological bases for welfare state expansion in the 1950s and 1960s.

With the memory of the Great Depression fresh in the mind, policy makers from all political persuasions found that the public sector had a key role to play in 'taming' the capitalist economy, through a wide range of regulatory, redistributive, monetary, fiscal and social conflict-resolution institutions. The post-war welfare state fundamentally redrew the boundaries between politics and economics. The extent of public intervention differed from one country to the next, but all advanced democratic governments assumed an active and strategic role in the economic management of the *mixed economies* of post-war Western Europe.

The defining feature of the post-war welfare state was that social protection came to be firmly anchored in the explicit normative commitment of granting industrial and social rights to workers and citizens, on a par with liberal and democratic rights (Esping-Andersen, 1994: 712). The pre-war practice of charity was replaced by the logic of social citizenship. In his seminal 1950 essays, *Citizenship and Social Class*, the British sociologist T.H. Marshall described social rights as 'the whole range from the right to a modicum of economic welfare and security to the right to share to the full in the social heritage and to live the life of a civilized being according to the standards prevailing in the society' (Marshall, 1992: 74). Marshall understood modern social policy as the use of democratic 'political power to supersede, supplement or modify operations of the economic system in order to achieve results which the economic system would not achieve on its own' (Marshall, 1992: 15). Gøsta Esping-Andersen aptly coined the political protection against economic risks as 'decommodification', defined in terms of 'the degree to which individuals, or families, can uphold a socially acceptable standard of living independently of market participation' (1990: 3). The guarantee of basic access to social protection and provisions of education and primary health care, made available to the population at large as a universal 'right', forced policy makers to expand the size of government, implement progressive taxation, and to make the best use of public resources and techniques in order to achieve the greatest social benefits at the lowest economic costs.

Keynesian economic policy analysis and full employment

Through John Maynard Keynes' path-breaking analysis of the Great Depression, macroeconomics became the key economic policy guide for post-war welfare state innovation and expansion. In *The General Theory of Employment, Interest and Money* (1936), Keynes introduced a completely new brand of macroeconomic policy analysis that allowed democratic governments to assume political responsibility for achieving full employment and comprehensive social protection without affecting the primacy of the free market economy (Hall, 1989). Keynesian economics focused on the macro behaviour of economic systems as a whole rather than on the micro behaviour of individual actors (Keynes, 1936). Fundamental is the idea that much economic activity is governed by 'animal spirits', best understood as waves of optimism and pessimism (see also Akerlof and Shiller, 2009). Left to their own devices, capitalist economies will therefore experience manias, followed by bouts of panic, generating self-fulfilling prophesies with fierce macro consequences for employment, output and investment (De Grauwe, 2010). To curb such fluctuations, Keynes argued, the modern state must sail into the wind of behavioural excess. Tools of countercyclical aggregate demand management such as discretionary monetary and fiscal policy were to be employed in order to sustain long-term economic stability and enhance productive capacity. The modern welfare state, in Keynes' ideas, played a key role in managing the business cycle, as comprehensive social security is inherently countercyclical, automatically compensating for recessionary declines and expansionary booms in private spending.

Keynesian economics provided William Beveridge, one of the founding fathers of the universal welfare state, with a unique political opportunity to fundamentally rethink the role of the state in welfare provision. In his wartime report, *Social Insurance and Allied Services* (1942), Beveridge defined the function of the welfare state in terms of the fight against the 'Five Great Evils of Want, Disease, Idleness, Ignorance and Squalor'. In his second report, *Full Employment in a Free Society*, 'freedom from idleness' was defined as the central purpose of the welfare state (1945). The basic form of social policy in the post-war decades was *social insurance*: the universal pooling of the social risks of unemployment and old age, for which private insurance would be inadequate. Workers contributed to social security, ensuring them future protection against the risks of cyclical and frictional unemployment through benefits that replaced a portion of their previous salary for a set period of time, usually long enough to return to work when labour demand increased. It should be emphasised that the original full employment objective both Keynes and Beveridge had in mind was defined in terms of full-time jobs for male workers only, 48 hours a week, with 48 working weeks in a year, for a period of 48 years. Their conception of full employment assumed that women, as housewives, would care for young children, frail elderly, and other dependent groups. Post-war social policy innovation, in this respect, very much consolidated the traditional gender roles of male breadwinners and female caregivers. Over the 1960s, social security coverage expanded to most workers and their families.

Class compromise

Politically, the success of the post-war settlement strongly relied on trade unions' acquiescence to wage restraint in return for full employment and expanded welfare provision (Crouch, 1999). Beveridge and Keynes both conceded that a combination of full employment and sectional wage bargaining was likely to produce inflationary spirals which could ultimately undermine the very policy objective of full employment that macroeconomic demand management made possible. For much of the 1950s and 1960s, managing the wage bargain acquired a new and strategic importance to the larger pattern of macroeconomic stabilisation, and all governments supported the active role of unions in wage determination and income policy, often anchored in effective tri- and bipartite social partnership institutions (Marglin and Schor, 1990).

Embedded liberalism

Within the wider geopolitical and economic international context, the post-war compromise was structured by two interlinked commitments: first, a dedication to international trade liberalisation; and second, a commitment to domestic compensation for the social costs associated with economic change and dynamism. At the Bretton Woods Conference of 1944, it was the towering figure of John Maynard Keynes, once again, who advocated for a rules-based global system of pegged-but-adjustable exchange rates, to be overseen by the IMF. This would allow national policy makers the freedom to pursue relatively independent social and employment policies, without undermining international economic stability and trade liberalisation. With the establishment of Bretton Woods, the twin objectives of full employment and welfare state expansion were thus anchored in what John Ruggie has described as a regime of 'embedded liberalism' at the level of the international political economy (Ruggie, 1994). In Ruggie's words, 'governments asked their publics to embrace the change and dislocation that comes with liberalization in return for the promise of help in containing and socializing the adjustment costs' (Ruggie, 1994: 4–5). Free trade, one of the key objectives of post-war European integration, was hereby made socially sustainable through the welfare state.

Measured by any yardstick of social institution building, the 'Golden Age' of welfare capitalism, class compromise and embedded liberalism was a tremendous success. It buttressed democratic governance and complemented the market economy with human solidarity. Affluence contributed to a high standard of living, full employment, decent wages, universal access to education and health care, a right to income for older people, ill people, those with disabilities, and unemployed and poor people, and a significant reduction of poverty and inequality. Far from being polar opposites, open markets and organised solidarity prospered together. Welfare state construction and expansion, together with significant declines in income inequalities, came to be viewed as essential ingredients in any strategy to boost economic growth. The painful memories of the Great Depression and World War II remained ever-present in the minds of post-war policy makers. In this respect, the impetus for the path-breaking establishment of the 'male breadwinner' welfare state, protected by the international regime of embedded liberalism after 1945, was as much progressive in design, based on organised labour support and class compromise, as it was conservative in intent. As Charles Maier notes, post-war reconstruction reflected, above all, a quest for normalcy and a search for stability (Maier, 1987).

Welfare growth to limits and the challenge of flexibility

Towards the late 1960s, however, the post-war celebration of unprecedented growth and social progress gave way to doubts. The resurgence of worker militancy and the 1960s wage explosion confronted the consensual political elites of the post-war decades with a highly charged political context. Policies complementing wage bargaining structures with automatic indexation formulae, introduced to maintain consumer purchasing power for minimum wage earners and social security beneficiaries, triggered a self-reinforcing inflationary dynamic (Crouch and Pizzorno, 1978).

The 'goodness of fit' between welfare expansion and market liberalisation was put to the test by the breakdown of the Bretton Woods monetary system and, subsequently, by the steep rise in oil prices in the 1970s. In March 1971, the Bretton Woods system of fixed exchange rates was replaced with a system of floating currencies, triggering considerable currency adjustments and economic instability. The oil shocks of 1973 and 1979 simultaneously accelerated inflation and pushed unemployment to unprecedented levels, triggering a dramatic increase in social security outlays. By the late 1970s, high inflation, mass unemployment and sluggish growth exhausted public patience with neo-Keynesian demand management and deadlocked corporatism. From the early 1980s on, European political economies no longer seemed capable of guaranteeing industrial full employment while preserving generous social protection. The coexistence of economic prosperity, full employment, income equalisation and expanding welfare provision had, in the words of Peter Flora, 'grown to limits' (Flora, 1986/87). The final quarter of the twentieth century has often been portrayed as the 'silver age' of the welfare state (Taylor-Gooby, 2004). This created a critical opportunity, intellectually, for the rise to hegemony of supply-side economics, from monetarism to rational expectations and unemployment hysteresis macro modelling.

Neoclassical economics, neoliberal politics and negative state theory

If Keynesian macroeconomics was the brainchild of the Great Depression, then neoclassical economics was the intellectual answer to the crisis of stagflation – the malignant combination of cost-push price inflation, economic stagnation and rising demand-deficient unemployment (Scharpf, 1991). Among academic economists, monetarism gained ground over Keynesianism by being better able to explain the predicament of stagflation as resulting from ineffective stop-and-go fiscal demand stimulus measures by governments. Monetarists argued that governments are best advised to keep money supply growing steadily at a rate equal to the growth of aggregate supply, so as to suppress inflationary expectations. Economists in the tradition of rational expectations claimed that economic cycles are not the result of endogenous 'animal spirits', because people form rational expectations. They returned to the theoretical models based on perfectly competitive and perfectly clearing markets.

The elections of Margaret Thatcher and Ronald Reagan sealed the political revival of self-regulating markets, followed by changes in government from the centre-left to conservative coalitions in polities on the European continent. Together, the supply-side revolution in economics and the politics of neoliberalism fostered a deliberate change in the hierarchy of social and economic policy objectives: the erstwhile primary objective of full employment of Keynes and Beveridge was traded for balanced budgets, low inflation, stable currency, central bank independence, privatisation and the drive towards labour market re-regulation and welfare retrenchment (Hay, 2004). Where the post-war welfare state was designed essentially to provide the institutional underpinning for an economy organised around stable industrial employment relations, the common quest in the wake of the two oil shocks became to enforce more flexible employment relations so as to encourage private sector expansion, falling prices and output demand growth. The key policy recipe of neoliberalism was to free markets, institutions, rules and regulations from the collective political decision making that had been the standard norm and operating procedure under embedded liberalism. In other words, the neoliberal turn was bent on a broad-based process of 'institutional liberalisation' of the form of 'organised capitalism' that was established after 1945.

At the core of both neoliberal politics and neoclassical economics was a deeply 'negative theory of the state'. To many neoliberal commentators, the crisis of welfare capitalism was rooted in the growth of unrealistic expectations, leading to an overburdened government incompatible with the tax burden level that citizens were willing to shoulder (Crozier et al., 1975). Neoliberal ideologues Friedrich von Hayek (1944, 1960) and Milton Friedman (1962) went as far as to argue that the coercive redistribution of the welfare state set the democratic polity on the slippery slope towards totalitarianism, cultures of welfare dependency and the demise of self-reliance and individual responsibility (Murray, 1984; Mead, 1986).

Assuming markets to be self-regulating, the neoliberal solution to the overburdened welfare democracy crisis lay in the return to the integrity of the market. Politics should be constitutionally prevented from interfering with the market's automatic 'clearing mechanisms' through a strict separation of economic and political spheres. A slimmed-down state, with public services run according to business principles, contracting-out and project management, with much stronger attention to meeting citizens' needs and wishes, was to give free reign to self-regulating markets. If social policy could not be banned, public support should not exceed targeted and means-tested minimum support for the deserving poorest citizens, and must be undergirded with strong workfare requirements. Following traditional neoclassical economic reasoning, income differentials are essential to economic growth as they constitute crucial incentives for improving economic efficiency and ensure that labour supply and demand are matched swiftly.

In the course of the 1980s, questions of real economy business profitability, international competitiveness and structural reform jumped to the forefront of the policy debate. For neoclassical economists, high unemployment and low growth were the consequences of labour market rigidities. Economic cycles were largely understood as outcomes of exogenous shocks – the oil shocks of the 1970s being the clearest cases in point – combined with slow transmission through the real economy as the result of market rigidities, including distortions related to welfare provision and labour market regulation. Unemployment thus came to be seen as a microeconomic problem of market distortions, and no longer as a macroeconomic problem of insufficient demand. Blanchard and Summers (1987) offered the paradigmatic explanation of 'hysteresis' to explain why wages did not fall and unemployment remained high in Europe in the 1980s: the structural rigidities of job preservation for employed workers was achieved at the expense of labour market outsiders, and this prevented real wages from falling enough to restore full employment. Long-term unemployment came to be viewed as the consequence of poor motivation and low search intensity resulting from the generosity of the welfare state, creating negative 'moral hazard' and 'adverse selection' externalities.

The OECD Jobs Study

In the early 1990s, the Organisation for Economic Co-operation and Development (OECD) received a mandate to examine the labour market performance of its member countries. The OECD Jobs Study, published in 1994, marked the beginning of a critical attack on the 'dark side' of double-digit unemployment of many of its European OECD members (OECD, 1994, 1997, 2006a). These reports proved highly influential in terms of the debate on welfare state reform, if not on actual policy. Hovering around 10% with few signs of improvement, unemployment rates in France, Germany and Italy were twice as high as in the USA. The employment rate was about 12 points below the USA. The OECD economists argued that Europe's generous welfare states, with their overprotective job security, high minimum wages and generous unemployment insurance, heavy taxation, and their overriding emphasis on coordinated wage bargaining and social dialogue, had raised the costs of labour above market clearing levels. Moreover, strong 'insider–outsider' cleavages, with unfavourable employment chances for young people, women, older people and unskilled people, prevented the rigid European labour markets from reaching employment rates on a par with the USA, the UK or New Zealand (Lindbeck, 1994).

Politically, the extension of employment protection legislation in Europe had moreover created self-serving constituencies of workers strongly opposed to necessary labour market deregulation (Rueda, 2007).

The fight against unemployment thus came to be seen as the quest for flexibility. Central policy recommendation of the OECD included making wage and labour costs more flexible by removing restrictions to better reflect local economic conditions and labour productivity, keeping the minimum wage low, reducing non-wage labour costs, restricting the duration of unemployment insurance, reforming employment security provisions that inhibit employment growth in the private sector, loosening employment protection and expanding fixed-term contracts. The OECD thus portrayed the fundamental dilemma of Europe's mature welfare states in terms of a tradeoff between welfare equity and employment efficiency. From this perspective, comprehensive welfare provision and economic security undermine the logic of the market. Well-functioning markets were seen as the best guarantee for wellbeing, self-reliance and autonomy. Inequality is inherent in markets and even necessary to motivate self-sufficient individuals as economic actors. The policy recommendations that followed from the OECD analysis included retrenchment of unemployment compensation, deregulation of job protection legislation, reduction of minimum wages, decentralisation of wage bargaining and lower taxation.

Single market, EMU and activation through social pacts

Although the English-speaking world spearheaded the rise of neoliberalism, Europe followed suit from the mid-1980s onwards. Nonetheless, different welfare states followed strikingly divergent social policy responses and labour market strategies. The social democratic welfare states of Scandinavia seemed to be able to sustain high levels of both employment and equality by expanding public sector service jobs. Liberal welfare states in English-speaking countries like the USA and the UK seemed to be able to create large numbers of private sector service jobs, following the additional neoliberal recipe of labour market deregulation and welfare retrenchment. The conservative or Christian Democratic welfare states of continental Europe, on the other hand, maintained budgetary restraint, but at the cost of low levels of employment in both public and private services, which not only led to growing divisions between labour market 'insiders' and 'outsiders', but also triggered a vicious spiral of increasing payroll charges, rising indirect costs and declining employment, which could eventually undermine the financial sustainability of the continental welfare states themselves. In Southern Europe, the continental 'inactivity trap' has been intensified by strict labour market regulation (Scharpf and Schmidt, 2000).

The Single European Market Act of 1986 and the Economic Monetary Union (EMU) of 1999 were negotiated at a time when neoliberalism was riding high. The understanding behind the introduction of the EMU, and the founding of an independent European Central Bank, was that an integrated market does not function properly when inflation and exchange rate fluctuations and competitive devaluations remain optional. The Maastricht convergence criteria for member states joining the EMU thus followed the neoliberal logic of the primacy of hard currency and balanced budgets. Membership required participants to achieve a stable inflation rate (within 1.5% of the three best performing states in the EU), a low government deficit (equivalent to no more than 3% of GDP), a low debt level (below 60% of GDP) and stable interest rates (within 2% of the three best performing states). A number of academic observers saw the single market and EMU policy package as a Trojan horse for a fully fledged neoliberal policy shift across the member states of the EU, believing that this would trigger a vicious cycle of deflationary 'beggar-thy-neighbour' strategies of internal devaluation through social dumping and competitive wage moderation (McNamara, 1998).

Partly as a result of the early 1990s currency crisis, most European countries went into recession, marking another rise in unemployment. As a result of high interest payments on the public debt and rising unemployment, public debt rose considerably in the majority of countries. This predicament left many member states little choice but to compensate for the loss of macroeconomic fiscal and monetary policy tools by strengthening the institutional responsiveness of domestic industrial relations systems and welfare state arrangements through labour market and social policy reform. Ironically, EMU pressures seemed to mobilise a far less hostile labour market policy response, marked by a shift towards activating social insurance and active labour market policies, in part based on the return of 'social pacts' between government, employers and trade union organisations (Ebbinghaus and Hassel, 2000). Apparently policy makers, especially on the European continent, did not dare follow the example of Thatcherist class warfare with the trade unions, but instead sought to negotiate with their unions, however much weakened by high unemployment. Under the slogan 'make work pay', specific attention was given to the removal of obstacles that hinder labour market participation, especially for the low skilled, women and elderly people (Blanchard, 2006; Eichhorst and Hemerijck, 2008). These social policy and labour market reforms included a broad range of in-work benefits, employment subsidies, tax deductions, individual counselling, working-time flexibility and social and family service provision. These proactive reforms, however, were accompanied by benefit cuts and a tightening of eligibility requirements, especially in the areas of unemployment insurance and social assistance, in countering poverty traps (Hemerijck, 2011). Towards the end of the decade, the experiences of the more successful European countries, like Denmark and the Netherlands, seemed to suggest that there need not be a tradeoff between equity and jobs.

Neoliberalism in the balance

How successful has neoliberalism been on its own terms? Has the scope of state intervention in the economy been rolled back? Has the policy strategy of institutional 'dis-embedding' unleashed a new epoch of market dynamism? Have greater income disparities encouraged higher levels of economic growth? Have 'insider' interests been sidetracked from the policy process? Important qualifications notwithstanding, the neoliberal transformation in the 1980s and 1990s has indeed made European capitalism more market-oriented. The strongest liberalisation has taken place in capital and product markets. The neoliberal policy shift to hard currency and balanced budgets also served to contain wage–price inflation. Neoliberalism's willingness to tolerate greater income inequality in the name of free markets has had a truly dramatic impact. The 1980s and 1990s were indeed decades of greater income inequality and relative poverty, including in the more egalitarian and stronger welfare states in Scandinavia and continental Europe, since the 1980s (Kenworthy, 2008; OECD, 2008). Most worrisome has been the progressive rise of child poverty and in-work poverty.

While neoliberal politics explicitly aimed at dismantling the welfare state is seen as an impediment to international competitiveness, it must be said that the achievements are rather elusive. In the 2000s, OECD governments 'spent more on social protection than at any time in history' (OECD, 2008). Statutory corporate taxes have been lowered, but by broadening the tax base the effective rates remained stable (Swank, 2002; Genschel, 2004). And with respect to supposedly immobile corporatism, it is striking to observe how many over the past two decades tried to seek a concertational style of policy making, inviting opposition parties and the social partners to encompass policy platforms over welfare reform and labour market regulation.

The social investment turn towards capacitating solidarity

By the end of the 1990s, political disenchantment with neoliberal policy measures began to generate electoral successes for the centre-left. Newly elected European social democrats like Tony Blair, Gerhard Schröder, Wim Kok and Poul Nyrup Rasmussen strongly believed that most European welfare states had to be transformed from passive benefits systems into activating, capacity building, social investment states. This policy platform was inspired intellectually by Anthony Giddens' 1998 book *The Third Way: The Renewal of Social Democracy*. By the late 1990s, Third Way ideas made their way to the European Commission (European Commission, 2000). But intellectually, and very surprisingly, it was the OECD that made the first about-face away from the neoliberal advocacy that had characterised their *Jobs Strategy* publications of the 1980s and 1990s, to spearhead the social investment perspective at their 1996 high-level conference, 'Beyond 2000: The New Social Policy Agenda' (OECD, 1996). Recent OECD studies like *Starting Strong* (2006b), *Babies and Bosses* (2007a), *Understanding the Social Outcomes of Learning* (2007b) and *Growing Unequal* (2008) are perhaps even more exemplary of the OECD's full-fledged endorsement of the 'social investment perspective' (see Chapter Three in this volume).

The EU, meanwhile, developed its own version of the social investment perspective, beginning under the Dutch EU presidency in the first half of 1997 (Hemerijck, 1997), when the Dutch Ministry of Social Affairs and Employment staged a high-level conference in cooperation with the European Commission, entitled 'Social Policy as Productive Factor'. The intention of the conference, chaired by Jacques Delors, was to correct the lopsided view that comprehensive social policy provisions, however morally commendable, only engender negative economic effects. The central tenet of the EU's turn to social investment is that social policy can potentially be a productive factor. Whereas neoliberal doctrines posited a tradeoff between these goals, the social investment perspective sees improved social equity go hand in hand with more economic efficiency. Social policy provisions are viewed as investments, potentially enhancing both social protection and productive potential.

In 2000, the Portuguese presidency of the EU further raised the social and economic policy ambitions of the EU, by putting forward an integrated agenda of economic, employment and social objectives, committing the Union to becoming the 'most competitive and dynamic knowledge-based economy in the world, capable of sustainable economic growth with more and better jobs and greater social cohesion'. The so-called Lisbon Strategy represented an attempt to relaunch the idea of the positive complementarities between equity and efficiency in the knowledge-based economy by way of 'investing in people and developing an active and dynamic welfare state' (Council of the European Union, 2000). In addition to the objective of raising employment rates throughout Europe, the Lisbon Agenda placed human capital, research, innovation and development at the centre of European social and economic policy. This broadened the notion of social policy as a productive factor beyond its traditional emphasis on social protection, to include social promotion and improving the quality of training and education. The Lisbon Strategy also prefigured a refocusing of equal opportunity policies with an eye on raising the employment rates of women and elderly workers.

Why We Need a New Welfare State

During the Belgian presidency in the second half of 2001, Frank Vandenbroucke, then Belgian Minister of Social Insurance and Health Care, eager to build on the Lisbon Agenda's social ambitions, invited a group headed by Gøsta Esping-Andersen, including myself, to draft a report on a 'new welfare architecture for 21st century Europe', later published with Oxford University Press under the title *Why We Need a New Welfare State* (2002). For Vandenbroucke, a towering intellectual of the active welfare state movement in European social democracy, the shift towards a knowledge-based society called for path-breaking social policy change. The assignment he gave Esping-Andersen and colleagues was to rethink the welfare state for the twenty-first century, so that 'once again, labour markets and families are welfare optimisers and a good guarantee that tomorrow's adult workers will be as productive and resourceful as possible' (Esping-Andersen et al., 2002: 25).

At the core of *Why We Need a New Welfare State* is the argument that the prevailing inertia in male breadwinner welfare provision results in increasingly suboptimal life chances in labour market opportunities, income, educational attainment and intra- and intergenerational fairness, for large shares of the population. European societies are confronted with problems of cumulative welfare failure because labour markets, families and existing social policy repertoires remain rooted in male breadwinner, passive transfer-oriented social insurance of workers with stable job biographies. The staying power of the 'passive' male breadwinner policy legacy, according to Esping-Andersen et al., frustrates more adequate responses to 'new' social risks of the post-industrial economy, ranging from rapid skill depletion, reconciling work and family life, caring for frail relatives, and inadequate social security coverage. These 'new' social risks adversely affect low-skill workers, young people, working women, immigrants and families with small children. Most troublesome is the polarisation between work-rich and work-poor families. Top income households are increasingly distancing themselves from the middle as a result of rising returns to skills, exacerbated by marital homogamy, that is to say family formation of spouses with similar educational backgrounds. At the bottom of the pyramid, less educated couples and especially lone-mother families face (child) poverty and long-term joblessness. As inequality widens, households' capacities to invest in their children's fortunes will become ever more unequal.

Perhaps the most important conceptual contribution of *Why We Need a New Welfare State* is that it adopts a 'life course perspective' in rethinking twenty-first-century welfare provision. Working poverty, obsolete skills and old age poverty are not predicaments that fall on citizens and families by chance. They are the end results of problems in the early stages of people's lives. Through the lens of the life course, Esping-Andersen et al. are able to identify and explicate better the intricate relationships that link care for children, the elderly and other vulnerable groups, to female employment and changing family structures. From a life course perspective, the real litmus test for future welfare state success will be the ability to resolve the tension between women's new career preferences and the continued desire to form families. In terms of public policy, this implicates an institutional realignment of the boundaries between work and family life, which during the heyday of male-breadwinner welfare states were viewed as functionally differentiated public and private spheres.

Because the heaviest burden of new social risks falls on the younger cohorts, in terms of policy redirection, Esping-Andersen et al. explicitly advocate a reallocation of social expenditures away from pensions and social insurance towards family services, active labour market policy, early childhood education and vocational training, so as to ensure productivity improvement and high employment for both men and women in the knowledge-based economy. There is, however, no contradiction between an explicit welfare effort towards privileging the active phases of life and sustainable pensions per se. As Vandenbroucke correctly states in the introduction to the volume: 'we should firmly keep in mind that good pension policies – like good health policies – begin at birth' (Esping-Andersen et al., 2002: xvi). It is important to add that Esping-Andersen et al. emphasised – contra the Third Way –

that social investment is no substitute for social protection. Adequate minimum income protection is a critical precondition for an effective social investment strategy. In other words, 'social protection' and 'social promotion' should be understood as the indispensible twin pillars of the new social investment welfare edifice.

The agenda-setting work of Esping-Andersen's group has been followed by comparable contributions by national think tanks, including the Irish National Economic and Social Council (NESC, 2005), the Dutch Scientific Council for Government Policy (WRR, 2006) and the Swedish Institute for Futures Studies (IFFS, 2006), and other agenda-setting publications by Giddens et al. (2006), Esping-Andersen and Palier (2008) and Delors and Dollé (2009). At the EU level, the *Renewed Social Agenda*, attending to the needs of children and young people, especially through education and actions to combat child poverty and the commitment to promote women's access to the labour market, has reinforced the social investment perspective as a central tenet of the European Union's action programme (European Commission, 2008).

The economics of social investment

The economic policy analysis of social investment is, however, far from self-evident. Unlike the Keynesian welfare state and the neoliberal retrenchment movement, the social investment perspective turn is not founded on one unified body of economic thought. Nonetheless, over the past decade both policy makers and expert academics have started to rethink the interaction between economic progress and social policy: from tradeoffs to mutual reinforcement. The protagonists of social investment, however, hold the relationship between substantive social policy and economic performance to be critically dependent on identifying institutional conditions, at the micro, meso and macro levels, under which it is possible to formulate and implement productive social policies. There are no 'quick fixes' comparable to the kind of straightforward micro or macro solutions dreamt up by the general theorists of neoclassical or post-Keynesian economics. The economic policy analysis of social investment relies heavily on empirical data and case-by-case comparisons. It is crucial to consider the 'fine' structures of the welfare state. Social policy is never a productive factor per se. One cannot turn a blind eye to the negative, unintended and perverse side-effects of excessively generous social security benefits of long duration, undermining work incentives, raising the tax burden and contributing to high gross wage costs. By the same token, rigid forms of dismissal protection, making hiring and firing unnecessarily costly, can result in high levels of inactivity.

Beyond such institutional contingencies, the social investment perspective does bring social policy as a potentially positive contributor to growth, competitiveness, social progress and political resilience back into the equation. Largely in agreement with the Keynesian welfare state, the social investment perspective makes a virtue of the argument that a strong economy requires a strong welfare state. Social protection expenditures remain powerful stabilisers of economic activity at the macro level as they consolidate effective demand during recessions. The experience of the early days of the 2007–10 financial crisis indeed reveals that this kind of Keynesianism through the back door is still operative. Basic minimum income protection serves to reduce poverty. Dire poverty is bad for any economy, especially when it is passed down the generations, permanently excluding disadvantaged groups from economic progress, wasting human capital and undermining social cohesion. In addition, institutions of social partnership permit macroeconomically responsive wage setting and employment-friendly welfare reform, while encouraging employers and trade unions to jointly invest in vocational training programmes, thus contributing to competitiveness through human capital upgrading and maintenance at the meso level. As today's organisation of knowledge-intensive production relies heavily on realising gains from cooperation (see Chapter Nine in this volume), social partnership at industry level is a prerequisite at the meso level, in addition to channelling industrial conflict in periods of structural adjustment at the macro level. At the micro level, social insurance, compensating workers and families who contribute to the common economic good by exposing themselves to periodic market contingencies, encourages private initiative and risk taking. But the devil is in the detail. High unemployment benefits of short duration, coupled to strong activation incentives and obligations, supported by active labour market servicing policy, are most successful in lowering unemployment and raising labour productivity (Blanchard, 2006; see also Chapter Seven in this volume). Effective policy mixes of this kind also have a moderating effect on wage developments.

The logic of 'social policy as a productive factor' stands in contrast to the neoliberal paradigm on two dimensions. In the first place, neoclassical economics, based on perfect information and market clearing, theoretically rules out the kind of social risks and market failures that the welfare state seeks to address. Second, because neoclassical economics focuses only on the (public) cost side of the welfare state, it is unable to appreciate its core macro- and microeconomic benefits (Atkinson,

1999: 8). Extensive comparative empirical research has since the turn of the century revealed that there is no tradeoff between macroeconomic performance and the size of the welfare state. The presence of a large public sector does not necessarily damage competitiveness; there is a positive relationship between fertility and high levels of female participation in most Scandinavian countries; and finally, high numeracy and literacy rates can be achieved with educational policies that abide by the principles of equal opportunities (Hemerijck, 2002; Lindert, 2004; see also Chapter Eight in this volume).

Alongside this nuanced reappreciation of the Keynesian welfare policy legacy, the economic policy analysis of social investment shares with the neoliberal approach a strong focus on the supply-side. Social investments today generate private and public dividends in the mid- to long term. Central to the notion of social investment is that the economic sustainability of the welfare state hinges on the number and productivity of future taxpayers. From this reading, social policy should contribute to actively mobilising the productive potential of citizens in order to mitigate new social risks, such as atypical employment, long-term unemployment, working poverty, family instability and lacking opportunities for labour market participation, resulting from care obligations or obsolete skills. There is also a deliberate orientation towards 'early identification' and 'early action' targeted on the more vulnerable new risks groups. The shift away from passive income compensation, through social insurance, to more active social policy support and servicing, is critically informed by the mounting evidence, collected over the past decades, of the enormous social cost of early failure and (too) late policy intervention across the life course. Early school dropout and youth unemployment massively narrow life chances in later life. Long-term unemployment easily turns into permanent labour exclusion with huge costs for individuals and society (OECD, 2007b; European Commission, 2008).

Rediscovering the state

This brings us to the more fundamental unifying tenet of the economics of the social investment perspective, bearing on its theory of the state. Distancing themselves from the neoliberal 'negative' economic theory of the state, social investment advocates view public policy as a key provider for families and labour markets. They do so on the basis of a far less sanguine understanding of efficient markets. Two economic rationales are at work here. The first relates to information asymmetries. Because citizens often lack the requisite information and capabilities to make enlightened choices, many post-industrial life course needs remain unmet because of the market failures of service under provision at too high a cost. In countering information asymmetries, the economics of social investment hark back to the original economic rationale for modern social policy as social security, offering collective insurance mechanism for redistribution over the life cycle. This is what Nicholas Barr has coined as the 'piggy-bank' function of the welfare state (Barr, 2001).

But the economics of social investment and its reaffirmation of the role of the state do not stop with 'piggy-bank' rationality. The more fundamental reason why the welfare state today must be 'active' and provide enabling social services is inherently bound up with the declining effectiveness of the logic of social insurance ever since the 1980s (Sabel et al., 2010). When the risk of industrial unemployment was still largely cyclical, it made perfect sense to administer collective social insurance funds for consumption smoothing during spells of Keynesian demand-deficient unemployment. However, when unemployment becomes structural, caused by radical shifts in labour demand and supply, intensified international competition, skill-biased technological change, the feminisation of the labour market, family transformation, and social and economic preferences for more flexible employment relations, traditional unemployment insurance no longer functions as an effective reserve income buffer between jobs in the same industry. Basic public income guarantees, therefore, have to be complemented with *capacitating* public services, a term coined by Charles Sabel, tailored to particular social needs caused by life course contingencies. Because it is difficult to privately and/or collectively insure new social risks, and as capacitating social services are not self-evidently supplied by private markets, it becomes imperative for public policy to step in for effective protection against new social risks. At the same time, however, capacitating services must be customised to individual needs across the life cycle to be effective.

In terms of substance, three areas of public policy stand out in the social investment perspective: bearing on human capital improvement, the family's relation to the economy and employment relations. The role of human capital, ensuring learning abilities during the life course, and its interaction with the welfare state, is the lynchpin of the social investment perspective. In an ageing economy with widening inequalities, raising the quality and quantity of human capital is imperative to sustain generous and effective welfare states, beginning in early childhood. One period of education at the beginning of one's life is no longer a good enough basis for a successful career. In economics, the case for human capital enhancement goes back to endogenous growth theory of the 1980s, suggesting that long-term growth is determined more by human capital investment decisions than by external shocks and demographic change (Lucas, 1988; Agell et al., 1997). It should, however, be emphasised that education and training as a means of raising the quality of the workforce take many years. The case of high-quality early childhood intervention is most powerfully argued by the economic Nobel laureate James Heckman. Since cognitive and non-cognitive abilities influence school success and, subsequently, adult chances in working life, the policy imperative is to ensure a 'strong start', that is, investment in the training of young children (Heckman, 2000; Heckman and Lochner, 2000).

As female participation is paramount to sustainable welfare states and parenting is crucial to child development, and thus to the shape of future life chances, policy makers have many reasons to want to support robust families, which under post-industrial economic conditions implies helping parents find a better balance between work and family life. The economic reasoning of the OECD in their *Babies and Bosses* (2007a) studies is that when parents cannot realise their aspiration in work and family life, including the number of children they aspire to, not only is their wellbeing impaired, but also economic progress is curtailed through reduced labour supply and lower productivity, which ultimately undermine the long-term fiscal sustainability of universal welfare systems. To the extent that low levels of education in less well-off groups depress productivity, underinvestment in education will engender stunted economic growth and decreased tax revenue. Overinvestment by work-rich families in their offspring offers little compensation for this fundamental market failure.

In the post-industrial context of new social risks and flexible careers, the goal of full employment has come to require far more differentiated employment patterns over the life course. In the aggregate, maximising employment, rather than fighting formal unemployment, should be the prime policy objective. A new model of employment relations is in the making whereby both men and women share working time, which enable them to keep enough time for catering to their families. Higher employment of women typically raises the demand for regular jobs in the areas of care for children and other dependants as well as for consumer-oriented services in general. If part-time work is recognised as a normal job, supported by access to basic social security, and allows for normal career development and basic economic independence, part-time jobs can generate gender equality and active security of working families. Accommodating critical life course transitions thus reduces the probability of being trapped into inactivity and welfare dependency and thus harbours both individual and economic gains (Kok et al., 2003; European Commission, 2006, 2008). Günther Schmid (2008) advocates that in an environment where workers experience more frequent labour market transitions, not only between employment and unemployment, but across a far wider set of opportunities and contingencies, including full- and part-time work, self-employment, training, family care, parental leave, child rearing and gradual retirement, policy supports are needed for individuals to successfully manage these transitions, preferably in accordance with productivity enhancing flexibility and higher employment levels. The issue is not maximum labour market flexibility or the neoliberal mantra of 'making work pay'. Instead, the policy imperative is for 'making transitions pay' over the life cycle through the provision of 'active securities' or 'social bridges', ensuring that non-standardised employment relations become 'stepping stones' to sustainable careers.

The explicit reappraisal of the role of the state as a necessary social investor is confronted with the overriding public finance limitation, anchored in the Maastricht criteria and the Stability and Growth Pact. As long as the neoliberal doctrine of balanced budgets and price stability continue to be viewed as sufficient conditions for overall macroeconomic stability, the shift towards social investment remains heavily constrained. While all the available evidence suggests that investments in child care and education will, in the long run, pay for themselves, existing public finance practices consider any form of social policy spending only as pure consumption. This may be true for the modus operandi of the post-war welfare state, which was indeed income-transfer biased. Today, as the welfare state is in process of becoming more service based, there is a clear need to distinguish social investments from consumption spending. A new regime of public finance that would allow finance ministers to (a) identify real public investments with estimated real return, and (b) examine the joint expenditure trends in markets and governments alike, has become imperative. This would be akin to distinguishing between current and capital accounts in welfare state spending, just as private companies do, as Esping-Andersen argues (2006).

Conclusion

In a deliberately stylised manner, this chapter has traced the evolution of the welfare state since the mid-twentieth century through three periods, each marked by distinct combinations of socioeconomic conditions, economic analysis and social policy prescription, shaped in turn by political contestation and compromise. Over the long run history of the modern welfare state we can observe how welfare Keynesianism and neoliberal policy prescriptions, in part, sowed the seeds of their own demise. Although neoliberal policy prescriptions helped to improve monetary stability, budgetary restraint, together with micro level labour market flexibility and social insurance activation, made conservative governments turn a blind eye to the political correlates of new social risks associated with the feminisation of the labour market, family change and the new demography of low fertility, ageing populations and the obvious market failures of private social service provision. As the epoch of welfare retrenchment gave rise to new inequalities and growth deficiencies, the social investment perspective, with employment participation, human capital formation, family and child care servicing at its core, emerged from the widespread disenchantment with neoliberal retrenchment and deregulation over the 1990s.

The rise of the social investment perspective thus exemplifies how political and economic developments are not tied together in any straightforward 'functional' manner (Hirschman, 1981). Over the 1990s it also became clear that dramatised neoliberal forebodings of the demise of the welfare state were much exaggerated. To wit, some of the most generous welfare states, with large public sectors devoted to human capital formation and family services, outperformed many of the most liberal political economies (Lindert, 2004). Especially the Nordic countries, in the words of André Sapir, proved best able to match 'high efficiency' in the economy with 'high equity' in the distribution of life chances (Sapir, 2006). In other words, an ambitious, generous and active welfare state, with a strong social investment impetus, proved to be an asset rather than liability in the emerging knowledge economy, before the onslaught of the early twenty-first-century Great Recession.

The current economic crisis will have profound repercussions for European welfare states. The years ahead will differ markedly from the epoch when the social investment ideas were first launched by Giddens, Esping-Andersen et al., Vandenbroucke and Delors, and diffused by the OECD and the EU. Will the determined fiscal response in 2008 and 2009, based on an emergency reconversion to the economic teachings of John Maynard Keynes, be followed by a more general reappraisal of generous welfare states, in the wake of the first crisis of twenty-first-century capitalism? Will the social investment perspective carry the day, or revert to marginality? Initially, the member states of the EU have responded to the crisis by extending short-term working arrangements, training and activation, gender equality in labour markets, and later retirement, fairly consistent with the social investment perspective. It remains, however, to be seen to what extent the pro-welfare consensus will be sustained once the calls for an 'exit strategy' of deficit and debt reduction, based on the mantra of balanced budgets and disinflation, grow louder. Social investment doesn't come cheap. To free up resources for social investment under post-crisis austerity conditions inevitably requires policy makers to step up social reform, particularly in the areas of pensions and labour market regulation, which endorse the principles of active ageing and transitional employment relations. It seems highly likely that the massive increase in fiscal deficits and public debt to levels not seen since World War II will force policy makers to restrain welfare commitments in order to sustain economic stability. After a two-decade loss of faith in public action ('blame-it-on-the-state'), the final downfall of the neoliberal efficient market and rational expectations hypotheses is no guarantee for the acceleration of welfare state renewal following the strictures of social investment policy analysis. But although the crisis is likely to put a strain on many welfare institutions, this could also engender positive consequences. For one, social policy has resurfaced at the centre of the political debate. People once again realise how important public institutions are to economic stability. Moreover, dire economic conditions will not make it politically opportune for policy makers to easily abandon welfare commitments. In this respect, the economic crisis may reinforce, rather than undermine, the portent of social investment welfare in the aftermath of the worst recession since the Great Depression.

References

Agell, J., Lindh, T. and Ohlsson, H. (1997) 'Growth and the public sector: A critical review essay', *European Journal of Political Economy*, 13 (1), 33–52.

Akerlof, G.A. and Schiller, R.J. (2009) *Animal Spirits: How Human Psychology Drives the Economy and why it Matters for Global Capitalism.* Princeton: Princeton University Press.

Atkinson, A.B. (1999) *The Economic Consequences of Rolling Back the Welfare State.* Cambridge, MA: MIT Press.

Barr, N.A. (2001) *The Welfare State as Piggy Bank: Information, Risk, Uncertainty, and the Role of the State.* Oxford: Oxford University Press.

Beveridge, W.H. ([1942] 1995) *Social Insurance and Allied Services.* London: HMSO.

Beveridge, W.H. (1945) *Full Employment in a Free Society.* New York: W.W. Norton & Company.

Blanchard, O. (2006) 'European unemployment: The evolution of facts and ideas', *Economic Policy*, 21 (45), 5–59.

Blanchard, O. and Summers, L. (1987) 'Hysteresis in unemployment', *European Economic Review,* 31 (1–2), 288–95.

Council of the European Union (2000) *Conclusions of the Lisbon European Council*, Ref. SN 100/00, March 23–24, 2000.

Crouch, C. (1999) *Social Change in Western Europe.* Oxford: Oxford University Press.

Crouch, C. and Pizzorno, A. (1978) (eds) *The Resurgence of Class Conflict in Western Europe since 1968.* London: Macmillan.

Crozier, M., Huntington, S.P. and Watanuki, J. (1975) *The Crisis of Democracy: Report on the Governability of Democracies to the Trilateral Commission.* New York: New York University Press.

De Grauwe, P. (2010) 'Animal spirits and monetary policy', *Economic Theory.* DOI: 10.1007/s00199-010-0543-0.

Delors, J. and Dollé, M. (2009) *Investir dans le Social.* Paris: Odile Jacob.

Ebbinghaus, B. and Hassel, A. (2000) 'Striking deals: Concertation in the reform of continental European welfare states', *Journal of European Public Policy*, 7 (1), 44–62.

Eichhorst, W. and Hemerijck, A. (2008) 'Welfare and employment: A European dilemma?', in J. Alber and N. Gilbert (eds) *United in Diversity? Comparing Social Models in Europe and America.* Oxford: Oxford University Press, pp. 201–36.

Esping-Andersen, G. (1990) *The Three Worlds of Welfare Capitalism.* Cambridge, UK: Polity Press.

Esping-Andersen, G. (1994) 'Welfare states and the economy', in N.J. Smelser and R. Swedberg (eds) *The Handbook of Economic Sociology.* Princeton/New York: Princeton University Press/Russel Sage Foundation, pp. 711–32.

Esping-Andersen, G. (2006) 'Putting the horse in front of the cart: Towards a social model for mid-century Europe', *WRR-lecture 2005*, pp. 31–69.

Esping-Andersen, G. and Palier, B. (2008) *Trois Leçons sur l'État-Providence.* Paris: Seuil, La Républiques des Idées.

Esping-Andersen, G., Gallie, D., Hemerijck, A. and Myles, J. (2002) *Why we Need a New Welfare State.* Oxford: Oxford University Press.

European Commission (2000) *Social Policy Agenda.* European Commission, Brussels.

European Commission (2006) *Implementing the Renewed Lisbon Strategy for Growth and Jobs: A Year of Delivery.* COM (2006), 816 final, Part I, 12 December 2006.

European Commission (2008) *Renewed Social Agenda: Opportunities, Access and Solidarity in 21st Century Europe.* COM (2008), 412 final, 2 July, 2008.

Flora, Peter (1986–7) *Growth to Limits: The Western European Welfare States since World War II,* vols 1–4. Berlin and New York: De Gruyter.

Friedman, Milton (1962) *Capitalism and Freedom.* Chicago: University of Chicago Press.

Genschel, P. (2004) 'Globalization and the welfare state: A retrospective', *Journal of European Public Policy,* 11 (4), 613–36.

Giddens, A. (1998) *The Third Way: The Renewal of Social Democracy.* Cambridge: Polity Press.

Giddens, A., Diamond, P. and Liddle, R. (eds) (2006) *Global Europe, Social Europe.* Cambridge: Polity Press.

Hall, P.A. (1989) *The Political Power of Economic Ideas: Keynesianism Across Nations.* Princeton: Princeton University Press.

Hay, C. (2004) 'Common trajectories, variable paces, divergent outcomes? Models of European capitalism under conditions of complex economic interdependence', *Review of International Political Economy,* 11 (2), 231–62.

Hayek, F.A. (1944) *The Road to Serfdom.* Chicago: The University of Chicago Press.

Hayek, F.A. (1960) *The Constitution of Liberty.* London: Routledge and Kegan Paul.

Heckman, J.J. (2000) 'Policies to foster human capital', *Research in economics,* 54 (1), 3–56.

Heckman, J.J. and Lochner, L. (2000) 'Rethinking myths about education and training: Understanding the sources of skill formation in a modern economy', in S. Danziger and J. Waldfogel (eds) *Securing the Future: Investing in Children from Birth to College.* Russell Sage Foundation: New York, pp. 47–83.

Hemerijck, A. (2002) 'The self- transformation of the European social model(s)', in G. Esping-Andersen with D. Gallie, A. Hemerijck and J. Myles, *Why we Need a New Welfare State.* Oxford: Oxford University Press, pp. 173–244.

Hemerijck, A. (1997) *Social Policy as a Productive Factor.* The Hague/ Brussels: Ministry of Social Affairs and Employment and European Commission.

Hemerijck, A. (2011) *Changing Welfare States.* Oxford: Oxford University Press.

Hirschman, A.O. (1981) *Essays in Trespassing: Economics to Politics and Beyond.* Cambridge: Cambridge University Press.

Institute for Futures Studies (2006) *Sustainable Policies in an Ageing Europe: A Human Capital Response*. Stockholm: Institute for Futures Studies.

Jenson, J. (2010) 'Diffusing ideas for after neoliberalism. The social investment perspective in Europe and Latin America', *Global Social Policy*, 10 (1), 59–84.

Jenson, J. and Saint-Martin, D. (2003) 'New routes to social cohesion? Citizenship and the social investment state', *Canadian Journal of Sociology*, 28 (1), 77–99.

Kenworthy, L. (2008) *Jobs with Equality*. Oxford: Oxford University Press.

Keynes, J.M. (1973 [1936]) *The General Theory of Employment, Interest and Money*. London: Macmillan for the Royal Economic Society.

Kok, W., Dell'Aringa, C., Lopez, F.D., Eckström, A., Rodrigues, M.J., Roux, A. and Schmid, G. (2003) *Jobs, Jobs, Jobs: Creating more Employment in Europe: Report of the European Commission's Employment Taskforce*. Brussels: European Commission.

Lindbeck, A. (1994) 'The welfare state and the employment problem', *The American Economic Review*, 84 (2), 71–75.

Lindert, P.H. (2004) *Growing Public: Social Spending and Economic Growth since the Eighteenth Century*. Cambridge: Cambridge University Press

Lucas, R.E. (1988) 'On the mechanics of economic development', *Journal of Monetary Economics*, 22 (1), 3–42.

Maier, C.S. (1987) *In Search of Stability: Explorations in Historical Political Economy*. Cambridge: Cambridge University Press.

Marglin, S.A. and Schor ,J.B. (1990) *The Golden Age of Capitalism: Reinterpreting the Postwar Experience*. Oxford: Clarendon Press.

Marshall, T.H. (1992 [1950]) *Citizenship and Social Class*. London: Pluto Press.

McNamara, K. (1998) *The Currency of Ideas: Monetary Politics in the European Union*. Ithaca, NY: Cornell University Press.

Mead, L.M. (1986) *Beyond Entitlement: The Social Obligations of Citizenship*. New York: Basic Books.

Murray, C.A. (1984) *Losing Ground: American Social Policy 1950–1980*. New York: Basic Books.

NESC (National Economic and Social Council) (2005) *The Developmental Welfare State*. Dublin: National Economic and Social Council.

OECD (1994) *The OECD Jobs Study: Facts, Analysis, Strategies*. Paris: OECD.

OECD (1996) *Beyond 2000: The new social policy agenda*. Paris: OECD.

OECD (1997) *The OECD Jobs Strategy: Making Work Pay. Taxation, Benefits, Employment and Unemployment.* Paris: OECD.

OECD (2006a) *OECD Employment Outlook: Boosting Jobs and Income.* Paris: OECD.

OECD (2006b) *Starting Strong.* Paris: OECD.

OECD (2007a) *Babies and Bosses.* Paris: OECD.

OECD (2007b) *Understanding the Social Outcomes of Learning.* Paris: OECD.

OECD (2008) *Growing Unequal.* Paris: OECD.

Pierson, P. (2002) 'Coping with permanent austerity: Welfare state restructuring in affluent democracies', *Revue Française de Sociologie,* 43 (2), 369–406.

Rueda, D. (2007) *Social Democracy Inside Out: Partisanship and Labor Market Policy in Advanced Industrialized Democracies.* Oxford: Oxford University Press.

Ruggie, J.G. (1994) 'Trade, protectionism and the future of welfare capitalism', *Journal of International Affairs,* 48, 1–11.

Sabel, C., Saxenian, A., Miettinen, R., Kristensen, P.H. and Hautamäki, J. (2010) 'Individualized service provision in the new welfare state: Lessons from special education in Finland', *Draft Report Prepared for SITRA,* Helsinki.

Sapir, A. (2006) 'Globalization and the Reform of European Social Models', *Journal of Common Market Studies,* 44 (2), 369–90.

Scharpf, F.W. (1991) *Crisis and Choice in European Social Democracy.* Ithaca/London: Cornell University Press.

Scharpf, F.W. (2003) 'The vitality of the nation state in 21st century Europe', in WRR, *De Vitaliteit van de Nationale Staat in het Europa van de 21ste Eeuw. WRR lecture 2002.* Groningen: Stenfert Kroese, pp. 15–30.

Scharpf, F.W. and Schmidt V. A. (eds) (2000) *Welfare and Work in the Open Economy: From Vulnerability to Competitiveness* (vol. 1). New York: Oxford University Press.

Schmid, G. (2008) *Full Employment in Europe: Managing Labour Market Transition and Risks.* Cheltenham: Elgar.

Swank, D. (2002) *Global Capital, Political Institutions and Policy Change in Developed Welfare States.* Cambridge, UK: Cambridge University Press.

Taylor-Gooby, P. (ed.) (2004) *New Risks, New Welfare: The Transformation of the European Welfare State.* Oxford: Oxford University Press.

Vandenbroucke, F. (2002) foreword in G. Esping-Andersen, D. Gallie, A. Hemerijck and J. Myles (2002) *Why We Need a New Welfare State.* Oxford: Oxford University Press, pp. i–xvi.

THREE

Redesigning citizenship regimes after neoliberalism: moving towards social investment

Jane Jenson

Long before the financial meltdown of autumn 2008 revealed the fundamental limits of financial deregulation and reliance on regulation by market relations, policy makers in many countries recognised that neoliberalism had reached its social policy limits. Rising child poverty rates and growing numbers of working poor, as well as gaps in benefit coverage and imbalances in programme financing, had already led social policy makers to rethink neoliberalism's understanding of what relations ought to be among states and markets, communities and families. Indeed the mid-1990s brought the spread of new ideas about the social investment perspective (Jenson and Saint-Martin, 2003; see also Chapter Two in this volume).[1]

This perspective has gained traction over the last 15 years and as it has done so ideas about social citizenship were transformed from those developed during the years of welfare state expansion described in Chapter Two. Social citizenship regimes that now rely on the social investment perspective are intended to sustain a knowledge-based and service economy, one quite different from that of the years after 1945 when welfare regimes were being built and consolidated. The announced goals of the social investment perspective are to increase social inclusion and minimise the intergenerational transfer of poverty as well as to ensure that the population is well-prepared for the likely employment conditions (less job security; more precarious forms of contracts) of contemporary economies. Doing so will supposedly allow individuals and families to maintain responsibility for their wellbeing via market incomes and intrafamily exchanges, as well as lessen the threats to welfare regimes and their programmes coming from ageing societies and family transformations.

Rather than advocating the minimalist state dear to neoliberals, proponents of the social investment perspective assign the state a key role in fostering these outcomes. In policy terms this implies increased attention to and investment in human capital, making work pay and early childhood, bringing new or different patterns of social spending: focused on education, particularly early childhood education; stressing support for labour market participation, particularly among categories such as lone parents and young parents; and seeking to make work pay, particularly for low wage and often service sector jobs. Policies include those for early childhood education and care (rather than day care), provision of in-work benefits (rather than social assistance or allowances), as well as support for job training and job searches (in addition to unemployment insurance).

The social investment perspective is historically located and rooted.[2] Governments that adopted it neither began from a clean slate nor developed the perspective in an independent fashion. It has been promoted by specific political forces, international organisations and policy networks. It has been grafted to existing welfare regimes, and many of the familiar differences across regime types remain visible even when the social investment perspective inspires policy design. Despite this variation, however, there is merit in undertaking a systematic analysis of the general terms of the social investment perspective. The goal of this chapter is to provide an ideal-type overview of the social investment perspective, by focusing on the ways in which the main principles that inform it have altered the notions of social citizenship embedded in post-1945 welfare regimes. These principles of the perspective are: (i) that learning is the pillar of the economies of the future, and therefore early childhood and school years are key moments for intervention; (ii) policy should focus on assuring the future of today's young people, so as to break the intergenerational cycle of poverty; and (iii) that investing in individual success enriches our common future and is beneficial for the community as a whole, now and into the future (Jenson and Saint-Martin, 2006: 435).

The proposition of the chapter is that the characteristics of the social investment perspective result from the joint legacies of post-1945 welfare regimes and of their encounter with neoliberalism, particularly its critiques of the state. They are neither the simple result of a shift in the structure of social needs nor yet another example of path dependency within a fixed institutionalised trajectory. The perspective emerges from policy thinking by think tanks, international organisations and particularly by governments seeking to recalibrate social policy interventions in the light of the criticisms and the political conflicts they sustained. Governments that have adopted the social investment perspective have not tried to return to the Keynesian past; nor did they reject all of the social thinking of neoliberalism. They did, however, begin to retreat from classical neoliberalism's emphasis on markets and communities as the only legitimate pillars of wellbeing and started to identify ways to better address the new social risks of contemporary economic and social relations. In doing so, they were redesigning social citizenship and relations between the state and citizens more broadly.

What is going on ...?

There is, of course, no academic consensus that the social investment perspective is any different from the neoliberal ideas – whether Thatcherism, Reaganism or the Washington Consensus – that have assaulted centre-left positions since the late 1970s. While the promised slashing of state expenditures and cutbacks in the welfare state threatened by neoliberal ideologues never happened,[3] it was nonetheless also clear that 'something was going on...'.

One position in this debate is that social-investment thinking is nothing but the wolf in new sheep's clothing. Some argue, for example, that we are simply seeing the rollout of neoliberalism (Peck and Tickell, 2002).[4] As recently as 2007 the Marxist geographer David Harvey published this broad-brushed picture of worldwide neoliberalism (2007: 23):

> there has everywhere been an emphatic turn, ostensibly led by the Thatcher/Reagan revolutions in Britain and the United States, in political-economic practices and thinking since the 1970s. State after state, from the new ones that emerged from the collapse of the Soviet Union to old-style social democracies and welfare states such as New Zealand and Sweden, have embraced, sometimes voluntarily and sometimes in response to coercive pressures, some version of neoliberal theory and adjusted at least some of their policies and practices accordingly.

Other analysts, however, identify sufficient change in policy logics to argue that 'after neoliberalism' is under construction (Larner and Craig, 2005). Yet even for the latter, there is little agreement about how to label what is emerging. Multiple candidates are suggested: simply a 'new welfare state' (Esping-Andersen et al., 2002); 'inclusive liberalism' (Porter and Craig, 2004; Mahon, 2008); the 'LEGO™ paradigm' (Jenson and Saint-Martin, 2006); a 'developmental welfare state' (Hemerijck, 2007); or, as here, the social investment perspective.

In large part, whether one sees little change or some change depends on the focal point of the analysis. For those whose level of analysis is social structures and whose object of analysis is the social relations of capitalism, there is a tendency to gloss over policy differences, in order to describe unchanging deep structures and their adjustable political forms. Just as post-1945 liberal democracy, even its labour-inclusive forms, was sometimes described as the 'best possible political shell for capitalism' (Jessop, 1978, for example), many see a redesigned and 'modernised' political shell playing the same role.[5] For others, however, whose object of analysis is public policy, this ongoing neoliberal hegemony is harder to find. Some policy analysts attest to 'the *different variants* of neoliberalism, to the *hybrid nature* of contemporary policies and programmes, or to the *multiple and contradictory aspects* of neoliberal spaces, techniques, and subjects' (Larner, 2003: 509, italics in the original). Others conclude that welfare regimes have the potential to change 'family' (Castles, 2005: 420–21) and new paradigms may emerge, even in the stickiest of welfare regimes, the Bismarckian ones (Palier, 2010: 365 ff., for example).

Such policy analysis has led to empirical findings that raise difficult questions for broad-brush characterisations of neoliberalism, such as that provided by Harvey. For example, well before Peck and Tickell (2002: 380) penned a sentence characterising neoliberalism everywhere as marrying 'aggressive forms of state downsizing, austerity financing, and public service "reform"', the failure of US and British neoliberal projects to downsize significantly had been amply documented (for example, Pierson, 1994), as were the variable consequences of neoliberal projects for social citizenship (for example, Jenson and Sineau, 2001). Analyses of some international organisations in the 1990s pointed to policy stances that could hardly be described as a 'neoliberal stalking horse' (Deacon and Kaasch, 2008; Jenson, 2010: 68 ff. on UNICEF, for example). Even the World Bank by 1997 has rediscovered the positive benefits of an active state.[6]

This lack of consensus either about naming a policy trend or about uncovering varied expressions and implementation of an idea about social investment is not unusual, of course. After 1945 even J.M. Keynes' ideas about macroeconomics were domesticated in a variety of ways by national governments, and often even labelled as something other than 'Keynesian'. After the fact, however, the general trend toward countercyclical spending linked to social protection was identifiable in numerous locations and jurisdictions, giving rise to the general descriptions of the 30 years after 1945 as those of the Keynesian welfare state.

The analytic task, then, is to go beyond local expressions and variations to uncover the policy logic. Doing so reveals growing policy enthusiasm for a social investment perspective and the adjustments in social citizenship that it implies. Its logic differs from those of the social state of the Keynesian era or the privatisation emphasis in neoliberalism, as this chapter maps in detail.

The social investment perspective and social citizenship

There are good reasons why a lack of academic consensus exists, however, and they go beyond the issues of level or object of analysis. History and ideas about its patterns have shifted greatly over the last three decades. By the 1980s social citizenship and macroeconomic policy seemed at loggerheads. The assemblage put into place after 1945 is frequently described as the Keynesian welfare state in order to indicate that it both stressed countercyclical spending and contained a commitment to social citizenship (among many, Quadagno, 1987, provides a useful overview). As Chapter Two documents, in the 1980s Keynesians' inability to manage the theoretically unexpected stagflation – simultaneously ballooning unemployment and inflation – opened the door to neoliberals to attack both macroeconomic ideas and the principles of social citizenship that accompanied them. The Keynesian notion that there was 'no perceived trade-off between social security and economic growth, between equality and efficiency' disappeared (Esping-Andersen, 1996: 3).

Calls for retrenchment of public spending so vigorously proclaimed by neoliberals presented state spending itself as 'the problem'. Neoliberals argued that there was a choice to be made between employment growth and generous social protection based on egalitarian principles. There was, in other words, a choice between a growing economy and continued commitment to the principles of social citizenship. Many pointed to the liberal and ungenerous welfare regime in the USA where jobs were multiplying. They prescribed it as a universal model, especially for those who stubbornly clung to values of equality or even equity.

The first hints of the emerging social investment perspective appeared among those who refused to follow this prescription: 'Critics insist that the associated costs of the American route are too high in terms of polarization and poverty. They suggest a "social investment" strategy as an alternative' (Esping-Andersen, 1996: 3). This proposal, made in a publication sponsored by the United Nations Research Institute for Social Development (UNRISD), was simultaneously echoed by the

OECD. The 1996 high-level conference, *Beyond 2000: The New Social Policy Agenda*, concluded with a call for a 'new framework for social policy reform', labelled a social investment approach, in which 'the challenge is to ensure that return to social expenditures are maximised, in the form of social cohesion and active participation in society and the labour market' (OECD, 1997: 5–6). With such analyses, ideas about social citizenship were being reworked (Jenson and Saint-Martin, 2003).

Among other things, the social investment perspective is founded on a different notion of time than those associated with either Keynesianism or neoliberalism. In the Keynesian perspective the here-and-now was the most important timeframe and social citizenship focused on inequalities, inequities and challenges of the present that would be addressed in the present. The countercyclical economic instruments obviously supported such a notion of time. One innovation of the neoliberal perspective was its focus on the future. As the standard analysis put it, spending in the present would risk mortgaging the wellbeing of future generations; it was better to keep deficits and certainly debt low than to do that. The social investment perspective also looks to the future but in a somewhat different way. The profits of any investment are located in the future, whereas consumption is something that occurs in the present. In this perspective then, for social spending to be effective and therefore worthwhile it must not simply be consumed in the present to meet current needs but it must be an investment that will pay off, generating returns in the future (Jenson and Saint-Martin, 2006: 440).

In this discourse of social investment, it is acceptable for the state to have a significant role, but only when it is behaving like a good business would, seeking to increase the promise of future returns. Spending for current needs, in contrast, must be canny and limited. There are, however, certain core costs which must be met so as to keep the enterprise solvent – that is, to provide some protection against the costs of social exclusion. But such spending on items which are not really investments should be limited, directed only where it is 'really needed'. Spotlighting the future also focuses policy attention on results (outcomes) and to life course analyses based on time series information.

The rest of this chapter maps the general notions that underpin the policy model that follows from social investment perspective. Doing so, the chapter maps the ways the perspective is reconfiguring ideas and practices of social citizenship.[7] In order to undertake this mapping, I use the heuristic of the *citizenship regime*, an analytic grid that permits one to make visible three intersecting dimensions of social citizenship: rights and duties, access and governance, and the responsibility mix

(Jenson and Phillips, 1996, 2001). Doing so in a comparative fashion provides a documentation of the characteristics of the social investment perspective compared to two other policy logics, those of Keynesianism and neoliberalism. These differences are also summarised in a more stylised way in each of the tables.

The responsibility mix

The responsibility mix refers first and foremost to the distribution within what we can label the welfare diamond. This four-cornered image captures the distribution of responsibility for wellbeing among the market, family, community and state. That which is assigned to the state constitutes the essential elements of social citizenship. Characteristics of the responsibility mix in the three eras of social policy are summarised in Table 3.1.

In the era of the Keynesian mixed economy all welfare regimes allocated a major role to the market as the foundation of wellbeing for most citizens and their family. The role of the other three sectors was to fill gaps left by market provision of income or services, while the state in particular would compensate for inadequate or limited market access (because of age, illness, family circumstances, lack of education and skills, and so on) or to make decommodification possible (so as to engage in training, parenting, and so on). Under the influence of Keynesian macroeconomic thinking the prevailing assumption was that social spending 'would complement the market economy: it would be an instrument of automatic countercyclical stabilization, it would ensure an educated and healthy workforce; and it would provide the complex social infrastructure essential to an urban economy' (Banting, 1987: 185). It would also complement the family's contribution to intergenerational wellbeing and reproduction. The community corner of the welfare diamond was important because many social services were publicly funded but actually provided by organisations in the third sector and anchored in the community (Evers, 2009: 247; and passim). After 1945, the mutualist movement, private philanthropic foundations and churches all continued to sponsor hospitals, seniors' residences, schools and so on, providing many health and education services, often using public funds. Sometimes the partnership was quite explicit, as in the Bismarckian welfare regimes of continental Europe, where religious institutions and unions organised and ran pension funds and provided social services. Sometimes the partnership was very important but less visible, as in liberal welfare regimes where the growth of the welfare state also involved the expansion of non-profit

Table 3.1: Three perspectives on the responsibility mix of the citizenship regime

	Keynesian perspective	Neoliberal perspective	Social investment perspective
Responsibility mix principally involves	Market, state, family	Market, family, community	Market, family, state, community
Market	Can provide wellbeing for all, with a few exceptions	Should provide wellbeing for all	May not provide sufficiently for all
Family	Children are the responsibility of the family	Families need to take responsibility and make choices for themselves	Families have primary responsibility for children, but the state has responsibility too
State	Should spend to provide protection against social risks	Spending should be limited, because the state can create the risk of dependency	Spending should be investments, such as in human capital to support labour market participation in the future as well as the present, or to confront new social risks and poverty
Community	Represents citizens and advocates Provides services in the shadow of the welfare state	May serve as a cushion to spending cutbacks and market failure	Potential partner in the provision of services, and source of local as well as expert knowledge

agencies providing services of all kinds and usually at least partially with public funds.

In post-1945 Keynesian welfare states, policy communities tended to describe government spending on social programmes and services as support for 'social security' or for 'social protection'. In contrast to this formulation, the neoliberal enthusiasts of the 1980s assumed that markets could and should generate all wellbeing and they promulgated the notion that social spending and state intervention were in conflict with economic prosperity. Such ideas generated neoliberals' vision of the proper responsibility mix, downplaying the role of the state. Neoliberals advocated redesigning relationships across the welfare diamond, so as to allow markets especially but also community-based organisations to reclaim their 'rightful' space in the allocation of wellbeing. Families were also called on to 'exercise greater responsibility' for themselves. The goal of these ideologues was to shrink the space of social citizenship.

Under the influence of neoliberals, governments limited access to social programmes and redesigned benefits. Those for the unemployed and recipients of social assistance were targeted for cutbacks if not elimination, at the same time that programmes were intended to ensure that the 'employables' (particularly young people and lone parents) would take up work rather than relying on social transfers. The neoliberal perspective was particularly enthusiastic about the role of the community sector, seeing it as an alternative source for collective solidarity to that of the state. Communities and organisations were called on to organise themselves to become more businesslike, and as such they could hope to be given contracts to provide services such as job training or for vulnerable older people (Newman et al., 2004).

The social investment perspective's macroeconomic analysis retains the focus on the supply-side that neoliberalism instituted; it is in this context that talk of social 'investment' (rather than spending) provides discursive coherence. When enthusiastic about the market it is of course natural to speak of investments. Therefore, as more activities are organised according to market principles, individuals and their families are called upon 'to invest in their own human capital' so as to succeed in the labour market. At the same time they are called to invest in their own futures, via savings for their retirement pensions and their children's education. But, in contrast to neoliberal ideas, the state is also meant to share some of this responsibility, by ensuring services (for example, child care) are in adequate supply as well as by providing in-work benefits to compensate for the fact that market incomes are often not high enough to meet family needs and avoid working poverty. It must also ensure access to the means of acquiring human capital via education and training.

Such policy prescriptions clearly signal that the social investment perspective is not simply an antipoverty measure; social investments are for the middle class too. It is an understanding of public interventions, in other words, that rallies those who want social policy to focus on education, including early childhood education, on training and on making work pay, as well as those who are concerned about child poverty. Sharing the OECD's key notion developed in the mid-1990s that social spending is not a burden but an investment in economic growth, the European Union could quickly move towards its own version, beginning as early as 1997 to describe *social policy as a productive factor* (see Chapter Two in this volume).

Despite allocating a larger role to the state and opening up greater space for social citizenship, the social investment perspective does not reject the premise of either Keynesians or neoliberals that the market ought to be the primary source of wellbeing. It too emphasises the importance of paid employment and other forms of market income. But whereas neoliberals assumed that market participation was the solution, the social investment perspective is suspicious that the market may not be producing sufficient employment for everyone. When social citizenship came to be oriented by what Jane Lewis (2001) has termed the adult worker model (replacing the male breadwinner model), market failure and the existence of the working poor are a challenge. Therefore, a common social investment prescription is the need to 'make work pay', not simply by making it competitive with social benefits rates but also by supplementing wages, providing low-cost services, or both.[8] In other words, the market sector of the responsibility mix requires restructuring.

It is also in similar terms that early childhood education and care (ECEC) can become a support for economic growth and social development: it is the starting point for investments in human capital. In the mid-1990s, for example, Swedish Prime Minister and leader of the Social Democrats, Göran Persson, announced 'a major change' in the philosophical and organisational grounding of child care (quoted in Korpi, 2007: 61):

> Lifelong learning should be a foundation stone in Government policy for combating unemployment. Sweden should be able to compete with high competence, and the prerequisites for this are to be provided through high quality in all school forms, from pre-school to higher education. The pre-school should contribute to improving the important early years of the compulsory school.

Responsibility for child care was transferred from the Swedish National Board of Health and Welfare to the Ministry of Education, to ensure that the transition to a human-capital approach was fully institutionalised. By 1998 a national preschool curriculum had been developed, focused on the skills the child should have in order to enter and succeed in school. This curriculum replaced one from earlier decades that built on values of equality and democratic citizenship (Korpi, 2007: 63).

Policy communities' focus on both making work pay and ECEC requires the state to underwrite activities which for Keynesians as much as neoliberals were market-driven or private matters, assigned to the non-state corners of the welfare diamond. In both cases neoliberals' emphasis on individual and family responsibility is muted, but there is also care to avoid the so-called limits of early welfare programmes, such as those that might have encouraged families to choose parental care over labour market participation by having a stay-at-home parent.

Rights and duties of citizenship

One of the most discussed elements of social citizenship and citizenship regimes are their assumptions about rights and duties. These have not been stable over time, as Table 3.2 maps.

Beginning in the 1940s, citizenship rights were often distributed according to one's relationship to the labour market. In Bismarckian welfare regimes, access to social rights depended on contributions to various social security systems. In liberal regimes access to social safety was available when the labour-market relationship, either of oneself or a family breadwinner, broke. And, while social democratic regimes provided more universal rights, the employment nexus in social policy thinking was central to shaping decommodification rights, for retraining, pensions, leaves and so on. Nonetheless, whether universal, targeted or based on insurance, social rights were intended to provide a significant degree of security and social protection.

In social democratic and liberal welfare regimes, social policy was also intended to encourage equality.[9] Sometimes this was done by providing similar benefits to everyone in order to foster a certain equality of condition; this was the social democratic approach. Sometimes, as liberal regimes did, the emphasis was more on equal opportunity. In all cases, however, and in the old-fashioned wording of T.H. Marshall, the goal of citizenship in the years after 1945 would '… range from the right to a modicum of economic welfare and security to the right to share to the full in the social heritage and to live the life of a civilized being according to the standards prevailing in the society' (1965 [1949]: 78).

Neoliberals advocated dismantling many of these citizenship rights. For example, Margaret Thatcher called for entitlements to be cut in order to increase individual responsibility: 'By "the healthy society" I mean … a society in which the vast majority of men and women are encouraged, and helped, to accept responsibility for themselves and their families, and to live their lives with the maximum of independence

Table 3.2: Three perspectives on social rights and duties

	Keynesian perspective	Neoliberal perspective	Social investment perspective
Social goals	Provide social protection	Avoid policy instruments that foster dependency; promote autonomy	Invest in prevention and human capital, in order to ensure growth and prosperity
Vision of equality	Equality of condition and equal opportunities	Inequality is inherent in markets and is necessary to motivate economic actors	Equality of opportunity
Citizens' duties with respect to the labour market	All citizens have a duty to work, but only male breadwinners must have paid work	All citizens have a duty to ensure they have sufficient income	All citizens have a duty to work but they also may have a right to adequate income, if the market does not provide
With respect to women's labour market activity	'Choice'	'Choice' only for those women who can afford it	'Choice' only for those women who can afford it
With respect to education	Young people must remain in school until the end of mandatory schooling	Young people should remain in school until able to support oneself and one's family	Invest in human capital, from preschool through post-secondary education
Citizens' rights with respect to income security	Benefits when families fail to provide or when ill-health and age make employment impossible	A minimum of income security for the deserving poorest of the poor, with requirement of reciprocal responsibility (workfare)	Benefits when ill-health and age make employment impossible, and when markets fail to provide sufficient income
With respect to publicly funded services	Some universally provided, some targeted	Publicly funded services only for those without adequate income or other means	Publicly funded services for those without adequate income and/or in need of support to enter employment and/or when the market fails to provide the service at an affordable price

and self-reliance.'[10] Income transfers were meant to be minimised and services, such as daycare or even health care, to be left to markets.

The social investment perspective involves a rejection of this neoliberal formulation, albeit without calling for a return to the Keynesian perspective. A major innovation involves shifting the ambition of social rights from providing protection against social risks as they occur (as Keynesians did) to fostering prevention. The result has been the creation of social programmes that focus not simply on 'the poor' but more specifically on poor children and their parents. Social investments in children – in their healthy development and preschool education – will supposedly ensure their success in school and therefore accumulation of the human capital that will allow them to break out of poverty. Thus children as well as their parents, young people and adults have a duty as citizens to invest in their human capital by seeking education and training (and saving so as to pay for it).

Activation and labour market participation for all is also a policy tool for breaking the intergenerational transmission of disadvantage, a key goal of the social investment perspective. When Keynesians described 'full employment' as a target, they really only considered half of the population, and they grounded access to many social rights in the situation of the male breadwinner. Thus women did not have the same duty as did male citizens to participate in the labour market. If women did take a job, it was often described as being by 'choice'. In exchange for performing their citizen duty, however, men gained social protection rights, supporting them if they were sick, disabled, elderly or victims of unemployment.

Neoliberals, with their emphasis on families' responsibility for themselves, tried to chip away at these rights. They targeted retirement pensions, disability pensions, social assistance and so on as being too costly to maintain. They treated lack of market income as private matters (leading to calls in some places for promoting marriage so as to reintroduce a male earner in all families) or as justification for harsh forms of workfare (in which receiving social benefits depended on having a job). Their mantra was 'any job is a good job', with little attention going to supports such as transportation, training or child care needed in order to stay in work, or to the quality of the job.

Proponents of the social investment perspective recognised that social and economic change over 60 years had made the male breadwinner model less useful and a single wage often inadequate. If a single male wage supported several adults and children 60 years ago, this is less true in the 2000s, because of job losses in the industrial sector, where wages had been high, and the rise of the service sector, with its traditionally lower-paying jobs. More generally, the polarisation of the post-industrial income structure in many countries has generated an increase in low-income rates among young families, whether lone-parent or couples, and the appearance of what has been termed 'child poverty' in many policy circles.

Thus, in countries that have moved towards the social investment perspective, active labour market policies blossomed (see Chapter Seven). While policy makers retained the notion that all citizens have a duty to work (unless a family is rich enough to live on one income), they also recognised that the state has a role in facilitating labour market participation. There provisions range widely, from providing training and support to jobseekers to reorganising the provision of child care services so as to meet the growing needs of families with employed parents (Mahon, 2008; see also Chapter Six in this volume).

Indeed, social care needs pose a challenge to increasing employment rates. Overall, and in sharp contrast to the formulations of the Keynesian era, a discursive link was made between employment of parents and a variety of social programmes seeking to increase the human capital of children and young people. One version of this congeries is provided by Hemerijck and Eichhorst (2010: 328): 'Since life chances are so strongly determined by what happens in childhood, a comprehensive child investment strategy is imperative. Inaccessible child care will provoke low fertility, low quality care is harmful to children, and low female employment rates raises child poverty.'

Nor has this analysis remained at the level of rhetoric or academic analysis. New social citizenship rights have been instituted, as the OECD documents (2006: 92): 'despite a very low base in many countries, provision for children under 3 is undergoing profound change, and receives growing government attention and funding. Since [1998] countries have introduced or made progress in policies', including parental and family leaves as well as significantly more child care services. Such provision reflects a redefinition from the post-1945 years as well as the neoliberal era of the type of rights needed by workers and parents in order to be responsible citizens.

State-supported right to accumulate assets is another favourite of the promoters of the social investment perspective. It involves public and private strategies intended to encourage and enable low-income persons to save and accumulate capital and interest, including by providing public funds to do so. Described as investments, the plans often target adult savers, through microcredit programmes, but they are also popular as tools for promoting the capacity to invest in children and their human capital.[11] In the UK, beginning in 2002 the Child

Trust Fund made several payments into an account in the child's name (at birth and age seven); this money could not be accessed by parents and the amount the state provided was higher for low-income children.

Governance arrangements and citizenship regimes

Governance arrangements include relations within the public administration, across different levels of government, and between public and private partners. The expectations with respect to all three have varied in the three eras of the welfare state, as Table 3.3 maps.

Table 3.3: Three perspectives on the governance dimension of social citizenship

	Keynesian perspective	Neoliberal perspective	Social investment perspective
Preferred forms of governance	Weberian hierarchical/ bureaucratic	Corporate models plus privatisation	Networking and partnerships
Focus for evaluation of success	Inputs (spending)	Bottom line (costs)	Outcomes (cost-benefit)
Role of intermediary groups	An organised expression of social needs and solidarity, meriting public support as part of the institutions of representation	Part of the private sector, often representing a 'special interest' Might be harnessed by government to respond to pressing social needs	An organised expression of social needs and solidarity that requires public investment to build its capacity for partnerships
Expectation of private sector	Wealth-creating sector	Model for wealth creation and regulation	Wealth-creating partner and model for regulation

Policies to provide social protection and social security put into place during the *trente glorieuses* fit well with a Weberian form of state, relying on hierarchical relations of accountability and concerned about tracking and controlling expenditures. The consolidation of welfare regimes also coincided with the last decades of nation building in Europe and North America. The policy reach of the central government finally covered the whole national territory and therefore access to social benefits and public institutions reached into the most distant and remote communities. Smoothing out regional inequities and spatial inequalities was a goal of many post-1945 welfare regimes, and this was done via a penetration of state services into all corners of what had, in many cases, been quite isolated regional enclaves, whether the far north, mountainous areas or rurally isolated territories. A bureaucrat representing the central government was often the symbol of this spatial inclusion. Coming after the horrors of World War II and during the Cold War, this consolidation was also meant to be a validation of the legitimacy of liberal and representative democracy: 'The welfare state was therefore also a political project of nation building: the affirmation of liberal democracy against the twin perils of fascism and bolshevism. Many countries became self-proclaimed welfare states, not so much to give a label to their social policies as to foster national social integration' (Esping-Andersen, 1996: 2).

As is well known, neoliberals were strong advocates of the privatisation of state services. Sometimes they argued for privatisation in the name of market fundamentalism, denigrating 'bureaucrats' and calling on state employers to behave in more businesslike ways and to manage as the private sector does, including by focusing on the 'bottom line'. As ideas about new public management took hold, among other things governments shed state employees in favour of consultants hired from the private sector to inculcate supposedly businesslike practices or financial management in government departments (for example, Saint-Martin, 1998). But frequently privatisation was also advocated in the name of 'choice'. Citizens were praised as being 'their own experts', fully capable of exercising consumer sovereignty in relationship to the services – whether public, private or community-provided – they wished to consume Jenson and Sineau, 2001: Chapter 9 (Blomqvist, 2004).

In this rush to 'choice', neoliberals also agitated for a shift in the scale of government, vaunting the local. Doing so worked what is certainly the most common and well-known dimension of this shift in scale: the emergence of 'community', in the sense that 'community is not simply the territory of government, but a *means* of government: its ties, bonds, forces, and affiliations are to be celebrated, encouraged, nurtured, shaped and instrumentalized in the hope of producing consequences that are desirable for all and for each' (Rose, 1996: 355).

When proponents of social investment regrouped in the face of the neoliberal assault, they did not reject all of these ideas. Indeed, the very label 'social investment' served to project the image of the more businesslike, market-friendly and dynamic entrepreneurial state as well as one that was more responsive to community needs and concerns. It also fits well with the ideology of the new public management that many governments had embraced since the 1980s as well as the shift in scale and responsibility to the local.

The notion that the community was the proper scale was retained in the social investment perspective, a shift that also marked a willingness to collaborate with intermediary groups. As Tony Blair and Gerhard Schroeder put it in their 1999 manifesto: 'Modern social democrats solve problems where they can best be solved. Some problems can now only be tackled at European level: others, such as the recent financial crises, require increased international co-operation. But, as a general principle, power should be devolved to the lowest possible level.' Commitment to governance practices that engage communities and NGOs is found throughout the European Union and its member states, reflected in numerous funding programmes as well as rules of engagement for the open method of coordination (Jenson and Pochet, 2006).

Patterns of access to political power have also altered with changing citizenship regimes. In the Keynesian world organised interests and associations were acceptable, indeed valued parts of the representational system. With its critiques of 'statism' and too much reliance on the public sector for the provision of wellbeing, neoliberalism assaulted existing relationships of representation, especially those involving organised labour. Beyond their attacks on trade unions, neoliberals mounted an assault on the identities of advocacy groups, labelling them 'special interests' and seeking to delegitimate their claims in the eyes of the public (Jenson and Phillips, 1996). Neoliberals favoured forms of representation that appeared to allow 'individuals' and not groups to seek representation. The social investment perspective does not favour this idea that individuals are the appropriate unit of political representation. Instead, the social investment perspective's focus on the community demonstrates the influence of a growing belief in the advantages of citizen engagement in groups and associations. The design of governance arrangements in the emerging citizenship regime relies extensively on notions of consultation, communication and local involvement (Evers, 2009: 208 ff.).

Why the social investment perspective?

When this congeries of ideas about social investment is described together and identified as constituting a policy perspective, 1996 and

1997 come to the fore as years of major change for social citizenship. By the mid-1990s, straightforward neoliberalism had hit an ideational, political and economic wall. There were clear signs of an organised critique of neoliberals' premise that social policy generated negative economic outcomes. In the European Union, policy communities composed of European and national decision makers as well as academics argued that social policy provisions could be productive factors contributing to economic performance (Jenson and Pochet, 2006; see also Chapter Two in this volume). These critiques generated a contingent convergence around ideas touching on what we are calling the social investment perspective. Where did this come from?

This last section of the chapter points to two converging factors that moved policy communities towards the social investment perspective. One is the failure of neoliberalism to live up to its own promises about economic wellbeing and stability. When crisis struck much of the world outside Europe in 1997 and as centre-left governments regained office European countries in the late 1990s, political space opened for those who would reject the neoliberal mantra of TINA (there is no alternative). But having space for alternatives does not account for which perspective comes to the fore; alternative diagnostics and prescriptions are always available, including a return to the past. One of the key characteristics of the notion of social investment, however, gives it leverage over others. It is, just as Keynesianism was before it, profoundly ambiguous. This uncertainty can be its strength. Key terms such as 'active labour market policy' can be retrieved from the years of the *trente glorieuses*, washed of their neoliberal connotations and recycled for a social investment future. Human capital investments can be stretched backward in time from the secondary and post-secondary education to which they often referred in the 1960s to include preschool education and even the developmental stimulus of infants.

The contradictions of neoliberalism

The promised cutbacks in state activity and massive savings in state expenditures failed to materialise in the 1980s and 1990s, despite the insistence by neoliberals that their main goal was slashing state budgets (Pierson, 1994; Castles, 2005). Notwithstanding the continued spending, however, social problems deepened and poverty rates mounted. Resistance to retrenchment and neoliberal politicians began to generate electoral successes for the political left in Europe. And then, in 1997, the Asian crisis destabilised the international economy and the international financial institutions in a frightening way. It provided a foretaste of the 2008 crisis that struck North America and Europe so hard.

While the earlier crisis was dramatic in its extent and consequences, the fact that it had much more limited effects on those two continents meant that much of the work at dismantling neoliberalism and building the neoliberal perspective was happening in international organisations concerned with development and non-European regions of the world. It also meant that some of the initial policy work was done in isolation. Nonetheless, by the late 1990s cross-fertilisation was occurring, as ideas about pushing human capital development and child-centred investments flowed from continent to continent (Jenson, 2010).

The Asian crisis triggered fundamental reassessments of economic and social policy in much of the world outside Europe. In several international organisations it finally became possible to question neoliberal analyses. A poverty reduction paradigm, in gestation for a number of years, solidified in the early and mid-1990s around a set of explicit and quantifiable goals for international development. This set originated in agreements and resolutions of the world conferences organised by the United Nations in the first half of the 1990s were adopted by the development ministers of the OECD in 1996, and were confirmed by the United Nations Millennium Declaration of 8 September 2000.

These actions were only generating social policy thinking of a 'safety net' sort (Deacon et al., 1997: Chapter 3), but nonetheless they did constitute a rehabilitation of social policy as a legitimate form of state action. By 1997 the World Bank had also published its annual World Development Report with the title *The State in a Changing World*. Epistemic communities were shifting their analyses.

The OECD is an international organisation that bridges Europe and Asia. A number of its members (Mexico, for example) are only middle income countries while others have only recently joined the ranks of those with modern welfare states (Korea, for example). Therefore, it is not surprising that the OECD could serve as a conduit for much of the policy puzzling in post-1997 assessments of the Asian crisis as well as exploring in the European context the contradiction between the promises of neoliberalism and its outcomes. As Chapter Two describes in some detail, in the 1980s the OECD had been the leader of the 'welfare as a burden' position, diffusing among other things the key idea among its membership and within policy communities at its 1980s conference on the welfare state in crisis that 'social policy in many countries creates obstacles to growth' (quoted in Deacon et al.,

1997: 71). By the early 1990s, however, concerns about stability in the OECD and elsewhere bubbled up in the idea sets of OECD officials. Social cohesion became a key word in policy discussion, and warnings appeared of the need to balance attention to economic restructuring with caution about societal cohesion (Jenson, 1998: 3, 5). The result is that in recent years 'the ideas underlying the OECD's social and health policies are not primarily neoliberal but rather appear to balance the economic imperatives of the international financial organizations with the social concerns of the United Nations social agencies' (Deacon and Kaasch, 2008: 226).

The focus on child development and wellbeing that characterises the social investment perspective was given a significant boost by another international organisation that bridges both Europe and the Global South. UNICEF became a key actor within the United Nations system, promoting an alternative to neoliberalism because of what its analyses of 'rich nations' revealed about neoliberal policies' particularly negative effects on children (UNICEF, 2000). At the international level UNICEF confronted the Washington Consensus head on, in the name of social investments and children (Murphy, 2006: 223 ff.). It advanced its analyses of the effect of neoliberal policy choices by tracing rising poverty for children in both rich countries and the developing world (UNICEF, 2000). Indeed, it publicised widely that two decades of Thatcherism in Britain brought a tripling of child poverty rates and that the US child poverty rate, after taxes and transfers were taken into account, was the highest among 'rich nations' (UNICEF, 2000: 21, 15).

Nonetheless, identification of these contradictions cannot by itself account for the emergence of a social investment perspective. Why did so many settle on social investment?

Rallying around (the ambiguous notion of) social investment

Work on the diffusion of ideas has frequently noted that those that spread are ones that can draw together numerous positions and sustain a moderate to high level of ambiguity. Peter Hall's edited volume on the diffusion of Keynesian ideas after 1945 made this point: 'To be Keynesian bespoke a general posture rather than a specific creed. Indeed the very ambiguity of Keynesian ideas enhanced their power in the political sphere. By reading slightly different emphases into these ideas, an otherwise disparate set of groups could unite under the same banner' (Hall in Hall, 1989: 367). The ideas that work best are those that have scientific legitimacy, often having been generated by academic research, but that also provide a commonsense meaning open to multiple interpretations (McNeill, 2006). Social investment is one such idea.

Social investment as an idea is ambiguous in its simultaneous backward and forward gaze. For example, the OECD could use it both to refer back to neoliberals' preference for markets as decision locales and to make claims for new spending, all the while allowing a distinction to be made between the 'bad old days' of social protection and the promising future of social investment. Gestures in multiple directions of this sort could turn presentations of redesigned spending into both a force for solving social problems, such as social exclusion and intergenerational poverty, and for advancing economic growth. Both could be used to justify a new claim, very different from the neoliberal *Jobs Strategy* of the 1980s (see Chapter Two), that there was a need to spend rather than simply cut back in the social realm. OECD experts diffused a social investment argument structured in now familiar terms:

> Today's labour-market, social, macro-economic and demographic realities look starkly different from those prevailing when the welfare state was constructed ... Social expenditure must move towards underwriting social investment, helping recipients to get re-established in the labour market and society, instead of merely ensuring that failure to do so does not result in destitution. (Pearson and Scherer, 1997: 6, 9)

Alongside policy makers, intellectuals from a variety of milieux have become the promoters of the social investment perspective, including its child-centred and learning focus. Initially they contributed to the ambiguity of the concept further, as each put forward his or her favourite definition or programmatic future. Perhaps the best-known intellectual promoting social investment in the European context and in terms very similar to those already developed by the OECD in the mid-1990s is Gøsta Esping-Andersen. For him, a real 'child-centred social investment strategy' is what the Nordic welfare states have been doing, and is done best there (Esping-Andersen et al., 2002: 51). This strategy is essentially one to ensure social inclusion and a competitive knowledge economy via activation, making work pay and reducing workless households, the need for all of which are included in the chapter on child-centred social investment (Esping-Andersen et al., 2002: Chapter 2). But in the mid-1990s another well-known European intellectual was calling for a 'social investment state' that would invest in human and social capital. Anthony Giddens' proposal for a more active state was more supply-side oriented and limited in its proposed interventions than were Esping-Andersen's proposals. It is not surprising, therefore, that the latter is dismissive of New Labour, often considered as having followed Giddens' version. He trumpets instead his own 'truly effective and sustainable social investment strategy' (Esping-Andersen et al., 2002: 5). We see here, however, not only a battle between two well-known intellectuals struggling for policy influence but also the range and ambiguity of the notion. Policy communities can appeal to one version or the other, or even combine the two, mixing and matching as needed.

If ambiguity is part of the appeal of the concept and the perspective, the result is that a social investment perspective can, as said in the beginning of this chapter, take on multiple colorations. These will depend in the first instance on the welfare regime to which it is being grafted and the extent to which that regime must depart from its past path in order to take up the perspective. Bismarckian regimes have had the most difficulty doing so (Palier, 2010: 385 ff.). Social democratic ones, for whom Esping-Andersen and others claim paternity of the concept of social investment, have turned older institutions to new ends, as we saw above when child care was turned towards fostering school readiness more than good citizenship. In the liberal welfare regime under the influence of Britain's New Labour, the same ambiguity allowed the party to claim continuity with its history while waving the social investment banner in the name of new times and alternative views of citizenship. The next chapters in this volume point to other examples of the ambiguity of the perspective that is helping it in a variety of ways to make headway as a viable response to the many failures of neoliberals' vision of social citizenship.

Notes

[1] This analysis, and especially the tables, is the product of initial work for a research project funded by the Social Sciences and Humanities Research Council of Canada (1999–2004). The group was composed of Paul Bernard, Alexandra Dobrowolsky, Pascale Dufour, Denis Saint-Martin and Deena White. The research has also been supported since 2001 by the same research council, via the Canada Research Chair in Citizenship and Governance.

[2] Thus it was ignored by the US government under George W. Bush, is less present in Bismarckian than liberal and social-democratic style welfare regimes, and has spread to only some but not all Latin American countries (Jenson, 2010).

[3] Careful analysis documents two patterns: (1) the three post–1945 decades were hardly a 'golden age' of universal and generous spending; and (2) spending did not decrease during the 1980s, despite the election of neoliberals such as Margaret Thatcher and Ronald Reagan (Huber and Stephens, 2001: 2).

[4] The 2006 issue of *International Organization*, edited by Beth Simmons, Frank Dobbin and Geoffrey Garrett, begins with the claim that 'the worldwide spread of economic and political liberalism was the defining feature of the late twentieth century' (2006: 781). The articles in the symposium are written in the present tense, suggesting this was still the case in the first decade of the twenty-first century.

[5] Jamie Peck enthusiastically quotes Stuart Hall, who depicted New Labour in Britain as 'what Lenin might have called "the best shell" for global capitalism' (2004: 393).

[6] The World Bank's 1997 World Development Report, *The State in a Changing World*, is sometimes identified as a marker for the shift in international organisations away from neoliberalism and its structural adjustment prescriptions. Available at http://publications.worldbank.org/ecommerce/catalog/product?item_id=203593.

[7] The material used in this mapping is generally policy documents of governments and international organisations. This collection has been accumulated since 1999, with the aid of the research support identified in note 1.

[8] For example, a survey in 2003 found that eight of the EU 15 countries had instituted an in-work benefit (Immervoll et al., 2007: 35). Sweden added its own in-work tax credit in 2007.

[9] Bismarckian regimes, in contrast, with their notion of 'earning' benefits via contributions were an exception. Their goal was essentially to preserve status differences linked to employment histories.

[10] Speech to Social Services Conference Dinner, 2 December 1976. Available at www.margaretthatcher.org/speeches/displaydocument.asp?docid=103161.

[11] The OECD (2003: 17) makes the case for these instruments being social investments in this way: 'In a publicly funded asset-building scheme, the funds that match household savings or constitute the endowments of a "baby bond" programme really are not government current expenditures. They are savings, just like those of the households they benefit. Forget how government budgets may treat them; in the national economic accounts, they ought to be counted as "government saving", which is to say "government investment". In effect and under the rules of the schemes, governments transfer to households a portion of current revenues as a claim on human or physical capital. This forms

the foundation for the idea of social investment. Following the reasoning above, it ought to be possible to simulate ex ante and to measure ex post social investment's net return over time, in terms of both economic growth and reduced income transfers because (if the arguments for Asset Building are correct) fewer people would live in poverty.'

References

Banting, K. (1987) *The Welfare State and Canadian Federalism*, 2nd edn. Montreal: McGill-Queen's University Press.

Blair, T. and Schroeder, G. (1999) *Europe: The Third Way*, available on www.socialdemocrats.org/blairandschroeder6-8-99.html.

Blomqvist, P. (2004) 'The choice revolution: Privatization of Swedish welfare services in the 1990s', *Social Policy & Administration*, 38 (2), 139–55.

Castles, F. (2005) 'Social expenditures in the 1990s: Data and determinants', *Policy & Politics*, 33 (3), 411–30.

Deacon, B. and Kaasch, A. (2008) 'The OECD's social and health policy: Neoliberal stalking horse or balancer of social and economic objectives?', in R. Mahon and S. McBride (eds) *The OECD and Transnational Governance*. Vancouver: University of British Columbia Press, pp. 226–41.

Deacon, B. with Hulse, M. and Stubbs P. (1997) *Global Social Policy: International Organizations and the Future of Welfare*. London: Sage.

Esping-Andersen, G. (ed.) (1996) *Welfare States in Transition. National Adaptations in Global Economies*. Thousand Oaks, CA: Sage.

Esping-Andersen, G., Gallie, D., Hemerijck, A. and Myles, J. (2002) *Why we Need a New Welfare State*. Oxford: Oxford University Press.

Evers, A. (2009) 'Civicness and civility: Their meanings for social services', *Voluntas*, 20 (3) 239–59.

Hall, P.A. (ed.) (1989) *The Political Power of Economic Ideas. Keynesianism across Nations*. Princeton, NJ: Princeton University Press.

Harvey, D. (2007) 'Neoliberalism as creative destruction', *The ANNALS of the American Academy of Political and Social Science*, 610 (1), 21–44.

Hemerijck, A. (2007) 'Joining forces for social Europe. Reasserting the Lisbon imperative of "Double engagement" and more', lecture to the conference *Joining Forces for a Social Europe*, organised under the German Presidency of the European Union, Nuremburg, 8–9 February 2007.

Hemerijck, A. and Eichhorst, W. (2010) 'Whatever happened to the Bismarckian welfare state? From labor shedding to employment-friendly reforms', in B. Palier (ed.) *A Long Goodbye to Bismarck? The*

Politics of Welfare Reform in Continental Europe. Amsterdam: Amsterdam University Press, pp. 301–32.

Huber, E. and Stephens, J.D. (2001) *Development and Crisis of the Welfare State: Parties and Policies in Global Markets.* Chicago: University of Chicago Press.

Immervoll, H., Jacobsen Kleven, H., Thustrup Kreiner, C. and Saez, E. (2007) 'Welfare reform in European countries: A microsimulation analysis', *The Economic Journal,* 117 (527), 1–44.

Jenson, J. (1998) *Mapping Social Cohesion. The State of Canadian Research.* Ottawa: CPRN. Available on www.cprn.org.

Jenson, J. (2009) 'Lost in translation. The social investment perspective and gender equality', *Social Politics,* 16 (4), 446–83.

Jenson, J. (2010) 'Diffusing ideas for after-neoliberalism: The social investment perspective in Europe and Latin America', *Global Social Policy,* 10 (1), 59–84.

Jenson, J. and Phillips, S.D. (1996) 'Regime shift: New citizenship practices in Canada', *International Journal of Canadian Studies,* 14, fall, 111–36.

Jenson, J. and Phillips, S.D. (2001) 'The changing Canadian citizenship regime', in C. Crouch, K. Eder and D. Tambini (eds) *Citizenship, Markets and the State.* London: Oxford University Press, pp. 11–35.

Jenson, J. and Pochet, P. (2006) 'Employment and social policy since Maastricht: Standing up to the European Monetary Union', in R. Fishman and A. Messina (eds) *The Year of the Euro: The Cultural, Social and Political Import of the Common Currency.* Notre Dame, IN: University of Notre Dame Press, pp. 161–85.

Jenson, J. and Saint-Martin, D. (2003) 'New routes to social cohesion? Citizenship and the social investment state', *Canadian Journal of Sociology,* 28 (1), 77–99.

Jenson, J. and Saint-Martin, D. (2006) 'Building blocks for a new social architecture: The LEGO™ paradigm of an active society', *Policy & Politics,* 34 (3), 429–51.

Jenson, J. and Sineau, M. (eds) (2001) *Who Cares? Women's Work, Childcare and Welfare State Redesign.* Toronto: University of Toronto Press.

Jessop, B. (1978) 'Capitalism and democracy: The best possible political shell?', in G. Littlejohn et al. (eds) *Power and the State.* London: Croom Helm, pp. 10–51.

Korpi, B.M. (2007) *The Politics of Pre-School: Intentions and Decisions Underlying the Emergence and Growth of the Swedish Pre-School,* 3rd edn. Stockholm: Ministry of Education.

Larner, W. (2003) 'Neoliberalism?', *Environment and Planning D: Society and Space,* 21 (5), 509–12.

Larner, W. and Craig, D. (2005) 'After neoliberalism? Community activism and local partnerships in Aotearoa New Zealand', *Antipode*, 37 (3), 402–24.

Lewis, J. (2001) 'The decline of the male breadwinner model: Implications for work and care' *Social Politics*, 8 (2), 152–69.

Mahon, R. (2008) 'Babies and bosses: Gendering the OECD's social policy discourse', in R. Mahon and S. McBride (eds) *The OECD and Transnational Governance*. Vancouver: University of British Columbia Press, pp. 260–75.

Marshall, T.H. (1965) *Class, Citizenship and Social Development*. New York: Doubleday Anchor.

McNeill, D. (2006) 'The diffusion of ideas in development theory and policy', *Global Social Policy*, 6 (3), 334–54.

Murphy, C. (2006) *The United Nations Development Programme. A Better Way?* Cambridge, UK: Cambridge University Press.

Newman, J., Barnes, M., Sullivan, H. and Knops, A. (2004) 'Public participation and collaborative governance', *Journal of Social Policy*, 33 (2), 203–23.

OECD (1997) 'Beyond 2000: The new social policy agenda', *OECD Working Papers*, vol. V, no. 43.

OECD (2003) *Asset Building and the Escape from Poverty. A New Welfare Policy Debate*. Paris: OECD.

OECD (2006) *Starting Strong II*. Paris: OECD.

Palier, B. (ed.) (2010) *A Long Goodbye to Bismarck? The Politics of Welfare Reform in Continental Europe*. Amsterdam: Amsterdam University Press.

Pearson, M. and Scherer, P. (1997) 'Balancing security and sustainability in social policy', *The OECD Observer*, April/May (205), 6–9.

Peck, J. (2004) 'Geography and public policy: Constructions of neoliberalism', *Progress in Human Geography*, 28 (3), 392–405.

Peck, J. and Tickell, A. (2002) 'Neoliberalizing space', *Antipode*, 34 (3), 380–404.

Pierson, P. (1994) *Dismantling the Welfare State? Reagan, Thatcher and the Politics of Retrenchment*. Cambridge, UK: Cambridge University Press.

Porter, D. and Craig, D. (2004) 'The third way and the third world: Poverty reduction and social inclusion in the rise of "inclusive" liberalism', *Review of International Political Economy*, 11 (2), 387–423.

Quadagno, J. (1987) 'Theories of the welfare states', *Annual Review of Sociology*, 13 (August), 109–28.

Rose, N. (1996) 'The death of the social? Refiguring the social territory of government', *Economy and Society*, 25 (3), 327–56.

Saint-Martin, D. (1998) 'The new managerialism and the policy influence of consultants in government: An historical–institutionalist analysis of Britain, Canada and France', *Governance*, 11 (3), 319–56.

Simmons, B., Dobbin, F. and Garrett, G. (2006) 'Introduction: The international diffusion of liberalism', *International Organization*, 60 (4), 781–810.

UNICEF (2000) *The League Tables of Child Poverty in Rich Nations*. Florence: UNICEF Innocenti Research Centre.

Part II

Mapping the development of social
investment policies

FOUR

Towards social investment? Patterns of public policy in the OECD world

Rita Nikolai

Introduction[1]

The debate on social investment and activation policies implies a new perspective on the relationship between different social policy areas. From this perspective, economic and social change together with the fiscal constraints they produce necessitate the redrawing of boundaries between 'active' and 'passive' social policies. It is assumed that the 'passive' welfare state is being steadily restructured into an 'activating' welfare state guided by a social investment perspective (see Chapters Two and Three). The social investment approach has been formulated in terms of redeploying public spending from passive social transfers to investments in education and training, labour market activation measures, promotion of lifelong learning and other measures to reconcile work and family (Giddens, 1998; Esping-Andersen et al., 2002; Palier, 2006).

The questions addressed in this chapter are to what extent the social investment 'turn' actually finds expression in the social expenditure profile of welfare states? Which countries are social-investment oriented today and which are not? Furthermore, do we see some convergence towards a social investment approach? To answer our questions we start by discussing how we can identify social investment policies and their relative importance in various countries. We then trace the development of public social expenditure in 21 of the 34 OECD member states from 1980 to 2007. We focus on disaggregated programme expenditures and compare public expenditures for investment measures and compensation expenditures on the basis of the OECD Social Expenditure Database and the Education Spending Database[2] as a way to compare the diversity in spending priorities among countries. We also ask to what extent we can observe a convergence of welfare policy when comparing the situation of the 1980s with the situation in 2007. The focus is more on outcomes and less on the processes and causes underlying the results. The analysis takes into account expenditures for families, active labour market policies, education systems, old age and passive labour market policies. The reason for starting with the 1980s is not only influenced by data availability, but also by the fact that the 1980s is the period immediately preceding the rise of the social investment perspective in the 1990s (see Chapter Two).

In addition, we elaborate a typology of welfare states according to their policy mixes between social investment and compensatory social policies. Drawing on these two analytical dimensions we can outline four worlds of social spending profiles. Comparing countries as a whole, the patterns we can make out depend on how investment and compensatory related social policies are combined.

Identifying social investment policies

How can we measure the importance of social investment policies? In this section, we will discuss which policies can be labelled as 'social investment'. To start with, we can differentiate between investment-related and compensatory welfare policies (Allmendinger and Leibfried, 2003; Nikolai, 2007). Compensatory social policies secure against social risks such as unemployment and old age. These policies are mainly of a contribution-financed social security type, with some supplementing systems of welfare services, in some countries with the goal of maintaining the status differences of the insurants and in other countries providing flat-rate benefits. Spending on old age insurance aims to prevent poverty by providing basic security in old age, to secure the continuity of living standards and reduce income inequalities. Expenditures include programmes covering both old age and survivors' pensions. With respect to unemployment, passive labour market policy regulates the compensatory allowances for the loss of income. Expenditures for this field include expenditures on unemployment benefits for unemployment and early retirement funds (OECD, 2007b).

Investment-related social policies are more strongly oriented towards provision for the future and the needs of the younger generations. We understand active labour market policy, family policy and education and training as fields of social investment (Armingeon, 2007; see also Chapters Six, Seven and Eight in this volume).

Family policy can pursue several objectives. The aims can be: (1) to keep up the birth rate, at least at a level that ensures the reproduction of the population; (2) to ensure that more women can reconcile work and family; (3) to reduce child poverty; (4) to promote the development of children by providing early childhood education and care services (see Chapter Six); and (5) to bridge the gap between the incomes of men and women. It is possible to argue that there is a component of social investment in all kinds of family policy programmes, albeit in varying degrees, which we analyse below.

Active labour market policy aims to promote labour mobility and the adaptation of citizens to changing labour markets (Armingeon, 2007; see also Chapter Seven in this volume). Through active labour market policies people should quickly be reintegrated into the labour market and the economic loss due to repeated unemployment should be minimised. The expenditures for this field include expenditure on active labour market programmes, training, training for young people, employment services, career guidance, as well as programmes for long-term unemployed, low skilled and disabled persons.

Education enjoys a pivotal role in the social investment strategy (Giddens, 2000; Lewis and Surrender, 2004; see also Chapter Eight in this volume). According to Giddens: '[t]he key force in human capital development obviously has to be education. It is the main public investment that can foster both economic and civic cohesion' (Giddens, 2000: 73). In this perspective, social and education policies are interdependent. The changes in society over the previous century are testing all welfare states, albeit to different extents. Profound processes of deindustrialisation have subjected the labour markets of developed societies to lasting change. Physical capital (machinery and equipments) and manual labour power are no longer the determining variables for wealth accumulation. The distinguishing features of the present knowledge society are skills for dealing with information and communications technologies and metaknowledge for acquiring, using and producing information (Rohrbach, 2007; Allmendinger et al., 2010). The education level of the broad population is thus a crucial competitive factor – all the more so because demographic developments in many countries are leading to population decreases that cannot sustain the absolute number of well-educated people unless the size of that group expands proportionately. Moreover, today's longer life expectancy and the ever-shorter half-life of knowledge mean that one phase of education early in life no longer suffices and that phases of additional education and training are more necessary than ever. Expenditure on educational institutions relative to GDP shows the priority countries give to education in terms of their overall resource allocation. Spending for education covers expenditures on schools, universities and other public policies involved in delivering or supporting educational services from primary to tertiary education (Allmendinger and Nikolai, 2010; Busemeyer and Nikolai, 2010; OECD, 2010a).

The next section analyses the spending profile of different welfare states to see to what extent they follow a social investment approach.

Tracing the developments in the social expenditure profile of welfare states

Social expenditures development

We will first look at the development of social expenditures from 1980 up to 2007 (Table 4.1). The data in Table 4.1 takes into account the three phases of welfare state development identified in this volume (see Chapters One, Two and Three in this volume): the Keynesian, the neoliberal and the emerging social investment phase. The year 1980 described the situation at the end of the Keynesian phase the 'golden age' of welfare capitalism. The second phase – the neoliberal phase – had its heyday in the 1980s and began to be questioned in the 1990s. The Asian crisis at the end of the 1990s marked the starting point for the social investment turn. We start our description with the year 2007, for which the latest data is available.

Table 4.1: Public social expenditure as a percentage of GDP, 1980–2007

	1980	1990	2000	2007
Australia	10.2	13.1	17.3	16.0
Austria	22.4	23.8	26.7	26.4
Belgium	23.5	24.9	25.4	26.3
Canada	13.7	18.1	16.5	16.9
Czech Republic		16.0	19.8	18.8
Denmark	24.8	25.1	25.7	26.1
Finland	18.1	24.3	24.3	24.9
France	20.8	24.9	27.7	28.4
Germany	20.4	20.1	26.6	25.2
Greece	10.2	16.5	19.2	21.3
Hungary			20.4	23.1
Ireland	16.7	14.9	13.3	16.3
Italy	18.0	20.0	23.3	24.9
Japan	10.4	11.3	16.5	18.7
Netherlands	24.8	25.6	19.8	20.1
New Zealand	17.0	21.5	19.1	18.4
Norway	16.9	22.3	21.3	20.8

	1980	1990	2000	2007
Poland		14.9	20.7	20.0
Portugal	9.9	12.5	18.9	22.5
Slovakia			17.9	15.7
Spain	15.5	19.9	20.4	21.6
Sweden	27.2	30.2	28.4	27.3
Switzerland	13.8	13.5	17.8	18.5
UK	16.5	16.8	18.6	20.5
USA	13.2	13.5	14.5	16.2
Mean (OECD-21)	17.3	19.7	21.0	21.8
Range	17.3	18.9	15.1	12.4
Standard deviation	5.2	5.3	4.5	4.0
Variation coefficient	0.30	0.27	0.21	0.18
Catch-up (1980–2007)	$r = -0.6489*$			

Source: OECD, 2010b. Annotation: $*p < 0.05$, $**p < 0.01$.

On average, in 2007, the OECD states spent 21.8% of the gross domestic product (GDP) from public sources for welfare policies. The spending levels in the Scandinavian, continental European and most of the southern European countries are higher than the OECD average. By comparison, the English-speaking, East Asian, most of the Eastern European (except Hungary) and also economically less developed countries are characterised by social expenditure rates below average. In almost all OECD states (with the exception of the Netherlands and Ireland), the level of public social expenditures as a percentage of the GDP increased between 1980 and 2007. The salience of the welfare state has also increased relative to other state functions (Starke et al., 2008). The majority of the OECD states spend more than half of total government outlays for social purposes (Castles, 2007). With regard to social expenditure as a percentage of total government outlays, the welfare state has even tended to crowd out public expenditures devoted to other purposes (Kohl, 1980; Castles, 1998). Thus on an aggregate expenditure level the welfare state is not on the retreat (Pierson, 2001) and the data do not display a 'race to the bottom' (Obinger and Starke, 2008) scenario.

The statistical measures of dispersion in the lower part of Table 4.1 indicate to what extent the social expenditure rates converge over the years since 1980.[3] Measures such as the range, the standard deviation and the coefficient of variation are denoted as σ-convergence (sigma-convergence). Sigma-convergence is understood as the increase in similarity between countries over the years. The rise in public social expenditure goes hand in hand with a strong convergence as indicated by the declining measures of dispersion. There is also evidence for β-convergence. The concept of β-convergence is understood as a catching up by policy laggards. In the last row we report the correlation (Pearsons' *r*) between the starting value 1980 and the annual growth rate (1980–2007). The correlation is negative and statistically significant, which implies that the cross-national variation in social spending growth is driven by a catch-up process by welfare policy laggards.

For the expenditure profile of the welfare states, the distinction between cash benefits (as, for example, via income transfers) and benefits in kind (as, for example in the form of services) is crucial (Kohl, 1980; Castles, 1998). In the welfare state literature, the continental European welfare states are characterised as transfer-heavy and the Scandinavian countries as service-oriented. The role of services is often emphasised in the literature on social investment and on welfare reform (Castles, 1998; Daly and Lewis, 2000; Kautto, 2002). Welfare states with developed service infrastructure have been shown to be better able to deal with the 'new' challenges of post-industrial society (Bonoli, 2007) such as new forms of employment and family structures, declining birth rates and long-term care.

Figure 4.1 informs about the composition of public social spending in 2007.[4] To investigate the public role in providing services, we separated the expenditures for health from other social service expenditures, as health expenditure accounts for a large share of services (Kautto, 2002).

Figure 4.1: Public social expenditures as cash and as in-kind benefits in percentage of GDP in 2007 (source: OECD, 2010b)

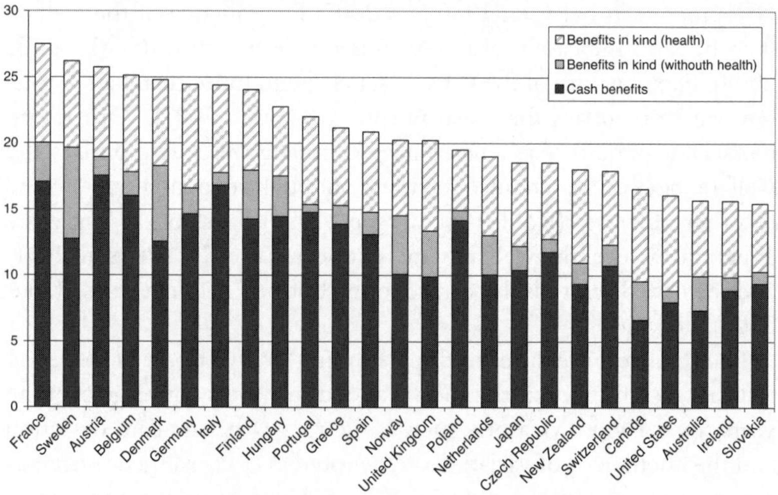

Compared to the OECD average, the traditional service-oriented Scandinavian countries still spend the most for benefits in kind in 2007. But also the transfer-heavy continental and southern European states expanded their expenditures for benefits in kind (Starke et al., 2008). With the exception of Canada and the USA, in some of the English-speaking countries such as Australia, New Zealand and the UK the in-kind expenditures have increased since 1980. The finding by Kautto, who states 'that with few exceptions relative service investments increased in Western Europe in the 1990s, contrary to the talk of welfare state retrenchment' (Kautto, 2002: 63) also holds true up to 2007. An ageing population, an emphasis on active rather than passive measures, increased labour force participation among women and calls for gender equality have apparently resulted in more investment in services in the majority of the OECD member states.

Programme-related spending categories

Analysis based on overall social spending tends to overestimate the coherence of welfare state regimes (Obinger and Starke, 2008). The architecture of individual welfare states is much more complex. We get a more nuanced picture of welfare state spending when we break down the total social expenditure into programme-related spending. Tables 4.2 and 4.3 show to what extent the dynamic of social expenditure is driven by the restructuring of social spending patterns. To contrast compensatory and investment-related expenditures we refer to the spending categories of active labour market policies, family policy, education, old age insurance and passive labour market policies. The breakdown by programme-related spending categories points out different developments in the single spending programmes and uncovers substantial asymmetries between the countries.

Since the 1980s it is mainly expenditure on old age insurance that has increased (Table 4.2). The gradual ageing of society has been a major preoccupation in developed countries for many years now and is reflected by steadily increasing levels of expenditures (Adema and Ladaique, 2009). Austria, Greece, Germany, France, Poland and Italy spend a large bulk of their financial resources on old age insurance. In the English-speaking countries and in the economically less developed countries expenditures are relatively low in this programme area. Here the English-speaking countries rely more on the private provision of social protection (Guo and Gilbert, 2007; OECD, 2007a). Although many countries have increased their spending on old age insurance due to an ageing population in the 1990s and 2000s, a number of countries restrained expenditure in the 2000s. In many countries pension reforms have followed a general trend of moving away from

Table 4.2: Public expenditures as a percentage of GDP for compensatory social policies, 1980–2007

	Passive labour market policy				Old age (including expenditures for survivors)			
	1980	1990	2000	2007	1980	1990	2000	2007
Australia	0.6	1.1	0.9	0.4	3.7	3.6	5.0	4.5
Austria	0.4	0.9	0.9	0.9	10.7	11.6	12.7	12.7
Belgium	2.4	2.9	2.8	3.1	8.9	9.1	9.0	9.0
Canada	1.2	1.9	0.7	0.6	3.0	4.3	4.3	4.2
Czech Republic			0.6	0.6		6.1	7.9	7.7
Denmark	4.8	4.2	3.0	1.9	7.1	7.4	7.1	7.3
Finland	0.6	1.1	2.2	1.5	6.0	8.0	8.4	9.2
France		1.7	1.5	1.4	9.5	10.8	12.0	12.8
Germany	0.5	0.8	1.3	1.4	9.8	9.2	11.2	10.7
Greece	0.2	0.4	0.4	0.5	5.4	9.9	10.9	12.0
Hungary			0.7	0.7			7.9	9.6
Ireland		1.7	0.8	1.0	5.7	4.2	3.4	3.9
Italy	0.6	0.6	0.4	0.4	8.9	10.2	13.6	14.1
Japan	0.5	0.3	0.6	0.3	4.1	5.0	8.1	10.1
Netherlands	1.6	2.5	1.3	1.1	6.9	7.3	5.7	5.5
New Zealand	0.5	1.9	1.3	0.2	7.1	7.4	5.0	4.3
Norway	0.4	1.1	0.5	0.2	5.7	7.5	6.8	6.5
Poland		0.003	0.9	0.3		5.1	10.6	10.7
Portugal	0.3	0.3	0.6	1.0	3.8	4.9	8.0	10.8
Slovakia			0.6	0.4			6.6	6.2

Spain	2.0	3.2	2.0	2.1	6.3	8.1	8.9	8.5
Sweden	0.4	0.9	1.4	0.7	8.3	9.2	9.7	9.5
Switzerland	0.1	0.1	0.5	0.6	6.0	5.8	6.8	6.7
UK	1.2	0.7	0.3	0.2	5.9	5.2	5.8	5.9
USA	0.7	0.4	0.2	0.3	6.3	6.1	5.9	6.0
Mean (OECD-21)	1.0	1.37	1.12	0.94	6.62	7.37	8.01	8.3
Range	4.7	4.1	2.8	2.9	7.7	8.0	10.2	10.2
Standard deviation	1.11	1.09	0.80	0.75	2.1	2.33	2.86	3.14
Variation coefficient	1.11	0.80	0.71	0.8	0.32	0.32	0.36	0.38
Catch-up (1980–2007)	$r = -0.7132*$				$r = -0.1652$			

Source: OECD, 1992, 2010a, 2010b. Annotation: $*p < 0.05$, $**p < 0.01$.

Table 4.3: Public expenditures as a percentage of GDP for investment-related social policies, 1980–2007

	Active labour market policy				Family				Education			
	1985	1990	2000	2007	1980	1990	2000	2007	1980	1990	2000	2007
Australia	0.3	0.2	0.4	0.3	0.9	1.5	2.9	2.4	5.6	4.7	4.6	3.8
Austria	0.3	0.3	0.5	0.7	3.1	2.6	2.8	2.6	5.6	5.4	5.4	5.1
Belgium	1.2	1.1	1.2	1.2	3.0	2.3	2.7	2.6	5.7	5.4	5.1	5.9
Canada	0.6	0.5	0.4	0.3	0.7	0.6	1.0	1.0	7.7	6.7	5.2	4.6
Czech Republic			0.2	0.3		2.5	1.9	2.0			4.2	4.1
Denmark	0.8	0.7	1.9	1.3	2.8	3.3	3.3	3.3		6.1	6.4	6.6
Finland	0.7	0.8	0.9	0.9	1.9	3.2	3.0	2.8	5.8	6.1	5.5	5.5
France	0.6	0.7	1.2	0.9	2.4	2.5	3.0	3.0	5.1	5.4	5.7	5.5
Germany	0.5	0.9	1.2	0.7	1.9	1.5	2.1	1.8	4.6	4.0	4.3	4.0
Greece	0.2	0.2	0.2	0.2	0.3	0.7	1.0	1.1	3.2	5.4	3.7	4.0
Hungary			0.4	0.3			3.2	3.5			4.4	4.9
Ireland	1.1	1.1	0.8	0.6	1.1	1.6	1.8	2.6	6.4	5.5	4.1	4.4
Italy		0.2	0.6	0.5	1.1	0.8	1.2	1.4	4.5	5.0	4.5	4.1
Japan		0.3	0.3	0.2	0.5	0.4	0.6	0.8	5.9	3.7	3.5	3.3
Netherlands	1.3	1.3	1.5	1.1	2.5	1.7	1.5	2.0	7.1	5.6	4.3	4.7
New Zealand	0.9	0.9	0.5	0.4	2.2	2.6	2.8	3.0	6.7	5.6	5.8	4.8
Norway	0.6	0.9	0.6	0.6	1.8	2.7	3.0	2.8	5.8	6.8	5.8	5.4
Poland		0.1	0.3	0.5		1.7	1.4	1.3			5.2	4.8
Portugal	0.2	0.5	0.6	0.5	0.6	0.7	1.0	1.2	3.7	5.5	5.6	5.1
Slovakia			0.3	0.2			2.0	1.8			4.0	3.4

Spain	0.3	0.8	0.8	0.7	0.5	0.3	1.0	1.2		4.4	4.3	4.2
Sweden	2.1	1.6	1.8	1.1	3.9	4.4	3.0	3.4	8.5	6.5	6.3	6.1
Switzerland	0.2	0.2	0.5	0.6	1.0	1.0	1.3	1.3	5.2	5.4	5.3	5.1
UK	0.7	0.6	0.2	0.3	2.3	1.9	2.7	3.2	5.7	5.3	4.5	5.2
USA	0.3	0.2	0.2	0.1	0.8	0.5	0.7	0.7	4.9	5.5	4.8	5.0
Mean (OECD-21)	0.67	0.67	0.78	0.63	1.7	1.75	2.0	2.1	5.67	5.43	4.9	4.88
Range	1.9	1.4	1.7	1.2	3.6	4.1	2.7	2.7	5.3	3.1	2.9	3.3
Standard deviation	0.48	0.40	0.51	0.35	1.03	1.13	0.94	0.91	1.28	0.79	0.80	0.82
Variation coefficient	0.72	0.6	0.65	0.6	0.61	0.65	0.47	0.43	0.22	0.15	0.16	0.17
Catch-up (1980–2007)	$r = -0.6982^*$				$r = -0.4842^*$				$r = -0.8308^*$			

Source: OECD, 1992, 2003, 2010a, 2010b. Annotation: expenditures for active labour market policies for Denmark and Portugal 1985=1986; $^*p< 0.05$, $^{**}p< 0.01$.

publicly funded to privately funded defined contribution schemes (Hinrichs and Lynch, 2010).

The male breadwinner–female carer family, which characterised the post-war welfare state, is no longer the norm (Taylor-Gooby, 2001). Changes in family forms and increased female and maternal employment have put pressure on welfare states. Between the 1980s and 2007 we can observe increased levels of spending for families (Table 4.3). On average the OECD countries spend 2.1% (in 2007) of their GDP on family benefits, with large variations across countries. Public spending on family benefits is above 3.0% of GDP in the UK, Sweden, Denmark and Hungary. Less than 1% of GDP is spent on family policy in Japan and the USA. It is noticeable that the social investment turn in the 2000s is not reflected in growing expenses for family policies. Only a few countries like Ireland, the Netherlands, Sweden and the UK have significantly increased their expenditure since 2000. In the other countries we can observe only slight increases (for example, Czech Republic), stagnation (for example, France) or even retrenchments (for example, Finland). Figure 4.2 shows how spending on family policy is divided between benefits in cash and benefits in kind. The majority of countries spend a higher proportion on benefits in cash than on services. Service-oriented countries with respect to family spending are the Scandinavian countries, Hungary, the UK, the Netherlands and France, which spent more than 1.0% of their GDP for benefits in kind for families.[5] It is assumed that the service-oriented expenditure has a stronger social investment content.

Figure 4.2: Family spending in cash and services in percentage of GDP in 2007 (source: OECD, 2010b)

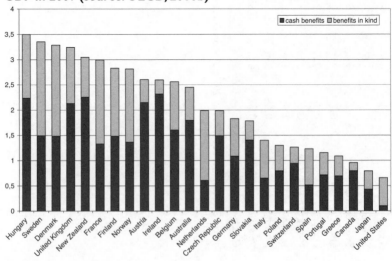

Active labour market policy as a policy idea has spread across countries, especially in the most recent period (Martin, 2001). In the field of active labour market policy the Scandinavian countries occupy top positions in 2007 (Table 4.3) and expenditure is also very high in the Netherlands and Belgium. But we see extreme levels of cross-national variation. Expenditure on active labour market policy ranges from 0.1% of GDP in the USA, up to 1.3% of GDP in Denmark. Despite the implementation of activation strategies in many OECD countries (Clasen, 2000), the activation turn in the 1990s and the rise of the social investment perspective in the 2000s are not reflected in higher expenditure on active labour market policy. While the mean for OECD states increased in the 1990s, it decreased between 1990 and 2000. The kind of activation strategies that countries have pursued in recent years have involved reductions in access to benefits and in the amount of benefits (Kenworthy, 2010: 438), but not necessarily the reinforcement of such things as training programme for example (see also Chapter Seven).

The examination of unemployment benefits indicates a very modest decrease in spending in the long run from the 1980s to 2007 (Table 4.2). The mean average of 2007 is similar to the situation at the beginning of the 1980s. Measures of dispersion like the range, the standard deviation and the variation coefficient are decreasing up to 2007. Compared to the increasing expenditure for old age or families, the expenditure for unemployment benefits remains stable. The highest expenditure for unemployment benefits is to be found in 2007 with more than 1.9% of GDP in Spain, Denmark and Belgium. Expenditure for passive labour market policy is relatively low, with 0.3% of GDP or less, in New Zealand, Norway and the UK. As a number of countries experienced high rates of unemployment beginning in the late 1970s and early 1980s, expenditures for passive labour market policies increased between 1980 and 1990. After 1990 expenditure on unemployment insurance has decreased. It is noticeable that the Scandinavian countries have substantially limited their expenses for unemployment benefits since 2000.

The social investment perspective highlights the importance of education. In the same vein, the concept of capabilities (Sen, 2000) unequivocally stresses education as vital to 'opportunities for self-realisation'. The educational system is regarded as one of the chief institutions governing the distribution of opportunities in life and is the fulcrum in combating social inequality (Nikolai, 2007; Wolf,

2009). Table 4.3 indicates that there is substantial variation in spending among OECD countries. The percentage of public investment in education is particularly high in Denmark and Sweden, amounting to over 6%, whereas private expenditure constitutes a relatively small share of the GDP in these countries (Wolf, 2009). The continental European countries are quite heterogeneous with regard to their educational spending: France and Switzerland show high rates of public educational investment by international comparison. By contrast, in Germany the public educational expenditure as a share of the GDP is below average and in the Netherlands it is barely average. In the southern European countries (with the exception of Portugal) public educational expenditure is below the OECD average. Also the East European countries and the English-speaking countries do not distinguish themselves by high public education expenditures. But the private educational expenditure is comparatively high in the English-speaking countries. Concerning the public–private mix in education funding, we find evidence for a growing weight of private financial contributions (Wolf, 2009; Wolf and Zohlnhöfer, 2009). At the end of the spectrum we find Japan and Slovakia. The statistical measures of dispersion are declining for education expenditures. There is evidence of a potential trend towards σ-convergence; however, this does not mean higher public expenditures for education. On average the OECD states spent less public resources as a percentage of GDP for education in 2007 than in 1980, 1990 and 2000. Since 1990 we notice considerable decreases in public expenditure for education. The social investment turn of the 2000s is not reflected in significantly higher public expenses for education in the mean of the OECD states. However, some countries, such as the UK, have increased their public spending since 2000 ,but in the majority of countries expenditures remain stable or have experienced excessive retrenchment, particularly in Australia, Canada and New Zealand. This might be influenced by two factors. First, demographic shifts have resulted in declining shares of pupils. The provision of educational services in primary and secondary education is largely demand-driven. Due to a declining fertility rate, the majority of the OECD countries are confronted with a diminishing younger population. Second, the decline in public expenditure may also reflect the growing role of private sources and shifts in the division of labour between the state and the private sector (Wolf, 2009; OECD, 2010a). Here students and their families shoulder a much greater burden for textbooks, private tutoring or student living costs than the state.

Summarising the programme-related expenditures, we find evidence for σ-convergence in the fields of active and passive labour market policies, family policy and education policy, as the measures of dispersion are decreasing between 1980 and 2007. We also indicate catch-up processes in these areas. The spending pattern for old age insurance is quite different with very modest catch-up and the indicators for σ-convergence are increasing, which means that the expenditure levels between the countries are not converging and the differences between the countries remain significant.

Towards social investment welfare states in expenditure terms?

With regard to their public performance structure and spending profiles, welfare states are commonly differentiated into social democratic, liberal and conservative welfare states (Esping-Andersen, 1990; Allmendinger and Leibfried, 2003). Usually, the main categorical distinction emphasised is that between generous and universal social democratic welfare states on the one hand and weakly developed social security systems of liberal welfare states on the other hand. Measured by social expenditure levels, conservative continental European welfare states reside in between those positions. Does this regime typology hold true when we compare expenditures for investment-related and compensatory social policies? Which are the countries that are the most social investment-oriented welfare states today? And which countries have been most prone to follow a social investment approach since the mid-1980s? To answer those questions, in Figures 4.3 to 4.6 we compare expenditures for investment-related and compensatory social policies in OECD countries for the mid-1980s,[6] 1990, 2000 and 2007. In all figures the y-axis depicts expenditures for investment-oriented social policies, while the x-axis refers to compensatory social policies. 'Investment policies' include expenditures for families,[7] education, as well as active labour market policies. Expenditures for old age pensions (including pensions for survivors) and passive labour market policies are defined as compensatory policies. By looking at the deviation of countries or country groups from the mean, we gain insights about the relative importance of investment-related versus compensatory social spending, predominating priorities and potential tradeoffs. Applying the statistical mean for both indicators, one obtains four clusters. To compare the development over time, we use the mean for the year 2007 to follow the typology of investment and compensatory social policies depicted in Figures 4.3 to 4.6 across four points in time. Cluster 2 refers to countries with high levels of spending for investment and compensatory social policies, however focusing more on social investment policies.

Clusters 1 and 4 represent cases of crossover: cluster 1 is characterised by countries with high expenditures for investment related social policies, but low or rather modest levels for compensatory social policies. In cluster 4, the allocation is reverse. Cluster 3 represents countries with low levels for investment as well as for compensatory social policies. The correlation between investment-related and compensatory social policies is not significant, even while showing a decrease since the mid-1980s to 2007.

We start with Figure 4.3 for the situation during the mid-1980s. Countries with high spending on investment as well as compensatory social policies (cluster 2) are Belgium and Austria. Countries with high expenditures for investment-related social policies, but low levels for compensatory social policies (cluster 1), are the Scandinavian countries, New Zealand, the UK, Canada and the Netherlands. Sweden appears here as an outlier: compared to all other OECD states Sweden spent considerably more of its GDP on investment-related rather than compensatory social policies. Spending on investment and compensatory social policies is modest in the USA, Switzerland, Australia, Portugal and Greece (cluster 3). In contrast to Sweden, Germany is a classical example of a compensatory-oriented welfare state (cluster 4): the expenses for age and unemployment are markedly higher than the expenses for education, families and active labour market policies.

The situation for the year 1990, the heyday of the neoliberal phase, is described in Figure 4.4. Sweden, the Netherlands, New Zealand, Finland and Norway now spend more for compensatory social policies, but their spending in investment-oriented social policies is still high. Figure 4.4 now also includes data for Italy, Spain, Japan, Ireland, Denmark and France, for which data for the 1980s was not available. Denmark belongs to a group with both high expenditures for investment and for compensatory social policies. The spending profile of Ireland is similar to that of the UK and Canada with higher expenditure on investment-oriented policies, but less for compensatory social policies. The composition of cluster 3 is similar to the mid-1980s, with the addition of Japan. Similarly to Germany, the southern European countries (except Portugal) concentrate their spending on compensatory social policies. The situation in France is similar to the ones in Austria and Belgium: expenditures for compensatory and investment-oriented social policies are high in these countries.

Following the Asian crisis at the end of the 1990s, the neoliberal paradigm has been increasingly questioned while the foundations of the social investment perspective were laid. Figure 4.5 depicts the starting

Figure 4.3: The nexus between the public expenditures for investment-related and compensatory social policies as a percentage of GDP mid-1980s

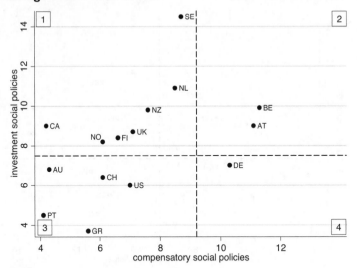

Annotation: $r = 0.4829$; $R^2 = 0.2332$.

Source: OECD, 1992, 2010b.

Figure 4.4: The nexus between the public expenditures for investment-related and compensatory social policies as a percentage of GDP 1990

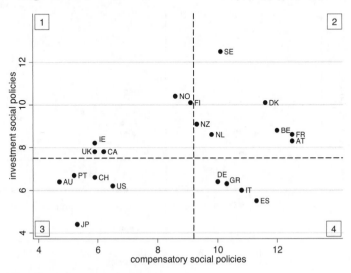

Annotation: $r = 0.3541$; $R^2 = 0.1254$.

Source: OECD, 1992, 2010b,

Figure 4.5: The nexus between the public expenditures for investment-related and compensatory social policies as a percentage of GDP 2000

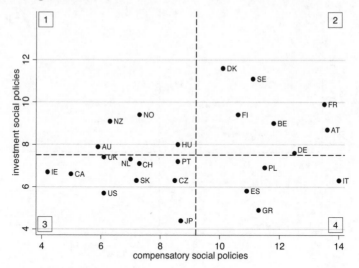

Annotation: $r = 0.2256$; $R^2 = 0.0509$.

Source: OECD, 2003. 2010b,

Figure 4.6: The nexus between the public expenditures for investment-related and compensatory social policies as a percentage of GDP 2007

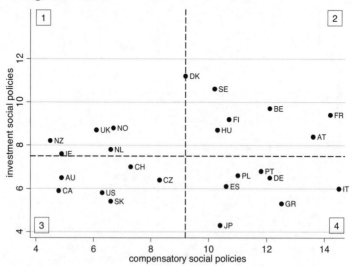

Annotation: $r = 0.0875$; $R^2 = 0.0077$.

Source: OECD, 2010a, 2010b.

point for the 'social investment turn' in 2000 and it also includes data for Eastern European countries. Hungary is the only East European country which spends more on investment than on compensatory social policies. Poland, Slovakia and the Czech Republic spend more on compensatory social policies and neglect the fields of education, families and active labour market policies.

Although in the overall picture of Figure 4.5 there have been slight changes for some of the countries in our analysis, the graphs for 2000 and 2007 are remarkably similar in their country distribution. Therefore, we will now take a closer look at the situation in 2007.

In 2007, the distribution of the countries along our indicators – the amount of expenses for investment and compensatory social policies – is very distinctive. Cluster 2 consists of Sweden, Finland, Hungary, Belgium, France and Austria. Within this grouping, the countries have a quite distinct profile: they are characterised by high spending for investment-related and compensatory social policies with the emphasis on investment-related social policies. The continental European countries Belgium and France belong to cluster 2 due to their high expenditure on families and their above-average expenditure on education (c.f. Table 4.3). Countries in cluster 2 protect their citizens at a high level against life risks such as old age or unemployment, but without neglecting investment-related policies. They follow a social investment approach with a double liability: in the backyard of the welfare state stands an education policy which exhibits an egalitarian distribution of education (Allmendinger and Nikolai, 2010).

Expenses for investment-oriented social policies are also high in Norway, the UK, New Zealand, Ireland and the Netherlands (cluster 1), but compared to the countries in cluster 2 the expenditures for old age and passive labour market policies are low. Compared to the situation in 1990, the Netherlands and New Zealand have retrenched expenditure on compensatory social policies and slightly increased expenditure on social investment. Norway belongs to this cluster 2 due to low levels of unemployment and thus less expenditures for passive labour market policies.

The third cluster consists of Australia, Canada, the USA, Slovakia, Switzerland and the Czech Republic. When we take into account only public expenditures, cluster 3 distributes less money for investment-related social policies compared to their expenditures for old age and passive labour market policy. Nevertheless, some countries in cluster 3 concentrate much more strongly on educational investments than on a broad state-sponsored social security. This is particularly true in view of the high private expenditure for education in the USA and

Canada. These countries invest much in education and research, but invest only little in public social policies and focus more strongly on private social protection. For example, in the USA the development of education services was advanced in place of the development of the social security system (Heidenheimer, 1981; Allmendinger and Leibfried, 2003). Thus, (private) educational policy is seen as a kind of welfare state replacement. The limited investment in public social policies is compensated through expanded education facilities. But this compensation holds true only for those individuals who successfully completed the educational system (Allmendinger and Nikolai, 2010).

Cluster 4 consists of the southern European countries, Poland, Switzerland, Germany and Japan. These countries spend higher levels on compensatory social policies but neglect investment-related social policies. For instance, these countries exhibit far lower levels of education spending than one might expect on the basis of their levels of social spending. These countries turn out to still be 'traditional compensatory welfare states'.

Drawing on our analytical dimensions, the social investment and the compensatory approach, we can outline four worlds of spending profiles. Both the English-speaking and the Scandinavian countries are examples of social investment in action, but the goals of these two welfare regimes are remarkably different. While both groups emphasise expenditures for investment-related policies, in the Scandinavian version of the social investment approach (cluster 2) countries spend a remarkable share on investment-related social policies without neglecting expenditures for old age and passive labour market policies. With this spending profile, welfare states promote activation and prevention but also protect against income insecurity in old age and unemployment phases. The British version of the social investment approach (cluster 1) also emphasises expenditures for education, families and active labour market policies, but spends less for compensatory social policies. The driving idea here is that of welfare state change from a safety net of entitlements to a springboard for personal responsibility (Blair and Schröder, 1999 [2000]). Following this idea, welfare states concentrate their public spending priorities on investments in human capital and scale back compensatory state benefits.

And finally, as the examples of France or Belgium show, not all continental European countries neglect investment-oriented social policies. In regard to the situation of 2007 it seems that traditional regime analysis (Esping-Andersen, 1990) no longer represents a valid framework for contemporary analysis.

Conclusion

This chapter analysed to what extent the social investment perspective finds its expression in the social expenditure profile of the OECD member states. Our findings are ambiguous. We find evidence for increasing levels of public social expenditure and convergence processes. A 'race to the bottom' in social expenditures cannot be confirmed. Since the 1980s, expenditure for old age insurances has increased. At a lower spending level, the welfare states have also increased public resources for families. In contrast to old age insurance and families, expenditure for active and passive labour market policies remains stable.

The results for education spending are puzzling. Although education plays an important role in the social investment approach, on average public expenditure for education has decreased since 1980. The perspective that social policies should focus more on prevention and social investment than on compensating for social risks does not find its expression in increasing levels of education spending. But here the division of labour between the state and the private sector in education funding is crucial. We have to consider a growing weight of private financial contributions. Whereas in Denmark, Sweden and Norway high levels of total investment in education is based almost entirely on public education funding, in New Zealand and the USA in contrast, funding is borne by substantial private engagement.

We also identified diverse spending priorities for different types of welfare states. There are considerable differences between the OECD member states in their compensatory strategies and social investment strategies during the 1980s and 1990s, and the differences between the transfer-heavy continental European welfare states and the service-oriented Scandinavian countries still hold true in 2007 with the Scandinavian countries spending most on benefits in kind. But in sum, an ageing population, an emphasis on active rather than passive measures, increased female labour force participation and calls for gender equality have resulted in more investment in services in the majority of the OECD member states since the 1980s. Still, we find mixed evidence to support the claim that welfare states are moving away from compensatory social policies towards a 'rechannel[ing] of social expenditures toward social investment' (Palier, 2006: 114). Countries which spend more for investment-related social programmes are the Scandinavian and, at a lower spending level, most of the English-speaking countries. Continental European countries such as Belgium, France and the Netherlands have relatively high expenditure levels on both scores, with still a predominance of compensatory-related expenditure. Germany, Japan, Poland and the southern European countries still display high levels of spending on compensatory social policies and little on investment-related social policies, especially in the sphere of education.

The Scandinavian countries (Finland, Norway, Sweden and Denmark) are extraordinarily strong in linking a high level of education for most of their population (see Chapter Eight) and a high degree of support in cases of unemployment, illness and old age. Countries in this group pursue a social investment approach with double liability. In contrast, most of the English-speaking states follow the neoliberal entreaty to scale back state benefits and to embark on the Third Way's priority investment in human capital. It remains an open question whether and to what extent the OECD countries will converge on the Scandinavian or the British version of the social investment state, or find new development paths.

Notes

[1] We would like to thank Simone Grellmann and Benjamin Edelstein for their support in the research and processing of the data used in this study.

[2] Data by EUROSTAT for social benefits by function are not as detailed as the data provided by the OECD.

[3] Due to data availability the measures of convergence include only the so-called 'established' 21 OECD member states. These are: Australia, Austria, Belgium, Canada, Denmark, Finland, France, Germany, Greece, Ireland, Italy, Japan, the Netherlands, New Zealand, Norway, Portugal, Spain, Sweden, Switzerland, the UK and the USA.

[4] The expenditures for cash benefits and benefits in kind include the following categories: old age, survivors, incapacity related, family, active labour market programmes, unemployment, housing and other social policy areas.

[5] A third type of public spending on family benefits is the financial support to families provided through the tax system. Tax breaks towards families are of considerable size in Germany, France, Japan, the Netherlands, and particularly in the USA (OECD, 2007a).

[6] We refer to the year 1985 due to data availability. The OECD data series for active labour market policies does not include data before 1985.

[7] Expenditures for families include benefits in kind as well as cash benefits. Both policies support families in the financial burden of child rearing.

References

Adema, W. and Ladaique, M. (2009) 'How expensive is the welfare state? Gross and net indicators in the OECD social expenditure database (SOCX)', *OECD social, employment and migration working papers, No. 92.*

Allmendinger, J. and Leibfried, S. (2003) 'Education and the welfare state: The four worlds of competence production', *European Journal of Social Policy*, 13 (1), 63–81.

Allmendinger, J. and Nikolai, R. (2010) 'Bildungs- und Sozialpolitik: Die zwei Seiten des Sozialstaats im internationalen Vergleich', *Soziale Welt*, 61 (2), 105–19.

Allmendinger, J., Ebner, C. and Nikolai, R. (2010) 'Education in Europe and the Lisbon benchmarks', in J. Alber and N. Gilbert (eds) *United in Diversity? Comparing Social Models in Europe and America*. Oxford: Oxford University Press, pp. 308–27.

Armingeon, K. (2007) 'Active labour market policy, international organizations, and domestic politics', *Journal of European Public Policy*, 14 (6), 905–932.

Blair, T. and Schröder, G. (1999 [2000]) 'Europe: the third way/die Neue Mitte', in B. Hombach (ed.) *The Politics of the New Centre*. Oxford: Blackwell, pp. 157–77.

Bonoli, G. (2007) 'Time matters: Postindustrialization, new social risks and welfare state adaptation in advanced industrial democracies', *Comparative Political Studies*, 40 (5), 495–520.

Busemeyer, M.R. and Nikolai, R. (2010) 'Education', in H. Obinger, C. Pierson, F.G. Castles, S. Leibfried and J. Lewis (eds) *The Oxford Handbook of Comparative Welfare States*. Oxford: Oxford University Press, pp. 494–508.

Castles, F.G. (1998) *Comparative Public Policy: Patterns of Post-War Transformation*. Cheltenham and Northampton, MA: Edward Elgar.

Castles, F.G. (2007) *The Disappearing State? Retrenchment Realities in an Age of Globalisation*. Cheltenham, UK and Northampton, MA: Edward Elgar.

Clasen, J. (2000) 'Motives, means and opportunities: Reforming unemployment compensation in the 1990s', *West European Politics*, 23 (2), 89–112.

Daly, M. and Lewis, J. (2000) 'The concept of social care and the analysis of contemporary welfare states', *British Journal of Sociology*, 51 (2), 281–98.

Esping-Andersen, G. (1990) *The Three Worlds of Welfare Capitalism*. Cambridge: Polity Press.

Esping-Andersen, G., Gallie, D., Hemerijck, A. and Myles, J. (2002) *Why We Need a New Welfare State*. Oxford: Oxford University Press.

Giddens, A. (1998) *The Third Way. The Renewal of Social Democracy.* Cambridge: Polity Press.

Giddens, A. (2000) *The Third Way and its Critics.* Cambridge: Polity Press.

Guo, J. and Gilbert, N. (2007) 'Welfare state regimes and family policy: A longitudinal analysis', *International Journal of Social Welfare*, 16 (4), 307–13.

Heidenheimer, A.J. (1981) 'Education and social security entitlements in Europe and America', in P. Flora and A.J. Heidenheimer (eds) *The Development of Welfare States in Europe and America*. New Brunswick, NJ: Transaction Publishers, pp. 269–306.

Hinrichs, K. and Lynch, J. (2010) 'Old-age pensions', in H. Obinger, C. Pierson, F.G. Castles, S. Leibfried and J. Lewis (eds) *The Oxford Handbook of Comparative Welfare States.* Oxford: Oxford University Press, pp. 353–66.

Kautto, M. (2002) 'Investing in services in West European welfare states', *Journal of European Social Policy*, 12 (1), 53–65.

Kenworthy, L. (2010) 'Labor market activation', in H. Obinger, C. Pierson, F.G. Castles, S. Leibfried and J. Lewis (eds), *The Oxford Handbook of the Welfare State.* Oxford: Oxford University Press, pp. 435–47.

Kohl, J. (1980) 'Trends and problems in postwar public expenditure development in Western Europe and North America', in P. Flora and A.J. Heidenheimer (eds) *The Development of Welfare States in Europe and America*. New Brunswick, NJ: Transaction Books, pp. 307–44.

Lewis, J. and Surrender, R. (2004) *Welfare State Change Towards a Third Way?* Oxford: Oxford University Press.

Martin, J.P. (2001) *What Works Among Active Labour Market Policies: Evidence from OECD Countries' Experiences.* OECD Economic Studies, No. 30. Paris: OECD.

Nikolai, R. (2007) 'Sozialpolitik auf Kosten der Bildung? Verteilungskonkurrenz in Zeiten knapper Kassen', *Zeitschrift für Sozialreform*, 53 (1), 7–30.

Obinger, H. and Starke, P. (2008), 'Are welfare states converging? Recent social policy developments in advanced OECD countries', in I. Dingeldey and H. Rothgang (eds) *Governance of Welfare State Reform. A cross National and Cross Sectoral Comparison of Policy and Politics.* Cheltenham and Northampton, MA: Edward Elgar, pp. 109–37.

OECD (1992) *Public Educational Expenditure, Costs and Financing: An Analysis of Trends 1970–1988*. Paris: OECD.

OECD (2003) *Education at a Glance*. Paris: OECD.

OECD (2007a) *Babies and Bosses — Reconciling Work and Family Life. A Synthesis of Findings for OECD Countries.* Paris: OECD.

OECD (2007b) *The Social Expenditure Database: An Interpretative Guide.* Paris: OECD.

OECD (2010a) *Education at a Glance.* Paris: OECD.

OECD (2010b) *Social Expenditure Database 1980–2007.* Paris: OECD.

Palier, B. (2006) 'The re-orientation of European social policies towards social investment', *Internationale Politik und Gesellschaft*, 1 (1), 105–16.

Pierson, P. (2001) *The New Politics of the Welfare State.* Oxford: Oxford University Press.

Rohrbach, D. (2007) 'The development of knowledge societies in 19 OECD countries between 1970 and 2002', *Social Science Information*, 46 (4), 655–89.

Sen, A. (2000) *Ökonomie für den Menschen. Wege zu Gerechtigkeit und Solidarität in der Marktwirtschaft.* München: dtv.

Starke, P., Obinger, H. and Castles, F.G. (2008) 'Convergence towards where: In what ways, if any, are welfare states becoming more similar' *Journal of European Public Policy*, 15 (7), 975–1000.

Taylor-Gooby, P. (2001) 'The politics of welfare in Europe', in P. Taylor-Gooby (ed.) *Welfare States under Pressure.* London: Sage, pp. 1–28.

Wolf, F. (2009) 'The division of labour in education funding: A cross-national comparison of public and private education expenditure in 28 OECD countries', *Acta Politica*, 44 (1), 50–73.

Wolf, F. and Zohlnhöfer, R. (2009) 'Investing in human capital? The determinants of private education expenditure in 26 OECD countries', *Journal of European Social Policy*, 19 (3), 230–44.

FIVE

Social investment or recommodification? Assessing the employment policies of the EU member states[1]

Caroline de la Porte and Kerstin Jacobsson

Introduction

In the 1990s a new approach to economic, employment and social policy emerged in the EU in the wake of the Economic and Monetary Union (EMU), to respond to low growth, to increase global competitiveness and to meet the challenges of ageing populations and new family patterns. An important component of this new approach was the European Employment Strategy (EES) formalised in 1997, in order to encourage member states to develop comprehensive, high-quality labour market policies to upskill workers' competencies. The means included shifting expenditure from passive to active labour market policies and increasing employment rates, which should in turn nurture economic growth (Goetschy, 1999). The EES became an important pillar of the Lisbon Strategy that was launched in 2000 to make the European Union 'the most competitive and dynamic knowledge-based economy in the world capable of sustainable economic growth with more and better jobs and greater social cohesion'. The new approach envisioned positive synergies between economic, labour market and social policies. Social policy was seen as 'productive', supporting economic growth and paving the way towards full employment, while minimising negative social consequences of the economic integration process. Investment in education and lifelong learning were identified as important features for increasing labour productivity, mobility and thus flexibility. Investments in child care were conceived as a crucial condition for increasing activity rates by allowing more women to work (see Chapter Six).

This chapter focuses on the 'social investment' dimension of the EES. According to the social investment perspective, labour market policy should be focused on investing in people in order to equip the labour force with the necessary skills to face change and on providing supportive services in order to reach full employment. The 'social investment' approach, in general, is focused on investing in people in order to meet the needs of future generations. It entails that public expenditure should be made in the form of investment rather than compensation, that is, be designed as to 'pay off' later on (see Chapter Three). The aim is to increase social inclusion through work and education and to ensure that the population is well prepared for changing requirements on the labour market, such as specific skills and higher educational requirements (see Chapter Three). In the social investment perspective, employment and labour market policy should focus on encouraging employment participation among all categories of citizens through an active approach to labour force participation. This requires a preventive rather than a curative approach and active measures rather than passive maintenance support.

The ideas of social investment are echoed in the EES. The social investment approach and the EES both call for a high rate of labour market participation among all categories of citizens, in line with the traditions in the English-speaking and Nordic welfare state traditions, but challenging the male-breadwinner/female carer model of the continental and Mediterranean welfare state regimes. The EES was formulated mainly to respond to core challenges of the continental and Mediterranean welfare state regimes: to increase labour market flexibility and to increase labour market participation.

The welfare states in Central and Eastern Europe, in contrast, have reorganised their institutions during the last 15 years, where market making has been the key priority. The problem in the new EU member states, from a social investment perspective, is not institutional adaptation, but ensuring institutional development and stabilisation as well as social security. The short-term political priorities and growth strategy based on attracting foreign direct investment (FDI) has been guiding the political agenda in welfare state reform in most of the EU-10[2] (Offe, 2009), which is at odds with high social expenditure and social investment (which requires a long-term perspective). The incentive structure for developing social investment in the EU-10 is not nearly as strong, as it requires *new investments*, compared to the EU-15, where the much higher levels of social expenditure allow for a *redirection* of social spending.

In this chapter, we will underline that, due to its political and malleable form, the EES can be used either as a comprehensive social investment strategy focusing on the development of human resources for the needs of the labour market, or, alternatively, as a liberalisation strategy with little or no social investment. This risk of using the EES as a liberalisation strategy (exclusively market making) is evident for all member states, but it is particularly perilous for the new member states, which are under more pressure to stabilise their economies and finances in preparations for Economic and Monetary Union (EMU) membership, which has included the reduction of social expenditure.

This risk is exacerbated because the EES is a soft policy mechanism which operates through policy coordination, consisting of common objectives and benchmarks as well as country-specific recommendations, towards which member states must show progress in regular national reports that should present policy implementation and policy planning (Borrás and Jacobsson, 2004).[3] Some authors criticise the softness and policy ambiguity of the strategy, arguing that there are no tangible effects (Lodge, 2007; Kröger, 2009), while others have argued that the EES has at least fostered ideational and discursive change (Jacobsson, 2004). The most optimistic authors have argued that the EES has been instrumental in shifting national agendas and policies towards a comprehensive full employment paradigm (Zeitlin, 2005, 2009). Our aim here is not to take issue with or review this literature (see de la Porte, 2010, for an in-depth literature review), but instead to make an empirical assessment of the achievements of the EES thus far. Has the EES helped countries and governments to move in the direction of social investment?

This chapter first presents the social investment aspect of the EES, after which it presents the analytical approach and methodology. In the empirical section, the chapter assesses the achievements and shortcomings of the EES in shifting national policies towards a social investment agenda, focusing on changes in labour market policy. While relevant, there is no scope to analyse changes in child care structures and education systems in this chapter (these issues are taken up in other chapters of this volume; see Chapters Four, Six and Eight). Using a qualitative approach, it assesses the progress made thus far, as well as the remaining challenges in two representative member states from respectively five distinct welfare state configurations: Nordic, English-speaking, continental, Mediterranean and East European. Based on the assessment of the achievements of the EES thus far, we draw conclusions on the prospect of the EES as a social investment strategy in the enlarged European Union.

The social investment component of the European Employment Strategy

The main aim of the EES has from the very beginning been to support economic growth by focusing on how to increase the employment rate of the EU and its member states. In the Employment Title of the Amsterdam Treaty (articles 125 EC–130 EC) the stated objective is to achieve a 'high' level of employment. This aim has been accompanied by quantitative benchmarks to achieve, by 2010, a 70% employment rate overall, a 60% female employment rate (European Council, 2000) and a 50% employment rate of older workers (55–64). The ambition was enhanced in 2010, with the new aim to increase the overall employment rate of the EU to 75% by 2020. If we look at how employment rates have been evolving among EU member states during the last decade (see Table 5.1), the EES appears to have borne fruit.

Table 5.1 shows that employment rates have increased – almost unequivocally – across the five welfare state configurations between 2000 and 2008. It is notable that between 2005 and 2008, employment rates increased for all member states. While the member states clearly converge towards a full employment model, it is far from certain whether the EES has been the main stimulus for this development. Different factors can explain the differences in degree of change. First, economic growth affects employment rates positively, particularly during periods of recuperation from economic recession. Second, more substantial changes are likely in countries with lower initial employment rates. Third – and this is where the social investment perspective comes in – changes differ due to divergence in public policy approaches by the governments.

In the following, the social investment strategy promoted by the EES – a specific policy frame – will be presented in more detail (see Table 5.2), after which the empirical developments in member states will be analysed. A policy frame is a specific way to conceive of a public policy issue, following which a particular course of action is prescribed. In the words of Rein and Schön (1993: 153) a policy frame 'provides conceptual coherence, a direction for action, a basis for persuasion, and a framework for the collection and analysis of data – order, rhetoric, and action'. Crucially, policy frames influence what the actors consider 'facts' (in the EES: low growth, unemployment, population ageing), thereby narrowing down the possible courses of action.

Table 5.1: Employment rates across welfare state configurations (2000, 2005, 2008)*

Welfare state configuration/ country	Employment rate 2000 (%)	Employment rate 2005 (%)	Employment rate 2008 (%)	±
Nordic				
Denmark	76.2	75.9	78.1	+
Sweden	73.0	72.5	74.3	+
Finland	61.8	63.1	67.2	+
English-speaking				
UK	71.2	71.7	71.5	+
Ireland	65.2	75.9	78.1	+
Continental				
Austria	68.5	68.6	72.1	+
Belgium	60.5	61.1	62.4	+
France	62.1	63.7	64.9	+
Germany	65.6	66	70.7	+
Luxembourg	62.7	63.6	63.4	+
The Netherlands	72.9	73.2	77.2	+
Mediterranean				
Greece	56.5	60.1	61.9	+
Spain	56.3	63.3	64.3	+
Italy	53.7	57.6	58.7	+
Portugal	68.4	67.5	68.2	−
East European				
Bulgaria	50.4	55.8	64.0	+
Czech Republic	65	64.8	66.6	+
Estonia	60.4	64.4	69.8	+
Latvia	57.7	63.3	68.6	+
Lithuania	59.1	62.6	64.3	+
Hungary	56.3	56.9	56.7	+
Poland	55.0	52.8	59.2	+
Romania	63.0	57.6	59.0	−
Slovenia	62.8	66.0	68.6	+
Slovakia	56.8	57.7	62.3	+
EU-27	62.2	63.5	65.9	+

*The employment rate is the total percentage of people aged 15 to 64 in employment (at least one hour per week), Labour Force Survey, Eurostat, 2010. ± indicates whether employment rates have increased or decreased in the period under consideration.

Source: Eurostat, 2010.

Table 5.2: Features of the EU employment policy frame and institutional structure of the EU's Lisbon Strategy defined in 2005

Dimension of the employment policy frame	Content of the employment policy frame
Problem perception	Low economic growth, low employment rates, high unemployment rates
Policy solution	• To achieve 'full employment' • To improve quality and productivity at work • To strengthen social and territorial cohesion
Supportive policy solution	• To promote a lifecycle approach to work • To ensure inclusive labour markets • To improve the matching of labour market needs • To ensure employment-friendly labour cost developments and wage-setting mechanisms • To expand and improve investment in human capital • To adapt education and training systems in response to new competence requirements • To promote 'flexicurity' (flexibility and employment security)
Overall outcome benchmark	• Overall employment rates 70% • Female employment rate 60% • Older worker employment rate 50%
Supportive policy benchmarks	• To provide every unemployed person a job, training or other employability measure within four months for young people and 12 months for adults • To activate 25% of the long-term unemployed by 2010 • To postpone the exit age of the labour force by an average five years by 2010 compared to 2001 • To secure coverage of child care for at least 90% of children between three years old and the mandatory school age and at least 33% of children under the age of three years by 2010 • To have an EU average rate of no more than 10% of early school leavers • To ensure that at least 85% of 22-year-olds in the EU should have completed upper secondary education by 2010 • To have 12.5% of the adult working population in lifelong learning schemes
Institutional structure: EU level	The EU Council sets the main policy direction and sectoral Council formations and committees set specific policy aims

EU instruments	Policy coordination, funding programmes (especially structural funds), legislation, partnership between EU institutions and Member States
Institutional structure: national level	Civil servants in employment, social and labour market ministries report policy to EU level (on basis of EU policy objectives)
	National Lisbon coordinator to ensure integration of EU policy aims in national policy

Source: European Commission, 2005.

A weakness of the EES frame is that it has to compete with the stronger frame for economic policy (stronger both because of its institutional backup with binding rules and an independent European Central Bank, as well as because of a clear anchorage in neoclassical economic theory). The economic frame is also reinforced by the strongly institutionalised internal market project. Since the EES – requiring considerable financial investments – is to be implemented in the context of the Economic and Monetary Union (EMU), with its requirements on governments to control public expenditure and to reduce public deficits, the risk is that the aims are not fully implemented in line with the social investment paradigm, which highlights the importance of *high-quality* social investments. A complication for the implementation of the EES, then, is the diverse and even contradictory pressures for reform from the EU level through the Lisbon Strategy: on the one hand, to curb public expenditure (EMU) and on the other to make social investments. The Lisbon Strategy, then, can be seen to communicate an ambiguous message, and is a hybrid of social-democratic *and* liberal political ideologies (de la Porte, 2008, 2011; Borrás and Radaelli, 2011). Ambiguity can be seen as an opportunity structure that is utilised intentionally or unintentionally by agents, resulting in different outcomes.

When the EES was first institutionalised, in 1997, special attention was paid to increasing the employment of youth and the unemployed, after which in 2000, the 'inactive' were included as a target group. After 2001, there was a special focus on increasing the employment rate of older workers, and after 2004, immigrants and disadvantaged groups were added as a target group for enhancing labour market participation. The core means identified to achieve high employment was by shifting expenditure from passive and curative labour market strategies to preventive and 'active' labour market policies. An important means through which to achieve high labour market participation, upgrading of skills and activation has been the modernisation of the Public Employment Services. The EES also encourages social partners to take up responsibility for the development and delivery of training, traineeships and other forms of activation that are implemented in the workplace. In addition, the EES calls for reform of the education systems to ensure that all pupils be trained in competencies related to the development of new technologies.

From 2005 onwards, 'flexicurity', consisting of flexible work contracts together with appropriate social security, became a central objective in the EES. It consists of 'flexible and reliable' contractual arrangements, comprehensive lifelong learning strategies, effective active labour market policies (ALMP), and last but not least, modern social security systems (European Commission, 2007). The implication for countries with heavily regulated labour markets (mostly countries from continental and Mediterranean parts of Europe) is that labour markets should be rendered more flexible, while in other countries (mostly countries from the East), the implication is that stronger labour market institutions should be developed (de la Porte, 2009).

The aim of achieving a high rate of labour market participation, and a highly trained workforce that is 'employable' for the needs of the economy, is at the heart of the EES. 'Employability' is the term in the EES which refers to the broad aim of increasing labour market participation, facilitating take-up of employment for individuals, but also putting responsibility on the individual for maintaining an 'employable' profile in line with the needs of the labour market.

The EES also includes a funding programme to support initiatives (via co-funding) developed on the basis of the EES policy objectives, the European Social Fund (ESF). While the two initiatives were initially separate, their integration has increased over time, after periodic revisions and adaptations (Hartwig, 2007). What is crucial for successful implementation of the EES as a 'social investment' strategy is long-term planning, to channel investment (supported by the ESF) effectively into human resource development in line with the needs of the labour market.

Empirical assessment on the basis of welfare state regimes

The qualitative research in the chapter is based on our own primary research that analyses implementation of the EES in the various member states. This data, which is triangulated, is based on official documents and approximately 100 semistructured interviews with key actors and informants in the member states and the European Commission between

2000 and 2010 (Jacobsson, 2005; Jacobsson and Vifell, 2007; de la Porte, 2008, 2009; Jacobsson and West, 2009; de la Porte and Al-Gailany, 2011). In addition, we have drawn on the work of colleagues that have also researched the national impact of the EES in detail.

In the following, the achievements and shortcomings of the EES in shifting employment policies towards a social investment agenda are presented, according to type of welfare state regime. We have identified five families of welfare systems: Nordic, English-speaking, continental, Mediterranean and Eastern European (Esping-Andersen, 1990; Ferrera, 1996; Aidukaite, 2009). For each family, the main institutional and policy legacy will be presented, followed by their current challenges. Thereafter, the influence of the EES in two representative countries of each regime will be presented in more detail. For the Nordic family, we analyse Sweden and Denmark in more detail; for the English-speaking family, we analyse the UK and Ireland; for the welfare states in continental Europe, we analyse France and Germany; for the countries of the Mediterranean rim, we analyse Italy and Spain; and finally, for the East European family, we analyse Estonia and the Czech Republic.

In order to analyse the influence of the EES, we distinguish two types of change, which we use in carrying out our empirical analysis.[4] First, we analyse how and the extent to which the EES has contributed to ideational change, indicated by the adoption and use of EU concepts and discourses by domestic actors. To what extent has the EES discourse been used, by whom and how? Second, we analyse how the EES has contributed to policy change, which is the development of new policies which are clearly in line with the intended effect of the EES and the social investment approach. To assess policy change in core areas of the EES – active labour market policies, policies to integrate different categories of people into the labour market (ESF supported), Public Employment Services, education, training – we present main national developments in this area. To support our analysis, we use the descriptive data from Eurostat[5] that is used to monitor implementation of the EES for 2005 and 2008.[6] Table 5.3 presents data on expenditure for active labour market policy as a percentage of GDP,[7] and indicates whether this has increased or decreased over time as well as data on the number of participants in activation progammes. Table 5.4 presents data for passive labour market policy as a percentage of GDP[8] and indicates whether this has increased or decreased over time (±) as well as data on the number of people receiving passive benefits. Table 5.4 also includes data on expenditure for running the PES[9] and on the number of unemployed people registered in the PES.

Table 5.3: Indicators on active labour market policy (ALMP expenditure as a percentage of GDP and number of participants in active labour market policy schemes (EU-25))

Welfare state configuration/MS	ALMP 2005	ALMP 2008	±	No. in ALMP 2005	No. in ALMP 2008	±
Nordic						
Denmark	1.267	0.979	–	143,977	149,899	+
Sweden	1.058	0.643	–	206,232	134,975	–
Finland	0.732	0.674	–	96,696	91,763	–
Anglo-Saxon						
UK	0.054	0.047	–	67,798	92,885	+
Ireland	0.49	0.54	+	63,177	71,172	+
Continental						
Austria	0.461	0.516	+	130,377	178,798	+
Belgium	0.911	1.083	+	338,661	516,789	+
France	0.659	0.603	–	1,523,797	1,538,663	+
Germany	0.604	0.529	–	1,508,310	1,572,787	+
Luxembourg	0.403	0.332	–	9,336	13,511	+
The Netherlands	0.856	0.714	–	349,050	325,923	–
Mediterranean rim						
Greece	0.057	0.14	+	na	42,899	na
Spain	0.53	0.528	–	2,721,158	2,716,406	–
Italy	0.477	0.358	–	1,765,390	1,460,834	–
Portugal	0.501	0.408	–	165,355	166,342	+
East European						
Bulgaria	0.432	0.262	–	88,781	89,788	+
Czech Republic	0.122	0.104	–	59,809	48,678	–
Estonia	0.047	0.035	–	2,194	1,263	–
Latvia	0.162	0.078	–	9,631	5,444	–
Lithuania	0.146	0.14	–	na	14,135	na
Hungary	0.203	0.208	+	71,359	68,260	–
Poland	0.356	0.469	+	463,401	779,388	+
Romania	0.108	0.06	–	99,421	85,455	–
Slovenia	0.194	0.093	–	16,564	7,149	–
Slovakia	0.169	0.15	–	137,890	91,568	–

Source: Eurostat, 2010.

Table 5.4: Indicators on passive labour market policy (PLMP expenditure as a percentage of GDP and number of people receiving passive benefits (EU-25), expenditure on public employment service (% GDP) and number of registered persons in PES.

Welfare state configuration/MS	PLMP 2005	PLMP 2008	±	No.PLMP 2005	No.PLMP 2008	±	PES 2005	PES 2008	±	Unemployed PES 2005	Unemployed PES 2008	±
Nordic												
Denmark	2.342	1.216	–	244,662	128,737	–	0.16	0.24	+	265,639	116,024	–
Sweden	1.156	0.448	–	358,800	196,795	–	0.18	0.29	+	690,385	524,877	–
Finland	1.902	1.354	–	302,066	227,202	–	0.14	0.12	–	505,185	415,907	–
Anglo-Saxon												
UK	0.183	0.197	+	881,493	1,021,545	+	0.38	0.26	–	881,493	1,021,545	+
Ireland	0.828	1.325	+	157,993	229,263	+	0.20	0.21	+	157,117	227,069	+
Continental												
Austria	1.517	1.161	–	292,063	246,127	–	0.17	0.16	–	268,252	224,788	–
Belgium	2.395	2.039	–	915,481	806,380	–	0.20	0.20	±	427,584	238,395	–
France	1.584	1.17	–	2,681,273	2,280,963	–	0.23	0.20	–	3,847,977	3,098,967	–
Germany	2.011	1.097	–	4,576,562	3,199,858	–	0.29	0.28	–	6,874,792	5,398,546	–
Luxembourg	0.653	0.525	–	8,725	8,915	+	0.05	0.05	±	8,948	9,916	+
Netherlands	2.008	1.265	–	724,830	534,100	–	0.44	0.33	–	717,200	454,900	–
Mediterranean rim												
Greece	0.406	0.462	+	na	219,385	na	0.01	0.01	±	481,913	399,672	±
Spain	1.45	1.885	+	1,294,893	1,814,630	+	0.09	0.10	+	3,036,910	3,587,968	+
Italy	0.81	0.81	±	791,153	766,260	–	0.04	0.04	±			
Portugal	1.279	0.989	–	316,665	253,476	–	0.14	0.13	–	522,062	470,927	–

Table 5.4 (continued)

East European

Bulgaria	0.213	0.156	−	78,519	66,711	−	0.07	0.05	−	427,584	238,395	−
Czech Republic	0.241	0.197	−	138,714	109,376	−	0.13	0.12	−	514,910	325,575	−
Estonia	0.119	0.206	+	17,568	11,858	−	0.02	0.03	+	25,349	21,308	+
Latvia	0.312	0.347	+	30,093	30,779	+	0.06	0.05	−	91,032	56,865	−
Lithuania	0.122	0.154	+	22,196	23,367	+	0.07	0.08	+	135,058	101,579	+
Hungary	0.392	0.37	−	135,104	155,079	+	0.08	0.13	+	410,649	477,351	+
Poland	0.857	0.35	−	875,916	454,903	−	0.07	0.09	+	2,835,107	1,459,978	+
Romania	0.393	0.174	−	236,206	127,579	−	0.04	0.03	−	534,393	363,369	−
Slovenia	0.39	0.268	−	14,330	14,545	+	0.10	0.09	−	334,605	254,521	−
Slovakia	0.266	0.431	+	54,776	79,790	+	0.17	0.11	−	91,889	63,216	−

Source: Eurostat, 2010.

Empirical analysis

The Nordic countries

In the Nordic countries, the welfare state is mostly universal and tax-financed. It aims to provide a high level of quality services and benefits for all citizens, independent of their status in the labour market (Esping-Andersen, 1990). Nordic countries have a high rate of labour market participation (see Table 5.1), which is a necessary condition for financing and providing access to high-quality social services for all citizens. Labour market participation has increased between 2000 and 2008, especially in Finland, often qualified as a 'latecomer' to the Nordic model (Kautto, 1999). Finland had a lower employment rate than Sweden and Denmark in 2000 (61.8% compared to 73% in Sweden and 76.2% in Denmark), and has designed public policy to enhance employment policy throughout the 1990s and 2000s (van Gerven, 2007). The employment rate in Finland increased to 67.2% in 2008, compared with an increase to 74.3% and 78.1% in Sweden and Denmark, respectively.

While the Nordic welfare state model was built upon the expectation that all citizens of working age would be in employment, if they were temporarily excluded from the labour market, then the public employment services would play an important role in educating and upskilling them and in reintegrating them into the labour market via active labour market policies. It is also relevant to note that these countries have a comparatively high level of passive expenditure, to provide a decent standard of living during spells of unemployment or due to early retirement from the labour market.

For Sweden and Denmark the EES has meant little on the ideational level, as activation and skills updating where an integral part of the labour market systems. However, the Danish 'flexicurity' model has been adopted at the EU level as a model for emulation (Kvist, 2007; de la Porte and Gailany, 2011). The Danish labour market model was first coined as the flexicurity model in 1999, when a Danish academic, Per Kongshøj Madsen, used the term with reference to the Danish labour market model (Barbier et al., 2009). It was then uploaded to the EU, and parallel to that, popularised in Denmark and used by politicians and government officials to refer to the Danish model. In a sense, then, the EES has had a discursive effect on Denmark, in that flexicurity was conceptualised to identify the particular features of the Danish model, which (further) legitimised the labour market model to the Danish electorate.[10]

Concerning policy change, both countries have repeatedly received recommendations that gender segregation together with important gender wage gaps represent a major structural problem. No specific initiatives have derived from the EES in these countries to respond to this problem (Jacobsson, 2005; de la Porte and Al-Gailany, 2011). Sweden and Denmark have also received recommendations to integrate immigrants on the labour market. For both countries, this has been a domestic priority and policy and programmes have been adopted to that effect (ibid). Both governments have been successful in increasing employment rates. However, increases in employment rates are not necessarily the result of comprehensive social investment.

Indeed, concerning changes in labour market policy itself, in Sweden and Denmark, there has been a shift to less costly forms of activation, suggesting a move away from social investment. In Sweden, there has been a shift to job counselling, rather than training. This is reflected in the substantial decrease in spending on active labour market policies in Sweden (from 1.058% GDP in 2005 to 0.643% GDP in 2008), but for a lower number of participants in 2008 (134,975) compared to 2005 (206,232). At the same time, investment in passive labour market policy has been reduced drastically between 2005 (1.156% GDP for 358,800 recipients) and 2008 (0.448% GDP for 196,795 recipients). In Denmark, active and passive labour market policies were maintained throughout the 1990s, but there has been an incremental change throughout the 2000s. The number of participants in ALMP is comparable in 2005 (149,879) and 2008 (143,977). The municipalities have a financial incentive to activate the unemployed rather than to allocate passive benefits without any conditionality. Overall, conditionality ('activation') has been increased for the reception of passive benefits (Clasen and Clegg, 2007). Despite this, the expenditure on activation has decreased from 1.267% GDP in 2005 to 0.979% GDP in 2008, suggesting that less costly activation measures, not necessarily in sync with the social investment approach, have been used. The activation approach has been criticised by social partners for not leading to concrete results in terms of skills updating and enhancement of competencies for the labour market (de la Porte and Al-Gailany, 2011). Instead, it potentially has a perverse stigmatising effect for those actually participating in the schemes (Barbier et al., 2009). The expenditure on passive measures has been halved between 2005 (2.342% GDP) and 2008 (1.216% GDP), roughly reflecting the decrease in number of recipients, which went from 244,662 in 2005 to 128,737 in 2008. This is likely to decrease more in the future, since the maximum period for receiving unemployment benefits has been halved in the wake of the financial crisis from four to two years. The ESF has not contributed significantly to any changes, and the earmarked money for regional development in Denmark was unutilised for many years. Now, in the wake of the financial crisis, that is changing (de la Porte and Al-Gailany, 2011).

In the countries from the Nordic welfare state configuration, then, the EES has not led to major changes. It supports the main logic of the existing systems, but the governments in the Nordic welfare states are decreasing the quality of labour market services, due to domestic reforms. Some structural issues – gender segregation, wage gap – addressed through the EES have not induced any major reforms, while others – increasing labour market participation of immigrants – have led to major reforms, but mainly or solely due to domestic electoral pledges. Concerning an important component of the social investment strategy – high quality of activation – this seems to have decreased over time in both countries.

The English-speaking countries

In the UK, the system related to employment and labour market policies is Beveridgian, where health care and education are central components, in order to develop an able workforce. The aim from the outset was to have a high overall employment rate. Thus, the concept of activity on the labour market was built into the system, but without the comprehensive system of unemployment benefits that is such a crucial feature of the Nordic countries. Furthermore, union power and membership are low. A crucial component of the system in the UK is the welfare-to-work strategy which began to take shape in the 1980s during the Thatcher administration. This included mandatory interviews for the unemployed after 12 months of unemployment in order to continue to receive benefits. The conditionality (in different forms: interviews, activation, training, and so on) for receiving benefits has incrementally increased throughout the 1980s up to the mid-1990s (Büchs, 2007: 76–77; Clasen and Clegg, 2007; van Gerven, 2007). The Irish welfare state model is often considered a latecomer in terms of social policies. Irish female labour market participation has until the 1980s been lower than in the UK, due to more traditional family models because of Catholicism. Labour market policy is clearly workfarist. Since the 1980s, the Irish model has a particular feature – the involvement of civil society actors in the development of the policy agenda and implementation of policy. However, similarly to the UK, trade unions are weak and union membership is low if compared to those in the continental or Nordic social systems.

When New Labour came to power in May 1997 in the UK, the New Deal programmes, consisting essentially of a supply-side welfare-to-work strategy, were immediately enacted. The New Deal programmes were the transposition of the most important electoral pledge of the New Labour Party. Most of New Labour's plans were introduced during Blair's first term in power, after which minor changes and reforms were undertaken (Büchs, 2007: 26). The New Deal programmes are created for different target groups, each focusing on the specific problems related to a target group. These were introduced successively, and some are mandatory while some are voluntary.

The EES did not have an effect on the development of these programmes in this initial phase, although the EES can be considered to justify the main direction of reform in the UK. After 1999, the Third Way policy also involved a re-organisation of the Public Employment Services, which took place between 1999 and 2002 where the national services and the individual local offices were harmonised across the territory (Büchs, 2005; van Gerven, 2007). The costs of running the Public Employment Services were 0.38% GDP in 2005, which decreased to 0.26% GDP in 2008; expenditure on ALMP was 0.054% GDP in 2005, which decreased to 0.047% GDP in 2008, while the number of people in activation schemes continued to increase, from 67,798 in 2005 to 92,885 in 2008. The already low level of expenditure on activation has thus continued to decrease, although participants have increased by 30% between 2005 and 2008 (see Clasen and Clegg, 2007 for a more detailed analysis). Expenditure on passive measures has increased slightly (but is at a low level) from 0.183% GDP in 2005 for 881,493 participants to 0.197% GDP in 2008 for a considerably higher number of participants (1,021,545).

The major reforms in labour market policy and the Public Employment Service were domestically driven. The Commission recommended the UK government to improve the level of passive support for jobseekers, and to provide the unemployed immediate access to the New Deal programmes and, with it, the jobseekers' allowance. However (this is also reflected in the data above), the government has not taken these recommendations on board (Büchs, 2007). The New Deal programmes were determined independently of the EES in a domestically driven path-dependent logic, although reference was made to the EES ex-post, especially in reports on UK employment policy to the European Commission. On the other hand, the government used the EES and the Lisbon Strategy to strengthen its political focus on the permanent updating of skills in the 2003 Skills White Paper, but did not use the EES or elements of it in actual policy planning documents (Büchs, 2007).

In Ireland, the local employment service was reformed from 1994 onwards with the help of European Social Funding. Activation schemes were introduced for young people from 1988, and for all persons aged 25–54 from 2000. The national training agency has been a key actor in this process. All people unemployed for more than six months are referred to the training office that finds new jobs for the unemployed or puts them into training schemes (O'Donnell and Moss, 2005: 323–24). Since 1997, there has been a focus on other groups – single parents and those on disability allowances. But the development of activation has been through cost-efficient measures, and there is no evidence to suggest that it was the EES that led to this change (Murphy, 2002; Lynch, 2003; de la Porte, 2008). Expenditure on ALMP was 0.49% GDP in 2005 for 67,798 participants compared to 0.54% GDP in 2008 for 92,885 participants. Expenditure for passive benefits increased from 0.828% GDP in 2005 for 157,993 recipients to 1.325% GDP in 2008 for 229,263 recipients. Through the EES Ireland has been advised to invest in skills updating but has not, to the regret of the social ministry, taken these recommendations on board. Ireland is one of the countries which has been worst hit by the financial crisis. It is badly equipped to respond to challenges of relaunching the economy because there has not been susbstantial investments in skills development during the last decade.

Concerning policy change, the direction of change is similar: in both countries, activation has been enhanced, but via welfare-to-work policies that were defined by domestic reform priorities. The EES, then, has not contributed to the development of a social investment approach in the Anglo-Saxon welfare states, although it has in the UK been used to justify reforms. The recommendations in both countries – pointing to the need to develop policy more in line with the social investment approach via better means for skills updating – have, ultimately, not led to substantial changes in these countries.

The continental countries

In continental Europe, the welfare systems are traditionally based on a male-breadwinner/female-carer model. For the countries based on this model, the EES has addressed core challenges: increasing labour market participation, facilitating the reconciliation of work and family life, and tackling early retirement. Here we will analyse the effects of the EES in France and Germany. It is clear that in both countries, activation, at least at the level of political discourse, became more pronounced throughout the 1990s in response to the high rates of structural unemployment recorded at that time. It was, at least, in the direction proposed by the EES (Coron and Palier, 2002; Barbier et al., 2009).

In France, the main reason for shifts to activation are labour market rigidities, and this has partially been put onto the agenda via the EES (Barbier with Symba-Salla, 2004; Erhel et al., 2005). The ideas of accessibility to child care institutions to facilitate female labour market participation have also been promoted through the EES (Barbier with Symba-Salla, 2004). In Germany as well, ideas of activation and high labour market participation were partially promoted through the EES. However, the 'modernists' in the SPD were more influenced by Third Way ideas and conceptions of the welfare state than by more comprehensive social investment ideas associated with the EES. One of the politically most salient manifestations of this shift in discourse occurred under Gerhard Schroeder, who wrote a paper with Tony Blair that focused on supply-side policies, removing work disincentives from the social security system and rebalancing rights and obligations.

In both France and Germany, policy reform began in the mid-1990s. In France, the key reform packages that were adopted in labour market policies at the moment of the introduction of the EES are the 'nouveau départ' programme for young people in 1998, and in the 2000s, various reforms that aim to enhance financial incentives to work, especially through tightening eligibility, and providing subsidies for employers (Erhel et al., 2005: 222-23). The EES has been used to support (but did not drive forward) the reform of Public Employment Services in France (Erhel et al., 2005: 224, 237). Expenditure in ALMP in 2005 has been quite stable, changing from 0.659% GDP in 2005 for 1,523,797 participants in ALMP to 0.603% GDP in 2008 for 1,538,663 participants. The tendency, however, is towards a decrease of expenditure for more participants. Concerning passive support, this has decreased substantially, from 1.584% GDP in 2005 for 2,681,273 recipients to 1.17% GDP in 2008 for 2,280,963 recipients. Overall, then, less is spent on active *and* passive measures. When flexicurity became a core aspect of the EES in 2004/05, the 'modèle danois' became a priority of the government and was widely debated in the media. The elites (the Villepin government: 2005–7) were favourable to EU policy, particularly as France had received recommendations to render its labour market more flexible. However, this attempt was met with resistance, including social protests, and in the end, the attempt to change labour market policy substantially led to the political defeat of the Villepin government in 2007 (Barbier et al., 2009). In a completely new area of relevance for the social investment approach, that of quality in work, a debate has developed among the social partners in France on the general issue of wellbeing at work (Barbier with Samba-Sylla, 2004).

The core changes to the German welfare state began in the mid-1990s in a Bismarckian welfare state that was deeply embedded and institutionalised. Until 2000, active policies were in line with the traditional (social-democratic) Keynesian model of economic and social growth. The policies were targeted at specific groups, but did not overhaul the male-breadwinner, female-carer model of welfare (Büchs, 2005, 2007). The most important policy changes were enacted after 2001 onwards, in the form of the 'Hartz' acts and the Act for reforming the labour market. These introduced new obligations for jobseekers and hardened sanctions in cases of non-compliance, cut benefits (especially passive ones) and changed conditions of eligibility (Büchs, 2005: 181–82). The level of expenditure on ALMP has decreased from 0.604% GDP in 2005 for 1,508,310 participants to 0.529% GDP in 2008 for 1,538,663 participants. The reduction in passive expenditure has been more substantial, from 2.011% GDP in 2005 for 4,576,562 recipients to 1.097% GDP in 2008 for 3,199,858 recipients. Ultimately, it was not the social investment approach but, instead, the 'Third Way' that had a more direct and tangible influence on the German reform process (Büchs and Friedrich, 2005: 265).

In both cases, the elites had decided on a reform objective, where the French government looked directly to Denmark, but was met by resistance. In the German case, it was the UK model which was a direct source of inspiration, rather than the EES itself. In both countries, issues addressed in EU recommendations (notably to reduce rigidities in the labour market) have incrementally been addressed, because they became acute.

The Mediterranean countries

In the countries of the Mediterranean rim, like the countries of continental Europe, the EES does address key challenges. These countries traditionally have low rates of female labour market participation, few and underdeveloped care structures, and very high reliance on pensions (and early pensions), especially in Italy, which has the highest rate of expenditure on pensions in Europe. Ideationally, activation, high labour market participation and lifelong upskilling were new for both countries, where these elements are underdeveloped compared to other (northern) European countries. While the EES as well as the OECD have promoted these ideas, domestically they have not been used to develop a social investment approach but, instead, a tighter form of activation with more obligations for the receipt of slimmed down passive benefits.

The EES has been used to justify reform, but in both Spain and Italy, our focus here, it has been to develop flexibility, and temporary and irregular work contracts with little protection. Child care institutions, modernisation of the Public Employment Services and human resource development have not been in the spotlight. In Italy, the EES was introduced parallel to various domestic reforms affecting labour market reform. The first was the Bassanini Law of 1997, which decentralised labour market policies to the regional and local levels. Two important milestones in the development of labour market flexibility in Italy were the Treu Law on flexibility of 1997, and the White Paper on Labour Market Policy of 2001, that set out a comprehensive reform of Italy's labour market. The latter draws extensively on the EES as a justification for the government's reform agenda, but interprets EES policy objectives in a way that is at odds with the social investment approach. Similarly, the discourse of 'quality in employment' has been used to increase flexibility on the labour market, which was the main priority government's employment policy at the time. Thus, the EES was clearly used for blame shifting (Ferrera and Sacchi, 2005) and reform has moved towards 'flexi-insecurity' (Berton et al., 2009). The constitutional reform (that included the 1997 Bassanini reform) resulted in the devolution of all (implementation) functions related to employment services and ALMP to the regions and the local authorities, although the overall normative framework was still to be established at the national level.

In Spain, reforms were carried out by governments from the left and the right, in conjunction with the social partners, at times of economic crisis, throughout the 1980s and especially the 1990s. The reforms sought to reduce the rigidity of the labour markets and to reduce wage and non-wage labour costs. The first wave of reform, during the 1980s, facilitated employment creation through temporary contracts. The second wave of reforms was initiated in the mid-1990s. In 1994, new forms of (precarious) employment contracts were introduced in conjunction with deregulation of the labour market. In 1996 the policy response was to counter precariousness through a new type of permanent contract, more social protection for temporary contracts and training schemes for the young unemployed. Further reforms in 2001 and 2002 also sought to reduce rigidities in the labour market. The OECD and the Bank of Spain had considerable political clout and were able to influence policy considerably. In addition, local and regional-level actors had been empowered by the institutionalisation of management and implementation bodies for the European Structural Fund, rather than the EES (López-Santana, 2006: 290).

In both countries, the ideas of the EES have had some influence, but they have not been interpreted or implemented as a comprehensive social investment approach. The EES has facilitated cooperation between different actors, at least at the level of the central government, but has excluded social partners. However, the EES is detached from the politics of decision making. The reforms in both countries move towards more flexibilisation and less security, which is the opposite of the social investment approach.

The East European countries

The influence of the EES in new member states has thus far been given little scholarly attention (de la Porte, 2009; Mailand, 2009; Jacobsson and West, 2009, 2010) but is nonetheless key for assessing the prospect of a social investment strategy in the EU. Under communism, the countries were officially full employment societies, with no unemployment problems (for example, Aidukaite, 2004). The systems were paternalist and all individuals had rights to comprehensive social protection (education, health care, housing) via their job status. The post-1989 development has involved (sometimes very extensive) recalibration of the former social and labour market policies and institutions, driven by the new elites in these countries, but in a context where external actors, including international organisations and the European Union, have had an important impact on institutional change and policy development (Offe, 2009; Ornestein, 2009). Aidukaite (2004, 2009) has argued that it is valid to refer to a 'post-socialist' welfare regime, which tends to be a hybrid of liberal and corporatist models and is characterised by programmes with high coverage but with low benefit levels. Most of the post-communist countries moved away from collective solutions towards individualised ones, even if they may not follow the same paths concerning institutional arrangements (Mayes and Mustaffa, 2010).

The EU has (co-)funded and supported the modernisation of the Public Employment Services. Access to the ESF and other EU funds has helped increase interest in active labour market policies, but they do little to contribute what is beyond the requirement for co-financing of the ESF. The Public Employment Services has been developed in most of the new member states since the early 1990s to cover significant parts of the population for placement. In the transition period there was a general reluctance in Central and Eastern Europe to allow the state to play a large role in social policy provision due to a shared liberal view that individuals should be able to cope on their own. Ornestein (2009) has argued that the Central and Eastern European countries have even aimed to 'out-liberalise' the EU-15. Nevertheless, in terms of reform outcomes, the EES has led to an increased focus on active labour market policies along with much-needed reform of vocational education and systems of lifelong learning. Most countries in the EU-10 have embraced flexicurity, but emphasising flexibility rather than security. The new member states are characterised by very low levels of social expenditure (see Chapter Four), and they are under pressure to meet the convergence criteria of the Stability and Growth Pact (Johnson, 2008). Very low benefit levels of unemployment discourage individuals from registering at public employment offices, contributing to the persistence of a shadow economy, which in turn reduces state revenues, which in turn makes it hard to increase social spending.

The national reports of the Central and Eastern European countries reveal that there is a change in discourse, in that the new member states recognise the need to invest in human resources. Ideationally, activation is taken on board, but is interpreted entirely in a neoliberal rather than a fully fledged social investment perspective. The EES is not considered a genuine reform agenda (de la Porte, 2009; Jacobsson and West, 2009). Policy makers in Estonia and the Czech Republic have taken greater interest in the ideas from the economic component of the Lisbon Strategy, rather than from the social component (Jacobsson and West, 2009, 2010).

Estonia is extremely liberal and very rapidly dismantled the old system. Initially, unemployment entitlements were financed from the state budget but in 2003 an unemployment insurance based on contributory financing was introduced. The current system consists of two tiers: the first tier comes out of the Unemployment Insurance Fund and is based on contributions; and the second tier is financed from the state budget and provides security for those who do not qualify for the unemployment insurance benefit. Hence, unemployment entitlements are based on a mixture of the corporatist and targeted models (Aidukaite, 2004: 61 ff.).

In Estonia, the expenditure for running the Public Employment Services is the lowest of the EU-25 (aside from Greece), and this has changed from 0.02% GDP in 2005 (25,349 were registered as unemployed) to 0.03% GDP in 2008 (21,308 were registered as unemployed). It is also the country with the lowest expenditure on activation (0.047% GDP in 2005 for 2,194 participants and 0.035% GDP in 2008 for 1,263 participants). Active labour market policies are thus virtually nonexistent in Estonia. Passive expenditure is also very low: 0.119% GDP for 17,568 recipients in 2005 compared to 0.206% GDP for 11,858 recipients in 2008. It is clear that there is virtually no money to 'shift' the direction of expenditure in labour market policy in Estonia.

The welfare model of the Czech Republic has been characterised as a continental, corporatist type (Mayes and Mustaffa, 2010: 24). Economically, it is considered to be a success in the transition to a free-market economy. However, the labour market is dualistic, and the people who have become unemployed due to industrial restructuration have only to a minor extent obtained new skills (de la Porte, 2009), which is a general problem in the East European countries. The Public Employment Services are well organised across the national territory, including monitoring and evaluation of all local centres' activities, which were developed with the support of European structural funds. The expenditure for running the Public Employment Services in the Czech Republic is the highest among the new member states, from 0.13% GDP in 2005 to 0.12% GDP in 2008, while the number of unemployed has decreased from 514,910 in 2005 to 325,575 in 2008. Expenditure on ALMP is still, however, very low: 0.122% GDP in 2005 for 59,809 participants, which decreased to 0.104% GDP in 2008 for 48,678 participants. While almost 80% of the ESF funds are earmarked for skills improvement (Kaluzna, 2008: 20), this has especially been used for the less costly forms of activation; that is, counselling services for job search. Passive support is also very low (although not as alarmingly low as in Estonia): 0.241% GDP for 138,714 recipients in 2005, which decreased to 0.197% GDP for 109,376 recipients in 2008. The EU has stated that ALMP are still small scale and not sufficiently targeted towards disadvantaged groups (European Commission, 2009). Indeed, the overall expenditure on employment services (running the Public Employment Services and activation measures) is still low, and has not increased substantially over time (de la Porte, 2009). Conditionality for receiving unemployment benefits has increased over time.

The new member states suffer from poor working conditions, low wages, regional disparities (between urban and rural areas) and income inequalities. The domestic agendas dominated by 'business friendly' free market considerations in many of these states is not compatible with the social investment ideals (see, for example, Woolfson, 2006). Moreover, in Estonia and the Czech Republic, trade unions are even weaker than in the Mediterranean countries. The level of trade union membership is extremely low in both countries, and collective bargains apply to at best half the total number of employees (National Reform Programme of the Czech Republic, 2008; Jacobsson and West, 2009). It is notable that the social partners in the Czech Republic did not approve of the National Reform Programme that outlines economic and employment policy, because worker security was not addressed (National Reform Programme of the Czech Republic, 2008). The model inherent in the EES, where social partners and local authorities are supposed to take an active role in implementation, does not fit well the context in the EU-10, due to the weakness of the social partners and the lack of resources at local level. The social partners in the new member states have not used the EES as a bargaining chip to gain more say in labour market affairs, and the EU, although calling for social partner involvement, has not directed country-specific recommendations to Estonia or the Czech Republic on this point. Another constraining factor for the EES to have an impact in the new member states is the centralised structure of policy making in many of those countries.

Overall assessment

Employment policies have been at the top of the reform agendas in member states at least since the late 1990s, when the EES was implemented. In the EU-15, the normative full employment model (and shifts to 'activation') that the EES embodies has become an ideational reference point in the domestic debates on employment policy, even if the EES did not bring about that debate. The evidence suggests that activation as conceived in the EES was not influential, but that the final aim of the EES – to reach full employment – has been embraced not only discursively but in terms of actual output. It has been used in some cases to extend key notions of (full) employment and/or activation, but it has only marginally been used as a resource through which to develop a comprehensive social investment policy. Our data suggests that there have not really been clear and massive shifts from passive to active expenditure on labour market policies in the EU-15, but that expenditure for both is depleting, while participants in ALMP are increasing in order to be able to receive benefits. Unemployment insurance has been reformed in most member states, increasing conditionality, decreasing the replacement rate, and decreasing the length of receipt of benefits. 'Activation' schemes are hardly comprehensive and individually tailored in line with the social investment agenda, but are instead workfarist, and there is more counselling than comprehensive training (see also Chapter Seven). The ESF has played a role in countries with underdeveloped regions

– notably countries from the Mediterranean welfare state regime but also Ireland.

As to the EU–10, the political context in which a social investment strategy would be implemented differs, if compared to EU–15. Political parties in many of the new member states represent a different cleavage structure than parties in Western Europe (that is, are organised around dimensions other than class and the left–right distinction, such as rural–urban, religious–secular and the ethnic cleavage). With weak social democracies and trade unions (Aidukaite, 2009), it is hard to see which policy actors in those countries would actively pursue the social investment agenda. As Morgan (this volume) points out, there needs to be a constituency for social investment reforms in the member states. Market making is the core priority of governments and business in the new member states, and this is typically what is retained from the EES. However, the ESF has contributed to the professionalisation of the Public Employment Services, but the development of human resources and the reform of education and training systems on which this hinges remains a major challenge (see also Chapter 9). Given the low political support and the weakness of industrial relations, pressure from the EU, coupled with financial incentives, is probably necessary for any substantive change to come about. Moreover, the governing elites feel the need to handle short-term issues rather than to make long-term investments. With the financial crisis of 2008–9, there are reverse tendencies involving cuts in social spending for most of the new member states. This has even been encouraged and in some cases actively supported by the IMF and foreign governments.

Conclusion: towards recommodification rather than social investment

In all types of welfare regimes it is first and foremost institutional legacies, creating particular constellations of reform challenges, and the predominance of economic and financial ministers over social affairs and labour ministers at EU and national levels, which shape economic and employment reform programmes. The EES can be used to legitimise domestic reform, not to actually drive policy change.

In terms of policy discourse, the full employment model as developed in the EES has been embraced by all member states. It mirrors, but hardly contributes to, the variations of 'new' political ideologies within the member states, from the Third Way in the UK to active liberalism in many countries, particularly in the new member states. However, in terms of reform outcome, activation policies and complementary reform of unemployment insurance systems have clearly contributed to recommodification in both the EU-15 and the EU-10. Work incentives and conditionality requirements have increased.[11] In most member states, public employment services have been developed and decentralised, organising the vacancy announcements, training and upskilling as well as access to benefits in periods of unemployment. While the institutional fit with the Public Employment Services model in the EES is comprehensive, the quality of activation services (and benefit levels) does not live up to the social investment approach inherent to the EES, particularly for the Mediterranean and new member states. Policies targeted at particular groups have been developed in order to increase the employment rate overall. But the reform of education, activation and training institutions, which is costly yet a key to sustainable and competitive economies for the future, has not been deep. Furthermore, conditionality has increased and benefit levels (of unemployment insurance) have decreased, ultimately decreasing the security level of individual citizens. Ultimately, the human resources strategy is not linked to the needs of the labour market, particularly for the new member states, where dual labour markets persist.

In summary, then, the ambiguity of the Lisbon Strategy has allowed policy makers a selective use of and reference to the message of the EES, and a bias in favour of commodification and flexibility rather than social investment. It is notable that despite the higher employment rates, there has not been a decline in people living at risk of poverty in the Union as a whole since 2000. On the contrary, income inequalities and in-work poverty have increased in many places (EAPN, 2007). A focus on employment rates without a parallel focus on quality (of jobs as well as services) and equality (of income as well as opportunity) may be misguided.

Moreover, the EES and the Lisbon Strategy were invented to respond to the needs of the EU-15. Yet the reform challenges partly differ between (and within) the EU-15 and the EU-10, as does the economic and political context in which reform is to be implemented. While the main challenge for EU-15 is to deregulate inflexible labour markets, the main challenge for EU-10 is to improve the security of workers and citizens, to develop protection against the market making, which is well underway in these countries. Thus far the EES has not been able to contribute to that end in the EU-10. For the EU-15, 'social investment' has implied the redirection of expenditure (without increases), but for the EU-10 the level of expenditure is much lower (17% of GDP in 2005, compared to 27.2% of GDP in 2005 for the

EU-27), implying that there is much less expenditure to redirect. In our view, the EES and the social investment paradigm that it embodies sidesteps the main challenges in the Central and Eastern European countries that face pressure to meet the convergence criteria of the Economic and Monetary Union, which has been exacerbated by the 2008 financial crisis. This has required making reforms to ensure the financial sustainability of the welfare state systems, which has had negative implications for their social sustainability, and where social investment for the future has been shelved until times look brighter.

Furthermore, other countries which have also been hit by the financial crisis, notably the Mediterranean countries and Ireland, have few real possibilities to develop a fully fledged social investment strategy. Ultimately, as is discussed in Chapter Eleven, the recent economic crisis casts a shadow upon the likelihood for governments to see social spending as productive, relative to other investments. A social investment strategy requires a long-term perspective. This is a crucial aspect of policy planning, which is hard to marry with the recent economic crises and financial instability, where short-term priorities about regaining financial stability and growth dominate the political agenda. Likewise, recommmodification may be the tempting option for governments in a short- or medium-term perspective. Arguably, the EES and its belief in positive synergies underestimates conflicts between long-term and short-term interests. Pressure on the unemployed to accept unskilled and unrewarding jobs may be detrimental to productivity in the long run. Likewise, for individual enterprises it may seem more rational to improve competitiveness by dismissals rather than investments in the labour force. And for governments, in their attempts to improve public finances, cuts in social expenditure or less expensive options are closer at hand than investments that promise to bear fruit in the distant future.

In conclusion, then, the problem for a social investment strategy in the EU is that it has had to be implemented within an institutional framework designed for something else, which is the stability of public finances. Consequently, in member states from all welfare state configurations, we have seen an uneven implementation of what was supposed to be a coherent package: governments have gone for less costly recommodification rather than social investment. If the EES is to be sustainable in the long run, then it is imperative that its objectives are consistent over time, coherent (internally but also with economic policies) and clear (that is, not open to interpretation across the political divide), but also that funding is allocated for the achievement of aims decided under the EES. There is clear evidence that the availability of co-funding for implementing reform objectives does contribute to the implementation of social investment, especially in the new member states where resources are scarce. The ESF, then, should be used strategically to be implemented in the East and the South, to meet Lisbon targets, particularly reform in education and training systems, but also the development of child care institutions, a precondition for the long-term integration of women on the labour market. The EES has helped shift the attention to activity rates rather than levels of unemployment, and by doing so has helped widen the agenda, for instance by placing family policy on the agenda in all member states (Jacobsson and Vifell, 2007). Yet thus far, the main policy outcome has been high employment rates, while activation has taken the form of recommodification rather than social investment.

Notes

[1] We would like to thank Johan Bo Davidsson and Moira Nelson for their reflections on our data. We would also like to thank the editors for relevant comments.

[2] We refer to the EU-10, that is the new EU member states in Central and Eastern Europe, excluding Malta and Cyprus, which have different trajectories.

[3] Since 2005 progress is reported in National Reform Programmes (NRPs), earlier in National Action Plans (NAPs).

[4] For an analysis of a third type of change, namely the impact of the EES on governance arrangements, institutional structures and actor relationships within the member states, see Jacobsson and Vifell (2007) and de la Porte (2008).

[5] To be more accurate, we tried to work out the expenditure on ALMP per person, by calculating the expenditure on ALMP in euros, divided by the number of participants and the expenditure on passive measures per person. However, the data seemed inaccurate for many countries, which is why we used more general descriptive indicators.

[6] We do not include data from 2000, as there is not Eurostat data from new EU MSs on active and passive labour market policies.

[7] 'Active' measures include: training, job rotation and job sharing, employment incentives, supported employment and rehabilitation, direct job creation and startup incentives (Eurostat, 2010).

[8] 'Passive' measures include out-of-work income maintenance and support (mostly unemployment benefits) and early retirement benefits (Eurostat, 2010).

[9] Costs of running the public employment service (PES) and any other publicly funded services for jobseekers.

[10] Recent developments, however, suggest that policies have been moving away from flexicurity since the 2008 financial crisis.

[11] For Esping-Andersen (1990) the concept of decommodification refers to the degree to which individuals, or families, can uphold a socially acceptable standard of living independently of market participation. Recommodification is a return to more of market reliance for a decent living standard.

References

Aidukaite, J. (2004) *The Emergence of the Post-Socialist Welfare State – the Case of the Baltic States: Estonia, Latvia and Lithuania.* Stockholm: Södertörn University College.

Aidukaite, J. (2009) 'Old welfare state theories and new welfare regimes in Eastern Europe: Challenges and implications', *Communist and Post-Communist Studies*, 42 (1), 23–39.

Barbier, J.-C. (with Samba Sylla, N.) (2004) 'La stratégie européenne pour l'emploi: genèse, coordination communautaire et diversité nationale'. Paris: Report for the French Labour Ministry.

Barbier, J.-C., Colomb, F. and Madsen, P.K. (2009) 'Flexicurity: an open method of coordination at the national level?', *CARMA Research Paper*, No. 3.

Berton, F., Richiardi, M. and Sacchi, S. (2009) *Flex-insecurity: Perché in Italia la Flessibilità Diventa Precarietà.* Bologna: Il Mulino.

Borrás, S. and Jacobsson, K. (2004) 'The open method of co-ordination and the new governance patterns in the EU', *Journal of European Public Policy*, 11 (2), 185–208.

Borrás, S. and Radaelli, C. (2011) 'The politics of governance architectures: Creation, change and effects of the EU Lisbon strategy', *Journal of European Public Policy*, 18 (4), 463–84.

Büchs, M. (2007) *New Governance in European Social Policy: The Open Method of Co-ordination.* Basingstoke: Palgrave Macmillan.

Büchs, M. and Friedrich, D. (2005) 'Surface integration. The national action plans for employment and social inclusion in Germany', in J. Zeitlin and P. Pochet, with Lars Magnusson (eds) *The Open Method of Coordination in Action.* Brussels: PIE Peter Lang, pp. 249–85.

Clasen, J. and Clegg, D. (2007) 'Levels and levers of conditionality: Measuring change within welfare states', in J. Clasen and N. Siegel (eds) *Investigating Welfare State Change: The 'Dependent Variable Problem' in Comparative Analysis.* Cheltenham: Edward Elgar, pp. 166–97.

Coron, G. and Palier, B. (2002) 'Changes in the means of financing social expenditure in France since 1945', in C. de la Porte and P. Pochet (eds) *Building Social Europe Through the Open Method of Coordination*. Brussels: PIE Peter Lang, pp. 97–136.

de la Porte, C. (2008) *The European Level Development and National Level Influence of the Open Method of Coordination: The Cases of Employment and Social Inclusion*. Florence: European University Institute.

de la Porte, C. (2009) 'The role of the OECD and the EU in the development of labour market policy in the Czech republic', *Journal of Contemporary European Research*, 5 (4), 539–56.

de la Porte, C. (2010) 'State of the art: Overview of concepts, indicators and methodologies used for analyzing the social OMCs', *RECWOWE working paper* 15/10, 53 pp.

de la Porte, C. (2011, forthcoming) 'Explaining the emergence and institutionalisation of the EES: Principal-agent theory and policy entrepreneurs', *Journal of European Public Policy,* 18 (4).

de la Porte, C. and Al-Gailany, Y. (2011) 'Analyzing the social OMCs: Case study Denmark', February, European Commission project (lead partners PPMI). *Assessing the effectiveness and the impact of the Social OMC in preparation of the new cycle.*

EAPN (2007) 'Strengthening the social dimension of the Lisbon strategy. Proposals from the European Anti-Poverty Network', available on www.eapn.dk.

Erhel, C., Mandin, L. and Palier, B. (2005) 'The leverage effect. The open method of co-ordination in France', in J. Zeitlin and P. Pochet (eds) with L. Magnusson, *The Open Method of Coordination in Action. The European Employment and Social Inclusion Strategies*. Brussels: PIE Peter Lang, pp. 217–48.

Esping-Andersen, G. (1990) *The Three Worlds of Welfare Capitalism.* Oxford: Polity Press.

European Commission (2005) Communication to the spring European Council, integrated guidelines for growth and employment (2005–2008), working together for growth and jobs: Guidelines for the employment policies of the member states (2005–8), COM (2005) 24 final, 2 February 2005.

European Commission (2007) Communication from the Commission to the European Parliament, the Council, the European Economic and Social Committee and the Committee of the Regions, Towards common principles of flexicurity: COM (2007) 359 final, 27 June 2007.

European Commission (2009) Volume I: Implementation of the Lisbon Strategy Structural Reforms in the context of the European Economic

Recovery Plan – Annual country assessments: Recommendation for a Council Recommendation on the 2009 update of the broad guidelines for the economic policies of the member states and the Community and on the implementation of member states' employment policies: COM (2009) 34 final, 28 January 2009.

European Council (2000) Presidency conclusions: Lisbon European Council, 23 and 24 March 2000.

Eurostat (2009) Labour Force Survey statistics.

Eurostat (2010) Labour Force Survey statistics.

Ferrera, M. (1996) 'The "southern model" of welfare in social Europe', *Journal of European Social Policy*, 6 (1), 17–37.

Fererra, M. and Sacchi (2005) 'The open method of co-ordination and national institutional capabilities: The Italian experience', in J. Zeitlin and P. Pochet, with L. Magnusson (eds) *The Open Method of Coordination in Action. The European Employment and Social Inclusion Strategies*. Brussels: PIE Peter Lang, pp. 137–76.

Goetschy, J. (1999) 'The European employment strategy: Genesis and development', *European Journal of Industrial Relations*, 5 (2), 117–37.

Hartwig, I. (2007) 'European employment strategy and structural funds: Spill-overs towards communitarisation', in I. Linsenmann, C.O. Meyer and W. Wessels (eds) *Economic Government of the EU: A Balance Sheet of New Modes of Policy Coordination*. Basingstoke: Palgrave Macmillan, pp. 119–40.

Jacobsson, K. (2004) 'Soft regulation and the subtle transformation of states: The case of EU employment policy', *Journal of European Social Policy*, 14 (4), 355–70.

Jacobsson, K. (2005) 'Trying to reform the "best pupils in the class"? The open method of coordination in Sweden and Denmark', in J. Zeitlin and P. Pochet, with L. Magnusson (eds) *The Open Method of Coordination in Action*. Brussels: PIE Peter Lang, pp. 107–36.

Jacobsson, K. and Vifell, Å. (2007) 'New governance structures in employment policy making: loose co-ordination in action', in I. Linsenmann, C.O. Meyer and W. Wessels (eds) *Economic Government of the EU: A Balance Sheet of New Modes of Policy Coordination*. Basingstoke: Palgrave Macmillan, pp. 53–71.

Jacobsson, K. and West, C. (2009) 'Joining the European employment strategy: Europeanisation of labour market policy in the Baltic states', in M. Heidenreich and J. Zeitlin (eds) *Changing European Employment and Welfare Regimes: The Influence of the Open Method of Coordination on National Labour Market and Social Welfare Reforms*. London: Routledge, pp. 112–33.

Jacobsson, K. and West, C. (2010) 'Europeanization of labor policy-making in the Baltic states', in B. Jacobsson (ed.) *The European Union and the Baltic States: Changing Forms of Governance.* London: Routledge, pp. 98–120.

Johnson, J. (2008) 'The remains of conditionality: The faltering enlargement of the euro zone', *Journal of European Public Policy,* 15 (6), 826–41.

Kaluzna (2008) 'Main features of the public employment service in the Czech republic', *OECD social, employment and migration papers,* No. 74. Paris: OECD.

Kautto, M. et al. (1999) 'Introduction: The Nordic welfare states in the 1990s', in M. Kautto et al. (eds) *Nordic Social Policy: Changing Welfare State.* London: Routledge.

Kröger, S. (2009) 'The open method of coordination: Underconceptualisation, overdetermination, de-politicisation and beyond', *European Integration online Papers (EIoP),* 13 (1).

Kvist, J. (2007) 'Denmark: From foot-dragging to pace-setting in EU social policy', in J. Kvist and J. Saari (eds) *The Europeanisation of Social Protection.* Bristol: Policy Press.

Lodge, M. (2007) 'Comparing non-hierarchical governance in action: The open method of co-ordination in pensions and information society', *Journal of Common Market Studies,* 45 (2), 343–65.

López-Santana, M. (2006) 'The domestic implications of European soft law: Framing and transmitting change in employment policy', *Journal of European Public Policy,* 13 (4), 481–99.

Lynch, B. (2003) National Report for Ireland (3rd Round), available on www.govecor.org.

Mailand, M. (2009) 'North, South, East, West: The implementation of the European employment strategy in Denmark, UK, Spain and Poland' ,in M. Heidenreich and J. Zeitlin (eds) *Changing European Employment and Welfare Regimes: The Influence of the Open Method of Coordination on National Labour Market and Social Welfare Reforms.* London: Routledge, pp. 154–72.

Mayes, D. and Mustaffa, Z. (2010) 'Social models in the EU', *Recon Online Working Paper 2010/20.*

Murphy, C. (2002) 'Assessment of the policy-making process', in P.J. O'Connell et al. (eds) *Impact Evaluation of the European Employment Strategy in Ireland.* Dublin: Department of Enterprise, Trade and Employment and ESRI, pp. 103–21.

O'Donnell, R. and Moss, B. (2005) 'Ireland: The very idea of an open method of co-ordination', in: J. Zeitlin and P. Pochet, with L.

Magnusson (eds) *The Open Method of Co-ordination in Action'*. Brussels: PIE Peter Lang, pp. 311–50.

Offe, C. (2009) 'Epilogue: Lessons learnt and open questions – issues of welfare state building in post-communist EU member states', Hertie School of Governance, Working Paper No. 40, March 2009.

Ornestein, M.A. (2009) 'Out-liberalizing the EU: pension privatization in Central and Eastern Europe', in *Journal of European Public Policy*, 15 (6), pp. 899–917.

Rein, M. and Schön, D. (1993) 'Reframing policy discourse', in F. Fischer and J. Forester (eds) *The Argumentative Turn in Policy Analysis and Planning*. London: UCL Press Limited and Duke University Press, pp. 145–66.

van Gerven, M. (2007) 'The broad tracks of path dependent benefit reforms. A longitudinal study of social benefit reforms in three European countries, 1980–2006', Studies in social security and health 100. Helsinki: Social Insurance Institution.

Woolfson, C. (2006) 'Working environment and "soft law" in the post-communist countries', *Journal of Common Market Studies*, 44 (1), 195–215.

Zeitlin, J. (2005) 'The open method of coordination in action: Theoretical promise, empirical realities', in J. Zeitlin and P. Pochet, with L. Magnusson (eds) *The Open Method of Coordination in Action*. Brussels: PIE Peter Lang, pp. 447–503.

Zeitlin, J. (2009) 'The open method of co-ordination and reform of national social and employment policies: influences, mechanisms, effects', in M. Heidenreich and J. Zeitlin (eds) *Changing European Employment and Welfare Regimes: The Influence of the Open Method of Co-ordination on National Reforms*. London: Routledge/EUI Studies in the Political Economy of Welfare, pp. 214–45.

Part III

Assessing the social investment policies

Promoting social investment through work–family policies: which nations do it and why?[1]

Kimberly J. Morgan

Work–family reconciliation policies are a lynchpin of the social investment approach. High-quality early childhood education and care (ECEC) programmes invest in both the cognitive development of young children and the labour market skills of their mothers by enabling them to participate in paid work. Employment continuity also bolsters household income, reducing child poverty and its potentially enduring effects. Parental leave and flexible work time promote women's paid work while enabling children to benefit from periods of parental care. Finally, ECEC services can be a source of employment for women who might otherwise struggle to find a foothold in the labour market.

Despite these apparent benefits, few countries have adopted work–family policies that fully promote social investment aims. In this chapter, I evaluate country policies according to how they perform on a social investment triad: *activation* of women's employment; promotion of gender *equality*; and fostering of child development through *quality* care. Very few countries emphasise all three dimensions; more commonly, countries focus on only one dimension while ignoring the other two. Evaluating nine Western European countries by these criteria, I qualify three as social investment 'pioneers' – France, Norway and Sweden – that were the first to adopt these kinds of policies; three as relatively recent 'path shifters' – Germany, the Netherlands and the UK; and three as 'slow movers' – Austria, Italy and Spain – that have made incremental changes to their menu of work–family policies.[2]

What political forces have driven or stymied movement towards the social investment approach in these nine countries? Governments generally have not followed a consistent template of social investment ideas. Instead, domestic political and economic circumstances have influenced the three policy dimensions. Policies to promote women's employment are often, but not exclusively, done under left governments, but only in a context of rising female workforce participation and intensifying electoral competition over the female vote. When middle-class women, in particular, are seen as an important voting bloc worth pursuing and these women are struggling with balancing paid work and family, left (and, at times, conservative) governments have often responded with supportive public policies.

The resulting policy matrix has not always been done in the most gender-egalitarian way, however, in part because of continuing ambiguities over how to treat parental care. Extensive periods of parental caring time can be justified by aspects of the social investment logic and have often been politically popular with the female constituency politicians are trying to reach. Yet, long leaves and feminised part-time work also undermine employment equality, creating a policy conundrum that no country – including social investment pioneers such as Sweden – has yet resolved.

Moreover, the drive to activate female employment in recent years has occurred at a time when many countries also have sought to contain the size of the public sector, relying instead on social welfare marketplaces to provide care services. These marketplaces often do a poor job in assuring broadly available and affordable high quality care. By contrast, the social investment pioneers sought to ensure broad-based access to publicly run and good-quality programmes. This is a crucial lesson of the social investment approach as developed by the pioneers that has been largely ignored by the more recent path shifters. Failing to learn this lesson and sacrificing quality to the goals of activation will impede the ability of states to fully achieve the stated goals of the social investment approach.

How can work–family policies promote social investment?

What types of work–family policies embody social investment goals? There is no *one* model of social investment policy, but multiple strands of policy argument that have become increasingly prominent among intellectuals and policy makers. I adopt three criteria based upon the claims of social investment advocates about their stated goals. Although my criteria might push some social investment thinkers further than they have gone thus far, the criteria are congruent with their averred objectives.

A central theme of the social investment discourse is the importance of *activating* the labour force, in this case by promoting women's participation in paid work (see Chapter Three). Child care, parental leave and part-time work policies should therefore be structured to support mothers' employment, with appropriate schedules for day care and preschools, availability of after-school care, and leaves that are decently paid and long, but not too long (see below). The development of early childhood programmes is also justified as a source of employment, particularly for women.

A social investment focus should do more than simply increase female employment rates, however, but lead policy makers to pay attention to the *quality* of care services. With their focus on the nation's future human capital, social investment advocates frequently emphasise the importance of breaking the intergenerational transmission of poverty and promoting social inclusion (Esping-Andersen, 2002: Chapter 2; Jenson, 2009: 447). Social investment thinkers also regard early childhood as a crucial time for shaping a nation's future workforce. Good-quality care services can contribute to both goals, helping to 'make work pay' for low-income parents while also providing developmentally enriching services to young children. The terminology increasingly used by policy makers and advocates – early childhood education and care (ECEC) – encompasses the two dimensions of these programmes.

Gender equality is another objective of the social investment approach as stated in EU policy papers, OECD documents and writings of some advocates (Esping-Andersen, 2002; OECD, 2005, 2007; Jenson, 2009: 448). 'Gender awareness' is a hallmark of the emerging social investment paradigm, and it represents a departure from the gender-blind understandings of the welfare state held by many Keynesian and neoliberal thinkers in the past (Jenson, 2009). Even so, social investment-minded analysts and policy makers sometimes view women's employment instrumentally – as a means to other ends, such as lower rates of child poverty or greater demographic sustainability – rather than as a goal in its own right. And although policy officials and advocates often emphasise the need to improve work–family balance, many fail to examine the deeper causes of gender inequalities, such as employment discrimination, pay gaps and the division of household work (Jenson, 2009). Yet, some of the goals of the social investment approach – such as the full development of women's 'human capital' and improved economic circumstances for families – require a reorganisation of the domestic division of labour so that men and women have meaningful choices in matters of paid work and care. Social investment-promoting family policies should therefore include paid parental leaves that are available to women *and* men, father-only parental leave time, equal rights to part-time work, or other measures that enable or encourage men to take on more domestic responsibilities, such as limiting the length of the working week.

Such policies are all the more important given the risks of promoting extensive parental caring time. Social investment advocates generally oppose the male breadwinner model, viewing it as outmoded and an obstacle to the full development of women's human capital (Esping-Andersen, 2002). On the other hand, a social investment approach should be sympathetic to some amount of parental caring time, particularly in the first year of a child's life when infants can gain the averred health and cognitive benefits of breastfeeding and intensive interaction with a small number of caregivers. It is for these and other reasons that some child development experts argue for parental leaves of up to a year (Waldfogel, 2006; Gornick and Meyers, 2009). Unless leave entitlements and take-up are equal for men and women, however, lengthy leaves may undermine gender equality goals if they render women less desirable candidates in the labour market, leading to occupational sex segregation and diminished employment opportunities. Even policies that aim to increase male take-up rates of parental leave may not be able to counteract economic incentives and cultural cues that influence decisions by parents about how to divide paid work and care (Charles, 2005).

In short, even under the most favourable policy circumstances, it may be difficult to attain all three legs of the social investment triad. With this in mind, we can still evaluate how close countries have come to attaining these ideals and the politics driving their efforts.

Comparing work–family policies

There are a small number of countries that developed social investment-promoting ECEC and parental leave policies long before the term 'social investment' came into being and that I refer to as 'pioneers'. Sweden and Norway are two such pioneers that have attempted for many decades to achieve all three objectives and come close to doing so. Workforce activation is promoted by the widespread availability of public ECEC, well-paid and job-protected parental leaves, options for part-time work, and the growth of a large public sector that offers decent jobs for many women. Women's employment rates in these countries are very high (Figure 6.1), including those of mothers.

Bolstering women's incomes through a combination of paid work and public subsidies also reduces the incidence of child poverty, while the high-quality ECEC programmes give children a 'strong start' in life (OECD, 2006: 130–31). Gender equality goals are embodied in the

Figure 6.1: Employment rate of women aged 25–49, 2009

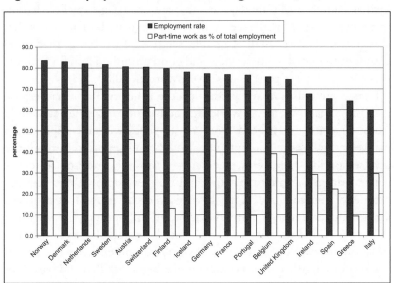

Source: Eurostat.

well-paid *parental* leaves of at least a year that include a fathers' quota – time reserved for the parent not taking the bulk of the leave (usually the father). Norway also allows a longer period of parental care at home – up to three years – and in both countries parents have rights to reduced work hours. Thus, social investment goals in these two countries are promoted by both extensive care services and the time parents have to spend caring for their children. However, although there are high male take-up rates for the fathers' quota days of parental leave, women still take the bulk of parental leave time, contributing to occupational sex segregation in the labour markets of these two countries and wage gaps, particularly for higher-skilled women (Mandel, 2010).

France is also a pioneer for its universal preschool system (the *écoles maternelles*) but it scores lower on other social investment criteria. Through the *école maternelle*, early childhood education is universally available for children aged three to six and is publicly provided (with some publicly funded yet privately run preschools), staffed by well-educated and remunerated teachers, and open for a lengthy school day.[3] France therefore is a fairly high achiever on the *quality* dimension, although some child development experts criticise the large class sizes of the *écoles maternelles* and/or question the emphasis on school preparation (OECD, 2006: 136–38, 331).[4] Provision for under-threes is inadequate: publicly provided *crèches* covered only 8% of children below the age of three in 2008, and subsidies for other forms of care have spurred the growth of more individualised forms of child care, such as nannies or home day care, that are of variable quality (Jenson and Sineau, 1998).[5] Reliance on these less-regulated forms of care has also prevented the growth of a public sector care workforce that could ensure both high-quality services and good unionised jobs for women, as is the case in the preschool sector (Morgan, 2005).

France presents a mixed picture on the other two criteria because it has not made women's workforce activation or gender equality a major priority, but instead tends to support mothers' employment inadvertently. Women's employment has been supported through the diverse subsidies and services described above, but resistance to the generalisation of part-time work and the development of a lengthy care leave (up to three years) have slowed the growth of mothers' employment. France is a 'middle achiever' on women's employment (Figure 6.1), and its matrix of work–family policies have contributed to labour market dualisation, as less-skilled women leave the labour market for lengthy periods of time while higher-skilled and wealthier women use subsidies for nannies and other individualised forms of care (Morel, 2007). There also have been few measures to promote changes in the gendered division of labour at home, such as daddy-only leaves or individual entitlements to paid leave. In short, France is internationally known for its universal preschool programmes but has done less to promote labour force activation or gender equality.

In all of the above cases, the ingredients of a social investment approach emerged by the 1970s and 1980s – well before the concept of 'social investment' had developed. In the past two decades, three other countries have moved towards embrace of a social investment approach: Germany, the Netherlands and the UK. All three were long the very embodiment of the male breadwinner model of social welfare policy (Lewis, 1992) but, in the past two decades, these 'path shifters' have made fundamental changes in their approach to work and family.

Since the early 1990s, Dutch governments have promoted the growth of child care services, largely through demand-side subsidies of parents who seek out child care in the marketplace. Activation received further impetus through the generalisation of part-time work, which helped augment the proportion of women, including mothers, in paid work. The Netherlands now has high rates of female workforce participation, albeit with large proportions of women working part-time (Figure 6.1). Gender equality has been an averred objective as well, evidenced by the fact that *all* employees have a right to request a part-time work schedule. One aim was to facilitate a *combinatie scenario* in which each parent symmetrically reduces work time and children are in ECEC for the remaining days of the week. However, in 2008 only 6% of couples with children worked part time, and in only 7% did both parents work full time. More commonly, one partner (usually the man) works full time while the other (usually the woman) works either part time (53%) or not at all (28%) (Merens and Hermans, 2009: 88). There have been no major changes to parental leave, which is often taken by reducing working time and is unpaid. On the *equality* dimension, then, the Netherlands has clearly moved away from the male breadwinner model yet women are still less integrated into the labour market than men.

Dutch policy also falls short on the *quality* dimension, as rapid growth in the child care marketplace over the past 15 years has come at the expense of good-quality care. While the Netherlands once ranked highly in an international comparison of child care quality, subsequent studies have shown a marked deterioration in quality (Vermeer et al., 2008; de Kruif et al., 2009). Some argue that the problems were exacerbated by the 2005 Child Care Law, which dismantled the centralised regulatory system in favour of local government oversight and 'light touch' regulation (Lloyd and Penn, 2010: 44). The 2005 law also fully shifted the Netherlands towards demand-side subsidies for market-based provision that spurred the growth of for-profit centres but also led to unequal geographic access, as child care centres increasingly locate in urban, high-income areas (Noailly and Visser, 2009). In sum, Dutch policy has successfully promoted activation but has done less to further the goals of either quality services for children or a more egalitarian division of paid and unpaid work.

The UK also has made significant changes in its work–family policy mix since the late 1990s. Policy developments since 1997 include the gradual expansion of paid maternity leave from 14 weeks to a 12-month entitlement in effect since 2010, improved maternity leave pay, enactment of an unpaid parental leave entitlement of 13 weeks (as required by the European Union), and the creation of a right for parents of children under six to request a more flexible work schedule. There also have been expanded tax subsidies for child care, obligations placed on local authorities to assure adequate access to these services, and guarantees of a certain amount of free nursery school care for all three and four year olds (Wincott, 2006; Lewis and Campbell, 2007).

The goals of activation, gender equality and improved child development rhetorically underpinned many of these changes, but aspects of policy design preclude a more complete achievement of any of them. Women's employment has been promoted but the high cost of private child care makes it difficult for many to work full time. Similarly, although maternity leave is open to men it is still called a *maternity* leave, sending a clear signal about its lack of gender egalitarian aspirations. Finally, the quality of care available in the marketplace has been much criticised, and access to quality care is stratified by income (Lloyd and Penn, 2010).

Germany is the path shifter that may come closest to reaching some social investment objectives once full implementation is achieved. In 2006, a Grand Coalition government enacted a major reform of the parental leave and benefit, which had been long (up to three years), means-tested and poorly paid (about €500 a month). The new leave/benefit is for 12 months and pays workers two-thirds of their salary, up to a ceiling (€1,800 per month). The new leave also tries to promote more active fathering: in addition to being gender-neutral, there are two additional months available to the parent who does not take the bulk of the leave, so that parents can lengthen the leave from 12 to 14 months. In addition to a law increasing the tax deductions allowed for child care expenses, in 2007 the Grand Coalition agreed to devote €4 billion over five years to expand the availability of child care and a 2008 law creates a right to child care for all children from the age of one starting in 2013 – the date by which there is supposed to be sufficient child care to cover 35% of children aged from birth to two years old (Leu and Schelle, 2009: 9–10).[6] Although it remains to be seen whether this goal will be met, German reforms combine an emphasis on gender equality, activation and quality services. Thus far, the economic crisis has not seriously undermined these new policies.[7]

Finally, there are some social investment 'slow movers' that have made incremental changes to their work–family policies; this chapter focuses on three – Austria, Italy and Spain. All three increasingly resemble France in the development of near-universal early childhood education services for children aged three to six. In Italy and Spain, these are long-day programmes that cover a significant part of the work day, while in Austria they are open for only part of the day. As in France, these are not strictly child care programmes but they do provide enriching, developmental services to young children. Less has been done for under-threes. In Austria, the availability of a lengthy but ill-paid parental leave has meant that parents (mainly mothers) provide primary care for children below age three. In Italy and Spain, by contrast, parents often rely on private child care alternatives – nannies, family members and formal care services available in the marketplace. These private options are often expensive and of varying quality, and while they have enabled the growing proportion of mothers in paid work, mothers' employment is still fairly low in these countries (below 60%) and the services do not further child development goals.[8]

The political forces driving the social investment approach to work and family

What political forces have produced these constellations of work–family policies? At first glance, one might think that an ideational argument is most appropriate, one that emphasises how new ideas about the imperatives of global competitiveness or the importance of human capital have shaped the kinds of programmes and policies adopted. A related approach would highlight the role of the European Union and OECD, as actors from both have preached the gospel of social investment for many years. Perhaps policy makers have imbibed these ideas and been driven to develop work–family policies reflecting them.[9]

There are several reasons why such an approach does not shed much light on the patterns described above. First, the social investment 'pioneers' embarked on their respective policy pathways long before the concept had been envisaged. Sweden has engaged in active labour market policies since the 1950s and began to build up supports for women's employment in the 1960s and especially the 1970s. Norway shifted more forcefully in this direction in the 1980s. The centrepiece of the French approach – the system of universal preschools – dates back to the late nineteenth century and expanded rapidly in the decades following World War II. Long before the social investment discourse came into fashion, all three countries had developed good quality, publicly provided early childhood education services that were universal or nearly so.

It is more probable that recent path shifters have been influenced by this model of policy reform. Certainly, New Labour couched many of its reforms in the language of activation, human capital and early years investments. Such ideas are less evident in the German reforms, which were propelled by Christian Democrats who emphasised the need to fight demographic decline. A more fundamental question is why some countries were influenced by these ideas while others were not. Why has Spain – a country often said to have enacted social policy reforms influenced by the European Union – not more fully embraced the EU's push for female labour force activation? Why have Austria and Italy also largely ignored these ideas? The social investment discourse provides a template of action but is not sufficient on its own to propel policy change. For that, we must investigate the forces that have shaped each of the three dimensions of policy making I identified earlier, moving some closer to the social investment approach while others remain far from it.

The politics of work and family in the social investment pioneers

When and why do governments choose to promote women's, and especially mothers', employment, and when is this done in a way that is congruent with social investment goals? In a number of countries, the foundations of the social investment approach were laid during the 'golden age' of welfare state expansion – a time of rapid economic growth, labour shortages and budgetary surpluses (Morgan, 2006). The overall economic context was thus propitious for policies to support female employment, while the strength of public sector unions and wide agreement on the role of the state in social affairs shaped the decision to develop high-quality and often publicly run services. Thus, for the pioneers, what mattered was not only the economic and political imperative to promote women's employment but also the temporal moment at which the foundations for their work–family policies were laid. As we shall see, economic downturn and the neoliberal turn in policy thought eroded those investments more in some countries (France) than in others (Sweden, Norway).

Of great importance in the Nordic countries was the calculation made by left parties about the electoral costs and benefits of promoting mothers' employment. In Sweden and Norway, social democratic governments were the architects of policies to support mothers' employment (Huber and Stephens, 2000), which they pursued as a way to continue expanding their electoral coalition beyond the working-class (Leira, 1989: 93; Morgan, 2006). The growth of the white collar workforce – including among women, many employed in the burgeoning public sector – generated strong demand for child care, leave time and other supportive measures. Work–family policies were a way to extend the social democratic model – which in its original incarnation had been male-breadwinner oriented, in tune with the views of its working class constituents – to address some of the concerns of white collar workers. Creating publicly run programmes also furthered the social democratic project of universal, equal access to social services and satisfied the growing public sector trade union movement, which resisted private or individualised forms of care (such as subsidised family day care) (Hinnfors, 1999; Morgan, 2005). By the 1970s in Sweden and Norway, Social Democratic policy makers embraced the two-earner model as the new norm (Leira, 1989: 92–93; Florin and Nilsson, 1999), and the supply of public child care began to expand.

Policies in both countries have had a strong gender egalitarian cast, as evidenced by the creation of paid *parental* leaves of at least a year, father-only parental leave quotas, and government campaigns to encourage 'men to be fathers' (Bergman and Hobson, 2002). The high proportion of women in parliament, left parties and labour unions contributed to this gender egalitarian emphasis (Mahon, 1997; Bergqvist et al., 1999; Kittilson, 2008; Bonoli and Reber, 2010) (Figure 6.2).

Figure 6.2: Percentage of women in parliament, 1960–2009

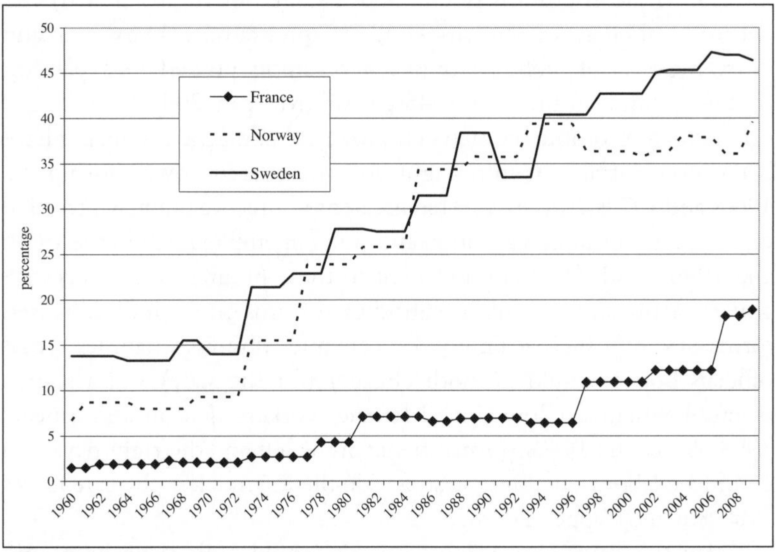

Source: IPU; Armingeon et al., 2010.

Yet, these two countries reveal how difficult it can be to attain all three social investment goals. The labour market in each is characterised by a high degree of labour market segregation, reflecting in part the effects of lengthy leave time on female employment prospects. Yet, efforts to award men and women an individual entitlement to an equal amount of leave have proven unpopular with much of the public, with some fearing this would reduce the total amount of time infants spend with their parents and thus have negative consequences for young children (Ellingsæter, 2006). In short, although Swedish and Norwegian work–family policies promote the triple goals outlined above – activation, equality and quality care – tensions between these three aims are readily apparent.

The political dynamics around work–family policies in France have been quite different, in part owing to the weakness of the political left. The golden age of welfare state expansion took place largely under centre-right governments, and by the time the left came to power in the early 1980s, full of promises about parental leave, child care and other redistributive objectives, the economy had sunk into crisis. Still, certain elements of the social investment approach were already in place as children aged three to six already had near universal access to publicly provided *écoles maternelles* by the 1980s. These programmes had been incorporated in the school system in the late nineteenth century as part of a drive to encompass the nation's children in a secular school system that would impart republican values. As a result, the *école maternelle* is integral to the education system and is staffed by highly trained and decently paid teachers. Much like ECEC programmes in Sweden and Norway, powerful public sector (teachers) unions pushed the expansion of these schools in the post-1945 period (Morgan, 2006).

Policies to promote women's employment and gender equality have been more variable. Centre-right governments in power during the 1960s and 1970s at times directed greater resources to publicly provided crèches, yet economic stagnation and rising unemployment in the 1980s and 1990s eroded the commitment to these programmes. Successive governments shifted public subsidies towards more individualised forms of care – such as family day care and subsidised nannies – that officials hoped would be both cheaper (for the state) and a source of employment for low-skilled female workers (Jenson and Sineau, 1998). Since the 1980s, governments of the left and the right have also embraced labour-shedding strategies in the form of lengthy care leaves (Morgan and Zippel, 2003).

Today, this mixed approach to work–family policy continues and weak representation of women in politics contributes to the lack of gender egalitarian objectives in French family policies. France long had one of the lowest rates of female representation in parliament and this has minimally improved since passage of the *parité* law in 2000 (see Figure 6.2). French policies support those mothers who decide to remain in paid work – rather inadvertently, in the case of the *écoles maternelles* – but have not prioritised maximisation of the female labour supply or the promotion of active fatherhood.

What can we learn about the politics of social investment from its pioneers? Left government and female empowerment are both important but do not preclude conflicts about how to balance parental caring time with activation and equality objectives. In the Nordic countries, those tensions are apparent in policies that promote female employment but also allow extensive caring time at home, which in turn undermines women's place in paid work. Lacking high levels of left or female political power, France adopted a less gender-egalitarian version of the social investment approach, one that concentrates most of its resources on preschool services, while other subsidies have contributed to labour market dualisation rather than equal access to paid work. Yet, a commonality in all three cases is the commitment to publicly provided services for many of the relevant age group. The foundations of these programmes were laid during a time of welfare state expansion, which included growth of the public sector and an accompanying unionised public sector workforce.

The politics of work and family in the path shifters

The three path shifting countries – Germany, the Netherlands and the UK – for years had done little in the way of work–family policies, yet all have made major policy shifts since the 1990s, albeit with different results. The Netherlands and the UK have put more emphasis on activation than either quality or equality, while Germany has adopted policies that appear closest to social investment ideals, assuming their full implementation in the years ahead.

In both the Netherlands and the UK, a similar political dynamic influenced the move towards female workforce activating policies, as left political parties faced with the demise of their traditional constituencies turned their attention towards the middle class, and women in particular. For British Labour, recurring electoral losses starting in 1979 spurred a drive to modernise the party. Recognising the inevitable further decline of their blue collar male constituency, Labour leaders turned their attention to women, whose tendency to vote somewhat more conservatively than men was changing, especially for younger women (Campbell and Lovenduski, 2005). In response, Labour sought to improve the representation of women in the party and advocate proposals of interest to the female electorate, such as greater spending on health care and education (Perrigo, 1996; Childs, 2008: 26–27). The 1997 election seemed to confirm the success of the strategy, as it was a resounding Labour victory – attributed in part to the closing of the gender gap – that ushered in the largest percentage of female (mostly Labour) parliamentarians in the nation's history.

During their 13 years in office, Labour governments made major changes to work–family policies that reflected both programmatic and electoral aims. Seeking a Third Way between Keynesian statism and Thatcherite neoliberalism, Labour thinkers developed a social investment discourse that inflected much of the party's social policy agenda. Thus, early childhood policy became a major focus in the aim of reducing welfare dependency, fighting child poverty and investing in the cognitive capabilities of the nation's children (Lewis, 2008). Sure Start was a centrepiece of this new approach, offering education, health and social services to disadvantaged families (Lewis, 2010). Labour governments also created an entitlement to a certain number of hours of free nursery education for all three and four year olds[10] and directed greater spending to ECEC services through both public programmes and new tax credits (Wincott, 2006; Penn, 2007; Lloyd, 2008).

Although much ECEC policy has been targeted to lower income families, the electoral imperative of attracting female voters helped bring about other initiatives that reach a wider swath of the population. Most significant was the development of rights to time off: during their 13 years in office, Labour governments significantly expanded paid maternity leave, granted fathers the right to take six months of the maternity leave, increased maternity pay, and enacted a right for parents of children under age 16 to request flexible work from their employers (under certain conditions). Persistent lobbying by female Labour MPs, coupled with concerns about the loyalties of female voters, pushed these initiatives into Labour party platforms and helped ensure their enactment.[11] In fact, starting with the 2005 election, competition for female voters led all three parties – Labour, the Liberal Democrats and the Conservatives – to embrace a similar package of parental leave and ECEC policies, although Labour's proposals were more generous (Morgan, 2010).

A similar electoral dynamic affected the Dutch Labour Party (PvdA) and was crucial to the abandonment of the male breadwinner model. By the 1970s, depillarisation and secularisation had eroded the bonds that long existed between social groups and the parties, creating volatility in the party system and a competitive scramble for voters (van Holsteyn and Irwin, 1989).[12] The female vote was also increasingly up for grabs, which helped prompt the PvdA to increase the proportion of women on electoral lists and in party organs (Leyenaar, 2004: 167; Oldersma, 2005: 158). The number of female PvdA parliamentarians grew rapidly throughout the 1980s and 1990s (Figure 6.3), as did the number of women serving as ministers in governments (Leyenaar, 2004: 129–30, 133–34). In the 1989 coalition between the PvdA and CDA, for instance, there were three women ministers out of 16 (and three junior ministers out of 11), with notably a PvdA woman in charge of the Ministry of Welfare, Health and Culture, and female junior ministers in the Ministries of Social Affairs and Economic Affairs (Leyenaar, 2004: 129).

This CDA–PvdA coalition government was the first to break with the male-breadwinner policies of the past, largely at the initiative of the PvdA. The government extended maternity leave from 12 to 16 weeks, created the right to a six-month, unpaid and part-time leave, and increased child care funding. Subsequent 'purple coalition' governments (Liberal and Social Democratic) supported child care services through

Figure 6.3: Average percentage of women in parliament, 1990–2009

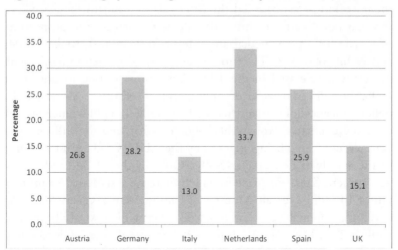

Sources: IPU; Armingeon et al., 2010.

demand-side subsidies and mandates for employer contributions (Lewis et al., 2008: 273). The Netherlands also developed a novel approach to work–family issues through the spread and protection of part-time work (Plantenga, 2002; Visser, 2002). Yet, while the vast majority of mothers work part-time only a small proportion of fathers do, undermining the egalitarian potential of these policies.

Moreover, reliance upon demand-side subsidies by both the Dutch and UK governments has propelled the growth of a child care marketplace but come at the cost of quality. Why have governments refused to create public care services? In the Netherlands, some female MPs within the PvdA opposed the shift to demand-side subsidies but were outmatched on this issue by the VVD and the CDA, both of whom employed a rhetoric of maximising parental 'choice'. There also is a longstanding tradition of publicly funded yet privately provided educational and welfare programmes; this traditional approach was reinvented to fit new market rationales that proclaimed the superior efficiency and responsiveness of market-based services (Morgan, 2006). In the UK, Labour governments embraced non-state provision of public services as a way to distinguish themselves from 'Old Labour' and associate their policies with the seeming dynamism of markets. In neither case were public sector unions strong enough to combat these developments.

The German trajectory towards Nordic-style work–family policies was somewhat different, owing to the slowness of the SPD to capitalise on female discontent with the lack of policies that support working parents. As in the UK and the Netherlands, the decline of their working-class base led the SPD to reach out to female voters through both platform shifts and efforts to increase the proportion of female SPD parliamentarians (Meyer, 2003: 406–7; Mckay, 2004; von Wahl, 2006: 468). The proportion of SPD women in parliament especially accelerated in the 1990s. Yet, upon coming to power in 1998, the SPD initially made only marginal reforms to work–family policies. Chancellor Gerhard Schroeder himself thought women's issues were mere 'chatter' (von Wahl, 2006: 474–75), and the SPD–Green government feared being attacked by the CDU/CSU for intervening in the family (Erler, 2009: 47–48). Only in the second red–green government (2002–5) – one in which there were six female ministers out of 14 – did a female Minister of Family Affairs, Renate Schmidt, develop a parental leave law much like that which would later pass, while a 2004 Day Care Expansion Act promised new funds to states and municipalities for child care (Korthouwer, 2008).

It took the return to power of the CDU in a Grand Coalition government to bring about a more comprehensive set of work–family policies. This time, the change reflected a drive by the CDU to staunch the exodus of female voters from the party. Throughout the 1990s and into the 2000s, the CDU lost support among women aged 30–49 and had low favourability among younger women and young people in general. Concerns about these developments were articulated in party debates over the proposed day care and parental leave laws, as supporters argued that the party needed to modernise in order to remain in touch with German society (Korthouwer, 2008; Clemens, 2009: 131). Moreover, owing to efforts to improve the role of women in the CDU, women were increasingly in positions of power within the party. Chancellor Angela Merkel is from East Germany and lacks the 'sentimental attachment' to the social traditionalism held by many in the CDU and CSU (Clemens, 2009: 126), and the architect of the new policy, Family Minister Ursula von der Leyen, had clout on this issue, being a mother of seven. Von der Leyen couched the reforms as a response to Germany's demographic decline in an effort to undermine conservative opposition to the changes (Von Wahl, 2006; Henninger et al., 2008).

Thus, between 2006 and 2008, the Grand Coalition government enacted transformative changes in Germany's work–family policies, including tax breaks for child care costs, the new parental leave law, and billions of promised investments in child care for under-threes. To assuage conservative critics inside and outside the Christian Democratic Party, the parental leave law that was originally to be ten months (plus two daddy-only months) was lengthened to 12 months, so as to provide a guaranteed full-year of (most likely) maternal care. Single-earner families also were allowed a benefit of €300 per month during 14 months, regardless of income (Hege, 2006).

What can we learn from the politics of work–family reform in the recent path shifters? Parties in all three were driven by changes in their electoral constituencies and strategies to modernise both politics and policy, bringing more women into their parties while also adopting policies to support mothers' employment. The entry of more women into these parties reinforced the strategy, as female politicians have lobbied for, or spearheaded, these policy changes. Yet, the political resonance of promoting more caring time for parents undercut some of the egalitarianism of these policy shifts, as Germany and the UK now have year-long leaves that are disproportionately taken by women. In addition, the push to activate women's employment came at the same time as a growing emphasis on market-based solutions to social welfare problems. In the Netherlands and the UK, this compromised the development of *quality* early childhood services.

The slower pace of reform in Austria, Italy and Spain

If policies to improve work–life balance are so electorally alluring, why have not all countries in Western Europe embraced them? In fact, even in the countries that have been moving more slowly, work–family policies have *not* been stagnant: to the contrary, *all* are doing more for working parents than in the past. Italy reformed its parental leave system in 1999, extending the paid leave to ten months and offering an additional month if the father takes three months of the leave (European Foundation, 2006). Spain in 2003 created a tax subsidy for working mothers of €100 per month per child under three, while an earlier measure created an unpaid, three-year leave that is in addition to the four-month leave reimbursed at 100% of wages (European Foundation, 2006). Spanish governments also have, since the mid-1970s, continually expanded the preschool system and there is now universal provision for children aged three to six (Valiente, 2009). Effective in 2010, Austria replaced an ill-paid, lengthy care leave with shorter and better-paid options – including a 12-month leave (14 if both parents take some time) paid at 80% of one's income up to a ceiling of €2,000 per month.[13] Thus, Austria's parental leave system is similar to the German one, although parents still have the option to take much longer leaves.

In sum, in all three cases we can see the popularity of work–family and early childhood policies, with Austria and Spain doing more in this area than Italy. However, thus far the reforms undertaken are incremental changes rather than outright path shifting. Spending on child care in Austria expanded under a Grand Coalition government (Obinger and Tálos, 2010: 120) but reaches at most 13% of children under the age of three (Auer and Welte, 2009: 400). The Austrian school system also remains ill-adapted to parents' work schedules, with very limited access to afterschool services (Haas and Hartel, 2010: 146). Spain and Italy similarly lack an infrastructure of publicly subsidised care services for under-threes, and Spain lacks a paid parental leave.

Part of the explanation lies in the lesser degree of female political empowerment and continued conservatism of female voters, factors that have only recently been changing. In most Western European countries, the gender gap in voting had flipped from benefiting conservatives to helping left parties by the 1990s, a trend that emerged later in Spain and Italy (Torres and Brites, 2006; Corbetta and Cavazza, 2008). Moreover, although left parties in Austria and Spain have worked to increase the representation of women in parliament – spurring a similar response by conservative parties – Italy has done little in this regard and has nearly the lowest percentage of women serving in parliament in Europe (Del Re, 2005; Köpl, 2005; Jiménez, 2009).

Where female electoral volatility has emerged and the proportion of women in politics increased, there has been some change in policy. For instance, the dynamism of Austrian family policy in recent years reflects competition between the political parties over who can 'own' family policy as a political issue – competition that emerged as electoral volatility and dealignment intensified in the 1980s and 1990s (Plasser and Ulram, 2008). In this more competitive environment, in which parties sought to distinguish themselves on 'hot issues' such as family policy, governments enacted a number of family policy reforms, including the various iterations of parental leave and parental benefits that were enacted in the 1990s and early 2000s (Sauer, 2007).

There are a number of reasons why, until recently, these reforms moved in a conservative direction. First, the electoral gains made by a populist right-wing party, the FPÖ, tipped the political spectrum rightward in the late 1990s and early 2000s. The FPÖ took a very traditionalist stance on gender and family issues, advocating payments to mothers at home and claiming that children were spending too much time in child care (Sauer, 2007: 27). Moreover, although a sizeable gender gap had opened up between the left and the right, this reflected the lack of female enthusiasm for the FPÖ rather than a steep decline in support for the ÖVP. Unlike in Germany, the Austrian Christian Democrats managed to hold onto much of their female constituency, in part because religion has remained a more significant source of voter identity and behaviour (Sauer, 2007: 31; Plasser and Ulram, 2008: 63–64, 72). Only when a Grand Coalition of the SPÖ and ÖVP returned did the latter move towards a more moderate position, opening up the possibility of the more gender egalitarian leave option that was recently created.

In Spain, the growing empowerment of women in politics also contributed to some gender-equality reforms. The expansion of the preschool system in the mid-1970s was largely driven by the impetus of societal modernisation of the country and the interest of the Catholic Church in receiving public funds to provide these services, but the growing role of women in the PSOE was also a factor (Valiente, 2009). Most notable are the actions of two PSOE governments since 2004 in which women have made up half or more of female ministers and women have had 36% of seats in the lower parliamentary chamber. These two PSOE governments instituted a wave of reforms, including new policies against gender violence, an equality law tackling sexual harassment and labour market discrimination, and new benefits for dependants over age six who need care (Calvo and Martín, 2009).

Yet, although Spanish governments have asserted the importance of helping parents reconcile work and family (Rodriguez et al., forthcoming), they have done little to develop public child care services for children under three (Nicodemo and Waldmann, 2009). In both Spain and Italy, existing programmes and policy measures enable parents to cobble together a 'solution' of sorts to their child care needs, thereby reducing the political pressures for reform. Like Spain, Italy has nearly universal, long-day preschool (open usually from 8.30 a.m. to 4.30 p.m.) for children aged three to six that is free and offers coverage for much of the day. These programmes likely undercut some of the urgency felt around work–family reconciliation. In addition, both countries are distinctive in their continued heavy reliance upon the extended family to care for children (Naldini, 2003). With most women of the older generations having been stay-at-home mothers, they are available to care for young children (Valiente, 2009: 83). The cobbling together of imperfect options has its price: mothers' employment rates are lower in these countries than in much of the rest of Europe, and fertility rates have plunged in the past decades. Still, in a 'vicious cycle' of informal family provision and inadequate family policies, the availability of family care seems to take some pressure off of Spanish and Italian political leaders to address the work–family issue in a more fundamental way (León, 2007).

In sum, the slower pace of change is explicable by the lesser empowerment of women (until recently), greater strength of conservatism in these countries and, in the case of both Spain and Italy, the existence of some services and family support networks that enable families to imperfectly cobble together some kind of solution to their work–family conflicts. In this, Italy and Spain look a good deal like France in the way in which the education system 'steps in', often unintentionally, to support working parents. These countries are thus inching closer towards a social investment approach in enabling broad-based access to good-quality programmes, but fall short on both the activation and equality dimensions.

Conclusion

This chapter explored the politics of social investment provision and thus offers insights into the feasibility of moving states towards these kinds of policies. The first lesson concerns the possibility of change: for years, social science analysts viewed welfare regimes as frozen in place, locked in path-dependent trajectories that were hard to break. As this chapter showed, however, a number of countries *have* engaged in major, path-shifting changes. In not all cases were these shifts in a full social investment direction, but they did move a number of states that were indifferent, or hostile, to mothers' employment towards a more supportive set of programmes.

What political forces were needed to bring about this change? Ideational shifts were less important than fundamental changes in the workings of electoral politics. The growing empowerment of women in the private and public arenas, reinforced by other large-scale structural changes such as the decline of religion and class identities, unleashed new political dynamics that, in Germany, the Netherlands and the UK, culminated in large-scale reform. The changing base of support for political parties and growing competitiveness of the female vote helped bring new issues on the political agenda, such as the need to promote women's employment and attend to the care and education of young children. One consequence is that, while ideational development is likely important in shaping the *content* of new social policy measures, changes in political party organisation and electoral interests are crucial for significant reform.

Third, even with these positive dynamics, politicians have not been implementing a cohesive social investment vision. To the contrary, governments have been driven by a mix of motives that may compromise the effectiveness of the policies they adopt. The British case exemplifies this: New Labour was one originator of many ideas that make up the social investment perspective, and they couched much of their family policy agenda in this language. Yet, their initial foray into work–family policy was fragmented and unhelpful to many families. Electoral pressures moved them towards a more encompassing set of policies, yet their determination to limit the growth of the state prevented them from developing a truly universal set of services and programmes. Thus, although social investment goals have underpinned many of the policies adopted in recent years, competing political considerations may impede the full realisation of these objectives.

Notes

[1] I am grateful to Brian Karlsson and Amanda Spencer for their superb research assistance and the George Washington University's Institute for European, Russian and Eurasian Studies for research support.

[2] This typology differs somewhat from the other chapters in this volume, in part because of the recent shift in German policy, which does not manifest itself in the data in Chapter Four, but also because of the specificities of the French case, where a strong early childhood education system developed for distinctive historical reasons elaborated on in this chapter.

[3] 2% of 2½ year olds were also in *écoles maternelles* in 2008 (and another 99,000 children attended an *école maternelle* on a part-time basis DREES, 2010).

[4] In 2009, the average number of children in a preschool class was 25.7; www. education.gouv.fr/pid338/l-education-nationale-chiffres.html.

[5] In 2008, 20% of under-threes were cared for by registered family day care providers, 4% by grandparents or other family members, 3% used another form of care, 2% received paid care at home, and 63% by parents (DREES, 2010).

[6] Employed parents can deduct two-thirds of the cost of employing someone in their home up to a level of €4,000 per year, per child.

[7] The planned new spending continues to flow into the development of public child care, for instance, although some local authorities argue that they are going to need more resources to meet the 2013 targets for child care provision (Bundesministerium für Familie, Senioren, Frauen und Jugend, 2010; Tichomirowa, 2010).

[8] The high proportion of Austrian women in paid work reflects how their employment figures count time on the lengthy parental leave. For instance, in

2006, 55.3% of mothers with children under three were counted as employed, yet only 28.2% were actually at work, whereas 25.2% were on parental leave and 1.8% on maternity leave (OECD, 2007: 48).

[9] See Jacquot et al. (forthcoming) on the impact of Europeanisation on work–family reconciliation policies.

[10] Currently, all three and four year olds are entitled to 15 hours per week of free nursery education for 38 weeks a year.

[11] For a detailed analysis of the passage of this legislation, see Morgan (2010).

[12] For example, the PvdA lost around one-fourth of its voters between 1963 and 1966 and faced challenges from new left-leaning parties, such as D66 (Oldersma, 2005: 155).

[13] Previously, parents could receive 30 months of job-protected time off from paid work and a flat-rate benefit (€436/month), with six more months for fathers taking the leave (Auer and Welte, 2009).

References

Armingeon, K., Engler, S., Potolidis, P., Gerber, M. and Leimgruber, P. (2010) 'Comparative Political Data Set 1960–2008', Institute of Political Science, University of Berne.

Auer, M. and Welte, H. (2009) 'Work-family reconciliation policies without equal opportunities? The case of Austria', *Community, Work & Family*, 12 (4), 389–407.

Bergman, H. and Hobson, B. (2002) 'Compulsory Fatherhood: the coding of fatherhood in the Swedish welfare state', in B. Hobson (ed.) *Making Men into Fathers: Men, Masculinities, and the Social Politics of Fatherhood*. Cambridge, UK: Cambridge University Press.

Bergqvist, C., Kuusipalo, J. and Styrkarsdóttir, A. (1999) 'The debate on childcare policies', in C. Bergqvist, J. Kuusipalo and A. Styrkarsdóttir (eds) *Nordic Democracies: Gender and Politics in the Nordic Countries*. Oslo: Scandinavian University Press, pp. 137–57.

Bonoli, G. and Reber, F. (2010) 'The political economy of childcare in OECD countries: Explaining cross-national variation in spending and coverage rates', *European Journal of Political Research*, 49, 97–118.

Bundesministerium für Familie, Senioren, Frauen und Jugend (2010) *Erster Zwischenbericht zur Evaluation des Kinderförderungsgesetzes*. Berlin: BMFSFJ.

Calvo, K. and Martín, I. (2009) 'Ungrateful citizens? Women's rights policies in Zapatero's Spain', *South European Society & Politics*, 14 (4), 487–502.

Campbell, R. and Lovenduski, J. (2005) 'Winning Women's Votes? The Incremental Track to Equality', *Parliamentary Affairs*, 58 (4), 837–53.

Childs, S. (2008) *Women and British Party Politics: Descriptive, Substantive and Symbolic Representation*. London: Routledge.

Clemens, C. (2009) 'Modernisation or disorientation? Policy change in Merkel's CDU', *German Politics*, 18 (2), 121–39.

Corbetta, P. and Cavazza, N. (2008) 'From the parish to the polling booth: Evolution and interpretation of the political gender gap in Italy, 1968–2006', *Electoral Studies*, 27 (2), 272–84.

de Kruif, R.E.L., Riksen-Walraven, J.M.A., Gevers Deynoot-Schaub, M.J.J.M., Helmerhorst, K.O.W., Tavecchio, L.W.C. and Fukking, R.G. (2009) *Pedagogische Kwaliteit van de Nederlandse Kinderopvang in 2008*. Amsterdam: Netherlands Consortium Kinderopvang Onderzoek.

Del Re, A. (2005) 'Italy', in Y. Galligan and M. Tremblay (eds) *Sharing Power: Women, Parliament, and Democracy*. Burlington: Ashgate, pp. 37–47.

DREES (2010) 'L'offre d'accueil collectif des enfants de moins de 6 ans en 2008', *Etudes et Résultats*, No. 715.

Ellingsæter, A.L. (2006) 'The Norwegian childcare regime and its paradoxes', in A.L. Ellingsæter and A. Leira (eds) *Politicising Parenthood in Scandinavia: Gender Relations in Welfare States*. Bristol, UK: The Policy Press, pp. 121–44.

Erler, D. (2009) 'La réforme du congé parental en Allemagne: vers le modèle nordique?', *Politiques Sociales et Familiales*, 95, 43–52.

Esping-Andersen, G. (2002) *Why We Need a New Welfare State*. Oxford: Oxford University Press.

Florin, C. and Nilsson, B. (1999) '"Something in the nature of a bloodless revolution…" How new gender relations became gender equality policy in Sweden in the nineteen-sixties and seventies', in R. Torstendahl (ed.) *State Policy and Gender System in the Two German States and Sweden, 1945–1989*. Uppsala: University of Uppsala Department of History, pp. 11–77.

Gornick, J.C. and Meyers, M.K. (2009) 'Institutions that support gender equality in parenthood and employment', in E.O. Wright (ed.) *Gender Equality: Transforming Family Divisions of Labour*. London: Verso Press, pp. 3–64.

Haas, B. and Hartel, M. (2010) 'Towards the universal care course model', *European Societies*, 12 (2), 139–62.

Hege, A. (2006) 'Pères, enfants, migrants: Changement de paradigme et résistances', *Chronique internationale de l'IRES*, 101, 11–21.

Henninger, A., Wimbauer, C. and Dombrowski, R. (2008) 'Demography as a push toward gender equality? Current reforms of German family policy', *Social Politics*, 15 (3), 287–314.

Hinnfors, J. (1999) 'Stability through change: The pervasiveness of political ideas', *Journal of Public Policy*, 19 (3), 293–312.

Huber, E. and Stephens, J.D. (2000) 'Partisan governance, women's employment, and the social democratic service state', *American Sociological Review*, 65 (3), 323–42.

IPU: Inter-parliamentary Union, Women in National Parliaments, Statistical Archive, www.ipu.org/wmn-e/classif-arc.htm.

Jacquot, S., Ledoux, C. and Palier, B. (forthcoming) 'A means to a changing end. European resources: The EU and the reconciliation of paid work and private life', *European Journal of Social Security*.

Jenson, J. (2009) 'Lost in translation: The social investment perspective and gender equality', *Social Politics*, 16 (4), 446–83.

Jenson, J. and Sineau, M. (1998) 'Quand "liberté de choix" ne rime pas avec égalité républicaine', in J. Jenson and M. Sineau (eds) *Qui doit Garder le Jeune Enfant? Modes d'Accueil et Travail des Mères dans l'Europe en Crise*. Paris: Librairie Générale de Droit et de Jurisprudence, pp. 141–72.

Jiménez, A.M.R. (2009) 'Women and decision-making participation within rightist parties in Portugal and Spain', *Análise Social*, 44 (191), 235–63.

Kittilson, M.C. (2008) 'Representing women: The adoption of family leave in comparative perspective', *Journal of Politics*, 70 (2), 323–34.

Korthouwer, G. (2008) 'How German Christian Democrats have said farewell to familialism', *Amsterdam School for Social Science Research*, Working paper 08/01.

Köpl, R. (2005) 'Gendering political representation: Debates and controversies in Austria', in J. Lovenduski (ed.) *State Feminism and Political Representation*. Cambridge: Cambridge University Press, pp. 20–40.

Leira, A. (1989) *Models of Motherhood*. Oslo: Institute for Social Research.

León, M. (2007) 'Speeding up or holding back? Institutional factors in the development of childcare provision in Spain', *European Societies*, 9 (3), 315–37.

Leu, H.R. and Schelle, R. (2009) 'Between education and care? Critical reflections on early childhood policies in Germany', *Early Years*, 29 (1), 5–18.

Lewis, J. (1992) 'Gender and the development of welfare regimes', *Journal of European Social Policy*, 2 (3), 159–73.

Lewis, J. (2008) 'Childcare policies and the politics of choice', *Political Quarterly,* 79 (4), 499–507.

Lewis, J. (2011) 'From Sure Start to Children's Centres: An Analysis of Policy Change in English Early Years Programmes', *Journal of Social Policy,* 40 (1), 71–88.

Lewis, J. and Campbell, M. (2007) 'UK work/family balance policies and gender equality, 1997–2005', *Social Politics,* 14 (1), 4–30.

Lewis, J., Knijn, T., Martin, C. and Ostner, I. (2008) 'Patterns of development of work/family reconciliation policies for parents in France, Germany, the Netherlands, and the UK in the 2000s', *Social Politics,* 15 (3), 261–86.

Leyenaar, M. (2004) *Political Empowerment of Women: The Netherlands and other Countries.* Leiden: Martinus Nijhoff Publishers.

Lloyd, E. (2008) 'The interface between childcare, family support and child poverty strategies under new labour: Tensions and contradictions', *Social Policy & Society,* 7 (4), 479–94.

Lloyd, E. and Penn, H. (2010) 'Why do childcare markets fail? Comparing England and the Netherlands', *Public Policy Research,* 17 (1), 42–48.

Mahon, R. (1997) 'Child care in Canada and Sweden: Policy and politics', *Social Politics,* 4 (3), 382–418.

Mandel, H. (2010) 'Winners and losers: The consequences of welfare state policies for gender wage inequality', *European Sociological Review,* 26 (6), 1–22.

Mckay, J. (2004) 'Women in German politics: Still jobs for the boys?', *German Politics,* 13 (1), 56–80.

Merens, A. and Hermans, B. (2009) *Emancipatiemonitor 2008.* Den Haag: Sociaal en Cultureel Planbureau.

Meyer, B. (2003) 'Much ado about nothing? Political representation policies and the influence of women parliamentarians in Germany', *Review of Policy Research,* 20 (3), 401–22.

Morel, N. (2007) 'From subsidiarity to "Free Choice": Child- and elder-care policy reforms in France, Belgium, Germany, and the Netherlands', *Social Policy & Administration,* 41 (6), 618–37.

Morgan, K.J. (2005) 'The production of child care: How labour markets shape social policy and vice versa', *Social Politics,* 12 (2), 243–63.

Morgan, K.J. (2006) *Working Mothers and the Welfare State: Religion and the Politics of Work–Family Policy in Western Europe and the United States.* Palo Alto: Stanford University Press.

Morgan, K.J. (2010) 'The end of the frozen welfare state? Innovation in work–family policies in Western Europe', paper presented at the Annual Meeting of the American Political Science Association, 2–5 September 2010.

Morgan, K.J. and Zippel, K. (2003) 'Paid to care: The origins and effects of care leave policies in Western Europe', *Social Politics*, 10 (1), 49–85.

Naldini, M. (2003) *The Family in the Mediterranean Welfare States*. London: Frank Cass.

Nicodemo, C. and Waldmann, R. (2009) *Child-care and Participation in the Labour Market for Married Women in Mediterranean Countries*, IZA Discussion Paper No. 3983.

Noailly, J. and Visser, S. (2009) 'The impact of market forces on the provision of childcare: Insights from the 2005 childcare act in the Netherlands', *Journal of Social Policy*, 38 (3), 477–98.

Obinger, H. and Tálos, E. (2010) 'Janus-faced developments in a prototypical Bismarckian welfare state: Welfare reforms in Austria since the 1970s', in B. Palier (ed.) *A Long Goodbye to Bismarck? The Politics of Welfare Reform in Continental Europe*. Amsterdam: Amsterdam University Press, pp. 101–28.

OECD (2005) *Extending Opportunities: How Active Social Policy can Benefit us All*. Paris: OECD.

OECD (2006) *Starting Strong II: Early Childhood Education and Care*. Paris: OECD.

OECD (2007) *Babies and Bosses: Reconciling Work and Family Life; a Synthesis of Findings for OECD Countries*. Paris: OECD.

Oldersma, J. (2005) 'High tides in a low country: Gendering political representation in the Netherlands', in J. Lovenduski (ed.) *State Feminism and Political Representation*. Cambridge: Cambridge University Press, pp. 153–73.

Penn, H. (2007) 'Childcare market management: How the United Kingdom government has reshaped its role in developing early childhood education and care', *Contemporary Issues in Early Childhood*, 8 (2), 192–207.

Perrigo, S. (1996) 'Women and change in the labour party 1979–1995', *Parliamentary Affairs*, 49 (1), 116–29.

Plantenga, J. (2002) 'Combining work and care in the polder model: An assessment of the Dutch part-time strategy', *Critical Social Policy*, 22 (1), 56–59.

Plasser, F. and Ulram, P.A. (2008) 'Electoral Change in Austria', in G. Bischof and F. Plasser (eds) *The Changing Austrian Voter*. New Brunswick, NJ: Transaction Publishers, pp. 54–78.

Rodriguez, A.M.G., Begega, S.G. and García, N.M. (forthcoming) 'Deconstructing the familist welfare state in Spain: Towards reconciliation through Europe', *European Journal of Social Security*.

Sauer, B. (2007) 'Reevaluating the "heart of society": Family policy in Austria', in M. Haussman and B. Sauer (eds) *Gender the State in the Age of Globalization: Women's Movements and State Feminism in Postindustrial Democracies*. Lanham: Rowman & Littlefield Publishers, Inc., pp. 19–38.

Tichomirowa, K. (2010) 'Wer zahlt für die Kinderbetreuung?", *Frankfurter Rundschau*. Available at www.fr-online.de/politik/wer-zahlt-fuer-die-kinderbetreuung-/-/1472596/2679424/-/index.html.

Torres, A. and Brites, R. (2006) 'European attitudes and values: The perspective of gender in a transverse analysis', *Portuguese Journal of Social Science*, 5 (3), 179–214.

Valiente, C. (2009) 'Child care in Spain after 1975: The educational rationale, the catholic church, and women in civil society', in K. Scheiwe and H. Willekens (eds) *Child Care and Preschool Development in Europe: Institutional Perspectives*. London: Palgrave Macmillan, pp. 72–87.

Vermeer, H.J., van Ijzendoorn, M.H., de Kruif, R.E.L., Fukkink, R.G., Tavecchio, L.W.C., Riksen-Walraven, J.M. and van Zeijl, J. (2008) 'Child care in the Netherlands: trends in quality over the years 1995–2005', *Journal of Genetic Psychology*, 169 (4), 360–85.

Visser, J. (2002) 'The first part-time economy in the world: A model to be followed?', *Journal of European Social Policy*, 12 (1), 23–42.

van Holsteyn, J.J.M. and Irwin, G.A. (1989) 'Toward a more open model of competition', in H. Daalder and G.A. Irwin (eds) *Politics in the Netherlands: How much Change?* London: Frank Cass, pp. 112–38.

von Wahl, A. (2006) 'Gender equality in Germany: Comparing policy changes across domains', *West European Politics*, 29 (3), 461–88.

Waldfogel, J. (2006) 'What do children need?', *Public Policy Research*, 13 (1), 26–34.

Wincott, D. (2006) 'Paradoxes of new labour social policy: Toward universal child care in Europe's "most liberal" welfare regime?' *Social Politics*, 13 (2), 286–312.

SEVEN

Active labour market policy and social investment: a changing relationship

Giuliano Bonoli

Introduction

Active labour market policies (ALMPs) seem an obvious component of any social investment project. Rather than simply paying a replacement income to jobless people, an active labour market policy aims to make sure that unemployment spells are as short as possible, by proactively helping jobless people re-enter the labour market. Reducing the duration and the incidence of unemployment, or, more generally, of worklessness, is an objective that is perfectly consistent with the social investment perspective as defined by Jenson (see Chapter Three). ALMPs provide help to disadvantaged people (the jobless) and take a long-term perspective by reducing the scarring effect of unemployment. They also provide returns for society as a whole by contributing to reduce outlays for cash benefits.

Upon closer scrutiny of the policies that usually go under the rubric of ALMP, the case for their inclusion within the social investment perspective is less obvious. In fact, ALMP is an umbrella term that refers to very different types of interventions. These include training, assistance in job search, subsidies paid to employers who accept to take on an unemployed person, work experience placement programmes or temporary job creation programmes in the public sector. Some consider sanctions and benefit conditionality also part of the ALMP toolbox (see, for example, Kluve, 2006) in so far as these are instruments that may provoke a change in the behaviour of the beneficiaries and speed up labour market re-entry. In short, given the broad variety of interventions that constitute ALMPs, it is simply impossible to make a general statement concerning their conformity to the social investment ideal.

The objective of this chapter is to focus on the different types of ALMPs that exist, or have existed, in OECD countries, and assess the role they play or have played from the point of view of the social investment perspective, as discussed by Jenson (Chapter Three). It begins by developing a two-dimensional classification of ALMPs. The first one focuses on the extent to which policies comprise an investment in beneficiaries' human capital. The second dimension considers the degree to which beneficiaries are expected to re-enter the labour market. Intersecting these two dimensions allows me to identify four different (ideal) types of ALMPs that reflect the social investment perspective to a different extent.

The chapter then moves on to look at how the various types of ALMPs have been in use in six European countries since the early post-war years. It finds that, unexpectedly, the strongest social investment orientation is found in the earliest period (1950s and 1960s) when, in the context of rapidly expanding industrial economies, the role of ALMP consisted in the upskilling of those who were nonetheless without work. Judging the social investment quality of current ALMPs is a more difficult question. They have a clear orientation towards the promotion of labour market participation, but, in spite of the fact that many countries are experiencing (skilled) labour shortage, the training content of ALMPs has declined in relative terms. By promoting quick labour market re-entry they reduce the scarring effect of unemployment. Often, however, for low-skilled people, the jobs that are available tend to be low paid and offer little or no prospects for advancement. Under these circumstances, the social investment quality of ALMPs is less obvious.

Four types of ALMPs

Active labour market policies have different origins. In Sweden, active labour market policies were developed as early as the 1950s, with the objective of improving the match between demand and supply of labour in the context of a rapidly evolving economy, essentially by financing extensive vocational training programmes (Swenson, 2002). At the opposite extreme, the term 'active' can be used to describe the approach developed in various English-speaking countries, which combines placement services with stronger work incentives, time limits on recipiency, benefit reductions and the use of sanctions, the so-called 'workfare' approach (King, 1995; Peck, 2001). In fact, as many have pointed out, active labour market policy is a particularly ambiguous category of social policy (Clasen, 2000; Barbier, 2001; Barbier, 2004; Clegg, 2005).

Some authors have attempted to deal with this problem by distinguishing between two types of active labour market policies, or activation: those which are about improving human capital, and those which use essentially negative incentives to move people from social assistance into employment. Examples of such classifications are found in Torfing (1999), who distinguishes between 'offensive' and 'defensive' workfare. Offensive workfare, which is the term used to describe the Danish variant of activation, relies on improving skills and empowerment rather than on sanctions and benefit reduction, as is the 'defensive' variant found in the USA. Taylor-Gooby makes the same point using instead the terms of 'positive' and 'negative' activation (Taylor-Gooby, 2004). In a similar vein, Barbier distinguishes between 'liberal activation', characterised by stronger work incentives, benefit conditionality and the use of sanctions, and 'universalistic activation', which is found in the Nordic countries and continues to rely on extensive investment in human capital essentially through training, though he recognises that a third type might exist in continental Europe (Barbier, 2004; Barbier and Ludwig-Mayerhofer, 2004) .

Dichotomies between human capital investment and incentive-based approaches to activation are a useful starting point in making sense of an ambiguous concept. However, they probably constitute an oversimplification of the real world and run the risk of carrying value judgements. In fact, these distinctions make reference to two underlying dimensions which should be examined separately.

The first dimension concerns the extent to which the objective of policy is to put people back into real jobs (that is, unsubsidised market employment), provided either by private or public employers. From the point of view of the social investment perspective this is important. Putting people back into jobs is a source of savings for the public purse, but it also reduces the duration of unemployment and hence its scarring effect on the beneficiary.

Many programmes have this objective, but some, especially in continental and northern Europe during the 1980s and early 1990s, looked more like alternatives to market employment. These took the shape of temporary jobs created in the public or in the non-profit sector. They were often used to recreate an entitlement to unemployment insurance rather than to increase the chances of landing an unsubsidised job. As will be seen in the narrative accounts below, the extent to which ALMPs favour labour market re-entry varies across countries and across time. I call this dimension the 'pro-market employment orientation'.

The second dimension refers to the extent to which programmes are based on investing in jobless people's human capital. Here the relevance of the social investment perspective is obvious. Upskilling jobless persons is likely to facilitate their labour market re-entry on the one hand, and to impact positively on productivity on the other, for the benefit of society as a whole. Investment can take the shape of vocational training or help in developing the sort of soft skills employers look for when selecting candidates.

Intersecting these two dimensions allows us to identify different types of labour market policy, and to map the variety that exists under the label 'active labour market policy' (Table 7.1).

Table 7.1: Four types of active labour market policy

		Investment in human capital		
		None	Weak	Strong
Pro-market employment orientation	Weak	(passive benefits)	**Occupation** • job creation schemes in the public sector • non-employment-related training programmes	(basic education)
	Strong	**Incentive reinforcement** • Tax credits, in-work benefits • Time limits on recipiency • Benefit reductions • Benefit conditionality	**Employment assistance** • Placement services • Job subsidies • Counselling • Job search programmes	**Upskilling** • Job-related vocational training

Of the six possible combinations between the two dimensions selected, four describe different orientations in active labour market policy. These can be labelled: incentive reinforcement, employment assistance, occupation – and human capital investment (the other two passive benefits and basic education – are not generally considered as part of ALMPs).

The first type of ALMPs, 'incentive reinforcement', refers to measures that aim at strengthening work incentives for benefit recipients. This objective can be achieved in various ways, for example by curtailing passive benefits, in terms of both benefit rates and duration. Benefits can also be made conditional on participation in work schemes or other labour market programmes. Finally, incentives can be strengthened through the use of sanctions. Elements of incentive reinforcement exist everywhere, but they are particularly strong in English-speaking countries.

The second type, which I term 'employment assistance', consists of measures aimed at removing obstacles to labour market participation. These include placement services or job search programmes that increase the likelihood of a jobless person establishing contact with a potential employer. Counselling and job subsidies may be particularly useful to beneficiaries who have been out of the labour market for a long time or have never had a job, who are often shunned by employers. For parents, an obstacle to employment may be the lack of child care, and help in finding (and paying for) a suitable day care service may also be included under the employment assistance variant. These interventions may provide modest improvements in the human capital of beneficiaries, mostly in the shape of better soft skills. Above all, however, they allow beneficiaries to put their human capital to good use. This approach is common in English-speaking countries (combined with incentive reinforcement), and since the mid- to late 1990s has also developed in northern and continental Europe.

A third type of active labour market policy can be labelled 'occupation'. Its objective is not primarily to promote labour market re-entry, but to keep jobless people busy, also in order to prevent the depletion of human capital associated with an unemployment spell. This type of ALMP consists of job creation and work experience programmes in the public or non-profit sector, but also training in some cases, such as shorter courses, which do not fundamentally change the type of job a person can do. Continental European countries in the 1980s and early 1990s have been among the main users of this type of ALMP.

Finally, ALMPs can rely on 'upskilling' or providing vocational training to jobless people. The idea here is to offer a second chance to people who were not able to profit from the training system or whose skills have become obsolete. The provision of vocational training to jobless people is most developed in the Nordic countries.

Whether the various types of ALMPs can be considered as part of a social investment approach depends largely on how one defines the latter. On the basis of Jenson's definition (this volume) at least two of the types of ALMPs identified in this paper qualify as social investment: upskilling and employment assistance. In the case of upskilling, or providing training that is work related and increases the chances of finding a job, the relevance for the social investment perspective is fairly obvious. Employment assistance does not aim at increasing human capital, but less ambitiously at removing obstacles to employment. However, given the very negative impact of joblessness on those who are hit by it and on their families, it is reasonable to consider employment assistance as part of a social investment agenda.

More difficult is to classify the other two types of ALMP. Incentive reinforcement may help get rid of poverty traps and hence reduce the duration of unemployment, an objective that is consistent with the social investment perspective. However, most of the tools that are part of this type of ALMP are much closer to a liberal view of employment regulation that sees strong work incentives as the key route to an efficient labour market. Occupation is also quite far from the notion of social investment, but can have a positive impact on the preservation of human capital and on jobless people's social integration.

It would be extremely helpful to operationalise these four ideal types with measurable indicators, and then map their variation across time and space. Unfortunately, available data allow only a very crude approximation of this exercise. There have been attempts to summarise with indicators the key institutional features of activation in different countries (Hasselpflug, 2005). The results obtained, however, are not entirely convincing, and do not match expectations based on more qualitative knowledge of many of the countries covered. This is due to a number of problems, among which the fact that these data sources are based on formal regulation, which can differ significantly from actual implementation. An alternative way to map, at least in part, cross-national variation in ALMPs on the basis of the ideal types discussed above is to use expenditure data on sub-programmes. The OECD provides this information since 1985 for most of its members. Available categories are: public employment services and administration, employment subsidies, job rotation schemes, start-up incentives, training and direct job creation.

These data allow us to operationalise three of the four ideal types presented above, as shown in Figure 7.1. Employment assistance, which includes the OECD spending categories 'public employment services and administration, employment subsidies, job rotation schemes, and start-up incentives'; occupation, which includes the category 'direct job creation'; and upskilling, which includes the category 'training'. In this way, we are able to trace the evolution over a 20-year period of the relative effort made in the different components of ALMP.

ALMPs spending profiles presented in Figure 7.1 reveal a number of important observations. First, there is obviously a cyclical effect, shown by the decline in overall spending between 1995 and 2005, which can be explained with the decline of unemployment (especially in Sweden,

Figure 7.1: ALMP spending profiles in six OECD countries, 1985–2005

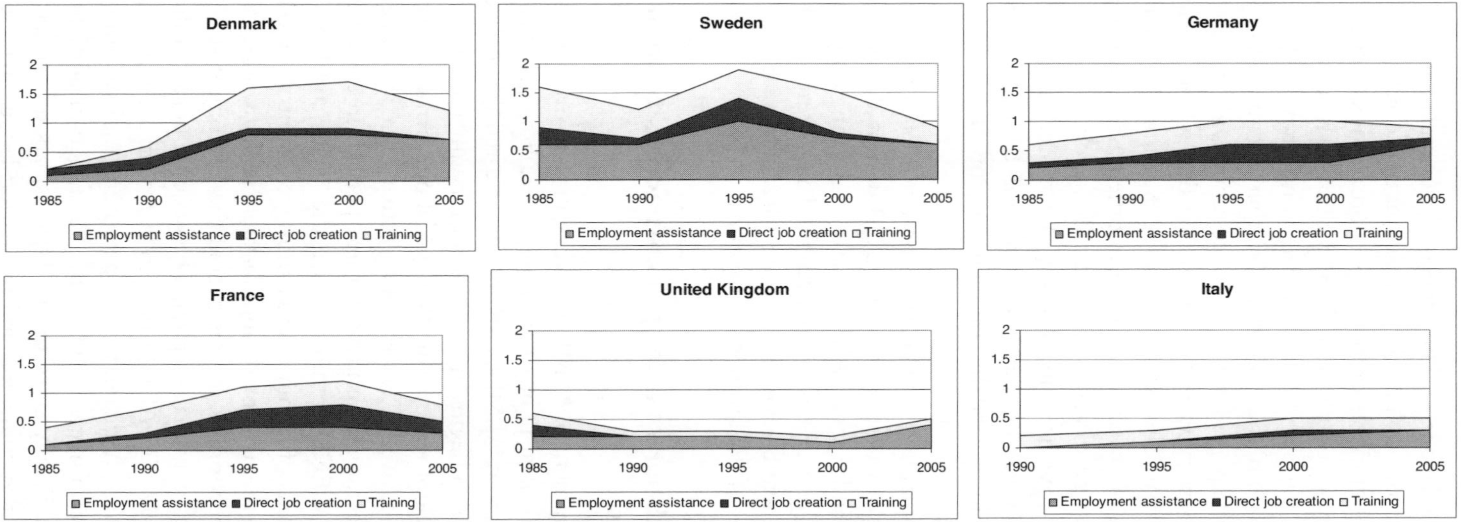

Source: Graphs constructed on the basis of data obtained from OECD.Stat (available on www.oecd.org).

Denmark and France). The increase in overall spending in the UK, instead, calls for a political explanation, as this took place in the context of declining numbers of jobless. Second, if one compares trends over the 20-year period covered, there is clearly a reduction in the size of direct job creation, which is relatively important in France, Germany and Sweden until the mid-1990s, but then declines everywhere. Third, over the same period of time, one sees employment assistance gaining importance everywhere, except in Sweden where spending on this function is basically stable over time. Spending on training, finally, shows a less clear trend over time, but there is a clear decline over the last five-year period covered, especially in relative terms (particularly in Denmark, Sweden and Germany). There are, however, big variations across countries, with the Nordic countries being the biggest spenders, the UK the lowest and the continental European countries somewhere in between.

OECD spending data need to be considered with caution since the distinctions adopted by the OECD do not always match national categories, and sometimes information is missing on given categories for several years. The results presented in Figure 7.1, however, are broadly compatible with the expectations put forward above, and with the findings of the qualitative literature.

Active labour market policies across time in six countries

The development of ALMPs spending profiles over time suggests that this area of social policy has undergone substantial change over the last two decades. ALMPs, however, pre-existed data collection by the OECD (which begins in 1985 for most countries). This section looks at the development in this field of labour market policy since the 1950s, when Sweden embraced an active approach in labour market policy. In fact, one can identify three periods in the development of ALMPs in OECD countries. First, the 1950s and the 1960s, when in the context of labour market shortage, countries developed active policies in order to provide appropriately skilled workers to expanding industrial economies. In this period the key objective of policy was investment in human capital. The second period follows the oil shocks of 1973–75. ALMPs have to face a considerably more difficult environment, characterised by persistent high unemployment. In this context, in many countries the key function of ALMPs becomes occupation. Finally, since the mid-1990s, labour market policy aims essentially at encouraging and facilitating labour market re-entry of unemployed persons and other non-working individuals. The tools adopted here consist of various mixes of incentive reinforcement and employment assistance.

What precisely happened during these three periods is reviewed next. The account focuses on six countries selected so as to represent the various types of welfare regime that exist in Western Europe: Sweden, Denmark (social democratic regime), Germany, France, Italy (conservative or Bismarckian regime) and the UK (liberal regime). Each period section adopts a different order in the presentation of country developments, starting each time with the 'pioneers' for the different types of ALMPs and then moving on to other countries. For the sake of brevity, only countries where a relevant development takes place are reviewed in each period.

The post-war years: ALMP in the context of labour shortage

Public policies affecting the supply of labour were developed in the post-war years. This period was characterised in many European countries by strong economic growth driven by industrial development. In this context, several countries ran into problems of labour shortage. Often, however, labour shortage was accompanied by unemployment, indicating a problem of skill matching. The issue was addressed with various tools that provided adequate job training.

In this respect Sweden played the role of a pioneer, with the implementation of the so-called Rehn–Meidner model. Put forward in 1951 by two trade union economists, Gosta Rehn and Rudolf Meidner, this strategy had several objectives: equality in the wage distribution, sustainable full employment and the modernisation of Swedish industry. Equality and full employment were to be promoted through a solidaristic wage policy, which basically meant identical wage increases across all sectors of industry. The egalitarian wage policy had both intended and unintended effects. Among the intended effects was a strong incentive for Swedish producers to invest in productivity-enhancing technologies. If productivity lagged behind, imposed wage growth would push out of the market less competitive companies. This represented a strong push for the modernisation of Swedish industry.

But, of course, not every industry would be able to keep up with the pace of wage increases agreed centrally. Low productivity industries were to be priced out of the market as collectively bargained wages increased. It was in order to deal with the workers that would as a result find themselves unemployed that Rehn and Meidner conceived ALMPs. As less productive companies were pushed out of the market, the workers they made redundant were to be retrained and made available for expanding, high productivity industries (see, for example, Mabbet, 1995: 141 ff.; Benner and Vad, 2000: 401; Swenson, 2002: 275; Anxo and Niklasson, 2006).

According to Swenson, however, ALMPs constituted also a response to one of Swedish employers' recurrent problems at the time: shortage of labour. By quickly retraining workers who had lost their jobs, ALMPs ensured a steady supply of appropriately qualified labour. If the idea of setting up an active labour market policy came from the trade unions, it was clearly acceptable to and possibly desirable for employers as well. In fact, according to Swenson, it was probably them who suggested it in the first place (2002: 275). On the basis of extensive historical research, he concludes that:

> Employers warmly endorsed activist training and mobility measures even before the labor confederation included them as the centerpiece of their plan for economic stabilization and industrial development (the 'Rehn-Meidner Model') ... Organized employers were not merely resigned to hegemonic Social Democrats and hoping to appease them for special consideration on particular details, for nicer treatment in other domains, or to avoid public disfavor. They knew what they wanted. Sometimes they liked best what they got and got what they liked best. (Swenson, 2002: 11)

The Rehn–Meidner model is a unique feature of Swedish economic history that was not repeated elsewhere. However, the idea of an active labour market policy in a rapidly modernising economy characterised by labour shortage was found appealing in other places as well. Sometimes, the tools used were different though, because the starting point was also different. This was the case of Italy, where unemployment was not the result of people being laid off by declining industries, but of labour surplus in the southern part of the country.

During the 1950s and 1960s, two decades of strong growth that Italians remember as the 'economic miracle', Italy was also concerned with a labour shortage problem. Expanding industries in the North needed adequately trained workers. The South still constituted a major reservoir of labour, but essentially unskilled. In order to improve the matching between skill demand and supply, a law on apprenticeship was adopted in 1955. It made provision for on-the-job training and lower salaries for trainees. The scheme, however, did not take off. Employers were generally not allowed to select apprentices, who were sent to them by labour exchange offices, and the trade unions complained that the law was being used to underpay young workers (Gualmini, 1998: 108).

Moves in this direction were also made in the case of France. In 1963, the Gaullist government embarked on a reform of the unemployment compensation system that would have facilitated access to (re-)training for unemployed people. This proposal encountered nonetheless the strong opposition of the trade unions, who feared increased state intervention in the management of unemployment insurance (UNEDIC). In France, unemployment insurance, as the rest of social security, is run jointly by the social partners who have traditionally resisted government intervention in what they consider a 'private' institution (Bonoli and Palier, 1997; Palier, 2002). The result was a watered-down version of the initial proposal. The episode highlighted the tension between an insurance-based unemployment compensations system run by the social partners and a public policy objective: the upskilling of unemployed people in the context of labour shortage. The social partners' and particularly the trade unions' narrow understanding of unemployment compensation as an insurance scheme severely limited the scope for injecting active and training measures into unemployment policy (Clegg, 2005: 176–79).

Only a few years later, Germany was to follow the same path, with the adoption of the 1969 Employment Promotion Act (*Arbeitsförderungsgesetz*). The law was adopted by the short-lived first Grand Coalition government in Germany's post-war history. The CDU–SPD coalition, led by the Christian democrats, lasted only three years (1966–69), but played an important role in shaping post-war labour market policy. The coalition came against the backdrop of the 1966–67 recession, after a row over budget broke out between the CDU and the FDP, the parties that formed the previous government. Its approach to social and economic policy anticipated many of the themes that have been popularised by political leaders in the 2000s. According to Alber:

> To combat the economic crisis, the new government intended to shift public expenditure from social consumption to social investment. Various transfer payments were curbed, and for the first time, educational issues were given priority ... As a first step towards a more active labour market policy, the competence of the unemployment insurance scheme was extended to include the promotion of vocational training. (Alber, 1986: 14)

The law was largely based on a proposal prepared by the SPD in 1966, at the time still in opposition. It emphasised a new, preventative, role for labour market policy, based on the adjustment of the workforce skills to technological change. The new law instituted the Federal Institute of Labour (*Bundesanstalt für Arbeit*) responsible for unemployment compensation insurance, but also for continuing education, re-training, employment services for disabled people and job creation programmes, and for training (Frerich and Frey, 1996). At the same time, a new law on vocational training was adopted, which significantly consolidated the system put in place 70 years earlier (Thelen, 2004: 241).

Contrary to a widespread perception among welfare state scholars, the post-war years were not an era of passive income protection. On the contrary, initiatives were taken in several European countries to introduce an active dimension of unemployment protection, essentially through vocational training. This made sense. In a context of rapid economic growth and labour shortage, to retrain jobless people so that they could provide the labour force needed by expanding industries was an obvious thing to do. The developments reviewed above show little consistency in terms of political determinants, however. The idea of linking training to unemployment policy came from political parties distributed across the political spectrum: the Swedish social democrats, the French Gaullists, Italian Christian democrats and a coalition government in Germany. These political forces have little in common, except perhaps a centrist orientation in economic and social policy matters.

Facing the employment crisis: ALMPs in the context of mass unemployment

The economic context of labour market policy changed dramatically after the oil shocks of 1973–75 and the subsequent economic crisis. All of a sudden, labour market policy had to deal with a new problem: rising unemployment. The idea of an active labour market policy was present in most countries, but the unfavourable economic context meant that the labour market policy, no matter how active, could achieve little. Against this background, we see the emergence of a different ideal type of ALMPs, the one I have labelled occupation, which does not really aim at putting jobless people back into the labour market, but more at keeping them busy and at weakening the deterioration of human capital associated with unemployment. It is intriguing that occupation, possibly the least 'liberal' type of ALMP, becomes particularly strong in the 1980s, a period characterised by the dominance of neoliberal ideas in economic and social policy (see Chapters Two and Three). In fact, the countries that expanded most this type of ALMP are also those that put up most resistance to the spread of neoliberal ideas (France, Germany, Sweden). The ALMPs adopted during those years can be seen as a form of compensation for the more liberal orientation taken in industrial policy (no more subsidies for declining industries or nationalisations).

This new function of ALMPs developed across countries, but through different channels that reflected previous policy.

In response to the employment crises of the 1970s, Sweden radically transformed its system of active labour market policy. It is noteworthy that the crisis years (mid-1970s to the late 1980s) did not result in open unemployment in Sweden. This was partly the result of the expansion of public sector employment, which took place over the same period of time, but also a consequence of the extremely widespread use of ALMPs. In fact, by providing an occupation to otherwise jobless persons, ALMPs allowed Sweden to keep employment at pre-recession levels (Mjoset, 1987: 430). This was obviously a rather new function for ALMPs, which was adopted by default in the context of a stagnating economy with little net job creation outside the state sector.

What role did ALMPs play during those years? To find out, we have to turn to the evaluation literature. In the Swedish case, from the 1970s and until the mid-1990s, ALMPs resemble increasing alternatives to market employment. On offer one finds essentially training programmes and relief works, that is, temporary jobs arranged mostly in the public sector. Typically, these jobs were used to renew entitlement to unemployment insurance (theoretically limited to 14 months). During these years, there was a relative shift away from supply-side measures towards demand-side interventions, that is, job creation programmes (Anxo and Niklasson, 2006: 360). Microlevel evaluations pointed out that most of these schemes were rather ineffective in terms of favouring labour market re-entry (Calmfors et al., 2001). The original aim of ALMPs, to upskill workers so that they can enter more productive occupations, had somewhat fallen out of sight. Swedish ALMP had clearly moved towards the 'occupation' type described above. During the same period (in 1974), Sweden adopted also a relatively strict employment protection law (Emmenegger, 2009). The 1970s can thus be characterised as a period of departure from the post-war Swedish model, with the country adopting many of the policy options that were being developed in continental Europe.

With unemployment rising from virtually nothing to 4% in 1975, Germany turned to active labour market policies in the second half of the 1970s. These measures were based on the Employment Promotion

Act of 1969. In a development that is reminiscent of the Swedish story, the objective of this law shifted from the general upskilling of the workforce to a tool aimed at reducing open unemployment, even though training continued to play an important role. The post-crisis years were characterised by a stop-and-go approach to ALMPs, partly due to the funding mechanism of these measures. Both passive and active unemployment benefits are financed out of the same fund. When unemployment is high, passive expenditure increases automatically, leaving fewer resources to finance active measures (Manow and Seils, 2000: 282). For example, after a sharp increase in the number of beneficiaries of ALMPs from 1,600 in 1970 to 648,000 in 1975, the numbers involved declined to 545,000 in 1982, under budgetary pressures (Frerich and Frey, 1996: 177; Seeleib-Kaiser et al., 2008: 43).

Active labour market policies were back with the return to power of the Christian democrats. The Kohl government, elected in 1982, expanded ALMPs in the context of a 'qualification offensive' based on various labour market and training programmes. Between 1982 and 1987, the total number of participants in such programmes rose from 555,000 to 1.4 million (Frerich and Frey, 1996; Seeleib-Kaiser et al., 2008: 43). Most of these concerned training and employment assistance, but an increasing number of people (some 10%) were on job creation schemes in the non-commercial sector (ABM). During the second half of the 1980s, Germany had yearly expenses on active labour market policy of around 1% of GDP, which was above the OECD average. The figure was slightly up from the first half of the decade (around 0.7% of GDP; see Clasen, 2005, Table 4.5).

Things were to change with unification in 1991. As former GDR companies underwent restructuring, redundant workers were given access to early retirement and labour market programmes which again had the objective of limiting open unemployment. Spending on ALMPs peaked in 1992 at 1.8% of GDP. At that time, however, the lion's share of active spending went to job creation programmes (Manow and Seils, 2000: 293; Clasen, 2005: 61–62). The move was effective in reducing open unemployment. It was not, however, able to prevent a massive surge in the unemployment rate following the recession of the 1990s.

Other countries, which did not develop extensive ALMPs before the crisis, were somewhat slower in introducing active elements in their unemployment policy afterwards. In France, tensions between the government and the trade unions arguably delayed the adoption of such measures (Clegg, 2005). However, starting from the mid-1980s, French active labour market policy is a rapid succession of different tools targeted sometimes to different groups. In general, their objective is 'occupation', that is, providing an occupation to jobless people rather than labour market re-entry. Typically, much emphasis is put on the notion of 'social insertion' or the possibility to participate in society without being in paid employment (Dufour et al., 2003; Barbier and Fargion, 2004). In practical terms, these measures consist of subsidised temporary jobs in the public or in the non-profit-making private sector.

The development of French ALMP started in 1984 with the adoption of the TUC (*Travaux d'utilité publique* – public utility works) for jobless youth by the Socialist government. These were soon complemented in 1986 with the PIL (*Programmes d'insertion locale*) targeted on the long-term unemployed and introduced by a Gaullist government. By 1989, these were replaced by CES (*Contrats emploi-solidarité*). In 1988 a general means-tested benefit was introduced (RMI, *Revenu minimum d'insertion*), which theoretically included an activation component in the shape of an insertion contract signed between the beneficiary and the authorities. In fact, as extensive evaluation of this programme showed, its ability to move beneficiaries into the labour market was extremely limited (Palier, 2002: 302–3). The French approach to labour market policy is characterised by a strong emphasis on occupation, accompanied by a strong rhetoric of social inclusion, or 'insertion'. This trajectory was confirmed by the Socialist government of the late 1990s (1997–2002). Beside the well-known law reducing weekly working hours to 35, the government introduced new job creation programmes, aimed at young people, subsidising jobs in non-commercial sectors for up to five years (Clegg, 2005: 222).

During the post-crisis years and well into the 1980s and early 1990s, occupation is an important function of ALMPs. Training continues to play a key role, as shown by the spending profiles presented in Figure 7.1. However, in such an unfavourable labour market context, training programmes can de facto become more akin to occupation than to effective human capital investment. The evaluation literature suggests that this might have been the case throughout most of the 1980s and early 1990s. This is a result reached in one of the first meta-analyses of evaluation studies of ALMPs, where two OECD economists conclude that many labour market programmes are ineffective or even counterproductive in terms of their ability to bring jobless people back to the labour market (Martin and Grubb, 2001). This may be the result of the predominant orientation of ALMPs (occupation) in the time-span covered by the study (1980s and early 1990s).

ALMPs since the mid-1990s: the 'activation turn'

The mid-1990s signal a new reorientation of ALMP in OECD countries. The economic context has changed. First, after the mid-1990s labour market conditions in most OECD countries begin to improve. Second, unemployment is essentially the result of an excess supply of low-skilled labour, and low-skilled workers may find it difficult to earn more from work than what their benefits are worth. The result is the development of a new role of ALMPs, which emphasises stronger work incentives and employment assistance. This reorientation is signalled also by a change in the language used and the increasing reference to the term 'activation'. OECD countries clearly move in this direction, but in a perhaps surprising order. The pioneers of this new phase are clearly not those who initiated ALMP in previous periods. Arguably, the pre-existence of active policies with a different objective slows down the development of activation.

Among the first to embrace the new activation paradigm in employment policy is Denmark, a country which up to then had done relatively little in the field of ALMPs (see Figure 7.1). The Social Democratic government elected in 1993 adopted a series of reforms that transformed the Danish system of unemployment compensation. The 1994 reform removed the possibility of regaining entitlement to unemployment insurance through participation in labour market programmes. It also set a seven-year limit to unemployment benefit. This period was subdivided in two phases: first a passive period of four years and then an active period of three years. Work availability requirements were also strengthened and individual action plans were introduced (Madsen, 2002; Kvist et al., 2008: 243). In addition, the reform also introduced the decentralisation of employment services, making it possible for labour offices at the regional level to develop labour market programmes suitable for their area.

The reform was based on the recommendations made by a tripartite outfit known as the Zeuthen committee, consisting mostly of representatives of both the trade unions and employer organisations. The social partners obtained important concessions, such as an important role in the implementation of labour market measures. At the same time, however, they agreed to reorient unemployment policy in the direction of activation (Kvist et al., 2008: 245). This important reform is seen as a major step towards the introduction of 'flexicurity', a new and influential model of labour market regulation. The Danish variant of flexicurity is based on a flexible labour market with regard to the rules concerning hiring and firing, generous benefits for those who are unemployed, and strong pressures and help for re-entering the labour market through a highly developed activation system (cf. Chapter Nine).

Subsequent reforms further strengthened work incentives and employment assistance elements. The duration of the entitlement period was reduced first to five years (1996), then to four years (1998). The 'passive' period was also shortened to two years and to six months for unemployed people younger than 25. After this period, claimants had both a right and an obligation to a labour market programme.

The year 1998 signalled a further acceleration of the trend towards activation. First policy for unemployed youth took a strong step towards strengthening work incentives and investment in human capital. Measures adopted included a six-month limit on standard unemployment benefit for the under 25s and the obligation to participate in training for 18 months, with a benefit equal to 50% of the standard unemployment benefit. Second, with the adoption of a 'law on active social policy', the principle of activation was extended to social assistance claimants (Kvist et al., 2008: 241–43). Like in past reform, together with incentive-strengthening measures, more inclusive instruments are also adopted. This is the case of a programme known as flexjobs, which subsidises up to two-thirds of labour costs for disabled people, without time limits (Hogelund, 2003).

Other countries followed the Danish lead in reorienting their unemployment compensation systems towards activation. Under Conservative rule, the UK had developed an approach clearly based on incentive reinforcement, with a series of reductions in unemployment benefit (Atkinson and Micklewright, 1989; King, 1995). A more significant step in the direction of activation is taken by the New Labour government elected in 1996, on the basis of a centrist orientation in social and economic policy which became known as the Third Way. Concretely, a whole range of programmes targeted on various groups of non-employed persons were developed since the mid-1990s. These consist mostly of employment assistance. They are coupled with incentive reinforcement, for instance with the introduction of a tax credit programme in 1998 (Clasen, 2005; Clegg, 2005). This orientation was further pursued in subsequent years, and is visible in the spending profile of the UK's ALMPs, which especially in 2005 put by far most of the emphasis on employment assistance.

Sweden was somewhat slower to reorient its ALMPs towards activation, but since the late 1990s labour market policy places considerably more emphasis on incentive reinforcement and employment assistance than in the past. Work requirements have been strengthened so that those who are still jobless after 100 days of unemployment may be required to accept a job anywhere in the country and a wage up to 10% lower than the unemployment benefit (Clasen et al., 2001: 211). The unemployment insurance reform of 2001 further strengthened the pro-employment orientation of active labour market policy. This was done through a number of measures. First, the possibility to renew entitlement to unemployment insurance through participation in labour market programmes was abolished. Second, the reform introduced an 'activity guarantee' for long-term unemployed people or people at risk of becoming long-term unemployed. This consists of more individualised activities clearly geared towards re-employment (Swedish Government, 2002; Timonen, 2004).

Germany is another latecomer to the activation paradigm, even though since the mid-1990s policy has clearly adopted this overall orientation (Clasen, 2005). One important step in this direction was the adoption of the so-called Job Aqtiv Act in 2001. The reform included several of the measures that one finds in the standard activation toolbox: stricter monitoring of job search, the profiling of jobless people, reintegration contracts and wage subsidies (Clasen, 2005: 72).

These changes, however, were not regarded as going far enough by the Schroeder government. In fact, only a few months after the adoption of the Job Aqtiv Act, a new commission was set up and given the task of making proposals for the modernisation of labour market policy. The commission was headed by Peter Hartz, a former manager at Volkswagen. Its proposals included several measures, ranging from support to unemployed people who want to set up their own business, to the creation of a 'personal service agency', a temporary placement service for unemployed people. However, the most visible and controversial proposal was the merger of long-term unemployment benefit and social assistance (the so-called Hartz IV reform), which resulted in benefit reductions for many recipients (Fleckenstein, 2008).

The activation paradigm, combining the incentive reinforcement and employment assistance, has clearly gained influence over the years. Combined with an expanding economy until 2008, it has also produced more encouraging results than in previous years, so that more recent meta-evaluations of the microlevel effects of ALMPs provide a more optimistic picture of the potential of ALMPs (OECD, 2006; Eichhorst et al., 2008). Their macrolevel impact is more uncertain, though it may be the case that an emphasis on activation reduces the negative impact of job protection regulations on the long-term unemployed (Pontusson, 2005). But activation has not reached every corner of Europe. Italy, for instance, is clearly lagging behind in this respect (Samek Lodovici and Semenza, 2008), France may have started moving in this direction in the late 2000s, with the merger of employment services and benefit agencies, and the transformation of RMI into RSA (*Revenu de solidarité active*), effective since 1 June 2009.

Conclusion

It is clear from the evidence presented in this chapter, based both on country expenditure profiles and on narrative accounts of policy developments, that the notion of active labour market policy can encompass very different policies, with respect to their objectives, the tools they use and the way they interact with passive unemployment compensation systems. This results in a fundamental ambiguity which may actually be partly responsible for the success experienced by this policy idea over the last 20 years or so, since ambiguous concepts can act as focal points of political agreement (Palier, 2005). However, lack of clarity makes it difficult to use the notion of ALMP as an analytical tool. This observation calls for a more fine-grained distinction between different types of active labour market policy, according to objectives pursued and tools used.

The empirical part of this chapter has shown that the orientation of ALMP has evolved over time, in a way that reflects changing economic circumstances, to some extent regardless of welfare regime. The three periods identified above are characterised above all by very different economic and labour market conditions. The first period, the 1950s and 1960s, is a time of rapid economic growth and labour shortage. Under these circumstances, at least four out of the six countries covered developed an ALMP system geared towards upskilling the labour force, so as to provide adequately trained workers to expanding industries. Steps in this direction were taken by Sweden, Germany, Italy and France, though only Sweden succeeded in developing a fully fledged re-training system.

In the second period (mid-1970s to mid-1990s) sluggish growth and industrial restructuring dominate the economic context. ALMPs turn into an alternative to market employment, and provide mostly occupation to jobless people. During this period, even programmes labelled as training tend to fulfil this function rather than genuine upskilling, as shown by the evaluation literature. Here, too, welfare regimes do not seem to matter much. Instead, the existence of a tradition in ALMPs plays an important role. The turn towards occupation concerns above all countries that had developed ALMPs during the previous period (Sweden, Germany and France), belonging to different welfare regimes.

Finally, in the third phase (mid-1990s to late 2000s), better economic and labour market conditions push countries towards activation. This is also a development that spans across regimes: in fact, all the countries covered (except Italy) turn to the activation paradigm in labour market policy, putting emphasis on employment assistance and on the reinforcement of work incentives.

Rather paradoxically, the laggards of the second phase become the leaders in the third one. The first countries turning to activation are Denmark and the UK, with high-profile reforms adopted in 1994 and 1996–97 respectively. Other countries follow suit, but at a slower pace. In Sweden, the 2001 reform can be seen as a milestone in this process. For Germany, one could identify the 2004 Hartz IV reform as the tipping point. Quite clearly, countries without an extensive system of ALMPs in place in the early 1990s have an advantage when it comes to re-orienting policy towards the objective of re-entry into market employment. Using ALMPs as an alternative to market employment created expectations among actual and potential beneficiaries, for example in terms of the ability to renew the entitlement to unemployment insurance. These practices, which are incompatible with the activation paradigm, are difficult to abandon.

This brief account of the development of ALMPs over more than half a century suggests that the social investment orientation of policy is not a recent phenomenon. On the contrary the notion that labour market policy should increase the re-employment chances of jobless people by investing in their human capital was probably stronger in the 1950s and 1960s than today, at least in those countries that intervened in this field (most notably Sweden).

This type of intervention was justified by the simultaneous presence of labour shortage in the expanding industries and unemployment in the declining ones or in some regions (like in southern Italy). This situation is in fact not so different from the one that prevails today in most of Europe. Shortage of skilled labour, which will be exacerbated by the process of population ageing, combines with high rates of unemployment among unskilled people. However, rather than turning to upskilling, governments seem more inclined to adopt measures that facilitate and promote labour market entry in low-skilled jobs. A number of explanations can be given for this puzzle. First, upskilling is a costly exercise and the current overall context of permanent austerity makes it more difficult to finance extensive vocational training than in the high growth decades of the 1950s and 1960s. Second, it may be the case that the distance in terms of skills between today's unemployed and the employers' requirement in the high-skill sectors is simply too big to be bridged by continuing education or training courses. It was arguably easier to re-train Swedish forest workers to work in the expanding manufacturing sectors than current unskilled service workforce to staff health and social services or other expanding high value-added sectors.

Yet the reluctance of European countries to embark on a major re-training for the low-skilled offensive seems a real obstacle to the deployment of the social investment strategy. The imbalance between supply and demand in the low-skilled segment of the labour market is such that standard compensatory measures (tax credits, family benefits) alone are unlikely to prevent poverty, child poverty and the transmission of disadvantage across generations: precisely the evils that social investment advocates want to get rid of.

References

Alber, J. (1987) 'Germany', in P. Flora (ed.) *Growth to Limits: the Western European Welfare States since World War II*. Florence, European University Institute, pp. 4–149.

Anxo, D. and Niklasson, H. (2006) 'The Swedish model in turbulent times: Decline or renaissance?', *International Labour Review*, 145 (4), 339–75.

Atkinson, A.B. and Micklewright, J. (1989) 'Turning the screw: Benefits for the unemployed 1979–88', in A. Dilnot and I. Walker (eds) *The Economics of Social Security*. Oxford: Oxford University Press.

Barbier, J.-C. (2001) *Welfare to Work Policies in Europe. The Current Challenges of Activation Policies*. Paris: Centre d'études de l'emploi.

Barbier, J.-C. (2004) 'Systems of social protection in Europe: Two contrasted paths to activation, and maybe a third', in J. Lind, H. Knudsen and H. Jørgensen (eds) *Labour and Employment Regulation in Europe*. Brussels: Peter Lang, pp. 233–53.

Barbier, J.C. and Fargion, V. (2004) 'Continental inconsistencies on the path to activation – Consequences for social citizenship in Italy and France', *European Societies*, 6 (4), 437–60.

Barbier, J.-C. and Ludwig-Mayerhofer, W. (2004) 'Introduction: The many worlds of activation', *European Societies*, 6 (4), 424–36.

Benner, M. and Vad, T. (2000) 'Sweden and Denmark: defending the welfare state', in F.W. Scharpf and V. Schmidt (eds) *Welfare and Work in the Open Economy*. Oxford: Oxford University Press, pp. 399–466.

Bonoli, G. and Palier, B. (1997) 'Reclaiming welfare: The politics of French social protection reform', in M. Rhodes (ed.) *Southern European Welfare States. Between Crisis and Reform*. London, Portland: Frank Cass.

Calmfors, L., Forslund, A. and Hemström, M. (2001) 'Does active labour market policy work? Lessons from the Swedish experiences', *Swedish Economic Policy Review*, 85, 61–124.

Clasen, J. (2000) 'Motives, means and opportunities: Reforming unemployment compensation in the 1990s', *West European Politics*, 23 (2), 89–112.

Clasen, J. (2005) *Reforming European Welfare States. Germany and the United Kingdom Compared*. Oxford: Oxford University Press.

Clasen, J., Duncan, G., Eardley, T., Evans, M., Ughetto, P., van Oorschot, W. and Wright, S. (2001) 'Towards "single gateways"? – A cross-national review of the changing roles of employment offices in seven countries', *Zeitschrift für Ausländisches und Internationales Arbeits- und Sozialrecht*, 15 (1), 43–63.

Clegg, D. (2005) 'Activating the multi-tiered welfare state: social governance, welfare politics and unemployment policies in France and the United Kingdom', PhD dissertation, Florence: European University Institute.

Dufour, P., Boisménu, G. and Noël, A. (2003) *L'Aide au Conditionnel. La Contreparties dans les Mesures Envers les Personnes sans Emploi en Europe et en Amérique du Nord*. Montreal: Presses de l'Université de Montreal.

Eichhorst, W., Kaufmann, O. and Konle-Seidl, R. (eds) (2008) *Bringing the Jobless into Work? Experiences with Activation in Europe and the US*. Berlin: Springer.

Emmenegger, P. (2009) *Regulatory Social Policy: The Politics of Job Security Regulations*. Bern: Haupt Verlag.

Fleckenstein, T. (2008) 'Restructuring welfare for the unemployed. The case of Hartz legislation in Germany', *Journal of European Social Policy*, 18 (2), 177–88.

Frerich, J. and Frey, M. (1996) *Handbuch der Geschichte der Sozialpolitik in Deutschland. Sozialpolitik in der Bundesrepublik Deutschland bis zur Herstellung der Deutschen Einheit*. Munich: Oldenburg Verlag.

Gualmini, E. (1998) *La Politica del Lavoro*. Bologna: Il Mulino.

Hasselpflug, S. (2005) 'Availability criteria in 25 countries', Working Paper No. 12. Copenhagen: Ministry of Finance.

Hogelund, J. (2003) *In Search of the Effective Disability Policy*. Amsterdam: Amsterdam University Press.

King, D. (1995) *Actively Seeking Work? The Politics of Unemployment and Welfare Policy in the United States and Great Britain*. Chicago: University of Chicago Press.

Kluve, J. (2006) 'The effectiveness of European active labour market policy'. Bonn, IZA Discussion paper 2018.

Kvist, J., Pedersen, L. et al. (2008) 'Making all persons work: modern Danish labour market policies', in W. Eichhorst, O. Kaufmann and R. Konle-Seidl (eds) *Bringing the Jobless into Work? Experiences with Activation in Europe and the US*. Berlin: Springer, pp. 221–55.

Mabbet, D. (1995) *Trade, Employment and Welfare. A Comparative Study of Trade and Labour Market Policies in Sweden and New Zealand, 1880–1980*. Oxford: Clarendon Press.

Madsen, P. (2002) 'The Danish model of flexicurity: a paradise with some snakes', in H. Sarfati and G. Bonoli (eds) *Labour Market and Social Protection Reforms in International Perspective*. Aldershot: Ashgate, pp. 243–65.

Manow, P. and Seils, E. (2000) 'Germany: Adjusting badly', in F.W. Scharpf and V. A. Schmid (eds) *Welfare and Work in the Open Economy*. Oxford: Oxford University Press, pp. 265–307.

Martin, J. and Grubb, D. (2001) 'What works and for whom: A review of OECD countries' experiences with active labour market policies', *Swedish Economic Policy Review*, 8, 9–56.

Mjoset, L. (1987) 'Nordic economic policies in the 1970s and 1980s', *International Organization*, 41 (3), 403–56.

OECD (2006) 'General policies to improve employment opportunities for all', *Employment Outlook*, 2006, 47–126.

Palier, B. (2002) *Gouverner la Sécurité Sociale. Les Réformes du Système Français de Protection Sociale Depuis 1945*. Paris: Presses Universitaires de France.

Palier, B. (2005) 'Ambiguous agreement, cumulative change: French social policy in the 1990s', in W. Streeck and K. Thelen (eds) *Beyond Continuity. Institutional Change in Advanced Political Economies*. Oxford: Oxford University Press, pp. 127–44.

Peck, J. (2001) *Workfare States*. New York: Guildford Press.

Pontusson, J. (2005) *Inequality and Prosperity. Social Europe vs. Liberal America*. Ithaca: Cornell University Press.

Samek Lodovici, M. and Semenza, R. (2008) 'The Italian case: From employment regulation to welfare reforms?', *Social Policy and Administration*, 42 (2), 160–76.

Seeleib-Kaiser, M., Van Dyk, S. and Roggenkamp, M. (2008) *Party Politics and Social Welfare. Comparing Christian and Social Democracy in Austria, Germany and the Netherlands*. Cheltenham: Edward Elgar.

Swedish Government (2002) *Sweden's Action Plan for Employment*. Stockholm: Swedish Government Offices.

Swenson, P.A. (2002) *Capitalists Against Markets: The Making of Labor Markets and Welfare States in the United States and Sweden*. Oxford: Oxford University Press.

Taylor-Gooby, P. (2004) 'New risks and social change', in P. Taylor-Gooby (ed.) *New Risks, New Welfare?* Oxford: Oxford University Press.

Thelen, K. (2004) *How Institutions Evolve: The Political Economy of Skills in Germany, Britain, the United States and Japan*. Cambridge: Cambridge University Press.

Timonen, V. (2004) 'New risks – are they still new for the Nordic welfare states?', in P. Taylor-Gooby (ed.) *New Risks, New Welfare*. Oxford: Oxford University Press.

Torfing, J. (1999) 'Workfare with welfare: Recent reforms of the Danish welfare state', *Journal of European Social Policy*, 9 (1), 5–28.

EIGHT

Do social investment policies produce more and better jobs?

Moira Nelson and John D. Stephens

Introduction

The argument for the social investment strategy depends on the ability of the strategy to produce employment and particularly employment in high-quality jobs, jobs that are attractive in terms of remuneration and in terms of quality of work. It is really that latter ambition that distinguishes the promise of the social investment strategy from a neoliberal strategy which creates employment by increasing wage dispersion and creating a large number of low-paid private service jobs in sectors such as hotels, restaurants and personal services, which has been the US path to high employment (Esping-Andersen, 1999).

Our analysis is an evaluation of whether this strategy has delivered on these aforementioned promises. First, in a pooled time series analysis of data on 17 OECD countries from 1972 to 1999, we examine the effect of various policies we identify as related to the social investment paradigm on employment levels, both for the economy as a whole and for a subset of knowledge-intensive industries. We consider employment in knowledge-intensive services to be a good measure of the level of quality employment. We find that short-term unemployment replacement rates, active labour market policy, day care spending, sick pay, education spending and educational attainment are very strongly related to employment levels, and that all of these policies with the exception of sick pay are very strongly related to employment levels in knowledge-intensive services.

Second, in a cross-sectional analysis we examine whether social investment is associated with high levels of discretionary learning employment, arguably the best available measure of quality employment (see Chapter Nine). For this analysis we bring literacy into the equation to understand the relationship between social investment policies, skill acquisition and employment. It is, in fact, the accumulation of human capital which links social investment policies to employment outcomes. Establishing a relationship between these three factors is therefore critical to sustaining the validity of the theoretical arguments put forth thus far. Because our key variable is only available cross-sectionally, our analysis is necessarily tentative, but we do find strong evidence affirming a positive relationship between social investment policies, human capital and quality employment. In short, the results provide substantial evidence that the policies associated with the social investment perspective lead to the expansion of employment, particularly employment in quality jobs.

The rest of the chapter proceeds as follows. First, we define the research question and justify the inclusion of the independent variables in the literature review. The measurement of the variables and the analytic techniques are then reviewed. From there, the next section displays the results of the first analysis on employment levels, both in the aggregate and for a subset of knowledge-intensive industries, and the next section develops these results further by examining variation in skill levels. The final section concludes.

What we know about social investment outcomes

Analysing the effect of social investment policies on employment outcomes calls for a clarification of the social investment perspective as well as an elaboration of how various policies associated with this perspective should improve employment levels. To begin, the social investment perspective embodies the view that public policies should 'prepare' individuals, families and societies to adapt to various transformations, such as the development of new social risks (Armingeon and Bonoli, 2006), population ageing and climate change, instead of simply generating responses to 'repair' damages after existing policies prove inadequate (see Chapters One, Two, Three and Fourteen). By addressing problems in their infancy, the social investment perspective stands to reduce human suffering, environmental degradation and government debt. The practical pursuit of this perspective calls for a new social citizenship regime (see Chapter Three), which empowers an interventionist state along with a vibrant civil society to anticipate and then address issues of relevance for the future wellbeing of individuals and society.

This chapter addresses a particular line of argumentation within the social investment perspective which relates human capital investment to the expansion of good jobs. The ways in which public policies address new types of social risks are indisputably vast and we choose to limit the scope of our analysis to include only those measures that improve human capital. Facilitating the acquisition of skills addresses the production needs of various industries, develops the ability to learn and rapidly adjusts to changing conditions (Nelson, 2010; see also Chapter Nine in this volume), and creates active, forward-thinking participants for the associated social citizenship regime. Well-educated citizens (and denizens) therefore advance the social investment agenda in numerous ways. In the present analysis, we narrow our focus a second time to concentrate solely on how human capital policies address skill needs in today's knowledge economy. In doing so, we prioritise the direct labour market value of education and training.

Achieving high employment by promoting skill acquisition speaks to the social investment perspective 'to prepare rather than repair' in numerous ways. On an individual level, enabling individuals to participate in the labour market addresses the growing need to rely on market income to maintain a given standard of living, as family and state-based support become either less available or less sustainable. In this way, policies that promote labour market participation stem the rise of unemployment, precarious employment and poverty, which increase when individuals lack the necessary skills to be integrated successfully in the labour market. For society more broadly, improving the connection of individuals to the labour market increases national income, reduces long-term reliance on social benefits and therein budgetary pressure, and encourages new forms of business investment. Therefore, both individually and on more aggregate levels, promoting high-quality employment holds many advantages.

In light of the benefits to high employment, the precise types of policies which encourage human capital investments deserve attention. Of course, education and training policies constitute the most obvious method of improving skills relevant to the service-based, knowledge economy, particularly cognitive and social skills. Other types of public policies, though, such as sick pay, can also protect the value of individuals' skills. Since skills diminish if not used (a phenomenon economists refer to as skill atrophy (Pissarides, 1992)), policies that minimise periods of absence from the labour market uphold the value of workers' skills over time. Human capital policies that expand high-quality jobs therefore include those that aid in the acquisition of skills as well as protect the value of skills already acquired.

The theoretical arguments about the need to acquire and protect skill investments embody ideas about the centrality of skills to employment growth and the value of government intervention that are in part unique to the social investment perspective. As a case in point, the capacity to address unemployment through supply-side measures remains a topic of considerable debate; and the proposal for more government intervention flies in the face of the neoliberal orthodoxy that assumes that markets always function efficiently. In this way, in proposing a new paradigm for promoting economic growth in a socially just way, the social investment perspective challenges existing beliefs about why unemployment persists and what should be done to address it (see Chapters One and Two). In the space below, we develop hypotheses about how various policies invest in human capital and thereby enable individuals to succeed in the knowledge economy. We finish this section by explaining how these hypotheses challenge the neoliberal orthodoxy and by addressing possible scope limitations.

Education and labour market policies conducive to social investment

Skill acquisition in formal institutions begins in early childhood education and care (ECEC) and continues in the primary, secondary and tertiary stages of education. Skill acquisition during these stages of education is realised through policies which promote high enrolment and quality instruction. The state of the economy arguably plays the largest role in how many students participate in educational courses, with industrialisation coupled with nation building constituting the largest force behind compulsory education reforms and the growth of the knowledge economy provoking policies that encourage lifelong learning.

Participation in a course of education, however, does not directly translate into high achievement, and the precise policies which promote achievement remains a topic of considerable debate. In light of these debates, a brief discussion of the limitations of our education policy measures is in order. The literature proposes three critiques to measuring education policy as public spending as a percentage of GDP. First, spending effort alone does not provide any information about how spending is allocated and then translated into learning outcomes in the classroom. Second, this measure does not reveal how much is spent per student. UNESCO offers such a measure but unfortunately it is only available quite recently. Third, GDP as a denominator could pose problems since expansion or contraction of the economy influences the indicator even if spending effort over education has not changed at all. These limitations suggest caution in presuming a straightforward relationship between government spending and the accumulation of human capital.

To make a case that these four stages of education indeed lead to the acquisition of skills demanded in the labour market and the resulting expansion of jobs, and good jobs in particular, we discuss each stage of education in turn, focusing on how patterns of enrolment have changed over time and then working to build a case that each type of education delivers skills demanded in today's economy. Then the relationship between human capital accumulation and employment growth is considered. We also address these aforementioned concerns in the analytical section which analyses the relationship between spending, skill levels and employment.

To begin, ECEC has as much to do with promoting mothers' employment as it does with improving the cognitive and social skills of young children (see Chapter Six). With the large-scale movement of women into the labour market and the observation that policies which reconcile work and family help sustain fertility rates and thereby population replacement, public policies have been expanded which offer alternatives to parental care. ECEC therefore invests in mothers' skills by allowing them to return to work and thereby avoid skill atrophy. With the growth of the knowledge economy, ECEC has also received attention for delivering cognitive skills important for coping with an ever-changing, knowledge-intensive labour market, and numerous studies confirm a significant impact of attendance on cognitive development (Broberg et al., 1997; Campbell et al., 2001; Waldfogel, 2002; Brooks-Gunn, 2003; Magnuson et al., 2007; Burger, 2010). Finally, there does appear to be a correlation between average cost of ECEC and enrolment levels cross-nationally (OECD Family Database).

Whereas ECEC is often voluntary, school attendance is compulsory for about ten years between the ages of roughly six and 16 across advanced industrialised countries and students are encouraged to complete upper secondary school, which typically requires an additional two years. By the end of the nineteenth century, most advanced industrialised countries had implemented compulsory education laws, the length of which was extended throughout the twentieth century. Between 1935 and 1940, primary school enrolment ranged from 28.6% in Portugal to 100% in Canada with the rest of the liberal welfare states lying close to Canada and most continental and Nordic welfare states with about 70% enrolment (Benavot and Riddle, 1988). By the end of the century, enrolment had risen to incorporate almost all school-age children for the duration of primary and secondary education across advanced industrialised countries.

The content of compulsory education has changed over time as well. Up until about 1850, reading, writing and arithmetic made up most of the curriculum (Cha, 1992: 64). Since then, new subjects were introduced, such as social studies, science, art and physical education (ibid), in line with scientific and political developments. As of about 1950, technological change motivated fundamental curricula adjustments to incorporate new technologies into new types of courses or existing teaching methods (Rasinen, 2003; Tondeur et al., 2007). Much research has also focused on pedagogical techniques and the way in which teachers can encourage creative thinking, a facility found to play a more central role in adapting to a more changeable labour market (Hargreaves, 2003). The multifaceted aims of education systems and the particular way in which they reflect economic and social development can be seen in a UNESCO study which assessed national education reports for 161 countries across the world (Benavot and Brasavsky, 2006). Based on a set of educational aims drawn from the literature, the researchers coded the presence (coded as 1) or absence (coded as 0) of these aims in national educational reports. For the period since 2000, the study finds that 48% of country reports emphasised employability, 34% technological and scientific knowledge, 27% lifelong learning, and 22% creative development. For comparison, the highest scoring aim was personal and emotional development at 73%, followed by the norm of equality at 63% and national identity at 55%. Education policy today therefore tends to look beyond basic reading, writing and numeracy skills to address skills made more relevant by the growth of the knowledge, or learning, economy.

In a similar way, tertiary education has become more important over time as a source of advanced theoretical knowledge. The popular press talks about a massification of higher education due to reduced barriers to participation and resulting elevated enrolment rates. The World Bank also writes that:

> Tertiary education institutions support knowledge-driven economic growth strategies and poverty reduction by (a) training a qualified and adaptable labour force; (b) generating new knowledge; and (c) building the capacity to access existing stores of global knowledge and to adapt that knowledge to local use. Tertiary education institutions are unique in their ability to integrate and create synergy among these three dimensions. (World Bank, 2002: 4)

Once attended by only a handful of the elite, the university now educates between a third (particularly in countries with a strong apprenticeship system) to above 90% (Canada) of each cohort. St George observes that: 'Science, technology and innovation, the cornerstones of the knowledge based economy, are now clearly on the agenda of both developed and developing countries, as fundamental to achieving sustainable development across the globe' (St George, 2006: 607–8).

Having reviewed policies which primarily facilitate skill acquisition, the focus turns now to policies that protect the human capital of working adults, including active labour market policies, unemployment insurance and sick pay. Active labour market policies protect the employability of marginalised workers through either training or placement in employment positions. In doing so, these policies reduce the risk of skill atrophy and protect the value of workers' existing human capital. It should be noted, however, that training measures also supplement participants' skill set and therefore play a role in skill acquisition as well. The particular profile of active labour market policies pursued by governments has changed over time depending on the state of the economy (see Chapter Seven). Evidence exists that spending on these policies increases employment levels (Kenworthy, 2003; Bradley and Stephens, 2007).

Short-term unemployment replacement rates are also expected to protect the value of workers' human capital by facilitating the search for a job appropriate to the worker's skill set. The limited generosity of these policies over time, however, ensures that recipients feel sufficient financial pressure to re-enter the labour market. In this way, high replacement rates with short duration are strongly employment-friendly. High replacement rates may serve more to reward a worker for his/her skill investment while out of work than to create a reservation wage that prevents the worker from seeking re-employment, and they may allow workers with industry-specific skills to conduct longer and more costly job searches in order to find employment in which their skill set is fully utilised. The importance of social insurance for investment in especially asset-specific high skills is the central theme in Iversen (2005) and Estevz-Abe et al. (2001). High replacement rates also serve as a disincentive for workers to leave the workforce altogether.

In a similar way, sick pay helps individuals who leave the labour market temporarily due to illness to retain the means to re-enter the labour market. Rather than relying on savings during this period of absence and due also in part to other legislation regarding sick leave, individuals receive the financial means to recover completely and therefore return to the same position after their illness has subsided.

For this reason, generous sickness insurance helps to reduce the effect of health risks on deteriorating the value of workers' human capital. Bradley and Stephens (2007) show that short-term unemployment replacement rates and generous sick pay provisions are positively related to employment levels.

Hypotheses

The hypotheses for the social investment variables on employment are derived in a straightforward manner from the literature review. We expect spending on total education, educational attainment, short-term unemployment replacement rates, day care and active labour market policies to be related to higher levels of employment either through increased participation in education or improved quality of instruction if not both. All of these policies invest in or protect the human capital of (future) workers and therefore improve their chances of finding jobs in the labour market.

Countries with strong social investment policies, moreover, should develop a comparative advantage in knowledge-intensive services.[1] Since jobs in such industries involve higher levels of workplace autonomy (Deetz, 1994; Robertson et al., 2003) and relatively high wages, we consider these to be high-quality jobs. We therefore expect that social investment policies, beyond leading to higher employment rates, support the expansion of good jobs.

Critics of this theoretical argument question the effectiveness of creating jobs through high public spending, condemning this approach as wasteful overeducation. Intervention in the economy more generally is seen as inhibiting business investment when the costs of financing social policy fall on employers.

In justifying the various social investment policies included in the analysis, we have already provided theoretical reasons why policies which promote skill acquisition and protect existing investment are relevant to the accumulation of skills necessary to succeed in the knowledge economy. In order to respond to the criticisms raised above, we review briefly the reasons why the expansion of social investment policies indeed leads to superior employment outcomes as compared to deregulation, the core job-growth strategy of the neoliberal agenda (on this agenda, see Chapter Two and the analysis of the OECD jobs study). Three rejoinders to the neoliberal view are in order. First, contrary to the classical economics perspective, markets do not always allocate resources in a profit-maximising way. Socioeconomic actors may face substantial informational or costs restrictions in participating in what would otherwise be productive economic exchanges. Second, even where markets function well, collective action problems may obstruct the creation of good policy if participation in the policy cannot be guaranteed and defection is likely. As a case in point, since education is a public good, the benefits of which cannot be internalised, markets are destined to undersupply education policies (Evans, 2008) and therefore care needs to be used in judging existing levels of attendance and spending in educational institutions as an optimal equilibrium. Finally, employment growth today occurs either in high-skill or low-skill jobs. Difficulties of employers to find high-skilled workers demonstrates the extent to which demand for higher levels of skills remains high and therein the benefits to investing in social investment policies. For instance, the inability of many Western European companies to find software programmers has led them to search intensively in Eastern Europe. The market for these skills is so competitive that wages have largely equalised across the European Union. For these reasons, public policies that promote the accumulation of human capital stand to improve employment levels.

At the same time, there may be limits to the extent to which social investment policies can increase job growth and it is important to acknowledge the scope limitations of our theoretical framework and the political challenges inherent in changing national education systems. Although our approach proposes a supply-side solution to create jobs, attention needs to be given that educational courses address skills demanded in growth industries. In this way, the ability to expand employment through education relies on timely adjustments in educational courses to reflect growth areas (for example, green-collar jobs). Moreover, we are not suggesting that unrestrained upskilling is the answer. There are certainly jobs for which a lower level of education is more than sufficient. However, many individuals continue to fall below minimum literacy standards. To the extent that a significant proportion of youth continue to lack the necessary skills to obtain even a low-level employment position, investment in social investment strategies is too weak and there remains room for improvement.

Data, measurement and analytic techniques

The first analysis of the determinants of employment levels includes 17 advanced industrialised countries from 1972 to 1999. The countries in this analysis include Australia, Austria, Belgium, Canada, Denmark, Finland, France, Germany, Ireland, Italy, Japan, Netherlands, Norway, Sweden, Switzerland, the UK and the USA. For the analysis of knowledge intensive services (KIS), there are no data for Canada, Norway and Switzerland. In the second analysis of skills, data availability from the International Adult Literacy Survey (hereafter IALS)[2] leads us to drop the cases of Austria, France and Japan. However, since data from the IALS are only available cross-sectionally for the mid-1990s, we are able to include countries for which we lack time series data, including New Zealand, the Czech Republic, Hungary, Poland, Portugal and Slovenia. The measurement of the variables and the data sources are listed in Table 8.1. Details on the measurement and sources are listed in the appendix to this chapter. The analytic technique used in the pooled analysis is Prais Winsten regressions, that is, panel corrected standard errors and first-order autoregressive corrections. In Huo et al. (2008), we explain why this is the most appropriate technique for these data.

The metrics of the independent variables and employment variables are different, so it is not possible to say anything about the effect of each of them absolutely or relative to each other. To this end, we calculate the effect of a two-standard deviation change in the human capital variables on the dependent variables holding the other variables in the analysis constant. As mentioned previously, we have missing data for the three spending variables: education, day care and active labour market policies. The missing values are different for each variable and cumulatively, if entered in the analysis together, they would cause us to lose 48% of our cases. Thus, initially, we enter these variables, along with sick pay generosity, and one year replacement rates one at a time in the analysis (models 1–3). We calculate the two-standard deviation change effect on the basis of these models.

Model 4 enters educational attainment, our human capital stock variable, in the analysis and drops the human capital investment variables. In the final model, we enter both attainment and the human capital investment variables in the analysis together. Theoretically, we would expect the investment variables to operate entirely through their effect on human capital stock and thus not to be significant in this equation, but given the deficiencies of our stock variable, average years of education, this might not be the case.

Table 8.2 lists the values of the social investment variables and the dependent variables by country and welfare state regime. Let us begin by examining the variation by regime type in our dependent variables in the last three columns. Employment levels are highest in the Nordic countries followed by the Anglo-American countries, continental European countries and Eastern Europe, with the southern European countries at the low end. KIS employment follows a different

Table 8.1: Variables used in data analysis

Pooled analysis		
Dependent variables		
Employment: percentage of working age (15–64) population employed		Huber et al. (2004)
KIS employment: percentage of working population employed in knowledge-intensive services		EU KLEMS (2009), GGDC (2006)
Human capital investment variables		
Active labour market policy spending as a percentage of GDP/unemployment, cumulative average		OECD (2007)
Public education spending as a percentage of GDP, cumulative average		OECD (2007)
Early childhood education and care, day care spending as a % of GDP, cumulative average		OECD, Jaumotte (2003)
Sick pay generosity		Scruggs (2205)
Educational attainment: average years of education of the populations 25 or more years old		Barro and Lee (2001)
Gross replacement rate, one year, for an unemployment spell of one year for 2/3 median pay		OECD
Controls		
Gross replacement rate, 4–5 year, for an unemployment spell of fourth and fifth year for 2/3 median pay		OECD
Social security payroll taxes as a percentage of GDP		Huber et al. (2004)
Total taxes as a percentage of GDP		Huber et al. (2004)
Degree of coordination of wage bargaining		Kenworthy (2001)
Union members as a percentage of wage and salary workers		Ebbinghaus and Visser (2000)
Capital market openness		Quinn and Inclan (1997)
Openness: Imports+exports as a percentage of GDP		Huber et al. (2004)
Cross-sectional analysis		
Skill acquisition index		Nelson (2008)
Literacy test scores: average for given percentile score of the adult population on the three parts (prose, quantitative, document) of the OECD/HRDC literacy test		OECD/HRDC (2000)
Discretionary learning employment		Valeyre et al. (2009)

Table 8.2: Measures of human capital investment, human capital stock, and employment circa 1995

	1 Public education spending cumulative average	2 Public education spending	3 Skill acquisition index	4 ALMP spending	5 Day care spending	6 1 year unemployment replacement rate	7 Sick pay generosity
Nordic countries							
Denmark	7.1	7.7	3.5	1.0	1.7	82	2.4
Finland	5.8	6.8	0.6	1.0	1.0	58	1.2
Norway	6.5	7.4	1.8	0.8	0.6	62	3.8
Sweden	7.5	7.2	1.5	2.1	1.8	90	3.1
Mean	6.7	7.3	1.8	1.3	1.3	73	2.6
Western continental Europe							
Austria	5.0	5.4		0.3	0.4	42	1.4
Belgium	5.5	5.2	0.3	1.2	0.1	55	2.0
France	5.3	6.6	0.2	0.9	0.4	69	0.3
Germany	4.6	4.6	−0.1	1.0	0.3	38	3.4
Netherlands	6.6	5.1	0.5	1.1	0.4	70	1.8
Switzerland	5.0	5.4	−0.0	0.3	0.1	70	1.1
Mean	5.3	5.4	0.1	0.9	0.3	57	1.7
Southern Europe							
Italy	4.3	4.9	0.0	0.3	0.1	15	0.3
Portugal		5.4	−0.2	0.4	0.0	65	0.7
Mean	4.3	5.2	−0.1	0.3	0.1	40	0.5
Eastern Europe							
Czech Republic		4.6	−0.5	0.2	0.1		
Poland		5.3	−0.0	0.3	0.5		
Hungary		5.3	−1.2	0.6	0.8		
Slovenia		6.0	0.4	0.0	0.7		
Mean		5.3	−0.3	0.3	0.5		
Anglo-American countries							
Australia	5.1	5.0	−0.9	0.4	0.1	32	−2.9
Canada	7.0	6.5	0.4	0.6	0.2	58	−2.4
Ireland	5.4	5.0	−0.6	1.1	0.1	38	−8.2
New Zealand	5.6	5.6	0.3	0.8	0.0	32	−4.4
UK	5.5	5.2	−0.3	0.6	0.0	26	−0.8
USA	6.2	4.7	−0.4	0.2	0.0	27	−8.3
Mean	5.8	5.3	−0.3	0.6	0.1	36	−4.5
Japan	3.6	0.5	0.2	0.3	0.2	32	−0.6

The data for discretionary learning are for 2005, the earliest for which data for the Eastern European countries are available.

8 Educational attainment	9 Score on OECD literacy test	10	11	12 Employment	13 KIS employment	14 Discretionary learning employment
	fifth percentile	Mean	95th percentile			
9.9	213	289	353	72.8	27.8	55.2
9.8	195	288	363	60.4	20.0	44.9
11.8	207	294	363	72.9		
11.2	216	304	386	72.2	28.5	67.5
10.7	208	294	366	69.6	25.4	55.9
7.6				68.8	17.2	47.3
8.6	163	277	359	55.2	20.3	43.3
7.7				57.6	21.9	47.7
9.6	208	285	359	64.8	18.7	44.3
9.0	202	286	355	64.7	24.2	51.6
10.2	150	271	349	79.8	24.2	
8.8	181	280	356	65.2	21.1	46.8
6.6	114	237	325	51.0	14.1	36.8
4.5	96	229	334	63.2	12.2	24.9
5.6	105	233	329	57.1	13.2	30.9
9.3	195	283	361	69.4	15.7	28.0
8.5	157	254	337	52.9	12.4	33.3
9.7	99	230	328	58.1	11.3	38.3
7.2	109	235	328	66.6	12.7	34.9
8.7	140	250	338	61.8	13.0	33.6
10.3	146	274	359	68.4	22.2	
11.2	145	280	372	67.3		
8.8	151	263	353	55.1	15.3	39.0
11.3	158	272	361	69.7		
9.0	145	267	360	68.0	25.3	31.7
12.2	133	272	371	72.6	26.6	
10.5	146	271	363	66.8	22.3	35.4
−0.8				74.0	16.2	

pattern with the Nordic countries followed by the Anglo-American countries and the continental European countries at the same level with Eastern and southern European countries at the bottom. Note that the KIS figures (like the overall employment figures) are expressed as a percentage of the working age population, which means that the percentage of total employment that is KIS employment is lower in the Anglo-American countries than in continental Europe. We should also note that the KIS employment figures are the percentage of the working age population working in KIS *sectors*, not the percentage working in KIS *jobs*. Thus, the discretionary learning employment figures, which are the percentage of employees working in discretionary learning *jobs*, has greater face validity as a measure of quality employment. In terms of discretionary learning employment, the Nordic countries are again at the top, followed by the continental European countries, with the other three groups at the bottom.

The Anglo-American countries stand out as doing well in overall employment performance but not in the production of quality employment. These countries are liberal market economies and have liberal welfare states. With high levels of wage dispersion and ungenerous welfare states, they have high levels of employment in low-wage service sector jobs, that is, employment but not quality employment. This fits with the fact that these countries do not invest heavily in human capital as indicated by our social investment variables in columns 1–7.

Columns 8–11 contain our measures of human capital stock in the adult population. Educational attainment is the average years of education of the adult population. Columns 9–11 are the average IALS scores at the fifth decile, the mean and the 95th decile. Figure 8.1 shows the relationship between the mean IALS score and average years of education. There is a moderately strong relationship between the two variables but not one that is sufficiently high to claim that they are measuring the same thing. Of the two variables, the IALS clearly has greater face validity as the more accurate measure of human capital stock. One can see that the Anglo-American and Nordic countries are similar in terms of average years of education but differ in terms of average literacy scores with the Nordic countries scoring much higher on the latter, arguably a result of their high levels of social investment. One can see from Columns 9–11 of Table 8.2 that the differences between these two groups of countries are concentrated in the bottom half of the skill distribution. The differences at the fifth percentile are particularly striking.

Figure 8.1: Average years of education of the population over 24 and mean score on the International Adult Literacy Survey

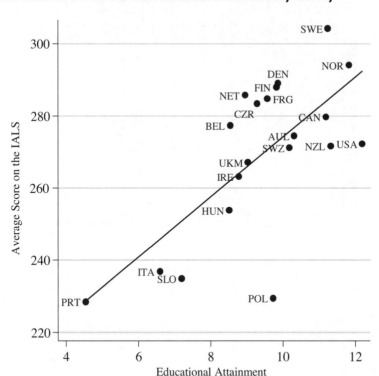

Analysis I: Pooled times series analysis of employment and employment in knowledge-intensive services

Our central hypothesis is that social investment policies increase employment, particularly employment in high-quality jobs. We began our examination of the empirical evidence with a pooled time series analysis of the data which are available for 17 countries over the span of 18 years, from 1972 to 1999. First, we examine the impact of social investment policies on total employment to answer the question of whether such policies increase employment. Then we examine their impact on knowledge intensive service (KIS) employment, to answer the question whether they produce quality employment.

The results from the pooled time series analysis are shown in Table 8.3. The results largely support the hypotheses. Day care, short-term unemployment replacement rates, sick pay generosity, active labour market policies, education spending and higher educational attainment

Table 8.3: Labour market and social policy determinants of employment levels

	Model 1	Model 2	Model 3	Model 4	Model 5
Direct investment outflows	.178 **	.192 **	.182 **	.162 *	.108
Openness	-.085 ***	-.049 **	-.055 ***	-.037 **	-.052 **
Payroll taxes	-.548 ***	-.429 ***	-.492 ***	-.253 ***	-.481 ***
Government revenue	-.132 *	-.247 ***	-.038	-.020	-.148
Wage coordination	.020	.244	.077	.150	.081
Union density	-.089 **	-.108 **	-.063 *	.051	-.164 ***
Long-term unemployment replacement	-.009	-.083 ***	-.077 ***	-.056 **	-.021
Short-term unemployment replacement	.086 ***	.065 *	.043 **	.123	.123
Sick pay	.698 ***	.779 ***	1.052 ***		.796 ***
Active labour market policy spending	28.842 ***				26.178 ***
ECEC (day care spending)		8.161 ***			4.334 *
Total educational spending			.761 *		0.561
Educational attainment				1.55 ***	1.326 **
Constant	78.363 ***	82.869 ***	73.496 ***	55.058 **	67.376 ***
Common rho	.85	.83	.85	.86	.88
R²	.95 ***	.95 **	.95 ***	.90 ***	.96 ***
Observations	287	286	423	473	246

* significant at 5%; ** significant at 1%;,*** singnificant at 0.1%; ^ significant opposite hypothesised direction.

Cell entries are Prais Winsten coefficients; significance level calculated with panel corrected standard errors.

R² proportion of variation in the employment levels explained by the variables in the equation.

increase employment levels. The final model indicates that day care, active labour market policy and sick pay have effects on employment levels independent of their effect on average years of education. That is, even independently of raising the level of formal education, these social investment policies increase employment by increasing the quality of skills. The model also indicates that average years of education has effects independent of the human capital investment policies. That is, average years of education does have an effect which is not simply a product of the social investment policies. Table 8.4 shows the estimated effect of the human capital variables on employment. To interpret the figures in the table, it is useful to know that the mean level of employment is 66% of the working age population and the standard deviation is 7.8%. Thus, the estimated effect of day care and active labour market policy is larger than a standard deviation and thus enough to move across more than 34% of the country years in the data set. These are impressive effects by any standard. The employment effects of sick pay generosity and educational attainment are also large.

Table 8.4: Estimated effect of a two-standard deviation change in human social investment variables on employment

Short-term unemployment replacement	2.8
Sick pay	5.1
ECEC (day care spending)	8.3
Active labour market policy spending	8.5
Educational attainment	5.0
Educational attainment with investment variables	4.3
Education spending	1.5

Table 8.5 displays the results of the regressions of employment in knowledge-intensive services on the human capital variables and controls. Day care, active labour market policies, education spending and higher educational attainment are associated with higher levels of KIS employment. Model 5 indicates that these investment variables have strong effects independent of their effect on average years of education. We interpret this to mean that they raise the quality of education. Referring back to Figure 8.1, they explain why the Nordic countries are all above the regression line and the Anglo-American settler colonies are all below it. That is, in the figure, the literacy skill levels of the Nordic countries are higher than one would expect given the average level of education. The analysis in Table 8.5 indicates that this helps these countries to produce high levels of KIS employment. Short-term unemployment replacement rates and sick pay generosity

Table 8.5: Labour market and social policy determinants of employment in knowledge intensive-services

	Model 1	Model 2	Model 3	Model 4	Model 5
Direct investment outflows	.184 ***	.154 ***	.236 ***	.113 ***	.165 ***
Openness	-.031 **	.001	-.026 **	.003	-.014
Payroll taxes	-.326 ***	-.196 ***	-.204 ***	-.088 **	-.245 ***
Government revenue	.100 *	.083 *	.181 ***	.220 ***	-.009
Wage coordination	-.427 ^	-.189 ^	-.124	.016	-.338 ^
Union density	-.097 ***	-.141 ***	-.068 ***	-.018	-.118 ***
Long-term unemployment replacement	.055 ^	.029 ^	.013	.005	.040 ^
Short-term unemployment replacement	.087 ***	.015	.025 **		.020
Sick pay	.123	-.006	.212 **		.153
Active labour market policy spending	18.373 ***				12.009 ***
ECEC (day care spending)		8.449 ***			3.352 **
Total educational spending			2.455 ***		1.966 ***
Educational attainment				2.149 ***	-.103
Constant	19.120 ***	19.837 **	2.557	-6.960 **	14.537 **
Common rho	.78	.82	.81	.88	.78
R^2	.82 ***	.84 **	.80 ***	.68 **	.87 **
Observations	235	251	334	371	216

* significant at 5%; ** significant at 1%; *** singnificant at 0.1%, ^ significant opposite hypothesised direction.

Cell entries are Prais Winsten coefficients; significance level calculated with panel corrected standard errors.

R^2 proportion of variation in the employment levels explained by the variables in the equation.

are not robustly related to KIS employment. This makes theoretical sense as these two policies are probably most important to the least skilled members of the workforce and not to KIS workers. Table 8.6 displays the estimated effect of the human capital variables on KIS employment. Again the mean level of KIS employment, 19.6%, and the standard deviation, 6.1%, are relevant data in interpreting the strength of the effects. By this standard, the effects of educational attainment and day care are very large and the effects of active labour market policy and education spending large.

Table 8.6: Estimated effect of a two-standard deviation change in human social investment variables on knowledge-intensive service employment

ECEC (day care spending)	8.6
Active labour market policy spending	5.4
Educational attainment	6.9
Education spending	4.3

Analysis II: Social investment policies, literacy skills and employment

As mentioned previously, the IALS data, which are direct measures of the quantitative, prose and document interpretation skills of the adult population, and thus are the most accurate measure of stock of general skills in the adult population, are only available at one time point. The discretionary learning employment data, the best measure of quality employment available, are not available at enough time points to make pooled time series analysis feasible. Thus in Table 8.7 we employ cross-sectional correlations to examine the effects of social investment policies on the IALS scores and the effects of both social investment policies and the IALS scores on the three employment variables.

The shaded area of Table 8.7 shows the correlations of the social investment measures with the IALS scores at three points in the skills distribution. With the exception of cumulative average educational spending, one sees that the impact of social investment variables is greater at the middle and bottom end of the distribution. These results provide insight into the relative position of the Anglo-American countries at the top and bottom ends of the skill distribution in Table 8.2. At the fifth percentile, the Anglo-American countries, weak as they are in social investment policies, do poorly, but at the 95th percentile, they score only slightly behind the Nordic countries. The contrasting position of the USA is particularly striking: at the top, it ranks third

Table 8.7: Correlations between social investment policies, literacy scores and employment outcomes

	Bottom fifth percentile literacy	Average literacy	Top 95th percentile literacy	Employment levels in 1995	Employment in KIS in 1995	Discretionary learning employment
Top 95th percentile literacy				.54	.81	.63
Average literacy				.53	.79	.72
Bottom fifth percentile literacy				.37	.61	.72
Sickness insurance	.66	.47	-.03	.15	.16	.50
Short-term unemployment replacement	.54	.49	.30	.42	.37	.67
ECEC (cumulative day care spending)	.53	.38	.21	.20	.38	.79
Cumulative ALMP spending in 1995	.68	.64	.58	.04	.55	.87
Skill acquisition index	.60	.51	.27	.41	.53	.70
Educational spending in 1995	.42	.41	.30	.40	.39	.64
Cumulative educational spending	.52	.72	.68	.50	.83	.82

behind Sweden and Canada; at the bottom, it scores behind all the countries in the Nordic, continental European, Anglo-American groups, but also behind the Czech Republic and Poland. Tentatively, one could interpret these findings in the following way: at the high end of the skill distribution (which is certainly correlated to high levels of parental education and income), private educational investment and residential segregation, both characteristics of the inegalitarian Anglo-American countries, make low levels of public human capital investment less consequential for skills at the high end. Expressed another way, elites across all countries manage to pass on valued skills and their related advantages to their children. Whereas a disadvantaged person is likely to develop greater literacy skills in Sweden than in the USA, for instance, well-to-do people in both these contexts should demonstrate high literacy because they are not dependent on public policies for skill development.

Figure 8.1 suggests an additional explanation to the contrasting performance of the Anglo-American countries at the top and bottom end of the distribution. The Anglo-American settler colonies (USA, Canada, Australia and New Zealand), all of which have a tradition of very broad access to secondary education, are well below the regression line, which indicates that they score poorly on the IALS given the average years of education of the adult population. The low values on the Anglo-American settler colonies on the human capital investment variables indicate the reason for this is probably that the quality of education at the primary and secondary level is not high on average in these countries. We should note here that two of these countries, the USA and Canada, were actually the countries with the highest level of educational spending in 1970, spending 8.5% and 7.4% of GDP on education, respectively. Their relative position deteriorated after that point.

Below the shaded area in Table 8.7 one finds the correlations of the social investment variables and the three employment variables. As one moves from total employment to KIS employment to discretionary learning employment, the correlations between the social investment variables and the employment variable increase in strength. Thus, social investment policies are much more consequential for the production of quality jobs than they are for the production of jobs regardless of quality. the correlations of the IALS and the employment variables (the box on the lower right-hand corner of the table) indicate a similar pattern: the measures of the stock of human capital are much more strongly related to quality employment than they are to the overall level of employment. These findings suggest that social investment policies therefore steer countries on a route to high employment that also improves the quality of work. Deregulation and slashing wages are often touted as necessary measures to increase jobs by those supporting the neoliberal orthodoxy. Our results show that investing in people is another viable path to high employment.

Conclusion

In our pooled time series analysis, we find strong support for the hypothesis that social investment policies have large effects on employment and quality employment more specifically. Short-term unemployment replacement rates, sickness insurance, day care spending, education spending, active labour market policy and average years of education all have significant effects on total employment levels and all of them except sickness insurance have significant effects on employment in knowledge-intensive services. The effects of active labour market policy spending and ECEC on both dependent variables are particularly strong. Moreover, there are effects of sickness insurance, active labour market policy and ECEC on employment, and of active labour market policy, ECEC and education spending on KIS employment independent of average years of education.

In our correlational analysis, we were able to include data from the International Adult Literacy Survey on the prose, quantitative and document interpretation skills of the adult populations of the countries studied, which is by far the best indicator of the human capital stock of the adult population. Moreover, since OECD/HRDC (2000) reports the average national scores at different deciles of the skill distribution, these data allow us to pinpoint where in the skill distribution the cross-national differences lie. For EU member states, we could also include data from the fourth European Working Conditions Survey on the level of discretionary learning employment, the best available indicator of quality employment (Valeyre et al., 2009). We found that there were strong effects of the social investment policies on the human capital stock and these effects were concentrated in the bottom half of the skill distribution. That is, social investment policies are particularly important in improving the skills at the mean of the skill distribution and below. In terms of the effect of social investment policies on employment, we found their effect on quality employment to be much larger than their effect on overall employment, regardless of quality. Moreover, the effect of social investment policies was greater for discretionary learning employment, our best-quality employment measure, than for KIS employment. Similarly, the IALS skill measures were more strongly related to the two measures of quality employment than to the measure of overall employment. In sum, we present strong empirical evidence that social investment policies do indeed produce more quality jobs, precisely the type of jobs characteristic of the emerging knowledge economy.

In pooled time series analyses, we and our co-authors have shown that social democratic government is associated with high levels of all of our human capital variables (Huo et al., 2008; Iversen and Stephens, 2008; Nelson and Stephens, 2009). The links between some of these variables, such as educational spending, and social democratic government are not as obvious as in the case of policies aimed primarily at redistribution. It would seem that parties across the spectrum would be in favour of upgrading the skills of the workforce. The additional motivation for left governments to invest in education is to expand secondary and tertiary school enrolment to open up educational opportunity to sons and daughters of workers. The expansion of secondary and tertiary education also expands the supply of educated workers, which reduces the education premium in income, which in turn results in greater income equality, the traditional goal of social democracy. Conservative parties by contrast may want to protect the educational privileges of their upper income constituencies, so they oppose expanding secondary and tertiary education. The average human capital level of the working age population suffers as a result: a World Bank study by Thomas et al. (2001) shows that there is an extremely high correlation between inequality of education as measured by the Gini index and average years of education, suggesting that it is almost impossible significantly to increase the average level of education without increasing equality in the distribution of education.

Had we historical data reaching further back than 1970, when our education spending time series begins, the relationship between social democratic government and education spending would probably not have been so strong. In 1970, the three highest education spending countries were Canada (8.5% of GDP), the USA (7.4%) and Sweden (7.4%), followed by the Netherlands (7.0%) and Denmark (6.7%). This is right after the Johnson administration's Great Society programmes, many of which involved education investment, and a long period of Liberal government in Canada (19 of 26 years since the end of the war). This suggests that centrist parties may invest in education in order to improve the workforce's skills and to increase educational opportunity and social mobility, so that social democratic government is not a necessary condition for social investment.

Higher spending in Canada and the USA in the early 1970s still would have an effect on total employment and KIS employment in our data analysis because people in school in this period were still in the workforce at the end of our time series or in the mid-1990s cross-section. One can see in Table 8.2 that the USA and Canada are higher on the cumulative average education spending variable than they are on education spending in 1995. Arguably, this had a positive impact on employment and especially KIS employment in those two countries. The decline in education spending in the USA and Canada does not bode well for the ability of the two countries to continue to produce high levels of high-quality employment.

Notes

[1] Eurostat classifies the following service sectors as knowledge intensive: (61) water transport, (62) air transport, (64) post and telecommunications, (65) financial intermediation, (66) insurance and pension funding, (67) other financial intermediation, (70) real estate, (71) renting of machinery and equipment, (72) computer and related activities, (73) research and development, (74) other business activities, (80) education, and (85) health and social work. The numbers of sector are codes according with the NACE (French acronym for Statistical Classification of Economic Activities in the European Community) classification scheme.

[2] Consistent with the usage in the IALS publications, we refer to the IALS as measuring 'literacy' skills, but we emphasise that it measures quantitative skills and document interpretation as well as verbal skills.

References

Armingeon, K. and Bonoli, G. (eds) (2006) *The Politics of Post-Industrial Welfare States: Adapting Post-Industrial Social Policies to New Social Risks.* Oxford: Routledge.

Barro, R.J. and Lee, J.W. (2001) 'International data on educational attainment: Updates and implications', *Oxford Economic Papers,* 53 (3), 541–63.

Benavot, A. and Riddle, P. (1988) 'The expansion of primary education, 1870–1940: Trends and issues', *Sociology of Education,* 61 (3), 191–210.

Bradley, D. and Stephens, J.D. (2007) 'Employment performance in OECD countries: A test of neo-liberal and institutionalist hypotheses', *Comparative Political Studies,* 40 (12), 1–25.

Broberg, A.G., Wessels, H., Lamb, M.E. and Hwang, C.P. (1997) 'Effects of day care on the development of cognitive abilities in 8-year-olds: A longitudinal study', *Developmental Psychology*, 33 (1), 62–69.

Brooks-Gunn, J. (2003) 'Do you believe in magic? What we can expect from early childhood intervention programs', *Social Policy Report*, 17 (1), 3–14.

Burger, K. (2010) 'How does early childhood care and education affect cognitive development? An international review of the effects of early interventions for children from different social backgrounds', *Early Childhood Research Quarterly*, 25 (2), 140–65.

Campbell, F.A., Pungello, E.P., Miller-Johnson, S., Burchinal, M. and Ramey, C.T. (2001) 'The development of cognitive and academic abilities: Growth curves from an early childhood educational experiment', *Developmental Psychology*, 37 (2), 231–41.

Cha, Y. (1992) 'The origins and expansion of primary school curricula, 1800–1920', in J.W. Meyer and D.H. Kamens (eds) *School Knowledge for the Masses: World Models and National Primary Curricular Categories in the Twentieth Century*. London: Routledge.

Deezt, S. (1994) 'The micro-politics of identity formation in the workplace: The case of a knowledge intensive firm', *Human Studies*, 17 (1), 23–44.

Ebbinghaus, B. and Visser, J. (2000) *Trade Unions in Western Europe since 1945*. London: Palgrave Macmillan.

Esping-Andersen, G. (1999) *Social Foundations of Postindustrial Economies*. Oxford: Oxford University Press.

Estevez-Abe, M., Iversen, T. and Soskice D., (2001) 'Social protection and the formation of skills: A reinterpretation of the welfare state', in P. A. Hall and D. Soskice (eds) *Varieties of Capitalism: The Institutional Foundations of Comparative Advantage*. Oxford: Oxford University Press, pp. 145–83.

EU KLEMS (2009) *EU KLEMS Database*. Available at www.euklems. net/.

Evans, P. (2008) 'In search of the 21st century developmental state', Working Paper #4. Centre for Global Political Economy, University of Sussex.

GGDC (2006) *Groningen growth and development centre, 60-industry database*, September 2006. Available at www.ggdc.net.

Hargreaves, A. (2003) *Teaching in the Knowledge Society: Education in the Age of Insecurity*. New York: Teachers College Press.

Huber, E., Ragin, C., Stephens, J.D., Brady, D. and Beckfield, J. (2004) Comparative welfare states data set, Northwestern University, University of North Carolina, Duke University and Indiana University, 2004.

Huo, J., Nelson, M. and Stephens, J.D. (2008) 'Decommodification and activation in social democratic policy: Resolving the paradox', *European Journal of Social Policy*, 18 (1), 1–20.

Iversen, T. (2005) *Capitalism, Democracy, and Welfare, Cambridge Studies in Comparative Politics*. New York: Cambridge University Press.

Iversen, T. and Stephens, J.D. (2008) 'Partisan politics, the welfare state, and three worlds of human capital formation', *Comparative Political Studies*, 41 (4/5), 600–37.

Jaumotte, F. (2003) 'Female labour force participation: Past trends and main determinants in OECD Countries', in *Economics Department Working Paper No. 376*, edited by OECD. Paris: OECD.

Kenworthy, L. (2001) 'Wage-setting measures a survey and assessment', *World Politics*, 54 (1), 57–98.

Kenworthy, L. (2003) 'Do affluent countries face an incomes–jobs trade-off?', *Comparative Political Studies*, 36 (10), 1180–1209.

Magnuson, K.A., Ruhm, C., and Waldfogel, J. (2007) 'Does prekindergarten improve school preparation and performance?', *Economics of Education Review*, 26 (1), 33–51.

Moller, S., Huber, E., Stephens, J. Bradley, D. and Nielsen, F. (2003) 'Determinants of Relative Poverty in Advanced Capitalist Democracies', *American Sociological Review*, 68 (1), 22–51.

Nelson, M. (2008) *Education Policy and the Consequences for Labor Market Integration in Denmark, Germany, and the Netherlands*. Chapel Hill: University of North Carolina at Chapel Hill.

Nelson, M. (2010) 'The adjustment of national education systems to a knowledge-based economy: A new approach', *Comparative Education*, November, 46 (4) 463–86.

Nelson, M. and Stephens, J.D. (2009) 'Human capital policies and the social investment perspective: Explaining the past and anticipating the future', in N. Morel, B. Palier and J. Palme (eds) *What Future for Social Investment?* Stockholm: Institute for Future Studies, pp. 67–78.

OECD (2007) *Education at a Glance 2007*. Paris: OECD.

OECD Family Database, www.oecd.org/els/social/family/database.

OECD/HRDC (2000) *Literacy in the Information Age: Final Report of the International Adult Literacy Survey*. Paris: Organization for Economic Co-operation and Development and Ottawa: Human Resources Development Canada.

Pissarides, C.A. (1992) 'Loss of skill during unemployment and the persistence of employment shocks', *The Quarterly Journal of Economics*, 107 (4), 1371–91.

Quinn, D.P. and Inclan C., (1997) 'The origins of financial openness: A study of current and capital account liberalization', *American Journal of Political Science*, 41 (3), 771–813.

Rasinen, A. (2003) 'An analysis of the technology education curriculum in six countries', *Journal of Technology Education*, 15, 31–47.

Robertson, M., Scarbrough, H. and Swan, J. (2003) 'Knowledge creation in professional service firms: Institutional effects', *Organization Studies*, July, 24 (6), 831–57.

Scruggs, L. (2005) 'Comparative welfare entitlements dataset'. Department of Political Science, University of Connecticut.

Simmons, B. (1999) 'The Internationalization of Capital', in H. Kitschelt, P. Lange, G. Marks and J. Stephens (eds) *Continuity and Change in Contemporary Capitalism*. Cambridge: Cambridge University Press, pp. 36–69.

St George, E. (2006) 'Positioning higher education for the knowledge based economy', *Higher Education*, 52, 589–610.

Thomas, V., Wang, Y. and Fan, X., (2001) 'Measuring education inequality: Gini coefficients of education'. Washington, DC: World Bank Policy Research Working Paper No. 2525.

Tondeur, J., van Braak, J. and Valcke, M. (2007) 'Curricula and the use of ICT in education: Two worlds apart?', *British Journal of Education Technology*, 38 (6), 962–76.

Valeyre, A., Lorenz, E., Cartron, D., Csizmadia, P., Gollac, M. and Illéssy, M. (2009) *Working Conditions in the European Union: Work Organization*. Luxembourg: Office for Official Publications of the European Communities.

Waldfogel, J. (2002) 'Child care, women's employment, and child outcomes', *Journal of Population Economics*, 15 (3), 527–48.

World Bank (2002) *Constructing Knowledge Societies: New Challenges for Tertiary Education*. Washington, DC: World Bank.

Appendix: Measurement of the variables

The first dependent variable in the pooled analysis is employment levels, which are measured as the number of employed individuals as a proportion of the working age population (15–64 years old). Our measure of knowledge-intensive services is based on the Eurostat classification of industrial sectors into classes based on technological and knowledge intensity. Eurostat classifies the following service sectors as knowledge-intensive (see note 1 for a list of the sectors). The data sources were GGDC (2006) and EU KLEMS (2009). The GGDC and EU KLEMS data were incomplete for sector 92, recreational, cultural and sports activities, so this sector was not included in our analysis. Only an average of 1.1% of the working age population worked in this sector compared to 19.6% in all other KIS sectors, so it is unlikely that the exclusion of this sector affected our results. (Initially, we intended to include sectors which Eurostat classifies as high technology manufacturing. However, two of these sectors, manufacture of pharmaceuticals, medicinal chemicals and botanical products (244), and manufacture of aircraft and spacecraft (353), are defined at the three-digit level and, apparently for this reason, there were no data for many country years and a number of countries had no data at all for one or both of the sectors. An average of only 1.4% of the working age population worked in these sectors. It is not surprising that when we reran the analysis including these sectors for only country years for which complete data were available, the results were essentially the same.)

The main explanatory variables include day care spending, active labour market policy spending, total educational spending, sick pay generosity, educational attainment and the short-term unemployment replacement rate (see Table 8.1). Day care effort, our measure of early childhood education and care, is measured by public day care spending as a percentage of GDP. These data are drawn from the OECD and Jaumotte (2003) series on day care spending. We use the OECD series and fill in with Jaumotte for 28 observations for which she has data and the OECD does not. There are 286 observations in this series for the period 1980–99 but of varying length depending on the country. The measure of active labour market policies is the level of government spending on active labour market programmes as a percentage of GDP. The variable is further divided by the unemployment rate in order to control for the number of individuals actually in a position to use these policies. There are 287 observations in this series of varying length, depending on the country. Education spending is measured as a percentage of GDP. We reasoned that these spending variables would have little immediate effect but rather would play out over time, so we measure them as cumulative averages.

Our measure for sick pay generosity is drawn from Scruggs' (2005) data. He provides measures for replacement rates, coverage, waiting days and qualifying conditions. We standardised each measure and then added the standard scores of replacement rates and coverage and subtracted the standard scores of waiting days and qualifying conditions.

The measure for educational attainment comes from Barro and Lee (2001). We use their measure of average years of schooling for those aged 25 and over. Total years of schooling is preferred over attainment of a given level of schooling (primary, secondary, and so on) in order to recognise all forms of education participation regardless of whether or not it culminated in an official qualification.

We use the OECD summary indicator of 'benefit generosity' of unemployment insurance at two-thirds of the average earnings level for our measures of short- and long-term unemployment replacement rates. One of our social investment variables, the one-year replacement rate, and one of our control variables, the replacement rate in the fourth and fifth year, are the average replacement rates across three different family situations (single, married with dependent spouse, and married with spouse in work). The OECD data are gross replacement rates. Both the income and the transfer are pre-tax. Net replacement rate is clearly the preferable measure. Scruggs (2005) has recently released data on net replacement rates and duration of benefits, but there it is not possible to calculate the replacement rate for bouts of unemployment of long duration from the data, which is essential for our purposes. As we have shown in previous work, these variables have the opposite effect on employment, which makes theoretical sense. Work by other scholars has shown that generous short-term replacement rates have positive effects on skills while generous long-term replacement rates, which tend to lengthen unemployment bouts, are associated with deterioration of skills (Huo et al., 2008). To check the validity of the gross replacement rates data, we calculated a net replacement rate for a bout of unemployment one year long from the Scruggs data. The one year gross and net replacement rate series are highly correlated (0.85), which increases our confidence in the analysis using the OECD measure.

The remaining controls follow from Huo et al. (2008) and consist of factors that were found to significantly influence employment levels, including long-term unemployment insurance, payroll taxes, government revenue, wage coordination, union density, capital market openness and trade openness. The variable for payroll taxes is payroll and social security taxes as a percentage of GDP. Government revenue is the total value of current receipts for general government as a percentage of GDP. Our measure of wage coordination is Kenworthy's (2001) indicator. This measure is preferable to measures of bargaining centralisation because it taps institutionalised practices such as pattern setting, tacit coordination and government intervention, which are missed by measures of bargaining centralisation. Our measure of union strength is net union membership as a percentage of wage and salary workers.

As control variables, we include two measures of economic openness or 'globalisation'. Following Moller et al. (2003), we use the Quinn/Inclan (1997) measure of capital and current account controls as our measure of capital market openness. As a general measure of capital market openness, we favoured the control measures over the flow measures (inward and outward FDI as a percentage of GDP) because, as Simmons (1999) and others have argued, it is the possibility of easy exit that changes the behaviour of actors not variations in actual flows. In the Quinn/Inclan measure, the maximum score indicates no capital controls. For these same reasons, our preferred measure of trade openness would be a measure of tariff and non-tariff barriers to trade. Unfortunately, no such time series exists, so we use the conventional measure of trade flows, imports plus exports as a percentage of GDP.

The Skill Acquisition Index measures the extent to which education policy expands opportunities to acquire skills. The index is made up of nine variables which cluster into four groups. Four variables capture investment in (future) workers' cognitive capacity; one variable measures access to further education at the end of compulsory education; two variables tap the openness of access to tertiary education; and two variables measure access to continuing education and labour market training (see Nelson (2008) for details on the measurement of the variables and construction of the index).

The International Adult Literacy Survey has produced highly comparable measures of the human capital stock, at least in terms of general (rather than firm or industry-specific) skills of the adult population (OECD/HRDC, 2000). In this study, a cross-nationally comparable test of respondent skills in prose, document handling and interpretation and mathematics (roughly analogous to the American SAT) was administered to a random sample of the adult population in 24 countries. We include the average scores of the fifth and 95th deciles, and the mean in our correlational analysis.

The data on discretionary learning employment are taken from the fourth European Survey on Working Conditions (Valeyre et al., 2009). Discretionary learning jobs are jobs that involve high levels of problem-solving and learning on the job and high levels of freedom for the worker to organise his or her work activity (see Chapter Nine for a fuller discussion).

NINE

Social investment in the globalising learning economy: a European perspective

Bengt-Åke Lundvall and Edward Lorenz

Introduction

The social investment perspective depends on correctly understanding the characteristics of the economy as a basis for identifying appropriate policies for promoting growth and competitiveness. In this chapter we start from a characterisation of the current phase of capitalism as a 'globalising learning economy', where the speed of adaptation and innovation is seen as crucial for the competitiveness of firms (Lundvall and Johnson, 1994; Archibugi and Lundvall, 2001). While the concept 'the knowledge-based economy' is associated with the need to invest in research and in the formal education of scientists and engineers, the learning economy signals the importance of institutional design in relation to labour markets and national education and training systems. We shall provide evidence to support the view that social investments in the form of expenditures on further education and training and in support of flexible labour markets combined with security (flexicurity) play a crucial role in sustaining the learning economy.

We build on previous research linking the dynamics of learning at the firm level to the innovative performance of national economies. In particular we build on work showing:

- that innovation requires a combination of science-based and experience-based knowledge (Jensen et al., 2007);
- that innovation thrives in countries where a big proportion of the employees are engaged in work activities involving problem solving and learning (Arundel et al., 2007);
- that the dramatic differences within Europe in how people learn at the workplace reflect differences in national institutional settings in relation to education and labour markets (Holm et al., 2010).

We also present evidence indicating a link between social investment, social capital, income inequality and organisational learning. Countries with a high frequency of organisational learning supported notably by social investments in education and training tend to display low degrees of income inequality and high degrees of social capital. Egalitarian income distribution goes hand in hand with equal access to jobs offering opportunities for learning and creative problem solving.

The learning economy

The concept 'the learning economy' refers to a specific phase of capitalist development where a combination of factors such as globalisation, deregulation of finance and the widespread use of information and communication technologies *speeds up the rate of change* in different dimensions (on the demand-side user needs change rapidly and on the supply-side there is acceleration in the creation, diffusion and use of new technology) (Lundvall and Johnson, 1994). While the term 'knowledge-based economy' refers to the growing importance of investment in knowledge the learning economy concept signals that another important new characteristic is that knowledge becomes obsolete more rapidly than before. Therefore, it is imperative for firms to engage in organisational learning and for workers to constantly engage in attaining new competencies.[1]

We see the growing emphasis in management literature on 'learning organisations' as reflecting the new context. In a context of rapid change, flat organisations with extensive horizontal communication are more efficient than hierarchical organisations with barriers between functions (Senge, 1990; Drucker, 1993). In a rapidly changing environment it is less efficient to operate in a hierarchical organisation with many vertical layers. It takes too long to respond if the information obtained at the lower levels first needs to be transmitted to the top of the organisation and then, in the form of directives, back down to the bottom of the pyramid.

We see references to 'the network society' (Castells, 2000) and 'open innovation' (Chesbrough, 2003) as pointing to another important dimension of the learning economy. In an era of growing complexity and rapid change, it becomes increasingly difficult to establish all relevant competencies inside the organisation. Therefore, firms engage in networking and alliances. Relational contracting and networking is used to enhance functional flexibility. When engaging in innovation, firms need to draw upon collaboration with external partners (Lundvall, 1985).

The learning economy is characterised by cumulative circular causation. The selection by employers of more learning-prone employees and the market selection in favour of change-oriented firms accelerate further innovation and change. In this context the key to economic success for a national or regional economy is its capacity to renew competencies in order to be able to move into activities that are less exposed to global competition. In the following section we show that the opportunities employees have for learning in their daily work activity are distributed across the member states of the European Union in a highly unequal manner.

Mapping forms of work organisation in Europe

Today it is generally accepted that competition is knowledge-based and that governments need to invest in knowledge through formal education and research efforts. Differences in national efforts in these respects are well documented and attempts are made to use lead countries as benchmarks. But there is no corresponding attention to workplace learning. This is problematic since in the learning economy the skill formation that takes place at the workplace is crucial for economic performance. And as we shall see, international differences are huge, even within Europe.

Lorenz and Valeyre (2005) and Arundel et al. (2007) develop an EU-wide mapping of the adoption of different types of work organisation. Drawing on the results of the Third European Survey on Working Conditions,[2] cluster analysis is used to identify four different systems of work organisation:

- discretionary learning (DL);
- lean production;
- Taylorist organisation;
- traditional organisation.

The two most important dimensions used to distinguish between them are respectively problem solving and learning on the job, on the one hand, and the degree of freedom that the worker has to organise his or her work activities, on the other. Discretionary learning involves complex problem solving and freedom to choose or change one's work methods and pace of work. A typical example would be managers, experts or skilled workers with great autonomy.

The principal difference between the discretionary learning and the lean clusters is the high levels of discretion or autonomy in work exercised by employees grouped in the former. Over 85% of the employees grouped in the DL cluster affirm that they have control over their work pace and work methods whereas only slightly over 50% of the employees grouped in the lean cluster affirm this. Another difference is that such core 'lean' or 'high performance' work practices as team work, job rotation and the use of quality norms are at average, or below average, levels in the DL cluster, whereas they are considerably above average in the lean cluster. Task complexity is higher in the DL cluster than it is in the lean cluster. Workers in automobile factories where modern management techniques are applied would typically fall in the lean category.

Discretionary learning thus refers to work settings where a lot of responsibility is allocated to the employee who is expected to solve problems on his or her own. Business service jobs are typical examples where employees continuously are confronted with new and complex problems. Although some of the tasks take place in a team, teamwork is not seen as imposing narrow constraints on the work. Rather, team work may involve brain-storming by professional experts as much as collectively solving narrowly defined problems.

Lean production also involves problem solving and learning but here the problems appear to be more narrowly defined and the space of possible solutions less wide. The pace of work is more constrained, notably by constraints linked to the use of numerical production targets or performance targets. This points to a more structured or bureaucratic style of organisational learning that corresponds rather closely to the characteristics of the Japanese or 'lean production' model.

The other two clusters are both characterised by lower levels of learning and problem solving. Taylorism offers the employee very limited access to learning and little autonomy when it comes to organising daily work. This is a kind of work widely used in textile factories in the south of Europe. In the traditional cluster, task complexity is the lowest among the four types of work organisation, while at the same time constraints on the pace of work are relatively low. This category groups traditional forms of work organisation where methods are for the most part informal and non-codified. This kind of work may be found in small shops and in paid domestic work.

The first four columns of Table 9.1 reproduce the figures from Lorenz and Valeyre (2005), showing the frequency of the four forms of work organisation for the EU-15. The figures show that DL forms of work organisation are most widely diffused in the Nordic countries and the Netherlands, and to a lesser extent in Germany and Austria, while they are little diffused in Ireland and the southern European nations.

Table 9.1: National differences in forms of work organisation, 2000

	Percentage of employees by country in each organisational class				
	Discretionary learning	Lean production	Taylorist organisation	Traditional organisation	Exposure Index
Austria	47.5	21.5	13.1	18.0	96.7
Belgium	38.9	25.1	13.9	22.1	101.2
Denmark	60.0	21.9	6.8	11.3	87.9
Finland	47.8	27.6	12.5	12.1	94.6
France	38.0	33.3	11.1	17.7	99.2
Germany	44.3	19.6	14.3	21.9	99.5
Greece	18.7	25.6	28.0	27.7	114.8
Ireland	24.0	37.8	20.7	17.6	106.5
Italy	30.0	23.6	20.9	25.4	107.6
Luxembourg	42.8	25.4	11.9	20.0	98.6
Netherlands	64.0	17.2	5.3	13.5	86.8
Portugal	26.1	28.1	23.0	22.8	109.6
Spain	20.1	38.8	18.5	22.5	109.2
Sweden	52.6	18.5	7.1	21.7	94.0
UK	34.8	40.6	10.9	13.7	98.7
EU-15	39.1	28.2	13.6	19.1	100.0

Source: Third Working Condition Survey 2000. European Foundation for the Improvement of Living and Working Conditions.

The lean model is most in evidence in the UK, Ireland and Spain and to a lesser extent in France, while it is little developed in the Nordic countries or in Germany, Austria and the Netherlands. The Taylorist forms are more present in Portugal, Spain, Greece and Italy, while the traditional forms are similarly more in evidence in these four southern European nations as well as in Germany, Belgium and Luxembourg.[3]

Globalisation, transformation of work and international competitiveness

In a globalising learning economy it constitutes a competitive advantage if most jobs in the national economy are skill-intensive and not directly exposed to competition from the rapidly growing Asian economies including China and India. Having a big proportion of workers in jobs where they continuously learn new skills while they work makes it possible to retain such an advantage.

It is in this light that the 'exposure index' presented in the last column in Table 9.1 should be seen. The basic idea is that different types of jobs are more or less exposed to global competition – highly exposed jobs might be outsourced or disappear when confronted with competition from low-cost countries. We assume that exposure increases with the degree of standardisation of the job and with the intensity of use of low-skilled labour.

Therefore, we assume that the least exposed jobs are jobs involving discretionary learning while Taylorist jobs and traditional organisations are most exposed with lean production in a middle position. We have calculated the index using the following formula:

$$\text{Exposure index} = 1.0DL + 1.5LP + 2.0(TAY + TRAD)$$

where DL=Discretionary Learning; LP=Lean Production; TAY= Taylorist organisation; and TRAD=Traditioanal organisation. The index has been normalised so that the unweighted average for the EU-15 equals 100. A high value for the index indicates that the economy is highly exposed to low wage competition from outside Europe. Greece, Portugal, Spain, Italy and Ireland are most exposed while the transformation of working life has gone furthest in the Netherlands and in the Nordic countries.[4] We would argue that *the inverse* of the exposure index provides an indicator of how capable nations are of sustaining their competitiveness in the longer term.

Applying the analysis to all of the EU-27 and Norway on the basis of survey data for 2005 also results in four clusters with similar characteristics to the ones referred to in this chapter. The 2005 data gives a similar pattern and shows that the majority of the new member countries have a structure similar to the one found in the south of Europe (Holm et al., 2010).[5] The Nordic nations (now including Norway) and the Netherlands stand out for their high use of the DL forms of work organisation and low levels of use of Taylorism. The lean forms are most present in the UK and Portugal amongst the EU-15 and Estonia, Slovenia, Latvia, Lithuania, Poland and Romania amongst the new member nations.

The Taylorist forms are relatively developed in all of the southern nations amongst the EU-15 and in a number of the new member nations including the Czech Republic, Cyprus, Hungary, Bulgaria, Slovakia and Romania. The simple forms are relatively frequent in Spain, Greece and Ireland amongst the EU-15 and in Hungary, Bulgaria, Lithuania, Cyprus and the Czech Republic amongst the new member nations (Holm et al., 2010). This implies that most of the new member countries are as exposed to globalisation as the countries in southern Europe.

Social investment policies and learning organisations

The learning economy needs the support from an active welfare state. A fundamental inherent contradiction in the learning economy has to do with the fact that while it thrives on the basis of social cohesion, if left to operate on its own, social cohesion is undermined. For example, the speed up of change makes it increasingly difficult for low-skilled workers to find employment while the demand for skilled workers tends to outgrow supply. Such processes were reflected in the outcome of the OECD (1994) *Jobs Study*, demonstrating a tendency towards polarisation of labour markets operating in *all* OECD member countries between 1985 and 1995. In the USA the polarisation was mainly in terms of income differentials while in most European countries it took the form of growing differences in access to employment between high-skilled and low-skilled workers. The UK was a worst case since it combined the two forms of polarisation.

In such a context public programmes that continuously upgrade the skills of workers, and especially low-skilled workers, are an especially important form of social investment. Expanding youth education and reforming initial education programmes to stay up-to-date in relation to changes in technology and skill demands is important but it cannot stand alone. In the learning economy the renewal of skills that comes from absorbing new generations of workers works too slowly (the annual inflow of new entrants coming from youth education and with the most updated competencies constitute only 2–3% of the total labour force). This implies a need to increase investments in lifelong learning, including continuous vocational training provided by employers.

In the learning economy it is also important to design labour market institutions and social policy so that they support the formation of learning organisations. *Flexicurity*, where mobility within and across organisational borders is combined with income security in case of unemployment, is an especially attractive institutional setup in the learning economy. Flexibility makes it possible to continuously reshape the capability profile of organisations through hiring and firing while high rates of substitution and reasonable length of the period of unemployment benefits make employees less risk-averse and more willing to take part in and contribute to change. In what follows we present evidence showing that well-developed systems of further education and training and labour markets characterised by flexicurity constitute institutional settings that support the learning economy.

Education and training for learning organisations

Since the discretionary learning forms of work organisation depend on the capacity of employees to undertake complex problem-solving tasks in relatively unconstrained or 'organic' work settings, it can be expected that nations with a high frequency of these forms will have made substantial investments in the development of the knowledge and skills of their labour forces. Countries with a high frequency of the DL forms of work organisation, however, are those that combine investments in formal education with investments in continuous vocational training. In what follows we focus first on formal education at the tertiary level, and second on the continuing vocational training offered by enterprises through both external and internal courses.

While most of the qualifications acquired through third-level education will be relatively general and hence transferable on the labour market, the qualifications an employee acquires through continuing vocational training will be more firm-specific. Some of this training will be designed to renew employees' technical skills and knowledge in order to respond to the firm's requirements in terms of ongoing product and process innovation. Other parts of continuing vocational training, notably the provision of in-house courses, will be more organisationally focused and designed to develop employee competence in the firm-specific routines and operating procedures that are required for daily production activities. This latter kind of vocational training will be highly complementary to the more informal forms of learning that occur on-the-job, as employees seek solutions to the problems they confront in their daily work.

There is a common understanding in most European countries that it is important to promote academic training and scientific research. The framework programmes and the Bologna process are examples of efforts aimed at promoting and coordinating such activities. The weak emphasis on vocational training and programmes for training adult workers reflects that in parts of Europe 'codified knowledge' carries higher status than experience-based knowledge. As we shall see below this bias may be problematic since it neglects the close connection between adult vocational training and jobs characterised by discretionary learning.

Figure 9.1 shows the correlations between the frequency of the DL forms and two of the four measures of human resources for innovation used in the European Innovation Scoreboard:[6] the proportion of the population with third-level education; and the number of new science and engineering graduates per 1,000 population aged 20–29 years in 2000. The results show a modest positive correlation

Figure 9.1: Formal education and discretionary learning

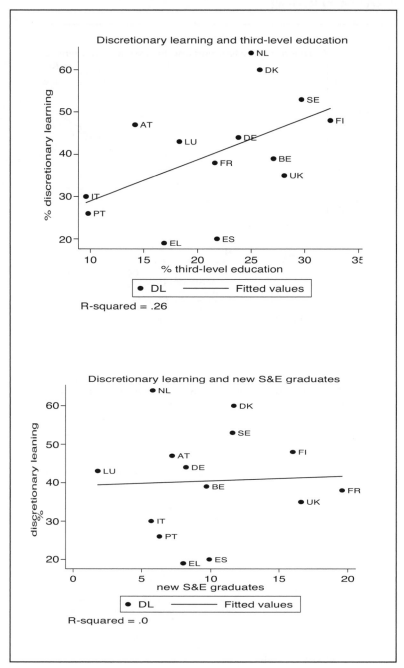

Source: Eurostat, Labour Force Survey and Education Statistics.

**Figure 9.2: Enterprise continuing vocational training and
discretionary learning**

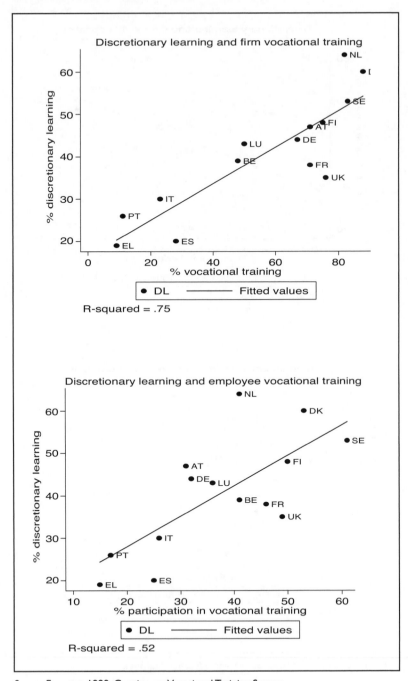

Source: Eurostat, 1999, Continuous Vocational Training Survey.

(*R*-squared = .26) between the DL forms and the percentage of the population with third-level education, and no discernible correlation between the DL forms and the measure of the importance of new science and engineering graduates.

Figure 9.2 shows that there are fairly strong positive correlations (*R*-squared = 0.75 and 0.52 respectively) between the frequency of the DL forms and two measures of firms' investments in continuing vocational training: the percentage of all firms offering such training and the participants in continuing vocational education as a percentage of employees in all enterprises.

Figure 9.2 also points to the north/south divide within Europe. The four less technologically developed southern nations are characterised by both low levels of enterprise continuing vocational training and low use of discretionary learning, while the more developed northern and central European nations are characterised by relatively high levels of vocational training and by high-level use of the discretionary learning forms.

The analysis suggests that an important bottleneck for constructing learning organisations in the less developed economies of Europe is at the level of further vocational training. Portugal, Spain, Greece and many of the new member nations have made important strides in increasing their production of science and engineering diplomas, but stand out for the weak development of continuous vocational training. This suggests that national systems that have emphasised the formal training of scientists and engineers to the neglect of vocational skills will find it harder to install participatory learning at the workplace. In the following section we argue that labour market systems that combine flexibility with unemployment security are complementary to the provision of continuous vocational training in supporting learning forms of work organisation.

Linking modes of learning to flexicurity

EU member nations display a large difference in systems of employment and unemployment protection. Systems combining high levels of unemployment protection with relatively low levels of employment protection may have an advantage in terms of the adoption of the forms of work organisation that promote learning and knowledge exploration. This is linked to the fact that organisations which compete on the basis of strategies of continuous knowledge exploration tend to have relatively porous organisational boundaries so as to permit the insertion of new knowledge and ideas from the outside. Job tenures tend to be short as careers are often structured around a series of discrete projects rather than advancing within an intra-firm hierarchy (Lam, 2005; Lam and Lundvall, 2006).

While absence of legal restrictions on hiring and firing will not necessarily result in the forms of labour market mobility that contribute to a continuous evolution of the firm's knowledge base, strong systems of employment protection may prove to be an obstacle. Well-developed systems of unemployment protection, on the other hand, may induce the efficient transfer of knowledge across organisations through the development of fluid labour markets. The security such systems provides encourages individuals to commit themselves to what would otherwise be perceived as unacceptably risky forms of employment and career paths. Further, such forms of protection contribute to the accumulation of knowledge for particular sectors or regions since in their absence unemployed workers would be under greater pressure to relocate.

Evidence in support of the view that systems of flexicurity coincide with DL forms of work organisation is provided in Figure 9.3. The top graph shows that there is a fairly strong positive relation (R-squared = 0.52) between a measure of the level of unemployment protection in a nation and the frequency of discretionary learning,[7] The middle graph shows a negative relation (R-squared = 0.36) between a measure of the level of employment protection and the frequency of the DL forms.

The bottom graph in Figure 9.3 shows an index of flexicurity constructed from the measures of employment and unemployment protection. The index is constructed so that a nation combining intermediate levels of both unemployment and employment security will score higher than a nation combining a high level of unemployment security with a high level of employment security, or a nation combining a low-level employment security with a low level of unemployment security.[8] The assumption is that the positive effects of a high level of unemployment protection (low level of employment protection) cannot compensate for the negative effects of a high level of employment protection (low level of unemployment protection). Rather, as the literature on flexicurity suggests, what is required is getting the right mix of flexibility and security. The index is positively correlated (R-squared = .48) with the frequency of the DL forms of work organisation.

In Holm et al. (2010) we have taken the analysis one step further towards addressing this research agenda by using multilevel logistic regression to explore the relation between individual level outcomes and national systems of labour market flexibility and regulation for the EU-27 and Norway. Factor analysis is used to identify differences in national labour market systems and the results show that in nations combining high levels of expenditure on active labour market policies

Figure 9.3: Correlations between discretionary learning and systems of social protection

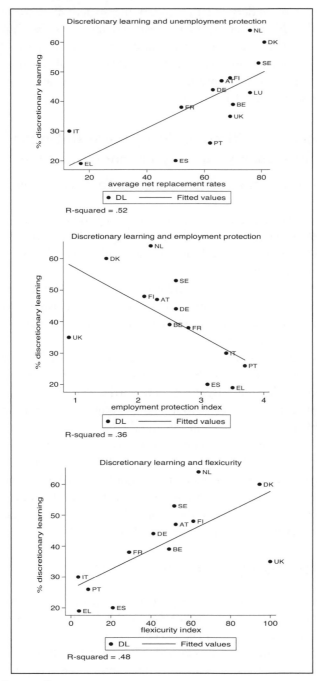

Source: See note 7.

with well-developed systems of further vocational training the likelihood of the DL forms of work organisation is higher.

In order to understand the underlying structural characteristics reflected in high levels of discretionary learning it is also important to reflect on the broader social conditions in which specific social investment policies are enacted. In what follows we focus first on the relation between inequality in income and learning, and second on issues of social capital and trust.

The social conditions for being successful in the learning economy: equality, openness and trust

Degree of inequality in access to organisational learning in Europe

The data referred to above on organisational models of learning in different European countries also makes it possible to develop a more dynamic and adequate indicator of inequality than the ones based upon income distribution.

In Table 9.2 we present an indicator for the social distribution of workplace learning opportunities. We distinguish between 'workers' and 'managers' and we compare their access to discretionary learning in different national systems.[9]

Table 9.2 shows that everywhere employees at the high end of the professional hierarchy have more easy access to jobs involving discretionary learning. But it is noteworthy that the data indicate that the inequality in access to learning is quite different in different countries. In the Nordic countries and the Netherlands the inequality in the distribution of learning opportunities is moderate while it is very substantial in the countries in the south of Europe. For instance, the proportion of the management category engaged in discretionary learning in Portugal is almost as high as in Finland (62% in Finland and 59% in Portugal), but the proportion of workers engaged in discretionary learning is much lower in Portugal (18.2% versus 38.2%).

Inequality in learning and in income

Sen (1995) has argued against using income distribution as an indicator when it comes to assessing wellbeing and the degree of inequality, and his capability perspective makes access to organisational learning an interesting candidate for an alternative indicator. On the other hand a high degree of skewness in income distribution may have an impact upon the 'social cohesion' on which interactive learning depends.

**Table 9.2: National differences in organisational models
(percentage of employees by organisational class)**

	Discretionary learning	Share of managers in discretionary learning	Share of workers in discretionary learning	Learning inequality index*
North				
Netherlands	64.0	81.6	51.1	37.3
Denmark	60.0	85.0	56.2	35.9
Sweden	52.6	76.4	38.2	50.3
Finland	47.8	62.0	38.5	37.9
Austria	47.5	74.1	44.6	39.9
Centre				
Germany	44.3	65.4	36.8	43.8
Luxembourg	42.8	70.3	33.1	52.9
Belgium	38.9	65.7	30.8	53.1
France	38.0	66.5	25.4	61.9
West				
UK	34.8	58.9	20.1	65.9
Ireland	24.0	46.7	16.4	64.9
South				
Italy	30.0	63.7	20.8	67.3
Portugal	26.1	59.0	18.2	69.2
Spain	20.1	52.4	19.1	63.5
Greece	18.7	40.4	17.0	57.9

*The index is constructed by dividing the share of 'workers' engaged in discretionary learning by the share of 'managers' engaged in discretionary learning and subtracting the resulting percentage from 100. If the share of workers and managers were the same the index would equal 0, and if the share of workers was 0 the index would equal 100.

Source: Lundvall, Rasmussen and Lorenz, 2008.

It is therefore of interest to see to what degree international differences in access to learning are mirrored in corresponding international differences in income inequality. In Table 9.3 we have compared the two forms of inequality for the EU-15. The data on income inequality emanate from a paper by Brandolini and Smeeding (2008) on inequality patterns and refer to the Gini coefficient with respect to disposable income. Both data sets cover the year 2000.

The most striking result is that the countries with the highest degree of income inequality (the UK and Portugal) are amongst those that are most unequal in terms of access to discretionary learning and that those countries (Denmark and the Netherlands) that have the most equal income distribution also offer the most egalitarian access to jobs with discretionary learning.

Table 9.3: Comparing income inequality with organisational learning inequality

	Income inequality Gini coefficient	Ranking income inequality	Inequality in organisational learning	Ranking inequality in organisational learning
Austria	0.257	11	39.9	12
Belgium	0.279	7	53.1	8
Denmark	0.225	15	35.9	15
Finland	0.246	12	37.9	13
France	0.278	8	61.9	6
Germany	0.275	9	43.8	11
Greece	0.334	4–5	57.9	7
Ireland	0.313	6	64.9	4
Italy	0.334	4–5	67.3	2
Luxembourg	0.260	10	52.9	9
Netherlands	0.231	14	37.3	14
Portugal	0.363	1	69.2	1
Spain	0.336	3	63.5	5
Sweden	0.252	12	50.3	10
UK	0.343	2	65.9	3

Sources: Brandolini and Schmeeding, 2008, p. 31; and the last column of Table 9.2.

This pattern shows that income distribution is more equal in countries where workers are given and take on more responsibility at the workplace. While income distribution may be of less relevance for individual welfare there seems to be a major 'system effect' from income distribution on the degree of participation in processes of work. In an era with growing income inequality in the USA and in most European countries this raises important questions about how increased inequality impacts upon participatory learning. One fundamental cause of the weakening of the competitiveness of nations may be 'below the radar' and reflect that growing income inequality reduces the willingness of workers to take an active part in processes of organisational learning.

When bosses get better off while workers experience more work for less pay it should come as no surprise if workers get less engaged in contributing to organisational and technical change. Perception of injustice linked to not receiving a fair share of the returns from economic activity can breed mistrust between workers and employers and reinforce more hierarchical forms of work organisation based upon high levels of control and characterised by a lack of autonomy. In what follows we raise the more general issue of the relation between social capital or trust, social investments and the development of learning organisations.

Social capital, trust and the learning economy

It is natural to think about *social investment* as related to *social capital*. Social capital is a multidimensional concept difficult to define and measure. It may refer to individuals' social network and to the resources that can be mobilised through such networks in critical situations. But it may also be defined at a societal level and refer to generalised trust and to the orderliness and predictability of co-citizens' behaviour. Here we define it as 'the willingness and capability of citizens to make commitments to each other, collaborate with each other and trust each other in processes of exchange *and* interactive learning across class and family boundaries'. While it may be argued that 'social capital' remains a nebulous concept (Jenson, 2010) it represents an attempt to capture this crucial dimension of the learning economy.

The impact of social investment on social capital is a controversial issue. Actually the impact of social investment on social capital may depend on national political culture – this was illustrated in connection with the debate on the Obama government reform of health care in the USA. What are regarded as fair and legitimate forms of government intervention in the Nordic countries were seen by many US citizens as a step towards 'communism'. In this context it is interesting to note that social investment with the aim to support knowledge and skill formation may be less controversial than other forms of government interventions with more clear impacts upon income distribution.

According to standard economic analysis, the Nordic countries should not perform as well as they do in a global context – especially not when it is assumed that knowledge is a key to economic success. One of the few clear conclusions of new growth theory is that small scale should be a handicap for economic systems. There are scale economies in the production of new knowledge, not least in high technology fields, and it is much less expensive to apply and use knowledge than it is to create knowledge.

The learning economy perspective may help to dissolve this paradox. Here tacit knowledge and experience-based learning are seen as important as codified knowledge and science-based learning. It is also taken into account that most interesting forms of learning take place in interaction between people. Scholars interact with colleagues, firms with customers and the master interacts with the apprentice. Within the business organisation interaction among specialised experts and across departments is a prerequisite for successful innovation. When it comes to implement innovation a close interaction between workers and managers is crucial for success. Firms that interact with customers, suppliers and knowledge institutions are more successful in terms of innovation than those that operate in isolation (Rothwell, 1977; Rosenberg, 1982; Lundvall, 1985).

How and with whom people interact will reflect the society they live in and the education system that shaped them. We argue that in the Nordic countries social capital and trust are fundamental resources that make national systems strong in terms of incremental innovation, absorption of knowledge produced elsewhere and rapid adaptation (Lundvall, 2002, 2006). Both the level of trust and the level of income equality are high in the Nordic countries. We also find that a fundamental and dynamic indicator of equality – equality in access to learning at the workplace – shows high values in the Nordic countries and Netherlands.

In the US-dominated literature social capital has been presented as rooted in civil society and the frequency of participation in civic activities has been used as an indicator of 'social capital' (Woolcock, 1998). It has been argued that big government undermines civil society and thereby also social capital. From the Scandinavian experience it is not clear that the growth in the welfare state has reduced the participation in civic organisations. In fact, the levels of trust are higher in the Scandinavian countries than in countries with small government. Especially there seems to be correlation between general (rather than selective) social welfare programmes and generalised trust. According to the European Social Survey, trust among agents seems to be consistently higher in the Nordic countries than in most other countries and combined with the small size of the system it results in dense *interaction* among agents both within and across organisations.

This gives rise not only to low transaction costs. More importantly, it facilitates processes of interactive learning where new insights about technologies and good organisational practices are diffused rapidly both within organisations and across organisational borders. The most important impact of high degrees of trust is *high learning benefits*. Low social distance between managers and workers and willingness to trust partners are key elements behind the relative success of the Nordic countries.

While the innovation systems in the Nordic countries may be handicapped in the production of codified knowledge, especially in certain scale-intensive science-based sectors, they have been highly successful in terms of learning by doing, learning by using and learning by interacting.

Summing up

Focusing upon EU-15, we have demonstrated that the differences among European member states in terms of organisational learning are dramatic and that the countries in the south of Europe are much more exposed to the competition from emerging economies than the Nordic countries where there are few Taylorist jobs left and where education systems and labour markets have adjusted to the needs of the learning economy.

Our results indicate that a movement towards a learning economy where a growing proportion of the citizens are engaged in jobs offering both learning and a delegation of responsibility can be promoted by developing more active and more ambitious labour market policies that combine mobility in the labour market with income security and access to training for workers. In the current crisis, establishing flexible security or 'flexicurity' in labour markets may be seen as a long-term supplement to short-term attempts that try to save existing jobs.

A major challenge in the learning economy is to establish links and reduce barriers between those who operate on the basis of formal codified academic knowledge and those who operate on the basis of experience-based and practical knowledge. Education and training systems therefore need to be designed so that they lower such barriers. This implies a need to make education systems more broad-based so that they give more equal weight to academic training and to vocational training. Academic training needs to be connected to the solution of practical problems and vocational training needs to demystify science and prepare workers for the use of advanced technologies (Lundvall et al., 2008).

Finally, we have pointed to the fact that social cohesion as reflected in egalitarian income distribution goes hand in hand with broad and democratic participation in organisational learning. Increasing income inequality may undermine the learning economy.

In most respects the Nordic countries stand out as being the ones best prepared to benefit from the opportunities offered by the globalising learning economy. But the Nordic countries are facing a dilemma emanating from globalisation. The demographic dynamics in these countries seem to result in an ageing population and to the need to open up labour markets to an inflow of young workers from other parts of the world. At the same time the current labour market and the welfare state institutional frameworks seem to face great difficulties when it comes to integrating workers from abroad – unemployment rates are high for foreign workers.

This points to a more general challenge for the social investment perspective. Historically nation states have functioned quite well as frameworks for economic growth. They have done so by developing institutions that promote the formation of human capital and through mechanisms of redistribution where resources have been transferred from those that benefit from change to those that become victims of change. 'Social investment' has been one important dimension of the framing of national economic growth.

The focus of most research on social investment, including this chapter, has been on comparing different national models. Much of the research has, more or less explicitly, indicated that the models practised in the Nordic countries have certain advantages that other countries could learn from. Today there might be a need to open up the discussion and to pose some new difficult questions. Worldwide, the EU represents the most ambitious attempt to make social investment and social rights transnational rather than national. Therefore, the EU is an interesting test case to study when it comes to understand the problems of social investment and social capital in a transnational setting. In Chapter Thirteen the new European strategy EU2020 will be discussed in this light.

Notes

[1] This can be illustrated by an extreme case referred to in a report from the Danish Ministry for Education. Here it is claimed that, on average, half the skills a computer engineer has obtained during his or her training will have become obsolete one year after the exam has been passed, while the 'halving period' for other categories of educated wage earners is estimated to be eight years (Ministry of Education, 1997: 56).

[2] The Third European Survey of Working Conditions on which the mapping is based was directed to approximately 1,500 active persons in each country with the exception of Luxembourg with only 500 respondents. The total survey population is 21,703 persons, of which 17,910 are salaried employees. The analysis presented here is based on the responses of the 8,081 salaried employees working in establishments with at least ten persons in both industry and services, but excluding agriculture and fishing; public administration

and social security; education; health and social work; and private domestic employees.

[3] In Lorenz and Valeyre (2005) logit regression analysis is used in order to control for differences in sector, occupation and establishment size when estimating the impact of nation on the likelihood of employees being grouped in the various forms of work organisation. The results show statistically significant 'national effect' also when controlling for the structural variables, thus pointing to considerable latitude in how work is organised for the same occupation or within the same industrial sector.

[4] While a low value on the exposure index indicates that the economy is less vulnerable to 'globalisation', it also may be seen as explaining difficulties with absorbing low-skilled labour and not least labour with a different ethnic background. Workplaces with Taylorist and traditional work organisations may be seen as 'entrance points' for immigrants with low skills since they offer jobs where workers with limited communication skills can operate efficiently. It means that the integration effort in order to be successful needs to be massive and focused upon upgrading skills, including communication skills, in the Nordic countries. The current high rates of unemployment among certain ethnical groups in these countries illustrates that this has not yet been fully understood among policy makers.

[5] The exception is Malta with a profile similar to the continental nations.

[6] See Pro Inno Europe: www.proinno-europe.eu/metrics.

[7] The unemployment protection measure in Figure 9.3 is the average net replacement rate of in-work income over 60 months averaged across four family types and two income levels including social assistance in 1999. See OECD, *Benefits and Wages*, 2002, p. 40. The employment protection measure is the OECD's overall employment protection index for the late 1990s. See OECD Employment Outlook, 1999, Chapter 2.

[8] The index is constructed by reversing the scoring on the employment protection index such that high values correspond to low levels of protection and multiplying this reversed score by the unemployment index. The resulting flexicurity index has then been rescaled so that the maximum score is 100.

[9] The class of managers includes not only top and middle management but also professionals and technicians (ISCO major groups 1, 2 and 3). The worker category includes clerks, service and sales workers as well as craft, plant and machine operators and unskilled occupations (ISCO major groups 4 through 9).

References

Archibugi, D. and Lundvall, B.-Å. (eds) (2001) *Europe in the Globalising Learning Economy*. Oxford: Oxford University Press.

Arundel, A., Lorenz, E., Lundvall, B.-Å. and Valeyre, A. (2007) 'How Europe's economies learn: A comparison of work organization and innovation mode for the EU-15', *Industrial and Corporate Change*, 16 (6), 680–93.

Brandolini, A. and Smeeding, T. M. (2008) 'Inequality: International Evidence', *New Palgrave Dictionary of Economics*, 2nd edn. Basingstoke: Palgrave Macmillan.

Castells, M. (2000) *The Rise of the Network Society, the Information Age: Economy, Society and Culture*, vol. I. Cambridge, MA: Blackwell.

Chesbrough, H. (2003) *Open Innovation: The New Imperative for Creating and Profiting from Technology*. Boston, MA: Harvard Business School Publishing.

Drucker, P. (1993) *Post-Capitalist Society*. New York: HarperCollins.

Holm, J.R., Lorenz, E., Lundvall, B.-Å. and Valeyre, A. (2010) 'Organisational learning and systems of labour market regulation in Europe', *Industry and Corporate Change*, 19 (4), 1141–73.

Jensen, M.B., Johnson, B., Lorenz, E. and Lundvall, B.-Å. (2007) 'Forms of knowledge and modes of innovation', *Research Policy*, 36 (5), 680–93.

Jenson, J. (2010) *Defining and Measuring Social Cohesion*. London: Commonwealth Secretariat and United Nations Research Institute for Social Development.

Lam, A. (2005) 'Organizational innovation', in J. Fagerberg, D. Mowery and R. Nelson (eds) *Handbook of Innovation*. Oxford: Oxford University Press, pp. 115–47.

Lam, A. and Lundvall, B.-Å. (2006) 'The learning organisation and national systems of competence building and innovation', in E. Lorenz and B.-Å. Lundvall (eds) *How Europe's Economies Learn: Coordinating Competing Models*. Oxford: Oxford University Press, pp. 109–39.

Lorenz, E. and Valeyre, A. (2005) 'Organisational innovation, HRM and labour market structure: A comparison of the EU-15', *Journal of Industrial Relations*, 47 (4), 424–42.

Lundvall, B.-Å. (1985) *Product Innovation and User-Producer Interaction*. Aalborg: Aalborg University Press.

Lundvall, B.-Å. (2002) *Innovation, Growth and Social Cohesion; The Danish Model*. London: Edward Elgar.

Lundvall, B.-Å. (2006) 'Interactive learning, social capital and economic performance', in D. Foray and B. Kahin (eds) *Advancing Knowledge and the Knowledge Economy*. Cambridge, MA: Harvard University Press.

Lundvall, B.-Å. and Johnson, B. (1994) 'The learning economy', *Journal of Industry Studies*, 1 (2), 23–42.

Lundvall, B.-Å., Rasmussen, P. and Lorenz, E. (2008) 'Education in the learning economy: A European perspective', *Policy Futures in Education*, 6 (2), 681–700.

OECD (1994) *The OECD Jobs Study: Facts, Analysis, Strategies*. Paris: OECD.

Rosenberg, N. (1982) *Inside the Black Box: Technology and Economics*. Cambridge: Cambridge University Press.

Rothwell, R. (1977) 'The characteristics of successful innovators and technically progressive firms', *R&D Management*, 7 (3), 191–206.

Sen, A. (1995) *Inequality Reexamined*. Oxford: Oxford University Press.

Senge, P. (1990) *The Fifth Discipline: The Art and Practice of Learning*. New York: Doubleday.

Woolcock, M. (1998) 'Social capital and economic development: Toward a theoretical synthesis and policy framework', *Theory and Society*, 27 (2), 151–207.

Part IV

Meeting the challenges ahead?

TEN

Social investment in the ageing populations of Europe

Thomas Lindh

Introduction

At different points in the life course families and individuals differ in both their needs and in terms of the resources they can command. Large shares of children require large expenditure on education and family resources. Large shares of young adults put the labour and housing markets under strain. In a stable population that would not make much of a difference to public policy since the relative shares of different age groups in that special case remain the same. But modern populations are far from stable. The demographic transition from high mortality and high fertility to a state of low mortality and low fertility results in a secular change where the initial population pyramids undergo what demographers call a 'rectangularisation'.

To begin with this is a highly beneficial change where an economy increases its economically active population in relation to the dependants. This demographic gift can be tracked in the old European welfare states as well as in the emerging economies of Asia. This gives ample room for social reform and in most countries, especially in Europe, the public sector has taken over more and more responsibility for intergenerational transfers of many different kinds: public pension schemes, public care systems, education and a variety of family support systems.

As the structure of the population changes these public commitments often come under strain or, more rarely, tend to become overly generous. In any case the slow inertial change of the population structure, not only with respect to age, but also in ethnic composition, and even, in some Asian countries, in gender composition, creates new challenges to public policy in terms of financing as well as in terms of new needs arising from the demographic change.

In Europe fast ageing populations are now emerging and worry public policy makers as tax bases are projected to shrink and demands for decent care and a worthy life for elderly people become harder and harder to fulfil. At least that is the picture we have got used to from media and politicians eager to save for this bleak future. Change and adaptation will indeed become necessary as the composition of the population changes its point of gravity towards ever older ages. But change and adaptation provide opportunities as well as problems. One of these opportunities is to invest more in health and education in order to improve the future support capacity of the working population. This deserves to be taken seriously when everyone worries about government debts in the wake of the financial crisis. This preoccupation with financial debt risks crowding out investments in education and health, as well as the social inclusion of large groups of young people.

Sweden has already gone through a dramatic ageing episode in the 1960s and 1970s when it became the world's oldest country. Morel et al. as well as Sommestad (see Chapters One and Twelve in this volume) discuss in more detail the demographically motivated social policy that is a legacy from the 1930s and the Myrdals in Sweden. Here I will focus more on how Sweden's early ageing led not only to problems but also to opportunities for social investment in many different forms: investment that today brings returns in the form of a very strong economy that could grasp new opportunities as a new ageing episode is upon us. Could – if public policy makers would abandon the illusion of health care, education and investment in social cohesion as a form of public 'consumption', that is.

Most European countries will soon start to age at a faster rate, and it may be fatal for the future of Europe if policy makers cannot embark on more far-sighted agendas than the current preoccupation with short-term stabilisation at the cost of eroding the future productive capacity by increasing social exclusion in particular for young people in the life phase of becoming established in the labour market, forming families and obtaining affordable housing.

Ageing and intergenerational redistribution

It has, over the last decades, become clear that macroeconomic performance and population structure are intimately tied together (see, for example, Bloom et al., 2003). When the population above 65 starts to grow faster than the active population this is associated with declining growth, decreased savings, increasing inflation pressure and difficulties in keeping down the public budget deficits.

Ageing European populations have therefore raised concerns about the sustainability of current welfare systems. While some concern is well motivated, the doomsday prophecies predicting an end to social welfare as we know it are vastly exaggerated. True enough, economic growth will wane and the support ratio for elderly care and welfare will diminish. But most of the pressure from an elderly population will not come within the next decade and for most European countries not until we are well into the 2030s or even the 2040s. There is plenty of time to prepare for a rational adaptation to the situation. Some adaptations require very long run investments, however, that have to be financed right now so timing of policies is becoming crucial. A central point of this chapter is therefore that attention to demographic detail and interaction with the economy has to be country-specific rather than EU harmonised.

Even with growth rates of the real economy of a paltry 1% (2%) per capita this means a more than 22% (or 49%) increase in an already comfortable standard of living after 20 years. To make such a number comprehensible consider that a 22% increase in GDP/capita in, for example, Germany represents more than the GDP/capita of Albania in 2008 or in West Germany and Finland in 1950. It is a quite substantial increase in resources per capita and far from any catastrophe scenario. Starting from a rather comfortable level of income per capita today the problem of ageing is not really the average level of income. The problem of ageing is not so much lack of resources but the fact that there will be fewer active income earners relative to the non-active population, hence a need for increased redistribution of resources across generations. This redistribution can take place through adaptations on several different margins.[1] Longer work lives, tax redistribution, increased female labour force participation, increased education, immigration and related issues have been extensively discussed as 'solutions' to the ageing problem.

In the European discussion of ageing the intergenerational perspective on human society and economies is still quite crude and primitive and all too often based on the strange concept that children and young adults form a social group of individuals competing with another social group of old people. Every individual will, however, live through these stages unless prematurely deceased. It is a basic fact of human life that all of us are born with the need for adults to support our consumption needs for many years. In every society redistribution of resources from the economically active population to dependants is a basic economic function that has created constraints within which the human species and societies have evolved (see, for example, Robson and Kaplan, 2003). For most of human history very few people survived into a physical state of old age dependency and this is still the case in many countries. Most adults continued to generate surpluses above what was necessary for their own consumption until they died or at worst spent a very short period of illness being dependent on the surplus generated by the adult population.

The capacity of human adult populations to generate very substantial surpluses has also made it both possible and a moral duty to take care of other individuals who, due to disabilities, accidents or old age, are incapable of producing enough for their own consumption. As longevity has increased more and more people live long enough for ageing to proceed to a stage where the individual no longer is self-supporting. Institutional responses to this development have created a diversity of social security measures like pension plans and elderly care systems. Often we primarily think of public interventions in this respect but there are a lot of other institutions, within or outside the family, that mediate these intergenerational transfers.

There are essentially three mechanisms for mediating intergenerational transfers. The first and obvious is family transfers primarily to children but also to elderly parents. For orphans and childless elderly there have always been alternative private, cooperative or public transfer flows that have taken on a much larger scale in modern societies. Across countries we find quite a large variation in institutions mediating these transfers where Scandinavian countries rely on public transfer systems to a much larger extent than other European countries. But there is still another mechanism for intergenerational transfers that is often not recognised as such, viz. the financial markets. Capital reallocation is de facto an exchange of resources across generations. In the case of bequests this is obvious but it holds also for other capital transactions. As one person abstains from consumption by buying an asset, another person sells the asset and obtains resources for consumption. Netting out all transactions, a capital reallocation across generations takes place.

With increasing longevity elderly dependency expands and a growing proportion of elderly persons are becoming dependent on transfers and redistribution across generations. Through technological change, trade and education, GDP per capita has increased exponentially for a long time and with it the potential to also increase the intergenerational resource flows. New research is now mapping out these transfer flows across generations within the National Accounts framework (Mason et al., 2009). The National Transfer Accounts (NTA) provide evidence that the intergenerational flows of resources are no less important today than they have been historically. On the contrary the flows have expanded outside the original family and kinship group and even outside the national context. This holds especially for financial markets but is also true for migration, remigration and generated remittances and social security benefits. EU subsidies are another example of how the intergenerational redistribution system exceeds national boundaries. It is troubling that this function of the subsidy system is very seldom recognised.

The central concept of this NTA accounting is the life cycle deficit, defined as consumption less labour income.[2] This deficit must at every age and time period be financed by public or private transfers, or alternatively by credit or assets and capital income generated by previous saving. In this context it is therefore natural to define net wealth as claims on future income either from existing capital assets or from public or private transfer systems.

Transfer wealth essentially consists of claims on the surplus income of economically active adults, or with another terminology the present value of returns to the human capital stock. Those claims can be realised through taxation in the case of public transfers or by familial obligations, charity or other private or cooperative insurance. From this perspective then much of both public and private consumption is actually investment in the future human capital stock that is needed to sustain the consumption needs of dependants in society.

Figure 10.1: Life cycle deficits per capita expressed as part of average labour income between ages 30 and 49

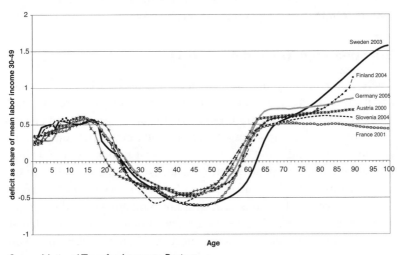

Source: National Transfer Accounts Project.

In Figure 10.1 per capita life cycle deficits for seven European countries normalised by average labour income between 30 and 49 years of age are compared. It is obvious that although the general pattern of youth and elderly dependence is common, there are strong dissimilarities between the countries. For example, in Austria the average young adult becomes independent at a much younger age than in the other countries, a fact linked both to a fairly small share in higher education and a traditional apprentice system with paid professional training. On the other hand Austrians tend to retire early and elderly care traditionally takes place within the family. Thus the patterns of intergenerational transfers within the official economy are strongly dependent on the institutional context in each country.

When the proportion of elderly dependants increase in an economy this creates tensions in the transfer system, no matter what the main mechanisms might be. In a country with mainly public redistribution systems, tax revenue and public transfers in cash and kind in the long run must balance and a tradeoff has to be made between elderly welfare and welfare and education for the young. In a traditional family system the tradeoff has to take place within the family and does not necessarily show up directly in the National Accounts. Family care for elderly people will rather show up in decreasing female labour supply, for example. This will certainly have an impact in terms of lower GDP per capita, but the resources spent will not show up in the accounts. Where transfers are primarily mediated by capital reallocation, consequences may be even harder to trace, but will still indirectly affect asset prices and the scope for capital accumulation. In both the latter cases inequality within cohorts will be a rising concern.

European ageing and prospects

There is a general awareness now both within the EU Commission and most of its member states as well as in the Russian Federation and other countries outside the Union that Europe is ageing and ageing fast. It has long been recognised that this will put pressure on pension systems, elderly care, and in general the social welfare system. In the media this is frequently turned into a major catastrophe story that makes the dismantling of the welfare state a historic necessity, a conclusion that for ideological reasons sounds quite sympathetic in the ears of some people. In evaluating these claims we should first of all recall that 'crying wolf' in order to obtain a short-run benefit before the wolf has actually shown up is in general a very dangerous strategy. In this particular case it is important to make three observations:

1. Ageing is a slow inertial process which we in fact can predict much better than climate change. It does not require hasty panic measures

but well-debated, deliberated and contemplated long-run reforms of social policies. At the same time some windows of opportunity have already opened and others will open in the future while still others have already closed. So focus must be on the windows that are currently open.

2. While all of Europe is ageing, its ageing burdens grow at different rates. This is due partly to different institutions and partly to demographic path dependence. Maximum pressures as well as windows of opportunity will come at different times for the European countries and the mix of measures required to adapt will be institution-specific and thus must necessarily differ across countries. Thus EU harmonisation may in this context be a very counterproductive policy.

3. Any ageing country will need to adapt its transfer system no matter whether this today relies on public intergenerational transfers, private family transfers or transfers mediated by the capital markets. The set of adaptations that is appropriate and permissible within different countries will differ but keeping the status quo is in no case an option that is available.

In Figure 10.2 the ageing of Europe is illustrated in some EU countries by the development since 1980 of the population share above 64. This is commonly taken as the definition of how old a country is. According to this definition Sweden ranked oldest in the late part of the past century but has been replaced by Italy, which is currently being caught up by Germany. According to the UN forecasts Italy will, however, take the lead again until caught up by Germany again in the late 2030s. Most other countries are projected to converge to a share of 65+ between 20 and 25% of the population around 2030, except Ireland, which is way behind in its ageing process. It is easy to see that although all countries are ageing, the variation in the process is quite large, suggesting that different countries will tend to feel the need for action at rather different points in time. Their fiscal resource bases will also vary in a non-coordinated way.

While 65 and above is a conventional marker of retirement ages, the average age of retirement in fact varies quite a lot, being in general lower in the countries of southern Europe. These differences in actual retirement age modify the actual dependency burdens and generally put southern Europe at a disadvantage.

We know that morbidity and mortality accelerates around the age of 80 and that much of the total care expenditure during life is concentrated on the last few years of life. The groups above 80 are referred to as the 'oldest old'. Here the per capita transfers often reach very high amounts, but since mortality is high in this group the aggregate share of transfers in kind and cash is not that high.

In Figure 10.3 the 80 and above population is depicted for the same EU countries as above. In this sense Sweden was the oldest European country until recently (2007), when Italy caught up. According to the UN projections Germany will be catching up with Italy around 2020 but then Italy takes the lead again. For this oldest-old group we see no tendency to convergence around 2030 but rather increased dispersion.

Figure 10.2: Estimates and projections of the population percentage 65 years old and above

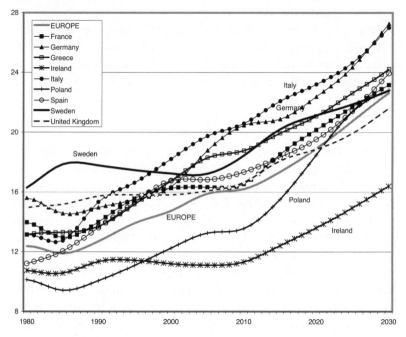

Source: UN World Population Projections, 2007.

While increasing life expectancy of course plays a role for this ageing process it is not at all the main factor shaping the ups and downs that we see in the ageing trends. In Table 10.1 current life expectancy for both sexes (2000–5) in some of the countries in the graphs is listed and it is quite clear that current accelerations in the age share measures has little or nothing to do with life expectancy. It is differences in the fertility rates both currently and historically that provide the main explanation of differences in the pace of ageing.

Figure 10.3: Estimates and projections of the population percentage 80 years old and above

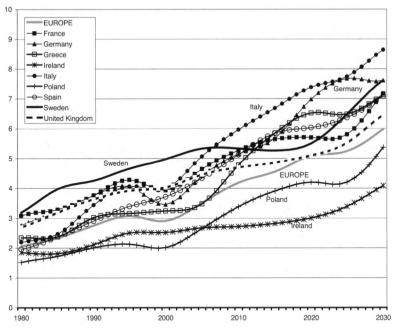

Source: UN World Population Prospects, 2007.

In spite of their small cohorts of children the predicted total dependency rates of our country sample rises much more steeply in low-fertility countries such as Germany, Italy and Spain than in countries with more moderate fertility trends like France, Sweden and the UK (Figure 10.4). While Sweden and France need to set young people in their 20s in focus for investment in education and labour market entry, the low-fertility countries need to consider their family policies a main priority.

Table 10.1: Life expectancy in 2005 (years)

Sweden	80.09
Spain	79.99
Italy	79.93
France	79.60
Germany	78.73
UK	78.47
Greece	78.26
Ireland	77.78

Source: UN World Population Prospects, 2007.

Figure 10.4: Estimates and projections of the dependency rate as a percentage: population 0–14 and 65+ divided by the population 15–64

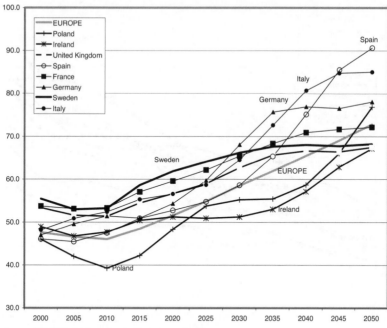

Source: UN World Population Prospects, 2007.

At this point it is prudent to note that there is a tendency in the public debate to take demographic projections far too seriously. The actual development is, however, far from deterministic and projections in 2050 have a wide margin of uncertainty (see Lutz and Scherbov, 1998, for an example). Although the general age structure projections are highly reliable for a decade or two and for the older population many more years, the uncertainty surrounding the projections for the young population increases strongly as time goes by. It is the inertia of demographic structural change that makes projections reliable and not any deep knowledge about what drives demographic change. Inflows and outflows into the population are very hard to predict with any reasonable degree of accuracy, and the smaller the country, the harder it gets. The more borders open for migration, the harder it gets, and so forth. Having pointed this out it is obvious that demographic change, at least in part, also is susceptible to policy interventions both in terms of actions to make it easier for people to achieve their desired fertility and in terms of migration policies. From a more negative view, negligence of appropriate health policies also affects mortality. In an ageing Europe the question of immigrant integration into the labour force becomes a matter of welfare preservation.

The ageing of populations in most developed countries has been going on for many years already. The problem is neither new nor unavoidable in the very long run although in Europe it will persist for many decades ahead. Demography is not fate incarnated but a reaction, a kind of memory resulting from social and economic events. An unfavourable ageing trend often has its roots in baby booms and busts generations ago. The trend of ageing and its economic and social consequences will not be avoidable in the near future (of this century) but consequences can be substantially ameliorated by political action. Immigration and fertility can be affected by political measures and current status of these variables is, among other things, also a result of the current social policy regime. Increased labour force participation and education can, at different time horizons, economically shore up shortages of people in active ages. Even the age boundaries for phases of the life cycle can be changed by ensuring incentives for later retirement and faster education.

Policies that make society a nicer place to have babies in will decelerate the ageing trends in the long run secular scale. In the shorter run decadal time-scale integration of immigrants also helps slow down the economic consequences of the ageing trend.

In either case it is no universal panacea to rejuvenate the population. Sooner (immigrants) or later (babies) also grow old. There are other adaptations though that will help to sustain social welfare. We can work longer, a reasonable proposition if we live longer and healthier lives. Current workplaces and working life demands may not today be consistent with that but this can change too.[3] Although a common EU policy against this background seems rather unrealistic there is clearly scope for learning between the EU countries about how to deal with ageing problems. Policies have to be adapted to the specific timing of demographic change and the institutional setup in different countries because transition problems will arise in the adaptations that are idiosyncratic to each country. Nevertheless, it is clear that youth unemployment and difficulties in integrating immigrants into the labour market are common European stumbling blocks in preparing for the ageing society.

The European Community can learn from each other but simple best-practice reasoning should, however, be avoided with great emphasis. The ageing challenge is common to all industrialised societies. It is a challenge with no simple solutions but with a wealth of potential adaptations available with the common denominator that a society has to reproduce itself in order to sustain increasing needs for intergenerational redistribution. Whether through native fertility or foreign immigration is not the crucial issue but different strategies in social policy will tend to force either the one or the other to dominate. Moreover, it should be noted that reproduction of a society should be defined as reproducing the production capacity necessary to maintain the intergenerational redistribution system. This does not imply that the population maintains its current size; education and technological change may very well uphold the necessary capacity with a lower number of workers. Prolonging working life or increasing labour force participation are other measures that increase productive capacity per capita.

Measures designed to simply increase the labour input of the current population have rather immediate effects and will in general not be very costly financially although the political costs may be substantial. Measures like increasing education or raising fertility require quite long gestation periods and may be quite expensive. Only when the individuals are middle aged will the investment costs be recovered and thus such measures have a planning horizon stretching from 20 to 50 years ahead. Immigration is intermediate between these cases but the details depend on source countries and the capacity of the host country to integrate immigrants into the labour market.

Macroeconomic effects of ageing

The changing age structure in Europe will have macroeconomic effects that are much more pervasive than just increasing the number of dependants to be supported (Lindh and Malmberg, 2008). Space does not permit a detailed argument but based on empirical regularities observed in the relation between age structure and macroeconomic variables, the following scenario has a high likelihood.

Saving goes down as the number of people saving for retirement decreases. The prediction of the pure life cycle hypothesis (Modigliani and Brumberg, 1954) that elderly people will live off their assets has been largely falsified; they are generally found to keep on saving after retirement (Börsch-Supan and Stahl, 1991). Still it is found on the macrolevel that national savings generally decrease as the 65+ age group increases. One of the reasons why elderly people can keep on saving is that pension income is sufficient for their consumption and increasing numbers of retirees deplete pension funds or government budgets. In many European countries the pensions are paid on a pay-as-you-go basis and represent claims on the active population that are not backed by assets and thus pressure builds up on public budgets as well as on corporate pension funds. At the same time other public expenditure on elderly care and health care starts to expand and the tax base in the active population decreases relative to expenditure.

Some countries need to expand the education system either for demographic reasons or to increase competitiveness in production. Increasing pressure on the government budget then becomes unavoidable. Strict budgetary discipline will depress aggregate demand dangerously close to a depression situation so the most likely outcome will be to finance budget deficits either by loans or by issuing new money. Loan financing also has depressing effects on the economy so at some point inflationary pressures start to build up.

The depressing forces will tend to dampen growth with further repercussions into the vicious circle of a weakening tax base and increasing public expenditure. The most sensible way to deal with this situation is to increase the taxes, but this option will also be limited, at least politically. Economically tax hikes will in many cases disrupt efficient allocation of resources but given the expansionary effects of government expenditure the final outcome is far from clear.

Connected to the above scenario is a deterioration of the current account and increased dependence on the global environment, while increased redistribution of resources is required both across birth cohorts and across regions, since the ageing trend will be stronger in economically weak regions.

In fact, we recognise in this scenario many of the ingredients in Swedish macroeconomic development in the 1970s and 1980s (Lindh, 2000). Swedish post-war developments illustrate both problems and opportunities in designing appropriate policies to meet the challenges of ageing. Thus it is of interest to go into a little more detail regarding the social policy changes that Swedish politicians met this early ageing wave with.

Swedish post-war social investment in human capital

Sweden was ageing faster than other countries in the post-war period mainly because of the very low fertility experienced in the 1930s. As Nikolai shows (see Chapter Four), Sweden was an outlier by 1980 in terms of social investment spending. This was very much the result of a public policy with roots in the 1930s that focused on investing in the population when the pace of ageing accelerated. Pension reforms were combined with school and education reforms, expanded elderly care systems were combined with highly subsidised housing programmes, and public day care was introduced and expanded quickly as female labour demand grew with the growing care sector.

Without a healthy and educated population that also reproduced itself the protection of social rights as well as the productivity of the economy could not be sustained. Providing good health care, healthy housing and expanding the investment in education of children were important parts in this endeavour that has survived as a mainstay in Swedish political debate, notwithstanding that a more individualistic policy perspective has become dominant.

Fertility started to rise in Sweden already at the end of the 1930s and in the midst of World War II a baby boom occurred that peaked in 1945. This baby boom substantially increased the demand for welfare services and family transfers. As the large cohorts born in the beginning of the twentieth century started ageing towards retirement, demands for pension reform grew and were satisfied at the end of the 1950s in a prosperous economy.

When the large cohorts born in the 1940s started to enter the labour market in the 1960s and onwards, the education system was expanded along several dimensions. This had as a consequence that (unlike US baby boomers) the Swedish boomers were not at all or to a much smaller extent victims of cohort-crowding[4] due to explicit education policies as emphasised by Nelson and Stephens (see Chapter Eight). Expansion of the care and education systems in turn provided females with labour market opportunities. This set off a demand for child care facilities that was met with a heavily subsidised public system of high-quality day care (see Chapter Six).

Total fertility rates (TFRs)[5] then again fell to low levels towards the end of the 1970s due to factors such as increased higher education for females, higher female labour force participation and the economic crisis. In 1974 the previous maternal leave system was replaced by parental leave with 90% income replacement for six months. In 1980, parental leave was further extended to nine months with income replacement at 90% and three months at a flat rate. At the same time a speed premium on having the next child within 24 months was introduced together with two months of paid leave to attend to sick children and some other minor changes. In the mid-1980s a new baby boom wave started and peaked in 1990 (TFR 2.1). After the 1993 collapse of the Swedish economy, benefit levels were first limited to 80% of income in 1995 and 1996 to 75%. TFR fell dramatically over the 1990s and although the 80% level was restored in 1998 fertility hit an all-time low (TFR 1.5) in 1999 when recruiting to the public sector had grinded to an almost full stop. Then birth rates resurged concurrent with further improvements in family policy. In 2002 two months of the parental leave were reserved for each parent and paid leave extended to 13 months and a special child allowance for parents in higher education was added to the system. In the child care sector, unemployed parents in 2001 got the right to have children in day care. This right was extended to parents on parental leave with another sibling in 2002, and a ceiling on day care fees (previously income-related) was introduced. Mörk et al. (2008) estimate that just this latter reform explains a substantial part of the increase in fertility 18 months after the reform. The latest official TFR calculation in 2009 has almost reached the fertility levels around 1990 (TFR 1.94).

This short story of the Swedish fertility 'roller coaster'[6] omits a lot of details (such as housing subsidies) but illustrates my argument that fertility in Sweden has been shaped by a number of social policy responses to circumstances, making it harder to achieve the desired norm of at least two children per woman. Desired fertility in Sweden has been firmly anchored around two children for a very long time (and completed fertility is actually close to two for all cohorts born since 1900).

It is, however, easy to understand why a forward-looking government wanting to preserve welfare for elderly people would also like to keep fertility not too far from the reproduction rate. I will not argue that the policies I describe were fully premeditated and implemented for rational reasons of amending ageing problems. That was certainly not the case, and the roller coaster variation is per se not a very rational response because it causes excessive variation in public budgets as well as public employment. I do believe that it was a long-term ingrained political tradition in Sweden to see fertility falling below reproduction rates as a symptom of social problems, and not without good reasons (see Lindh et al., 2005, for more elaborated arguments).

It is now the case that Sweden still has a very old population compared to most other countries in spite of massive immigration (13% of the population was foreign-born in 2009). Nevertheless, Swedish demographic projections look less dramatic and less worrisome than those of countries that have viewed fertility as a completely private issue.

Deliberate or not, the policy reactions to Swedish ageing in the past resulted in investment in the young. That does not involve only fertility, of course; it was also a matter of expanding health care and education for the young, allowing labour immigration in the 1950s and 1960s and in the 1960s and 1970s to provide good housing opportunities, study loans, pensions, and so on. Sometimes this was done to ridiculously high costs that could not be sustained in the long run. Many policies were later abolished such as most of the housing subsidies but many are still very much with us like the child care system and the parental leave transfers.

Although these investments in both the human and social capital of the young baby boomers from the 1940s caused temporary costs in terms of the GDP level – as the ageing burden increased in the 1970s – they are also a very important factor behind the recovery of the Swedish economy in the late 1990s when the pay-off to higher educated middle-aged boomers from the 1940s stimulated the economy. This is a much more important lesson to learn from the crisis than budgetary caution in the present situation.

Most of these investments in the young generation are not generally recognised since they go under the headings of 'public consumption' or 'government transfers'. This terminology is grossly misleading. No farmer would fail to differentiate what can be eaten from the harvest from that which must be sown in the spring. Such mistakes would put the farmer's survival at stake.

Where does Sweden stand today?

Sweden is now in the middle of a generational shift. A large chunk of the working population is retiring from working life while another large chunk of the population is entering adulthood. If the entrants could simply enter into the vacancies created by retirement there would not be much of a problem to discuss. In reality this will, however, set in motion a very complex chain of promotions, new vacancies and closing of some of the old job slots. Not least will it deepen the regional disparities. Thus, in Sweden today, demography, in the form of generational shift, will further contribute to the factors mentioned by Lundvall and Lorenz (see Chapter Nine) that speed up the rate of change in the labour market.

From a long-term perspective an older population will require more services and less goods production. Globalisation further reinforces the same pattern of replacing labour-intensive low skill and not place-dependent jobs through import substitution with specialised services and skill-intensive export production to pay for the imports. Structural change of the economy is therefore implied both by domestic demographic change and by global competition. The re-matching of the labour force needed in order to implement this change could be favoured by the generational shift providing lots of mobile and well-educated labour to help it along.

In Figure 10.5 the annual changes in the number of people in age group 15–29 and 65+ are displayed. Like in 1970 we now have a group of young adults that has been increasing in numbers and at the same time strongly increasing numbers of retirees. This was not the case in the 1990s. Although there was an increase in young adults it was not as strong and the increase in the 65+ group was slow and even decreased towards the end of the decade.

Figure 10.5: Annual changes in the number of young adults (15–29) and in the elderly (65+)

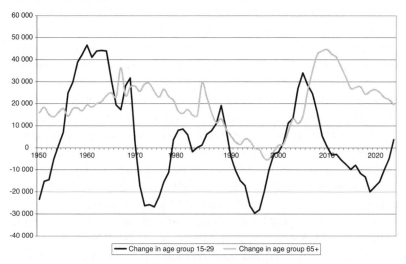

Source: Estimates and projections from Statistics Sweden.

An opportunity to renew and prepare the care and education sector for the future has now opened. The return from investments in human capital is likely to be vast, borrowing is cheap, and a more painless structural adjustment of the economy than Sweden had in the 1990s is possible although not likely as long as budgetary discipline arguments remain unchallenged, and indeed institutionalised in EU treaties. There is not necessarily anything wrong with budgetary discipline: waste should be condemned. But when the accounting in state budgets does not allow for the periodisation of investment expenditure, budgetary discipline spells underinvestment, and in particular in such parts as education and family support that still go under the name of 'public consumption' in the National Accounts. There is today a growing dissatisfaction with 'core' macroeconomics not being able to produce much in terms of answers to the questions of today. Still, there is most likely a long way before any consensus grows about exactly what is wrong.

Opportunities for social investment in the wake of the financial crisis

The financial crisis in 2008 may very well lead to further short-sighted decisions that undermine the opportunities to safeguard the welfare systems by a well-informed productive social policy. Massive investment in the future tax base of the European Union is needed and the financial crisis has already diverted substantial resources to emergency support for banks and automobile industries and strengthened xenophobic tendencies across Europe that makes immigrant integration harder. Sweden held the distinction of being the oldest country in the world for most of the time from the 1960s to the mid-1990s. The baby boomers of the 1940s came into the labour market at about the same time. The boomers helped not only to support this ageing population but to substantially increase the welfare for the whole population and in particular elderly people by contributing to the then new ATP pension system both for themselves and for their parents. Extensive labour immigration in the 1950s and 1960s with immigrant labour force participation rates that even exceeded those of the natives added to the tax base, making it possible to substantially increase social welfare along many different dimensions in the 1960s and early 1970s. In particular, education was reformed and made accessible to many more than before.

Later in the 1970s and 1980s a vast expansion of health care and elderly care also became possible within the tax revenue generated by the much better educated cohorts which were replacing the retiring cohorts born in the beginning of the twentieth century and greatly aided by a quick expansion of female labour supply. Without the expansion of the education system to harbour the boomers the tax revenue would have been substantially less. Thus the investment in the boomers was crucial to the welfare enhancement for elderly people.

But there were also mistakes made in the 1970s in terms of unsustainable subsidies to housing, too lax monetary policies and the use of devaluation to improve competitiveness in the world market. Some, although perhaps not all, of the mistakes could have been avoided if long-term planning had not extrapolated the record growth rates of the 1960s, which were caused by the coincidence of a demographically favourable situation and a fast growing and stable world market.[7]

As the boomers from the 1940s now retire, Sweden and its social policy again must adapt to a similar situation as in the early 1970s.

Although the social investment perspective was not defined in the 1970s, many of the aims and actions of that time were in the same vein of thought. After the deregulation of the economy in the 1980s and 1990s it is now up to Swedish politicians to decide whether the country will act as a warning beacon for other European countries to avoid or serve as an example to follow: an example for how a productive social policy can not only avoid future problems but at the same time solve a number of current social problems like immigrant integration, gender discrimination and youth unemployment.

The celebrated Swedish pension reform in 1994, seen as a model for many other countries, is now facing its first serious crisis by releasing the 'brake', that is, the financial solvency rule guaranteeing the financial integrity of the system. The buffer funds in the system have suffered depletion in the financial crisis. Together with negative income growth and inflation it has become necessary to lower pensions to preserve long-run financial stability. To avoid too large pension cuts in the election year 2010 politicians have already redesigned the system in order to spread out the cut in pension benefits over several years. As the automatic balancing mechanism was introduced everybody was assured that such an event was so highly improbable as to be negligible. But financial crises occur now and then within the lifespan of a generation and serve as a warning of relying too heavily on capital markets to transfer resources across the life cycle.

At the same time the young boomers born around 1990 are starting to fill up a higher education system that has been shrinking in the 2000s and where large parts of the staff are on the verge of retirement. Other young boomers try to become established in a labour market where both public and private employers have been cutting back. The age at which 75% of a Swedish cohort has become established in the labour market increased over the 1990s from 23 years to 28 or 29. This is partly due to higher enrolment in higher education, that is, an investment for the future, but partly also due to a swelling of the ranks of unemployed youngsters, undermining the future impact of the investment by marginalising large groups early in life, especially second generation immigrants (Rooth and Ekberg, 2003).

A new baby boom wave has been rising since 2000 and now fills the day-care centres and will soon require expansion of the school system again. The strain on the government budget would be hard even within normal economic activity. Starting from budget deficits in the wake of the financial crisis there is clearly a danger that short-sightedness will drain the resources needed for aiding young people's education, labour market experience and most likely also loom large over their housing prospects and family formation ambitions. The retirement of the baby boomers is at the same time slowly draining the tax base for state income taxes and capital taxes.

At the longer horizon looms the need for elderly care and health care for the now retiring boomers some time in the 2020s. The intergenerational transfer and care systems for the elderly are in Sweden almost exclusively administered through the public welfare institutions. Calculations at the Ministry of Finance (Pettersson et al., 2006) attribute 80% of the public budget expenditure to transfers in kind and cash over the life cycle. It is of paramount importance for the future welfare state in Sweden that the social investment activity does not tradeoff welfare expenditure for the elderly against investment in the generation who is expected to finance the elderly care and the pay-as-you-go pension system in the 2020s and onwards. In other European systems the strain of elderly dependency will also increase but depending on the design of the intergenerational transfer system the pressure may be hidden outside of the System of National Accounting. In family reliance systems it is often assumed that children can take care of elderly parents as well as two or more even older relatives. While that might have worked in the old days[8] the resource base for family care has eroded heavily in almost all countries due to decreased fertility, increased labour mobility and female labour force participation and increased higher education. The repercussions on female labour supply, because it will be females mainly who provide family care, will then further undermine the tax base for other social policies. In funded systems long-run returns within the country will wither as the labour force shrinks and domestic asset demand falters with diminishing aggregate saving. Only risky investment in developing and emerging countries provides a vent for these systems.

Sweden has now, somewhat ahead of other European nations, come to a critical juncture where competing resource demands must reach a new balance in the midst of crisis. The government in place since 2006 has learned from the crisis in the 1990s and their Social Democrat predecessor to be cautious with the public budget. Former Prime Minister Göran Persson's dictum 'Whoever is in debt is not free' has become the creed also of the right-wing government.

Unfortunately that is exactly the wrong lesson for the current crisis. The Swedish crisis at the beginning of the 1990s was a home-brewed crisis in a more favourable demographic situation. Yet it turned out that the burden of establishing a working public balance again was borne mainly by young adults, low-skilled labour, immigrants and families with children (Palme et al., 2003). In a situation where a baby boom is entering the labour market and another is withdrawing, tight fiscal policies are a recipe that jeopardises our welfare for decades to come, increasing inequality, decreasing potential future growth and undermining the sustainability of both the pension system and the public budget by shrinking the future tax base.

Conclusion

The challenges of an ageing Europe provide motivation as well as opportunities for social investments, equipping our societies with tools to adapt to a historically new situation. Never before have we been able to observe countries where up to a fourth of the population eventually will be above 65 years of age. In this chapter, I have argued that this requires massive social investment in the younger population to foster skills and social cohesion.

The experience from how Sweden in the 1970s and 1980s has met ageing emphasises the importance of offensive investment in the human and social capital of the young as crucial for the sustainability of elderly welfare. But the world has also changed since then, adding globalisation and climate change to the challenges Europe will meet. Increased labour mobility and immigration trends put new issues on the social investment agenda; many social security policies are designed with the implicit assumption that the individual lives within one system from birth to death. Social cohesion and social investment thus need to be rethought in stretching across previous borders.

The human capital life cycles do look different in the European countries. In family-conservative, German-speaking and Mediterranean countries fertility is at dangerously low levels, which is also the case for Eastern European transition countries. There is a difference between these two groups of countries though. In the transition countries the population is generally younger, making it easier to induce a recovery in birth rates, and also intensify investment in education. In the liberal and Scandinavian welfare states fertility is not of any prime concern, but rather the investment in improving education and labour market entry for the young. In Scandinavia integration of immigrants is far from satisfactory, making immigration a net fiscal burden. Rational strategies must be formed according to these differences as well as with respect for different histories, preferences and institutions.

Thus, the lesson from early Swedish ageing is not to attempt to duplicate more or less successful strategies (and avoid mistakes) but in the much more general conclusion that public policy and social investment must aim at providing citizens with the tools needed to uphold intergenerational redistribution and at the same time extend social cohesion across current borders. As Lundvall and Lorenz argue (see Chapter Nine), this will also mean redesigning outdated labour market institutions in order to achieve necessary learning flexibility.

The intergenerational redistribution approach in this chapter is obviously tailored for better understanding of the ageing issues but at the same time provides an alternative view of society and the economy, neither as an endeavour for individual satisfaction nor for serving the interests of static class collectives. Social investment from this point of view is investment not in the production but in the reproduction and extension of the intergenerational redistribution system.

Productive social policies have to be designed to fit current demographic structures as well as take into account their consequences for future demographics and the repercussions the population structure has on both economics and the sustainability of social welfare. This requires long-term perspectives as well as an integrated view of the policy system. The European Union has a long way to go before achieving such an integrated view on social investment (c.f. Chapters Four and Five).

Notes

[1] MacKellar (2000) discusses this in detail.

[2] The life cycle deficit $LCD_{it} = C_{it} - YL_{it} = YA_{it} - S_{it} + \square^+ - \square^-$, where C is public and private consumption, YL is labour income, YA is asset income and S is savings and the last two terms are the difference between transfer inflows and transfer outflows, both public and private.

[3] In Sweden the prime factor at this time may be to speed up education in order to prolong working life by starting it earlier. In Austria it may be more important to offer more higher education and instead improve incentives to work longer; see Figure 10.1.

[4] Easterlin (1961) put forward the hypothesis that labour at different ages are not perfect substitutes and thus relatively large supplies of young labour would compete within the cohort and put downward pressure on wages. In the USA this has been largely confirmed but evidence in Europe is mixed.

[5] The TFR is defined as the sum of the fertility rates at each age in a given year.

[6] The expression comes from an article by Hoem and Hoem (1996).

[7] This unwarranted optimism in the Long-Term Survey at the Ministry of Finance is sometimes referred to as the 'porcupine' since if you place the

GDP forecasts from the 1970s and 1980s in the same graph the picture will resemble that animal with ever lower revised forecasts.

[8] Except in countries with extensive emigration like Sweden in the nineteenth century.

References

Bloom, D.E. and Canning, D. and Sevilla, J.P. (2003) *The Demographic Dividend: A New Perspective on the Economic Consequences of Population Change*. Santa Monica: Rand.

Börsch-Supan, A. and Stahl, K. (1991) 'Life cycle savings and consumption constraints', *Journal of Population Economics*, 4 (3), 233–55.

Easterlin, R.A. (1961) 'The American baby boom in historical perspective', *American Economic Review*, 51 (5), 869–911.

Hoem, B. and Hoem, J. (1996) 'Sweden's family policies and roller-coaster fertility', *Journal of Population Problems*, 52 (3–4), 1–22.

Lindh, T. (2000) '1990-talets ekonomiska utveckling – vilken roll har åldersfördelningen spelat?', in J. Fritzell (ed.) *Välfärdens förutsättningar – Arbetsmarknad, demografi och segregation*, antologi från kommittén Välfärdsbokslut, SOU 2000:37. Stockholm: Fritze.

Lindh, T. and Malmberg, B. (2008) 'Macroeconomics and age structure in a welfare state – Sweden 1946–2005', in J.C. Tremmel (ed.) *Demographic Change and Intergenerational Justice: The Implementation of Long-Term Thinking in the Political Decision Making Process*. Berlin: Springer Verlag, pp. 51–95.

Lindh T., Malmberg, B. and Palme, J. (2005) 'Generations at war or sustainable social policy in aging societies', *Journal of Political Philosophy*, 13 (4), 470–89.

Lutz, W. and Scherbov, S. (1998) 'An expert-based framework for probabilistic national population projections: The example of Austria', *European Journal of Population*, 14 (1), 1–17.

MacKellar, L.F. (2000) 'The predicament of population aging: A review essay', *Population and Development Review*, 26 (2), 365–97.

Mason, A., Lee, R., Tung, A., Lai, M. and Miller, T. (2007) 'Population aging and intergenerational transfers: Introducing age into national accounts', in D. Wise (ed.) *Developments in the Economics of Aging*. National Bureau of Economic Research: University of Chicago Press.

Modigliani, F. and Brumberg, F. (1954) 'Utility analysis and the consumption function: An interpretation of cross-section data', in K. K. Kurihara (ed.) *Post-Keynesian Economics*. New Brunswick: Rutgers University Press.

Mörk, E., Sjögren, A. and Svaleryd, H. (2008) 'Cheaper childcare, more children', *Working paper 2008:29*. Uppsala: Institute for Labour Market Policy Evaluation.

Palme, J., Bergmark, A., Bäckman, O., Estrada, F., Fritzell, J., Lundbeg, O., Sjöberg, O., Sommestad, L. and Szebehely, M. (2003) 'A welfare balance sheet for the 1990s. Final report of the Swedish Welfare Commission', *Scandinavian Journal of Public Health*, Supplement 60, August.

Pettersson, T., Pettersson, T. and Westerberg A., (2006) 'Generational analyses – redistribution between generations in a growing welfare state', *report to ESS 2006:6*. Stockholm: Ministry of Finance (in Swedish).

Robson, A.J. and Hillard, S.K. (2003) 'The evolution of human longevity and intelligence in hunter-gatherer economies', *American Economic Review*, 93 (1), 150–69.

Rooth, D. and Ekberg, J. (2003) 'Unemployment and earnings for second generation immigrants in Sweden. Ethnic background and parent composition', *Journal of Population Economics*, 16, 787–814.

ELEVEN

Aftershock: the post-crisis social investment welfare state in Europe

Patrick Diamond and Roger Liddle

Introduction

This chapter discusses the prospects for social investment approaches in the wake of the worst financial crisis for more than 80 years.[1] It explores whether the pressures resulting from the crisis will prompt a reversal of social investment ideas and concepts aimed at changing the basic character of the welfare state from remedial to pre-emptive strategies.

The idea of social investment heavily influenced the European Union's (EU) Lisbon Strategy. The Lisbon Strategy saw itself as representing a new synthesis of competitive markets, knowledge-based investment and strategies for social inclusion, advocating a break with the neoliberal mindset of the previous two decades, while different in prescription to the Keynesian welfare state of the post-war era. This social investment 'turn' in policy thinking, as Hemerijck describes it, gathered momentum in the mid-1990s and owed a good deal to the intellectual influence of social scientists such as Gøsta Esping-Andersen. This new approach to the European social dimension was further developed in the landmark Belgian Presidency in 2001.

The Lisbon Strategy fell far short of its ambitious targets. Other chapters in this volume assess the diversity of social investment policies in Europe, analysing successes and failures and the tensions and synergies that have emerged over the last decade. The global financial crisis and recession, however, have added a new urgency to the debate about the future of social investment. Before the crisis, a great deal of discussion focused on the question of the Europeanisation of social and employment policy and whether EU processes were *effective* in promoting reform at member state level. Now the issue is whether a social investment strategy remains both *coherent* and *politically feasible* for the post-crisis era ahead. That is the focus of this chapter.

Crises are not only moments of catastrophe, but create unprecedented opportunities for social and economic reform. The current crisis has inevitably thrown up many challenges, but it also presents a window in which to transform the existing social and economic order. One outcome might be that Europe's political class will focus again on the importance of embedding a strong social dimension in Europe, echoing and building on Delors' conception of Social Europe in the late 1980s, but for a very different era.

Crises, however, do not necessarily lead to major ideological and political shifts. There is always the possibility that the order that prevailed prior to the financial crisis in 2008–9 will be restored. In particular the leadership of Germany, which has been forced reluctantly by events to assume the role of economic hegemony within the Eurozone, may well believe that tighter financial regulation, tougher fiscal rules and better crisis management capabilities will be sufficient in themselves to resolve the problems with the current EU economic and social order (Proissl, 2010). This chapter argues the case for a programme of radical reforms in the light of the crisis, but it has to be acknowledged that achieving this is by no means certain. There would have to be significant change in the prevailing economic orthodoxy that provides the context for social investment ideas and strategies.

The present structural context of the EU makes the term 'aftershock' just as appropriate as the notion of 'crisis': EU countries are confronted by the prospect of a series of aftershocks that will delay or even jeopardise the recovery, and constrain the options available to governments in the future. Unless concrete steps are taken to deal with the fallout of aftershocks, the EU's ability to overcome the social impact of the global financial crash over the next decade will be seriously impaired. In the wake of the crash, intellectual and political attention has unsurprisingly focused on immediate crisis management, in particular restoring stability and resilience to the financial sector and handling the rise in public indebtedness. But major questions about the sustainability of EU social protection regimes and the models of capitalism which underpin them still remain unanswered.

We may have entered a phase of societal development in the wake of the financial crisis which Colin Hay defines as 'catastrophic equilibrium', in which a series of accumulated economic and political pathologies act as roadblocks to change and reform (Hay, 2010).

The literature on social investment has lacked a comprehensive account of the structural barriers holding back the implementation of social investment strategies in the light of the multidimensional challenges that Europe faces. A central theme of this chapter is that these challenges have been exacerbated by the aftershocks of the global financial crisis. At the same time, the barriers to implementation have grown as the aftershocks put significant fiscal obstacles in the way of the social investment approach. It is clear that significant institutional and structural constraints now threaten the implementation of social investment strategies.

First, the banking crisis and its aftermath have diverted the attention of policy makers and politicians away from long-term strategic issues towards immediate crisis management. The emphasis tends to be on shoring up the existing models and their attendant paradigms, rather than contemplating deeply rooted institutional reforms. Second, public deficits are judged by what the debt markets are perceived to tolerate, not by what is economically rational when private sector activity is exceptionally weak. The 'golden rule' principle that even with the economy in a steady state, it makes sense for the authorities to 'borrow to invest' has been temporarily abandoned. This creates an environment in which it becomes less plausible to argue for investment in welfare state innovation that can raise the potential growth rate and curb the future public costs of social failure. Third, the financial crisis has heightened the significance of 'old' social risks such as poverty. Already millions of EU citizens lack access to the basic essentials of life, especially in the member states that joined the EU in 2004 and 2007. There are fears that the crisis and ensuing fiscal retrenchment will lead to rising income poverty among children and older citizens.

Taken together, this hardly constitutes a propitious backdrop to forging a new welfare state edifice in Europe. The crisis is deep and its nature highlights the links between three central framing arguments that run through the chapter. The first is the multidimensional nature of the crisis on which the first section expands, and the fact that its current aftershocks have originated not just in the financial sector crash itself, but in long-term structural trends. The chapter argues that it is not just one crisis that the EU faces, but five interlocking social crises: rising unemployment and the social consequences of the global financial crash; growing divergence throughout the EU, as countries seek alternative paths to entrenching macroeconomic stability and coping with new structural pressures; the long-term crisis of winners and losers that originates in economic globalisation; the structural trends of demography and rising life expectancy that bear down on the welfare state; and the impact of migration, integration and identity on social citizenship and cohesion. The 2008 crisis did not create these problems, but its aftershocks have intensified them. The crisis in public finances accentuates the difficulty of responding to long-term challenges such as Europe's ageing demography and climate change, which will prove as fiscally challenging as the present need for consolidation to reduce indebtedness. The question is whether robust social investment strategies can be developed against the backdrop of these multidimensional challenges that the 2008–9 crisis has accentuated the difficulty of meeting.

The second framing argument is that these aftershocks in combination put social and economic inequality back at the centre of the public policy agenda, but in a new context: highlighting the emerging problems of the 'squeezed middle'. This will force a reassessment of the strengths and weaknesses of the pre-crisis policy consensus. The social investment perspective has drawn heavily from the philosophical well of John Rawls and Amartya Sen. Its objective is not to secure equality of outcome, but to overcome the structural barriers to equality of opportunity and widen access to the capabilities that individuals need to realise those opportunities. Yet perceptions may have changed as a result of the crisis. At one level, the contrast between the relative fortunes of bankers and the young unemployed refocuses attention on inequalities of outcome, particularly the perceived grossness and unfairness of some rewards at the top. However, the economic realities experienced by the 'squeezed middle' appear to diminish public support for redistribution – as the British Social Attitudes Survey suggests has occurred in the UK[2] – and may make social investment the only viable approach by which deepening inequalities can be addressed by governments. The third framing argument concerns the structural barriers within Europe to the implementation of a social investment framework: both the institutional constraints within the nation state accentuated by the new politics of austerity, as well as the ambiguous role of the EU itself.

The third section then briefly discusses the future of the state and its relevance to the wider debate about the viability of a social investment perspective. This explores whether the necessary retrenchment in public spending in the wake of the crisis will result in a return to the 'cutting back of the state' ideology of the previous neoliberal hegemony. Many commentators have long predicted the demise of the post-war Keynesian welfare state. Whatever the ideological preferences of the major political actors in key European memser states, however, we urge a more cautious approach. While the halcyon days of the bounded national welfare state may be over, the state will continue to play a significant role in social and economic policy. There is no reason to believe that state spending as a proportion of GDP is set to fall dramatically in the industrialised countries (Flinders, 2010).

Attention then switches in the fourth section to the role of the European Union, highlighting the present tradeoffs between economic integration and a socially inclusive modernisation of Europe's welfare states, and considers how a strengthening of the EU's social dimensions might help to resolve these tensions. It argues that a Euro-Keynesian solution is both improbable and unrealistic as individual member states need to pursue distinctive reform strategies in order to improve their resilience in coping with present challenges and future social risks. The EU as a whole needs to develop a new policy paradigm based on a combination of social investment and regulatory intervention, implemented through policy reforms both within member states and action at EU level. The final section concludes with indications of how improved policy action and coordination at EU level could ensure a more favourable structural environment for the return to growth that would underpin the realisation of social investment policies, and provide important safeguards against the present risk of a destructive social 'race to the bottom' in Europe.

One of the central lessons of the crisis, particularly in countries such as Britain, Ireland and Spain, is that social policy cannot adequately compensate for the effects of models of capitalism that tend to amplify inequality and risk. This is also a lesson for some of the new member states; for example, those in the Baltic region. In the future, social investment and regulatory intervention have to be seen as two sides of the same coin. To be effective, social policy will have to operate within the context of robust regulation of markets, instead of relying solely on the post hoc cushioning provided by the central state.

The existence of a highly deregulated financial sector, for example, will impair social investment, as well as the resilience and stability of the wider economy. This does not mean that financial re-regulation is the only priority. In addition, new regulatory interventions are needed to rebalance the economy; to promote innovation through better linking research and enterprise; ensuring an adequate supply of capital to innovative and growing businesses; actively nurturing potential competitive strengths through both sectoral and spatial policies; and improving the supply of skills and human capital. In tackling the crisis aftershocks analysed in this chapter, social policy has to help shape market outcomes as a positive productive factor, instead of seeking only to correct adverse consequences after the event. This has clear implications for how the EU conceives its future policy for the Single Market, not simply as an instrument of liberalisation and deregulation, but as a common set of rules designed to combine economic efficiency with greater social justice.

The focus of this chapter on structural barriers should not imply an apocalyptic view about the long-term viability of the social investment paradigm. Crises do provide moments in which potentially far-reaching and radical social reforms become more attainable than in the past. The future remains open and is ours to shape.

The multidimensional nature of the crisis: five interlocking 'aftershock' challenges are at work

As we argued above, current aftershocks originate in long-term structural trends but the crisis has amplified the economic and social challenges those trends now pose. This section summarises those interlinking challenges.

Aftershock I: the direct social consequences of the crisis – rising unemployment, lost potential and public austerity

The first-round effect of the financial crisis was an increase in unemployment in most EU member states. Unemployment in October 2010 stood at 10% in the Eurozone and 9.6% in the EU-27. In the EU-27, however, unemployment has fluctuated since the beginning of the decade: from 8.5% in October 2000, to 8.8% in October 2005, to 7.3% in October 2008, and up to 9.4% in October 2009. There has been a reversal in the progress made in reducing unemployment from 2005 to 2008, when the EU was more successful than the USA in creating new jobs. The question is whether this rise in unemployment would prove to be of short-term cyclical impact, or have more lasting consequences that would leave permanent social scars.

One of the positive features of the current crisis is that although unemployment has increased in the core EU countries – the UK, France and Germany – unemployment has risen significantly more slowly than would have been expected by the experience of previous recessions. This suggests that government-led labour market interventions and stimulus policies have in the short term been effective. A good example was the German subsidy to support temporary short-time working. Moreover, German export growth has bounced back after an initial sharp decline in manufacturing output, as has economic growth overall. Unemployment in Germany at the end of 2010 was approximately three million and on a largely downward trajectory. This appears part of a longer-term labour market trend, to the extent that unemployment in the final months of 2010 was two million less than when the Schroeder government introduced the Hartz IV (Agenda 2010) labour market reforms in 2003.

Germany, however, is in a much more favourable position on unemployment than most member states. Unemployment rose between October 2008 and October 2010 in 25 of 27 member states – only Luxembourg and Germany have bucked the trend. In some countries the rise in unemployment over this timeframe has been especially marked: in Spain, it has risen from 13% to 20.6%; in Estonia, Lithuania and Bulgaria it has more than doubled to 16.2%, 18.3% and 10.1% respectively; and there have been big increases in Ireland (13.9%), Latvia (18.2%), Hungary (11.2%) and Slovakia (14.5%). There is a clear contrast between the core of the Eurozone, which has been more resilient, and a periphery of countries in which there are severe employment problems. This raises the issue of how unemployment is affecting social and geopolitical cohesion among various age groups and member states within the Eurozone.

Advocates of social investment strategies have focused their policy concerns on the problems of long-term unemployment, its concentration among particular social groups, and its tendency to reinforce the transmission of social disadvantage through the generations. The severe impact of the present crisis on young people in particular raises major social concerns about the long-term 'scarring' effects of youth unemployment, as well as the loss of productive potential for the future. Young people appear to have been disproportionately affected in many member states. Across the EU, youth unemployment (defined as ages 15–24) at the end of 2010 stood at one-fifth, rising to more than 40% in Spain and Latvia. The Netherlands is the only member state whose youth unemployment is ranked below 10%.

Unemployment has increased faster amongst workers on temporary contracts than those with permanent positions. The social impact of rising unemployment reflects the dualisation of labour markets in member states where those at the margins have proved to be most vulnerable. Not only are workers on temporary contracts easiest to dismiss: employers have had very little incentive to invest in their skills, accentuating the human capital deficiencies of member states, particularly those in southern Europe that have a large stock of poorly educated labour. The Spanish case is the most extreme. In 2009, temporary fixed-term employment fell by a staggering 35% in the Spanish construction sector, while at the same time the wages of Spanish workers on permanent contracts actually increased by 4% (Bentolila et al., 2010).

One key factor in explaining the diversity of employment outcomes is whether member states have made use of the fiscal policy space to stimulate their economies and intervene directly to save jobs. This, together with increased wage flexibility, probably explains why unemployment has not in the initial stages of the crisis risen as fast as expected in the UK and France. In the second round of the crisis, where measures are being taken to execute 'exit strategies' from public indebtedness, the social consequences will differ greatly in scale and social impact as member states face a wide divergence of fiscal challenges.

A central indicator of unemployment increases to come is how public deficits vary between member states. In 2009, no member state registered a government surplus and 25 member states recorded a worsening of the government balance relative to GDP compared with 2008 (only Estonia and Malta showed an improvement). Indeed, since the pre-crisis period in 2007, there has been a marked increase in the public deficit as a percentage of GDP in several member states. In Ireland, this has gone from a 0.1% surplus to 14.3% deficit; in Belgium the deficit has risen from 0.2% to 6%; in Greece the reported deficit almost trebled to 13.6%; in Latvia and Lithuania it has increased more than nine-fold to 9%; in Portugal it has increased from 2.6% to 9.4%; and in the UK it has rocketed to 11.5% from 2.8%.

Nonetheless, while in 2009 Ireland's budget deficit was 14.3% of GDP and Spain's 11.2%, in contrast Germany's was only 3.3% and Austria's 3.4%. As a result the imperative for fiscal consolidation varies widely. The European Commission has recently forecast that it expects there to be 1.5% growth in GDP in 2011, rising to 2% in 2012. About half of the EU-27 are anticipated to post lower deficits in 2010 than in 2009. Thanks to stronger growth, and the end of temporary stimulus measures and additional consolidation measures announced by most member states in their annual budgets, the overall government deficit in the EU-27 is expected to fall from 6.5% of GDP in 2010 to approximately 5% in 2011 and 4.5% in 2012. This will broadly be matched in the Eurozone, albeit at a lower level. However, debt ratio remains on an upward trajectory, reaching 83% of GDP in the EU-27 and 88% in the Euro area by 2012, which could in time jeopardise long-term fiscal sustainability if it is not reversed (European Commission, 2010a).

Despite these differences, common themes do emerge across the EU. Welfare spending on transfer payments is being reduced in many member states. For example, €30 billion have been cut from the budget in Germany, with parents on unemployment benefits losing their entitlement to *Elterngeld* (payments to parents supporting the cost of bringing up children) of €300 a month. €2.8 billion worth of welfare cuts were announced in the Republic of Ireland's December 2010 budget. In the UK, £19 billion in welfare benefit cuts have been announced in the period up to 2015.

From a social investment perspective, the scale of the planned fiscal consolidations at national level raises a number of concerns. First, in the general squeeze on resources, the scope for social investment will be restricted. Second, the danger is that fiscal retrenchment will reinforce the elderly bias that has predominated in many Western welfare state regimes (Esping-Andersen, 2009). Third, cuts in welfare benefits will reverse whatever progress has been made in recent years in tackling poverty, particularly child and family poverty, which is particularly negative for human development potential.

Aftershock II: the impact of EU divergence

For much of the last 60 years, Europe has witnessed increasing convergence among member states, but the present crisis appears to be leading to greater divergence. At the same time, the risk is that solidarity among member states will decline given the pressures of domestic austerity.

To take a starker example, in the second quarter of 2010, Greece's GDP fell by 1.5%, while Germany's grew in contrast by 2.2%. Several of the new member states have witnessed dramatic falls in GDP. For example, Romania's economy shrunk by 8.7% in the second quarter of 2009. This is in a country where the average standard of living of its weakest regions is little more than a quarter of the EU-27 average. It is worth recalling that in 2008 on the accepted EU measure of material deprivation – the inability of a citizen to afford three of nine key indicators – 51% of Bulgarians and 50% of Romanians were categorised as deprived; 30% of Bulgarians, 29% of Slovaks and 26% of Hungarians could not afford a proper meal every day.

The diverging impact of the economic crisis across the European continent is also exacerbating regional divisions within EU countries. The threat to national solidarity produced by such polarisation has been revealed in Germany, where liberal *FreieDemokratischePartei* (FDP) finance expert Frank Schäffler advocated the abolition of 'solidarity' payments by west German citizens to fund investment in the former East.[3] In January 2010, unemployment in eastern *Länder* stood at 13.5% in contrast to 7.4% in the west.

From a social investment perspective, growing territorial divergence increases the social challenges that Europe faces. Not only does it raise the issue of absolute poverty in weaker member states with its attendant impact on human potential. It also adds to migratory pressures within the EU and in particular the 'brain drain' of talent from the weaker regions. This is seen by some economists as precisely the kind of increased labour market flexibility that the European economy needs if the Single Market and its single currency are to prosper (Alesina et al., 2010). While such migration may have positive economic effects in the regions to which migrants transfer, it can also increase social pressures, in particular the failings of the education system and the problems of low skills and employability, even in the more prosperous parts of the EU. As for the poorest and weakest regions which migrants leave, while remittances back home are an important source of transfers, the question of the long-term sustainability of these regions are made more difficult. In summary, internal migration can be positive, but without complementary interventions that ease the social costs, the impact on solidarity and cohesion within the EU could be adverse.

Aftershock III: the long-term globalisation crisis of 'winners' and 'losers'

The impact of greater divergence *between* member states at the macroeconomic level is accompanied by the increasing polarisation of labour markets between 'winners' and 'losers' *within* member states. There is considerable dispute as to how far this trend towards polarisation is due to globalisation which is often blamed in popular discourse: changes in technology and decisions by firms within the EU to invest in lower costs locations within the Single Market may be just as important. However, the crisis has clearly accentuated the global competitive challenge, as Asian and other emerging economies race ahead and gradually build up their competitive capabilities in sectors higher up the value chain. From a social investment perspective, Europe is now in a position where it needs to address these economic and social challenges from a relatively weak economic base.

The labour market has been increasingly hollowed out, squeezing real wages for those in the middle and lower deciles of the wage distribution, as Maarten Goos and Alan Manning cogently argue in their seminal work, *Lousy and Lovely Jobs* (Goos and Manning, 2007). This is the case in the USA and UK but also across most of the EU-15, which has experienced a disproportionate increase in high-paid and low-paid employment since, 'in advanced countries, technologies are becoming more intense in the use of non-routine tasks concentrated in high-paid and low-paid service jobs at the expense of routine tasks concentrated in manufacturing and clerical work' (Goos et al., 2009). Lower-skilled workers are also increasingly vulnerable to the threat of redundancy and unemployment. While 84% of highly skilled Europeans have a job, more than half of low-skilled workers are currently unemployed (European Commission, 2010b). In France, 72% of those with higher-level qualifications have full-time jobs, whilst the figure for those without a diploma is 43% (Savidan and Maurin, 2009). Downward pressure on wages and the fear of unemployment have heightened economic insecurity for those on lower and middle incomes, compounded by the growth of income volatility. Across the industrialised countries, median income households experience much sharper changes in incomes over time than was the case 30 years ago (OECD, 2008).

The access to skills necessary for an individual to succeed in the global knowledge economy also remains unequally distributed. In the UK, as well as in the other OECD countries, the class divide in educational achievement between children from high- and low-income households remains stubborn and persistent (West, 2009). These educational inequalities exacerbate the polarisation between 'lovely' and 'lousy' jobs, ensuring that existing social inequalities in ethnic and class terms are hardwired into the diverging labour market. This has wider social ramifications, as the decline of stable working-class jobs fuels a loss of self-esteem and identity, particularly among younger and older men, leading to the rise of social pessimism across the EU and even disengagement from politics itself (Liddle and Lerais, 2007).

Overall, wage share as a proportion of national income has declined sharply since 1980 in the EU-15, Japan and the USA, implying that average wages have failed to keep pace with labour productivity. In 17 out of 20 countries, earnings at the top of the wage distribution rose sharply relative to those at the bottom after the early 1990s. There is also evidence of higher levels of income volatility and wage instability in the major industrialised countries (OECD, 2008).

Within the UK at one end of the income distribution, the City of London appears to be recovering rapidly from the initial impact of the financial crisis, with the return of large bonus payments. By contrast, the decline of relatively secure manual jobs is starkly illustrated by the rise in UK poverty rates among households where at least one parent is working: in 1999, 40% of children classed as living in poverty came from families with at least one working parent. By 2009, this had increased to nearly 50% (Tripney et al., 2009).

In Germany, the National Institute for Economic Research calculated that in 2008, domestically 11.5 million individuals were living in poverty, a third more than a decade previously (Grabka and Frick, 2010). Vital in this regard was the increase from the early 1990s to 2008 of the proportion of jobs paying only the subsistence wage, from slightly over a quarter, to over a third of the total.[4]

It is also important to focus not only on the pathways that the unemployed use to get back into work, but on the dynamics of low-paid jobs. The Institute for Social & Economic Research's British Household Panel Survey has tracked members of 5,000 households since 1991, demonstrating that the low-waged and low-skilled in the UK economy are most likely to experience spells of temporary unemployment; 30% of such men became unemployed for a period, compared to 12% in the top quartile. Skill levels have a significant impact on job tenure.[5]

The situation in the EU is, of course, characterised by considerable diversity, as well as convergence. Some member states have sought to cope with structural challenges by maintaining strong protections for those in work at the cost of higher unemployment and inactivity, while others have put employment activation first and tolerated more widespread low pay and in-work poverty. There has been a tendency to increased dualism in both labour markets and the design of welfare states, with employers restructuring their operations to offer near lifetime opportunities to a highly skilled core. On the other hand, welfare states need to adjust to the risks of in-work poverty among increasingly excluded groups of low-paid and low-skilled workers (Palier and Thelen, 2010). Of all the member states, the Nordic countries have by far the best record in navigating a way through this dilemma, but that is largely because their social investment strategy has strongly supported full-time employment participation by 'dual earner' couples (Palme, 2006).

The growth of such a dualism points to the need for continued labour market reforms at national level. High unemployment may make such reforms more difficult to achieve, except in member states where the internal crisis has become so severe that voters and interest groups see no alternative to acceptance of change, as may be occurring in Greece and Spain. On the other hand, a well developed model of 'positive flexicurity' may require additional public investment in active labour market measures and new forms of social insurance, the likelihood of which will be severely constrained by the public spending consequences of the crisis. It may also necessitate new labour market regulations to require employers to pursue family friendly employment practices, which may encounter stronger business resistance at a time of squeezed profitability.

Aftershock IV: demography and life expectancy – the long-term viability of the 'European Social Model'

The threat to social cohesion fuelled by the polarisation of the European labour market is heightened by the increasing strains imposed on the post-war welfare state by changing patterns of longevity and life expectancy, as the Commission has recently recognised in a green paper on pensions (European Commission, 2010c).

While member states are at different stages of their ageing process (see Chapter Ten), tensions will emerge between the increasing long-term costs of welfare provision in terms of additional health and social care costs as well as pensions, and member states' immediate drive for fiscal austerity. Once the painful fiscal consolidation resulting from the events of 2008 is complete, member states face the greater challenge of addressing the spending pressures of the EU's demographic crisis.

It should be remembered that for all the strengths of Europe's existing social models, nearly a fifth of Europe's older people are still prone to poverty in old age, particularly where they have an inadequate occupational pension and live alone. In addition to straining the capacities of national welfare systems due to inequalities of life expectancy and pension provision, the ageing of Europe's populations threatens to widen the gulf between rich and poor. The aftershock of the financial crisis on pensions has also to be considered. The sharp fall in equity markets has seriously affected the level of pension fund assets, squeezing pensioners' incomes in countries with large private sector provision (Hemerijck et al., 2010).

The favoured social investment response to the sustainability of the welfare state in the face of ageing demography has been to increase the retirement age, and to promote higher employment participation among older people. The financial crisis, the global recession and the increase in unemployment pose a potential threat to that strategy. While the first signs are that employers and unions are not following the restructuring strategies of the 1980s and 1990s in laying off older workers and encouraging early retirement, it is unclear whether the welcome rise in the employment participation rate among the over-50s in the last decade will be sustained.

The complexity of changing retirement patterns and the sustainability of pensions systems are challenging enough, but Europe will also need to cope with an increasing proportion of 'frail elderly' requiring care. Household service provision will be organised via partnerships where the state provides some financing, as well as direct medical care. But the system will increasingly rely on other forms of paid and unpaid care work. This potentially conflicts with gender equality priorities, since care and domestic provision for elderly people are predominantly provided by women in most European countries, where pay rates and job security are very low.

Aftershock V: migration, integration and identity

Given that demographic change poses profound questions about the future sustainability and structure of the welfare state in the EU, an obvious response is for European countries to be the welcoming recipient of younger migrants. Internal migration was a huge driver of economic growth in the past. From the 1960s, migrants came to Europe from Turkey, North Africa and former colonies throughout the world. In the last 15 years, there has been a huge growth in migration to southern Europe from Africa, the Balkans and Latin America, while the UK and Ireland saw a large influx of East Europeans after EU enlargement in 2004. From the perspective of Europe's demographic crisis, this should have been seen as a positive development.

Economically, however, the EU has failed to make the most of this potential talent pool and it is likely that the aftershocks of the economic crisis both on job opportunities and on social provision will worsen this situation markedly. In Germany in 2006/07, only 12.2% of boys and 14.8% of girls from a Turkish background attended an academic *Gymnasium*, in comparison to 41.7% and 47.4% of their native contemporaries. Turkish pupils are by contrast disproportionately represented at the lower end of the school system: 44.3% of Turkish boys attend a *Hauptschule*, as opposed to only 16.7% of Germans.

Similar inequalities exist in France where according to a 2003 study, 10.1% of second-generation Turkish pupils attend university, in contrast to 18.6% of those from low-income backgrounds (Windle, 2008). In the UK, children from some ethnic minority groups appear to do better at school; however, children of African-Caribbean, Bangladeshi and Pakistani origin perform significantly worse. A recent study demonstrated that only in Sweden does the second generation of migrants enjoy the same educational opportunities for their children as the native community (OECD, 2008).

There are growing concerns about the social and political impact of migration across the EU, despite the many economic and cultural benefits which migrants bring to member states. The 2009 European Parliament elections witnessed significant success by far-right political parties standing on an anti-immigration platform. Geert Wilders' anti-Islamic party came second in the Netherlands with 15% of the vote, with Jobbik, a Hungarian anti-Semitic party antagonistic towards Sinti and Roma, winning three of the country's 22 seats. Austria's two main far-right parties claimed over 28% of the vote in the 2008 national election. The British National Party is strong in particular areas of northern England, winning seats in the European Parliament in 2009. It can hardly be coincidental that the neo-Nazi National Party of Germany is most entrenched in two former eastern *Länder*, winning seats in their regional parliament.

The capacity of migration to emerge as a contested political issue is greatly exacerbated by divergences between the richer and poorer member states in the EU after the financial crisis. The combination of increasing migration and strained integration has potentially serious consequences for the welfare state and the foundations of social solidarity on which it depends. The 'squeezed middle' complains of wage competition from migrants – although the facts are in contention – and looks with increasing resentment at 'scroungers' not in work and on welfare benefits. On the other hand, if language, educational and labour market barriers result in migrants being disproportionately out of work, instincts of solidarity are undermined even further. The social contract behind a social investment welfare state depends on an explicit acceptance of rights and duties. A comprehensive social investment strategy must seek to invest in the skills and capabilities of every individual, regardless of ethnicity or background.

The role of the state and the politics of austerity

In the light of the five post-crisis aftershocks outlined in the previous section, the debate about the practical capacity and legitimate role of the state underpins all of the contemporary challenges of social investment, shaping the policy options and strategies that are viewed as credible and realistic (Flinders, 2010). Some commentators argue that the present conjuncture will lead to a significant 'rolling back of the state' which would, in turn, require a major rethink of the social investment model. This proposition appears questionable, however.

First, the necessity for fiscal consolidation should not automatically be interpreted as an ideological shift concerning the role of the state. While the present round of fiscal consolidations will lead to a downsizing of the welfare state, depending on the severity of the fiscal challenge that member states face, some adjustment was inevitable as current public spending plans were based on assumptions of economic growth that the crisis and its aftershocks have made unrealisable. While a powerful

Keynesian argument can be made to sustain public spending throughout a cyclical downturn, increased borrowing cannot be a substitute for long-term fiscal sustainability.

Second, although centre-right governments now predominate in the EU and their 'leitmotif' is fiscal caution and prudence, there is little evidence of any strong ideological commitment to changing the fundamental nature of the European welfare state. Even in the UK, the British Conservative Party has made much of its determination to protect the socialised National Health Service.

Third, what is significant about the state in almost all of the major industrialised countries is not only the sheer size of government, but its apparent capacity to withstand all efforts to reduce its scope and scale (Pierson, 1995). Public expenditure as a proportion of GDP has exhibited remarkable stability since 1970, fluctuating within a relatively narrow range. There are also considerable pressures for increased spending that will not disappear. Demographic pressures are already creating strains in health and social care systems. Tackling climate change, while driving forward the transition to a low-carbon economy, will prove costly for both the taxpayer and the electricity consumer (Latham and Liddle, 2009).

While the size of the state has not diminished in terms of resource allocation since the 1960s, the functions of the state have clearly evolved during that period. Perhaps the most important change is the impact of the New Public Management (NPM) paradigm, which clearly influences many governments in the industrialised world and has led to a shift in the role of the state from provider to commissioner of public services. In other words, a strategic state that aims 'to steer but not to row' (Osbourne and Gaebler, 1990). For the last two decades, debate has largely revolved around how public services should be delivered, the merits of increased patient and parental choice, the role of quasi-markets and diversity of provision.

The implications for the ideas and strategies associated with social investment are two-fold. On the one hand, the emphasis on efficiency and effectiveness implied by outcome-orientated approaches to service delivery does not necessarily weaken the traditional commitment to the state, particularly not in relation to the share of GDP invested in the welfare state and public services. Indeed, the changing functions of the state may open up additional oppurtunities for social investment, bringing in new providers and creating more vibrant quasi-markets in social policy and public services. A simplistic public–private dichotomy does not necessarily facilitate effective social investment strategies.

On the other hand, the institutional legacy of NPM, at least in Britain and the USA in particular, is a highly fragmented organisational landscape which makes the coordination of policy and delivery increasingly problematic (Rhodes, 2007). The fragmentation of responsibility and accountability among multiple 'arms-length' public bodies and quasi-autonomous delivery agencies makes it far more challenging to sustain coherence and a long-term view, as well as to ensure consistency of implementation. This governance challenge might constitute a significant structural barrier to the successful enactment of social investment strategies in the future.

Just as the pressures on the state will increase over the next decade, the role of the state is as likely to expand in socioeconomic terms. The state retains many capacities to mitigate the impact of markets and to advance the public interest. Indeed, the financial crisis has refocused attention on the importance of state intervention in dealing with policy catastrophes relating to economy management, the financial system and global security. While centre-left parties have failed to benefit from what has been interpreted in some quarters as 'the return of the state', there is nonetheless a greater sense of the range of options and tools available through which government might play an active role, rather than simply an acquiescent rush back to 1980s neoliberalism. This is an important backdrop to debates about the future of the social investment welfare state paradigm.

The role of the EU and how its social dimension might be strengthened

While a strong case in principle can be made for greater EU integration in the wake of the crisis, at the level of domestic politics there is a danger that member states will revert to welfare nationalism in labour market regulation and welfare spending. Crucially, major EU member states are currently committed to allying domestic austerity, based on the notion of a balanced household budget, with the cultivation of export surpluses as their route to economic recovery. Many economists are incredulous, however, about this export orientated approach to the recovery, as all the leading economies that are cutting back on public spending hope to compensate for the negative impact on growth by increasing exports. Leading *Financial Times* commentator Samuel Brittan, for example, describes such policies as 'beggar-my-neighbour' in scope, noting pessimistically that, 'countries now in surplus, including China and Germany, are not going to spend their way into payments deficit because of exhortations by the UK or even the International Monetary Fund'.[6]

The prevailing policy mindset is detrimental to the future cohesion and stability of Europe in a globalising world. There are strong arguments for greater economic coordination at the EU level as well as a social policy framework that would constrain the present tendency towards negative welfare nationalism. Some policy makers yearn for the creation of an EU-wide economic government in the wake of the crisis that, in its full-blown ideal, might recreate the powers of Keynesian economic intervention that nation states were able to exercise at the height of the post-war consensus. This ought to be based on a form of fiscal federalism focused on expansionary policies, bolstered by Europe-wide wage coordination, capital and exchange controls, and if necessary industrial intervention and the imposition of import quotas and external tariffs (see Bofinger and Ried, 2010; Collignon, 2010). These interventionist policies would then provide the basis for a wider and deeper framework of social protection across the EU, based on the revival of the traditional post-war welfare state.

The crisis has demonstrated why this model of full-blown Keynesian interventionism at EU level is unlikely to be enacted. There is little sign of significant political support for it: rather, the prevailing mood is currently one of a reversion to national sovereignty, and the rejection of the idea that a stronger EU offers a solution to the structural economic challenges facing the European continent. Even if the political support did exist, such a prescription would not deal with the major structural trends alluded to in this chapter that will dramatically transform patterns of need and dependency in the welfare state for generations to come, and need to be tackled through effective national reforms.

However, a viable alternative to full-blown fiscal federalism might be for the EU to develop a hybrid model that exploits the potential for multi-tier governance within the existing European polity based on pooled sovereignty in specific policy areas. As was noted earlier, what Europe needs is a new policy paradigm based on the combination of social investment and regulatory intervention, given the multiple risks of the demise of the social investment paradigm in the post-crisis world (Hemerijck, 2010). Policies of social investment require welfare state reforms which are largely implementad through individual member states. They will not succeed unless they are coupled with stronger regulatory interventions designed to shape market outcomes, rather than simply attempting to correct the social consequences of the market. This imperative for national action should be complemented by a stronger framework at the EU level which shapes and influences reforms to the economic and social models of member states.

This stronger social framework is urgently needed because the liberalisation enforced by the single market and European Monetary Union (EMU) requires ongoing and significant economic adjustment. First, strong social models are required to handle the ensuing shocks and transitional costs such as redundancy and the downward pressure on wages, particularly for the most disadvantaged. Second, effective social policies help to increase employment participation which makes the EU more economically efficient, adds to Europe's long-term growth potential, and improves the sustainability of the social model. Third, if it is to sustain popular legitimacy with EU citizens, Europe cannot be reduced to a neoliberal project which is simply concerned with enabling markets to function more efficiently. The EU needs a coherent vision based on greater equity and personal wellbeing which advances collective solidarity.

The crisis has not fundamentally altered the major long-term dilemmas facing the EU and its member states.[7] The crisis should also be seized as an opportunity to do better, otherwise the future dimension will be lost in short-term crisis management. The need to sustain social investment strategies in a climate of fiscal austerity is the real challenge.

Conclusion: pointers for the future

Solidarity at the EU level is problematic, given that many traditional forms of solidarity have waned both within and between member states. But there are practical and concrete initiatives that the EU can develop both to foster growth and shape more positive social outcomes. Here we outline six concrete steps for national and EU policy makers.

First, there is a strong argument that the EU's fiscal and budgetary rules should be rewritten and a new consensus established on what should be the basic principles of public finance for the period ahead. Steady consolidation is essential in order to reduce public debt, but not on a timetable that will threaten recovery. The concept of social investment should be given a central place in the new EU 2020 Strategy. In judging progress towards member state compliance with a revised set of fiscal and budgetary rules, the question of the quality as well as the quantum of public expenditure needs to become a guiding principle. This raises the issue of whether it would be possible to arrive at an operational definition of what constitutes 'social investment' on which member state policies could be compared and judged. The EU has gone a long way to develop statistically robust measurements of social inclusion that allow meaningful comparison between member states. A similar exercise should now be undertaken to measure member state performance on indicators of social investment.

Second, the EU must do more to promote wider acceptance of the free movement of labour which adds to both economic efficiency and personal freedom. It could ensure greater portability of social rights within the EU. At the same time, it could ease potential tensions from internal migration by revising the Posted Workers Directive. This would strengthen the protection of established terms and conditions of employment in host countries. This is vital to address populist fears of wage undercutting associated with migrant labour.

Third, the EU could also strengthen the capacity of its member states to fund a decent welfare state through fair taxation. In the new circumstances of post-crisis fiscal austerity, member states should look more favourably on an ambitious tax agenda. This should include strengthened tax coordination to clamp down on tax evasion and abuse. The combined power of the EU should be brought to bear in order to tighten the regulation of tax havens. Member states should more closely coordinate their approach to business taxation in order to prevent tax competition eroding the business tax base to the ultimate disadvantage of all. Member states should welcome proposals for new taxes levied at EU level for a financial activities levy and carbon tax. Such taxes will only raise significant revenue if imposed at an EU level. If levied at member state level, their effectiveness will be diluted by the fear that business will migrate to elsewhere in the EU.

Fourth, the EU should develop and finance a low-carbon transition plan. This will require large-scale public–private investments in cross-border energy grids and transport infrastructure. EU-wide measures should be enacted to stimulate growth and employment across the entire EU. This will be of particular benefit to those member states where the extent of fiscal austerity precludes the possibility of making sensible low-carbon investments of their own. It would both stimulate economic activity and improve long-term competitiveness. This low-carbon investment plan would be financed by issuing bonds at EU level. Far from being a radical step towards the federal EU that 'sovereignists' fear, this would simply extend the practice of the European Investment Bank in issuing bonds for productive purposes, taking advantage of the lowest possible interest rates at which capital can be borrowed within the EU. All that is needed is an extension of that principle.

Fifth, the EU Structural Funds should be used more effectively to mitigate the impact of economic shocks on dislocated regions across the EU. Structural fund transfers ought to be sustained, but with greater conditionality attached. That should include the pursuit of EU social objectives, as the Barca report recommends (Barca, 2009). Structural funds can also help to promote positive policy 'synergies', bringing together employment policy, urban regeneration, welfare provision, education, health, and so on.

Sixth, the EU should focus far greater attention on key social policy targets such as child poverty, school dropout rates, integration of ethnic minority groups and employability. The Europe 2020 Strategy rightly focuses on these social dimensions. The major development in EU policy, however, is the agreement by the June 2010 European Council to reduce poverty and social exclusion by 20 million by 2020. This is a significant breakthrough for the project of a 'Social Europe' and should assume great importance. If it is made operational and effective, it offers the potential to act as an EU-wide brake on the more extreme consequences of increasing welfare nationalism.

The framing of the new poverty target in terms of the three dimensions of relative poverty, absolute material deprivation and worklessness will require detailed technical work. But it could enable a broader policy framework to be developed that addresses the new social risks of poverty. This should include serious analysis of the structure of the labour market, the challenges of addressing low-wage equilibria, the effectiveness of minimum wages and in work benefits, and the need to modernise Europe's welfare states to cope with new social challenges, as well as the adequacy of existing social protection arrangements. The conclusion of the 2010 Joint Report on Social Protection ought to be noted:

> The crisis has highlighted great diversity within the EU. Its scope, magnitude and effects vary as does the capacity of national welfare systems to provide adequate protection. Not all Member States have the financial means to meet rising demand and some have large gaps in their safety nets. Narrowing these gaps is now a priority. (European Commission, 2010d)

The argument of this chapter is that there should be no return to 'business as usual' after the financial crisis and global recession has run its course. Instead, member states need to focus on the new challenges of the twenty-first century: economic globalisation, the low-carbon transition and the ageing society. Addressing these vast challenges – while coping with the long-term impact of the current recession – will require a stronger enabling and steering role for national governments.

This should, at the same time, occur within a stronger and more credible EU framework. Otherwise, the danger is that the EU will merely succumb to 'beggar my neighbour' policies among member states.

The 2008–9 financial crisis is unlikely to transform the economic and social architecture of the EU, although its long-term implications are still unclear. The crisis also presents new opportunities for fundamental social and economic reform. In the past, change has been extremely difficult to achieve in Europe's welfare regimes, precisely because many groups of beneficiaries have effectively defended the current constellation of social rights as being in the public interest. Periods of upheaval put renewed pressure on existing frameworks of provision, however, potentially thawing frozen welfare state landscapes. The crisis aftershocks that the EU is currently experiencing may indeed be the catalyst for rebuilding the collective solidarities that a strong Europe inevitably needs if it is to prosper.

Notes

[1] All statistics referred to in this paper are taken from datasets on the Eurostat website, http://ec.europa.eu/eurostat, or from official national statistics offices across the EU-27, unless otherwise stated.

[2] British Social Attitudes Survey, www.britsocat.com/.

[3] http://in.reuters.com/article/idINIndia-50988720100821.

[4] www.stern.de/panorama/armutsbericht-arbeit-schuetzt-nicht-vor-armut-620763.html.

[5] www.iser.essex.ac.uk/survey/bhps.

[6] www.ft.com/cms/s/0/fca56f34-b154-11df-b899-00144feabdc0.html.

[7] As argued by André Sapir at the Institute for Futures Studies Conference, in Stockholm, 7–8 May 2009.

[8] European Commission, *Global Europe: Competing in the World*, http://ec.europa.eu/trade/issues/sectoral/competitiveness/global_europe_en.htm.

References

Alesina, A., Ardagna, S. and Galasso, V. (2010) 'The euro and structural reforms', in A. Alesina and F. Giavazzi (eds) *Europe and the Euro*. Chicago: University of Chicago Press, pp. 57–98.

Barca, F. (2009) *An Agenda for Reformed Cohesion Policy: A Place-Based Approach to Meeting European Union Challenges and Expectations*. Brussels: European Commission.

Bentolila, S., Boeri, T. and Cahuc, P. (2010) 'Ending the scourge of dual labour markets in Europe', VOX. Available at www.voxeu.com.

Bofinger, P. and Ried, S. (2010) 'A new framework for fiscal policy consolidation in Europe', German Council of Economic Experts, *Working Paper 03/2010*. Wiesbaden: German Council of Economic Experts.

Collignon, S. (2009) *Report on Europe: Mastering the Crisis*. Rome: Centro Europa Ricerche.

Esping-Andersen, G.E. (2009) *The Incomplete Revolution: Adapting Welfare States to Women's New Roles*. Cambridge: The Polity Press.

European Commission (2010a) *European Economic Forecast – Autumn 2010*. Brussels: European Commission.

European Commission (2010b) *New Skills for New Jobs: Action Now. A Report by the Expert Group on New Skills for New Jobs Prepared for the European Commission*. Brussels: European Commission.

European Commission (2010c) *Green Paper on Pensions* MEMO/10/302. Brussels: European Commission.

European Commission (2010d) *Joint Report on Social Protection and Social Inclusion*. Brussels: European Commission.

Flinders, M. (2010) 'The future of the state', in V. Uberoi, A. Coutts, D. Halpern and I. McLean (eds) *Options for Britain II*. London: Wiley Blackwell, pp. 19–41.

Goos, M. and Manning, A. (2007) 'Lousy and lovely jobs: The rising polarization of work in Britain', *The Review of Economics and Statistics*, 89 (1), 118–33.

Goos, M., Manning, A., Fraumeni, B. and Salomons, A. (2009) 'Job polarization in Europe', *American Economic Review*, 99 (2), 58–63.

Grabka, M. and Frick, J. (2010) 'Weiterhin hohes Armutsrisiko in Deutschland: Kinder and junge Erwachsene sind besonders betroffen', *Wochenbericth des DIW Berlin*, July.

Hay, C. (2010) 'Pathology without crisis: The strange demise of the anglo-liberal growth model', Leonard Shapiro lecture, Political Studies Association Conference, Edinburgh, 13 May 2010.

Hemerijck, A. (2010) 'The end of an era: Economic crisis and welfare state transformation', paper presented at the conference on Economic governance in the eurozone and the EU: Drawing lessons from the crisis, Joint event ELIAMEP and Bruegel, Athens, 10–13 June 2010.

Hemerijck, A., Knapen, B. and Van Doorn, E. (2010) *Aftershocks: Economic Crisis and Institutional Choice*. Amsterdam: Amsterdam University Press.

Latham, S. and Liddle, R. (2009) 'How can the response to climate change be socially just?', in A. Giddens, S. Latham and R. Liddle (eds) *Building a Low-Carbon Future: the Politics of Climate Change*. London: Policy Network.

Liddle, R. and Lerais, F. (2007) *Europe's Social Reality*, BEPA, European Commission. Brussels: European Commission.

OECD (2008) *Growing Unequal? Income Distribution and Poverty in OECD Countries*. Paris: OECD.

Osborne, D. and Gaebler, T. (1990) *Reinventing Government: How the Entrepreneurial Spirit is Transforming the Public Sector*. New York: Plume.

Palier, B. and Thelen, K. (2010) 'Institutionalizing dualism: Complementarities and change in France and Germany', *Politics & Society,* 38 (1), 119–48.

Palme, J. (2006) 'Why the Scandinavian experience is relevant for the reform of the ESM', in P. Diamond (ed.) *The Hampton Court Agenda: a Social Model for Europe*. London: Policy Network, pp 37–48.

Pierson, C. (1995) 'Comparing welfare states', *West European Politics*, 18 (1), 197–203.

Proissl, W. (2010) 'Why Germany fell out of love with Europe', Bruegel essay and lecture series, July 2010. Brussels: Bruegel.

Rhodes, R.A.W. (2007) 'Understanding governance: Ten years on', *Organization Studies,* 28 (8), 1243–64.

Savidan, P. and Maurin, L. (2008) *L'état des inégalités en France 2009: Un panorama complet des inégalités*. Paris: Éditions Belin.

Tripney, J., Newman, M., Bangpan, M., Hempel-Jorgensen, A., Mackintosh, M., Tucker, H., and Sinclair, J. (2009) *In work poverty: a systematic review*, Department for Work and Pensions, Research Report No. 549. London: Department for Work and Pensions.

West, A. (2009) *Poverty and Educational Achievement: Why do Children from Low-Income Families tend to do Less Well at School?* Bristol: The Policy Press.

Windle, J.A. (2008) 'Ethnicity and educational inequality: An investigation of school experience in Australia and France'. Joint PhD: University of Melbourne, University of Bourgogne.

TWELVE

Climate policy and the social investment approach: towards a European model for sustainable development

Lena Sommestad

Introduction

Climate change is one of the major challenges facing humanity in the twenty-first century. Impacts and risks will grow over time and call for a double response: adaptation to new, often more severe climatic conditions; and a major transition to a low–carbon economy. Awareness of the potentially huge implications of climate change has grown in recent years, but attention from policy makers is still surprisingly limited outside the realm of environment and energy policy. This lack of attention is evident not least within the social policy community.

It is often observed that climate change tends to hit hardest those who are poor and vulnerable. Poor people suffer more than rich people and poor countries suffer more than rich countries. Policy measures to halt climate change can also put disproportionate burdens on the less affluent. These social dimensions of climate change need to be addressed not only in view of future social and economic problems but also because social policy has the potential to affect the ways in which individual countries and the global community respond to climate change.

In this chapter, I focus on social policy and climate policy in the EU. Special attention is given to two social policy areas with important implications for climate policy: income inequality and employment. EU member states have long since had well-established social policy regimes and the EU has also pioneered more extensive climate change mitigation policies. Taken together this makes the EU experience potentially instructive for other regions as well.

I argue that the future success of EU climate change mitigation policies will be dependent on successful social policy design. Social investment policies in particular can provide important backing. I also contend that successful climate policies have important features in common with social investment policies. Both policy areas build on a similar orientation towards investment in the future. Both policy areas also share a preoccupation for the quality of life and a tense relationship to the neoliberal economics paradigm.

European policy makers typically describe social and environmental targets as 'mutually supportive'. Climate policy and social policy are supposed to develop in tandem within a broader context of sustainable development. In practice, however, EU climate policy has hitherto been largely unrelated to social policy or social investment. In fact, the attachment of climate policy to the core ideas of sustainable development has been fairly weak as well. Instead, EU climate strategies seem to have been designed mainly on the basis of neoliberal doctrine, in support of liberalised energy markets, limited state intervention and European competitiveness. Cost efficiency has been at the centre of attention.

This chapter begins with an overview of the challenges and contradictions of current neoliberal European climate policies. I then explore interactions between climate and social policies. I finally discuss the broader conceptual context, in particular the need to disassociate current climate and social policies from the limitations of neoliberal doctrine. I argue that the time may be ripe for a fundamental change in the interpretive framework of EU policy making, the rise of a new economic policy paradigm: 'the economics of sustainable development'. In my view, an economic paradigm based on the concept of sustainable development can offer important new perspectives on economic policy and facilitate the closer integration of social and climate policies. Most importantly, a new paradigm of sustainable development can provide a consistent economic framework for the social investment perspective by acknowledging the need for state intervention and by giving priority to quality and sustainability in social and economic life.

European climate policies: origins and challenges ahead

Climate politics – the global framework

The first global agreement to combat climate change, The UN Convention on Climate Change, was reached at the 1992 UN Summit on Environment and Development in Rio de Janeiro. It was part of a broader effort to promote strategies of sustainable development worldwide. The Climate Convention came into force in 1994, sparking off a process of global environmental negotiations of unprecedented complexity (Kjellén, 2008).

Climate policies demand national mobilisation to protect truly global public goods: the atmosphere and the climate system. This distinctive feature of climate politics raises challenging issues of common responsibility and global fairness. A further challenge of climate politics is the huge divide between developed and developing countries. Although all countries in the world have a responsibility to contribute to climate change mitigation, their capacity to do so varies widely. On this basis industrialised countries have agreed to take the lead in combating climate change.

In 1997 parties to the Climate Convention agreed on a protocol that specified targets and measures, the Kyoto Protocol. The Kyoto Protocol states that only industrialised countries have quantified targets while developing countries have more limited commitments (such as reporting emissions).

In recent years global negotiations on climate change mitigation have come to a deadlock in the course of the long-standing attempts to agree on a new 'post-Kyoto' climate deal (in Copenhagen in 2009 and Cancún in 2010). Tensions grow between developed and developing countries. Equally important, the scope for policy renewal is limited due to the already established 'Kyoto mechanisms' that mirror a strong influence of neoliberal ideas on climate policy. Cost-effectiveness is the guiding principle of neoliberal climate policies and climate policy instruments are designed to maximise the play of market forces and to minimise the role of public actors.

Climate change mitigation policies became increasingly influenced by neoliberalism on the road from the Rio Conference (1992) to the Kyoto Protocol (1997). The rise of neoliberal ideas in climate politics parallels the neoliberal turn in social policy but came much later and was marked by a stronger adherence to economic models. In fact, when straightforward neoliberal thinking rose to predominance in climate policy it was already about to be replaced by 'inclusive liberalism' or 'the social investment perspective' in social policy (see Chapters Two and Three).

Looking ahead, climate politics stand out as a major challenge for the EU. Not only will EU member states be confronted with growing demands from poor and emerging economies for visible results in climate change mitigation, they will also have to make progress in climate policy while dealing with other major challenges such as the aftermath of the economic crisis, long-term population ageing and ever-more intense global competition. Concerns will grow over energy security. We find European climate policy at a crossroads.

Neoliberal climate policies at a crossroads

EU climate policy includes a diverse package of policy instruments, developed over the years and brought together since 2000 in the European Climate Change Programme (Damro and MacKenzie, 2008; Cooper, 2010). Well before the Kyoto summit EU climate policy instruments were market-oriented in the sense that policy instruments were designed to promote European competitiveness and the development of the internal European market. For example, uniform EU regulations were agreed on emission limits and technical standards. However, after the Kyoto summit – when US demands for emissions trading were accepted – the EU moved towards a more fully fledged neoliberal approach to climate change mitigation.

The key idea behind neoliberal climate policy is to put a market price on carbon, thereby internalising the externalities of CO_2 emissions. By trading emissions permits on a capped market, reductions are supposed to be made where costs are the lowest. The market price of carbon constantly varies (in contrast to a CO_2 tax rate which is fixed).

The EU has led the way in implementing market-based climate policies. The flagship of this new approach, the EU Emissions Trading Scheme (EU-ETS), came into force in 2005 (Christiansen and Wettestad, 2003: 5–9; Damro and Méndez, 2003). Emissions trading is complemented by other market-based instruments such as certificates of origin and ecolabel schemes (Bertoldi and Huld, 2006; Friberg, 2008: 169–70).

In 2009, EU leaders endorsed a new strategy, The EU Climate and Energy Package. In this package energy policy was for the first time fully integrated into the common European agenda. Joint measures were agreed to promote the liberalisation of European energy markets, thereby reinforcing the neoliberal context of European climate change mitigation.

Scepticism of neoliberal climate policy approach

Just as the social investment turn in social policy was triggered by disenchantment with neoliberal solutions, there has been a growing dissatisfaction with the neoliberal approach to climate change mitigation in recent years. This scepticism is not so much about the capacity to deliver on the Kyoto target as about the efficiency of current climate change mitigation policies. Apart from harsh criticisms regarding the level of ambition, critics call attention to several weak points of the neoliberal climate policy paradigm.

One line of criticism relates to lessons learnt about liberalised energy markets in Europe. It has been argued that liberalised markets are in fact not well designed to coordinate major infrastructure projects needed in the transition to a low-carbon society. Failed attempts in Europe to introduce large-scale heating systems (district heating) illustrate this point. District heating systems offer splendid opportunities for Europe to increase energy efficiency in urban areas by making use of surplus heat from power stations, waste incineration, industry and geothermal sources. However, the commercial strength of district heating lies in maintaining the value chain, from source to consumption, and these value chains tend to be fragmented by current market-oriented EU regulation. In addition, financing is difficult, since time horizons for energy infrastructure are distant and rates of return are low (Euroheatcool, 2006; Henning and Mårdsjö, 2009).

A second weakness of liberalised energy markets, according to critics, is a low level of investment in research and development. Anthony Giddens has studied the highly privatised and deregulated British energy market and argues that much-needed energy investments have been put off due to deregulation. At the same time, deregulation in the UK has resulted in 'short-termism' and a lack of controls for system risk. Power companies have become caught up in financial speculation. All in all, Giddens concludes that the liberalised British energy sector today fails to deliver any radical progress at a moment in time when innovation must be at the core of any successful climate change strategy (Giddens, 2009).

As regards the design of the European emissions trading system, the EU-ETS, critics point out that European energy companies have acquired huge windfall profits from emissions trading. These windfall profits are the combined result of the grandfathering approach of the EU-ETS in conjunction with marginal pricing practices on liberalised European energy markets (Ellerman and Joskow, 2008). Critics also bring to light the great volatility of prices on the carbon market. This volatility discourages low-carbon investment. Investors ask for a stable and predictable price on emission permits (Newbery, 2010).

Overall, the EU-ETS has met with significant resistance over the years, both at EU level and within member states, in spite of the widely praised efficiency of carbon pricing. In several member states, industry has forcefully resisted proposed allocation schemes – sometimes in concert with trade unions (Damro and MacKenzie, 2008: 75–77). This resistance should be seen in the context of an overall reluctance to accept a cost on CO_2. In fact, even conventional economic instruments such as CO_2 taxes have been difficult to implement in Europe. In 2010 only three EU member states had introduced a CO_2 tax: Sweden, Denmark and Finland. A government proposal in France was rejected in 2009. Subsidies for fossil fuels still prevail in several EU member states, instead of a price on carbon (EEA, 2004).

At present, impacts of the financial crisis serve to boost further scepticism about the adequacy – and the limits – of the current strong emphasis on market-based climate policies. In 2009, investment in green energy declined worldwide, due to the downturn of the economy. In this situation it became increasingly clear that market-based climate policy instruments such as emissions trading are in fact designed for economies working at full capacity. When demand and economic activity wane, so do prices and the profits on investment in climate change mitigation (Jones and Keen, 2009; Cooper, 2010).

Finally, the current crisis has raised doubts about the neoliberal doctrine of limited government action. In late 2008, the EU Commission launched a significant stimulus package, The European Recovery Plan. A key pillar of this plan was to kick-start smart, green investments. This should 'drive a competitive Europe ready for the low carbon economy'. However, results have fallen far short of expectations. While other global players such as the USA, India, China and South Korea have turned away from rigid neoliberal assumptions and invested massively in greening their economies, there are few indications of a substantial shift towards this kind of green investment strategies in the EU or in EU member states. All in all, public investments represent only a minor part of the European stimulus package. At a moment in time when the EU could have chosen to make a decisive turn towards a low-carbon future, Europe has lost, instead, its former leading role in greening investments.

Social investment and climate change

EU climate policies have until now been largely unrelated to social policy. I would argue that this is unfortunate, since social policy – and social investment policies in particular – do in fact influence the capacity of governments to mitigate climate change. In the following I will further explore two social policy issues of particular interest: income inequality and employment. I will then discuss possible ways to better integrate the social investment perspective and climate policy in the overall EU project.

Income inequality and climate change mitigation

There has been an apparent lack of interest in income inequality perspectives in European climate politics (Compston and Bailey, 2008). In fact, inequality within the EU has attracted much less interest over the years than between–country inequality, such as the North–South divide. However, income inequality is an important issue for climate change mitigation. Countries with more unequal income distribution tend to be less successful in climate change mitigation than more equal ones. This is shown in Figure 12.1. There is a statistically significant relationship between income distribution in a number of OECD countries and national reduction of CO_2 emissions since 1990 (the base year of the Kyoto Protocol).

Figure 12.1: Successful reduction of CO_2 emissions 1990–2007 (1990=100) by Gini coefficient

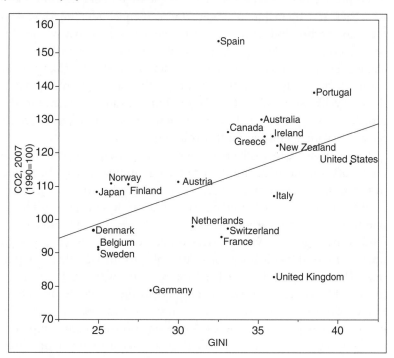

R-square, 0.206; p-value 0.0387.

Source: UNFCC (2010) for CO_2 index; Human Development Report (2005) for Gini coefficient.

How to interpret this figure? Clearly, income inequality is only one factor among others to analyse in the search for explanations to variations in climate policy performance. This can be seen in the figure where there are some obvious exceptions to the general trend as, for example, the UK. In the UK specific events such as the phasing out of the British coal mines resulted in significant emissions cuts in the broader context of high levels of inequality and an overall climate policy 'suffering from a severe mismatch between good political intentions and reality' (Lorenzoni et al., 2008). However, the overall correlation between inequality and unsuccessful climate change mitigation in this figure points to the need to consider in greater detail the mechanisms by which income inequality can make it more difficult to pursue effective climate change mitigation policies.

A possible explanation to the observed pattern is that income inequality relates to a political culture where individual interests are given precedence. This case has been made by Robert Wilkinson and Kate Pickett, who maintain that economic inequalities tend to weaken the public ethos and commitment to work together that we need if we are going to solve problems that threaten us all, such as climate change. They compare the demand for action on climate change with a war effort: people will contribute only if they see the burden as fairly shared (Wilkinson and Pickett, 2009). This explanation relates to the broader idea of the beneficial impacts of social cohesion (Jenson, 2010; see also Chapter Thirteen in this volume).

A more immediate explanation of the relationship between income inequality and unsuccessful climate change mitigation can be found in the realm of economics. It has been shown that inequality makes it difficult to use economic instruments in climate policy. This is due to the fact that carbon pricing and other economic instruments tend to be regressive. When prices on carbon – that is, energy – go up, it is more difficult for poor households to manage than for rich ones. Poor households have less money than do the rich and poor households also tend to use a larger part of their income on energy. Some governments try to overcome resistance to carbon pricing by compensating poor households. Compensation through lump sum transfers to poor households within the social security system or within the tax system is one way of maintaining the price signal of a carbon tax without unacceptable regressive effects. This type of compensation has sometimes been successful. However, the more unequal a society becomes, the greater the need for compensation will be (Jacobs, 1991: chapter 14; Metcalf, 1999; OECD, 2006: chapter 7).

Even more problematic, however, is the fact that poverty is so severe in many countries that people cannot pay their fuel bills even without a price on carbon. This means that most energy subsidies to poor households are not at all introduced with climate policy in mind. They simply address poverty. Such subsidies are often poorly designed from a climate policy perspective, since they subsidise the cost of energy instead of compensating poor households for lost income. Policies of this kind can help poor households to pay their energy bills but they cannot help them to save energy or to switch to non-fossil fuels. Compensation within the social security system or within the tax system would be a better option (IEA, 1999; OECD, 2006: chapter 7).

The challenge of energy poverty has attracted increasing attention in the EU in recent years, in particular as regards 'fuel poverty', that is, the inability to pay for residential heating. Although fuel poverty is most common in Eastern European member states (Brodén and Werner, 2003) it exists in many EU-15 member states as well. The UK, for example, is a member state where fuel poverty has clearly served to halt climate change mitigation efforts in the residential sector. British heating is still completely dependent on fossil fuels, but due to the fuel poverty problem there is no cost on CO_2 in residential heating. Climate-friendly heating options remain unprofitable (Defra, 2009; Henning and Mårdsjö, 2009). This contrasts sharply with the situation in Sweden, for example, where a more equal income distribution has made aggressive carbon taxation policies possible. In Sweden, fossil fuels have been almost entirely phased out in the residential heating sector (Friberg, 2008).

All in all, available evidence indicates that inequality impacts negatively on climate change mitigation efforts. This fact should encourage the EU climate policy community to join forces with members of the social policy community to actively promote policies to reduce income inequalities, including social investment policies. In equal fashion the social policy community should pay more attention to EU climate policy debates. The fact that greater income equality facilitates the fight against climate change can offer a new rationale for member states to engage in social policy development. All in all, both climate and social policy communities could benefit from developing win–win social investment programmes in more targeted areas. One example is housing programmes that can both reduce CO_2 emissions and raise living standards. Another example is cheap and climate-friendly public transport that can cut CO_2 emissions while improving, at the same time, labour market access and the quality of life for poor households.

Employment and climate change

Employment policies matter to climate change since the transition to a low-carbon economy will demand radically new approaches to energy production, manufacturing, construction and transport. As societies change, green employment opportunities will open up – but thousands of jobs will also be at risk. In the process of change, human capital investment can make the difference between successful adaptation and industrial failure. Upgrading of skills is needed both to manage the negative sides of the transition and to make the most of new business opportunities.

In spite of the huge transition expected, analyses of the impacts of climate change on future employment patterns are still few. Most authors draw attention to the employment potential of green jobs (Jones, 2009). Only a few try to project the overall impact of climate change on global and European labour markets (UNEP, 2008). Social policy considerations are clearly present, for example, in calls for a 'just transition' to the new green economy. However, there are until now few references to specific social policy approaches, such as the social investment perspective.

What do available studies tell us about the impact of climate change on European labour markets? The European report 'Climate Change and Employment' (2007) shows that we can expect significant redistribution effects between jobs, sectors and countries. Impacts will be greater in the south than in the north. Primary sectors such as agriculture, fisheries and forestry will be the most severely affected. Energy-intensive industries are at risk for relocation outside Europe, while new job opportunities will open up in transportation, construction and energy production. Overall, demand for more qualified labour is bound to increase. This underlines the key role of social investment policies for developing and renewing the competencies of the workforce but also for implementing labour market institutions that promote both flexibility and security to accompany the transition (see Chapters Eight and Nine).

Proposals so far on how to manage the green transition underscore that climate policies should be foreseeable and keep all social partners involved. Experience in the realm of European climate policy so far makes clear that labour unions, along with industry, will strongly resist aggressive climate policy measures if they perceive that they put jobs and competitiveness at risk. The report 'Climate Change and Employment' therefore suggests proactive industrial policies along with strong guarantees for workers' rights (including income security, retraining opportunities and participation). One key recommendation is to establish a European observatory on economic and socioeconomic changes associated with climate change. In line with this, it is also suggested that national, regional and European dialogue bodies should be set up to deal with adaptation to climate change and greenhouse gas reduction measures. This approach has been attempted in Spain, where a national pact on implementation of the Kyoto protocol was launched in 2005, involving government, employers and unions.

Another line of proposals calls attention to the key role of public investment, for example, investments in thermal renovation of older housing, combined heat and power systems and other neighbourhood renewal programmes. This type of programmes – that demands many different types of skills and competencies – can serve to integrate environmental and social policy aims such as lower emissions, improved housing, and more and better jobs (Pye et al., 2008).

Within the EU, Sweden pioneered green investment programmes in the 1990s in response to a severe domestic recession. These Swedish programmes were designed as part of a broader green welfare agenda with an explicit aim to generate both employment and improved environmental performance at local level. By giving priority to innovative projects, they also spurred ecological modernisation and 'eco-efficiency'. Evaluations show that the Swedish green investment programmes were clearly successful as a cost-efficient tool of climate policy. All in all, programmes launched from 1998 to 2008 have cut greenhouse gas emissions by more than two million tonnes a year, which equals 75% of the Swedish emissions reduction target. Programmes have also created employment in emerging green new business sectors such as biofuels (Eckerberg, 2000; Kåberger and Jürgensen, 2006).

After the 2008 global economic downturn, green investment programmes have attracted new interest worldwide as a combined response to the climate crisis and the financial crisis. Proposals have been launched from different parties under headings such as 'a Green New Deal' or 'a Clean Energy New Deal' (UNIDO, 2008; IEA, 2009; Barbier, 2010). However, as noted earlier, the EU has so far lagged behind other major economies in launching this type of greening stimulus programmes.

Most discussions on climate change and employment have revolved, as illustrated above, around specific sectors, measures and programmes. It is clear, however, that impacts of climate change will not, over longer time horizons, be limited to certain sectors. On the contrary, no sector will be able to cut itself off from global warming. Changes brought about by climate change will also be closely related to other challenges to future employment, such as global competition and technical progress. Against this background, the best way to prepare a member state for changing patterns of employment due to climate change would be well-designed overall policies. Policy makers need to give greater attention to issues such as innovation and green growth strategies but also income security, education and lifelong learning (cf. Chapters Eight and Nine). Active labour market policies, in particular, helping people to upgrade their skills and cope with rapid change, will be highly relevant in the climate change context (Chapter Seven).

To sum up, a successful European transition to a low-carbon society demands decisive social investment policies. Once again, it is urgent that the climate community becomes aware of the positive interaction between social investment and climate change mitigation and that advocates of the social investment perspective pay more attention to climate policy. Demands for greater labour market flexibility, education and skills in the transition to a low-carbon society, shaped by a warmer climate, can serve to strengthen the social investment approach.

Towards a new policy paradigm

I have argued in this chapter that there is much to gain from better integration between climate policy and social investment policies in the EU. But how can this integration be attained? Improved dialogue and greater awareness can be one step forward (Pye et al., 2008). However, the greatest challenge for the research community, in my view, is to sort out the inconsistencies and failures of current policies and pave the way for a new economic policy paradigm.

As pointed out in the introductory section of this chapter, neoliberal doctrine still supplies the logic of European climate policy. Neoliberal ideas are also still very present in social policy, especially in activation policies (see Chapters Five and Seven). However, scepticism is growing, not least in the social investment community. Although governments have moved towards embracing some kind of social investment thinking without rejecting all of the social thinking of neoliberalism (see Chapter Three), the social investment perspective as such goes in fact far beyond the limits of neoliberalism. It launches a long-term intergenerational perspective on human capital and in contrast to neoliberalism it pays attention to externalities – the social dimension. As noted by Anton Hemerijck (see Chapter Two), 'the social investment turn' does in fact strongly oppose the very core of neoliberal economics such as the idea of a tradeoff between social equity and economic efficiency. Lundvall and Lorenz (Chapter Thirteen) make a similar observation when they argue that the EU commitment to social cohesion has in fact never resulted in an explicit recognition of the claim that greater social cohesion can contribute to competitiveness rather than undermine it. What is still lacking is an alternative, distinct economic policy framework. As Hemerijck puts it: the 'economics of social investment' is not yet 'founded on a unified body of economic thought'.

In this section I suggest that there is in fact a new body of economic thought already in the making that can provide a more suitable economic foundation for both climate and social investment policies: the new 'economics of sustainable development'. The emergence of this new body of economic thought – embedded in the more comprehensive paradigm of sustainable development – is triggered not only by the 'social-investment turn' but also by a growing dissatisfaction with the limitations of neoliberal doctrine within the climate policy community.

Since 2006, Sir Nicholas Stern has led the way in challenging the unrealistic and short-term interpretations of cost efficiency that have too often taken the upper hand in mainstream climate economics. His acclaimed report, 'Economics of climate change', has drawn attention to the fact that uncertainty and long-time horizons must be taken into account in dealing with climate change (Stern, 2008; Touffut, 2009).

More importantly, recent proposals for a 'Green New Deal' have served to challenge the idea of perfect competitive markets. They have also revived insights in Keynesian macroeconomics. Demand management and long-term investments have come to the fore. In parallel, environmental economists have made their voices more often heard, challenging the lack of consideration for environmental concerns and social equity in mainstream economic theory. Finally, there is a growing interest in more complex dimensions of environmental politics such as adaptive ecosystem management and sustainable urban governance. This interest draws attention to the key role of governments, civil society and citizens in climate change mitigation; thereby challenging the one-sided neoliberal orientation towards carbon markets. Hence, critics open up for a more comprehensive climate and social investment policy framework, realising the key role of economic incentives but dismissing the limitations of neoliberal doctrine (Ostrom, 1990; Folke et al., 2005; Ackerman, 2008; Bartle, 2009; Hale, 2010).

Is it reasonable to believe that the paradigm of sustainable development will develop into a comprehensive alternative to the current neoliberal policy framework? In my view there are three main arguments in favour. First, the concept of sustainable development is well founded in an international ideational context. Second, the paradigm of sustainable development has increasingly shaped modern EU identity and policy making. Third, there is a strong economic case for the paradigm of sustainable development, based on empirical evidence.

Sustainable development: the global context

The modern concept of sustainable development was launched in the 1987 Brundtland Report 'Our Common Future' and laid the groundwork for the 1992 UN Conference on Environment and Development in Rio. Gro Harlem Brundtland coined the often-quoted definition of sustainable development: 'Sustainable development is development that meets the needs of the present without compromising the ability of future generations to meet their own needs.' The concept of sustainable development was used, in Rio, in the context of global environmental challenges: climate change and loss of biodiversity. However, from the very beginning it also embraced economic and social considerations. Brundtland called for a new quality of growth. She declared that even a narrow notion of physical sustainability demands a concern for social equity, not only between generations but also within generations. Governments must address both the carrying capacity of natural systems and the social challenges facing humanity. In contrast to the neoliberal paradigm, citizen participation is at the centre of sustainable development strategies. To this end, the 1992 Rio Conference was accompanied by the launch of Agenda 21, a bottom-up approach to environment and development. Agenda 21 encouraged the participation of 'major groups': children and youth, women, indigenous peoples, non-governmental organisations, trade unions, local governments, business, scientists and farmers.

In the last two decades, the concept of sustainable development has remained essential within the United Nations. In 2002, governments reaffirmed their commitment to sustainable development at the World Summit for Sustainable Development (WSSD) in Johannesburg. The UN Commission on Sustainable Development, CSD, continuously coordinates assessments of sustainability targets. Other international organisations such as the OECD and the EU have followed suit. This has resulted in ever-more advanced attempts to analyse and measure economic, social and environmental aspects of sustainable development (OECD, 2002; UNECE, 2008; Stiglitz et al., 2009).

Over the years, however, calls for sustainable development have repeatedly clashed with neoliberal doctrine. Global economic institutions such as the International Monetary Fund (IMF) and the World Trade Organization (WTO) have enforced the primacy of open global markets as a key driver of human wealth and progress, often in conflict with advocates for sustainable development. Lars-Göran Engfeldt, former Swedish ambassador for the environment, has described how the 'short-term paradigm' of neoliberalism made it increasingly difficult to implement the strategies for sustainable development agreed on in Rio (Engfeldt, 2009). It is clear, however, that the discourse on sustainability has gained strength in recent years in relation to neoliberal doctrine, not least as a consequence of the global financial crisis. After two decades, when the two strands of thought have run parallel, time may be ripe for advocates of the paradigm of sustainable development to challenge the tenets of neoliberalism. The current mix of ideas can be expected to erode as sharper conflicts arise.

Sustainable development in the EU

In the EU, the concept of sustainable development has since long been part of the political agenda, although it has remained in the shadows of the predominant neoliberal doctrine. From the early 1990s, following the Rio Summit, individual member states launched their own sustainable development strategies. In 1997, sustainable development became one of the objectives of the EU with the Amsterdam Treaty. The first EU Sustainable Development Strategy was agreed in 2001. The Lisbon Strategy (2000) confirmed a strong commitment to social cohesion and environmental sustainability. Today, the EU explicitly declares the aim of the union to work for sustainable development in the second article of the Treaty of Lisbon, following directly after the introductory statement that 'the union should establish an internal market'. In the same spirit, the *Europe 2020 Strategy* is based on the vision of 'smart, sustainable and inclusive growth' (see Chapter Thirteen).

As already noted, policy making within the EU has been fraught with ambiguity as regards the relationship between the vision of sustainable development on the one hand and the neoliberal ideas of competitiveness, open markets and limited state intervention on the other. In social policy and climate policy alike, ideas of neoliberalism and sustainable development have run parallel. However, the tide is turning.

Susan Baker observes that sustainable development has increasingly shaped the construction of EU identity over the years, even if actual policies are still 'merely symbolic'. This change in identity, she argues, can bear important transformative potentials (Baker, 2007). Her observation is in line with the reasoning of Peter A. Hall, who argues that ideas play a key role in policy making, in particular in transitions from one policy paradigm to another. When a particular set of ideas eventually gain credibility over another, this will structure the policy-making process in new ways and privilege some lines of policy over others. Eventually a new policy paradigm takes precedence, which will change 'not only the goals of policy and the kind of instruments that can be used to address them, but also the very nature of the problems they are meant to be addressing' (Hall, 1993: 279).

Shifts in policy paradigms are rare and difficult to foresee. However, a shift of policy paradigm in the EU away from neoliberalism is no doubt fuelled by accumulating policy problems both internally and externally. Apart from the apparent ambiguities of current social and climate policies, the financial crisis provides a moment of truth for neoliberal economic doctrine. Similarly, the stalemate of global climate negotiations calls for a new approach. I would argue, however, that the most important driver of change in the years to come can well turn out to be not policy problems but an increasingly persuasive economic case for the paradigm of sustainable development. So far, advocates of sustainable development have seldom explicitly addressed the key economic argument of the neoliberal paradigm: the claim that market mechanisms must be given maximal sway since dynamic, competitive markets are the drivers of economic wealth and prosperity. In my view, it is vital for advocates of sustainable development to present an alternative story to this neoliberal narrative of economic growth – not only to argue for the merits of a new quality of economic growth, but also to show that long-term economic wealth and prosperity can, in fact, be better achieved within a paradigm of sustainable development.

The economic case for sustainable development

When advocates of the social investment perspective talk about human capital as a core asset of the economy or suggest that a 'more equal income distribution is positively associated with economic growth' (Kap and Palme, 2009: 17), they expose the limitations of a one-sided neoliberal growth perspective, based on the narrative of liberalised markets as key drivers of wealth and prosperity. However, much of the social investment literature – including Esping-Andersen's influential *Why We Need a New Welfare State* (2002) – fail to bring this conflict between neoliberal thought and the social investment perspective to light. Similarly, advocates of policies for sustainable development rarely make explicit that they do in fact represent an alternative theory of economic growth or wealth creation. Instead, they tend to focus on aspects such as the quality of growth or the limits to growth (Baker,

2006). In my view, a successful future for policies of sustainable development demands that economic arguments for a sustainable development path are presented with greater commitment and coherence (Sommestad, 2010).

Although no explicit theory of sustainable growth has been launched to challenge the prevailing neoliberal paradigm, there is a growing body of research in support of new 'economics for sustainable development'. Apart from the long-standing argument that unregulated markets will result in short-sighted exploitation of natural and human resources (Raskin et al., 2002; Ackerman, 2008), this body of research includes one key message: lasting economic prosperity depends on long-term investments in public goods such as ecosystems, education, health and social cohesion. Within this strand of thought on sustainable growth, human capital is at the centre of attention.

In the European context, economic research on sustainable growth dates as far back as the 1930s. As noted by Morel et al. (Chapter One) and by Lindh (Chapter Ten), Swedish scholars Gunnar and Alva Myrdal at this time played a key role in the early launch of social investment policies in Sweden. Their ideas about investing in the productivity of the population served to supplement both the social rights perspective and the more widely adopted, economic framework of Keynesian-style full employment policies. Both Alva and Gunnar Myrdal contributed to the 'productivist' Swedish social policy tradition, linking social policy to economic performance. Later the Myrdals pioneered studies on human capital formation and women's role in work and family. Gunnar Myrdal also developed analyses of the impacts of population ageing, thereby preceding current discussions on the economic consequences of an ageing European population (Esping-Andersen, 1992; Sommestad, 1997; Andersson, 2007).

In recent years, research that explores the link between social investment and economic performance has proliferated. Following the neoliberal turn (when social spending was seen as inimical to economic prosperity) the idea of social policy as productive is once again at the centre of attention, not least in the realm of development economics. Current research on the beneficial impacts of social policy on economic performance relates to the social investment perspectives once pioneered by the Myrdals and point in particular to social equity, health and education as key elements in a new approach to economic development (Mkandawire, 2001).

I would argue that there are three crucial predictors of economic growth that stand out as particularly important in view of the challenges facing Europe ahead: health status, education and age structure.

Two Harvard economists, David E. Bloom and David Canning, were among the first to launch health as an important input to economic growth. In an article published in *Science* (2000), they concluded that the impact of health status on economic growth is strikingly large, and that it emerges consistently across empirical, cross-country studies. East Asia in the post-war decades is an illustrative example. According to Bloom and Canning, health investments must be seen as one of the major pillars upon which East Asia's economic miracle was based (Bloom and Williamson, 1998; Bloom and Canning, 2000). American economist Jeffrey Sachs pursued a similar argument in his path-breaking report for the World Health Organization, *Macro-Economics and Health. Investing in Health for Economic Development* (WHO, 2001). Sachs stressed that the linkages of health to long-term economic growth and poverty are powerful and much stronger than has been generally understood. Both studies serve to boost the importance of social policies but also point to the long-term impacts of action to protect the environment, since environmental damage is often intrinsically linked to health.

It has long since been assumed that education has strong impacts on economic growth, and in recent years this relationship has been convincingly demonstrated in cross-country studies. One key result is that greater investments in secondary education could give a strong boost to economic growth worldwide. However, as noted by population economists Lutz, Cuaresa and Sanderson, policy makers must realise that education is a long-term investment with near-term costs. 'The fruits of investments in education need a long time to ripen... but, in the long run, it is one of the best investments societies can make in their futures' (Lutz et al., 2008).

Finally, as regards age structure, it has been shown that youthful populations, with large cohorts of people in their working ages, tend to promote rapid economic growth, as in East Asia today. By contrast, growth rates tend to slow down in regions with ageing populations, such as contemporary Japan or Europe (Lindh and Malmberg, 1999, 2007; Bloom et al., 2003). These analyses point to the need for the EU to launch comprehensive policies for development of human resources, and to include as many citizens as possible in employment.

All in all, the growing body of research on health, education and age structure gives strong support to policies that put sustainable development at the centre of attention. A growth narrative on this basis strengthens calls for environmental protection, climate change mitigation and social investment. It makes clear that economic prosperity and human welfare depend not only on market competitiveness today but also on sustainable resources and productive investments made in the past.

Looking ahead: climate and social policies in the EU

If current developments eventually bring a shift towards sustainability in the overarching policy framework of the EU, this would imply huge changes for policy areas such as social policy and climate policy. So far, social policy and climate policy have developed more or less in isolation. In spite of serious efforts to boost the productive aspects of both policy areas – in terms of social investment, employment, ecological modernisation and eco-efficiency – they have nevertheless remained at the margins of the predominant, market-based EU project. Within a paradigm for sustainable development, social policy and climate policy would move instead to the centre of EU politics. This would strengthen the social investment perspective, facilitate full employment policies, bridge the gap between social policy and climate policy, and pave the way for more successful climate change mitigation.

In addition, a more systematic enforcement of the concept of sustainable development would add valuable dimensions to both climate policy and social policy. In climate policy, a future sustainability paradigm would serve to strengthen the role of citizenship. The citizenship perspective is largely absent in current market-based EU climate policies. Business and consumers predominate.

In social policy, a sustainability paradigm would inform the social investment perspective by relating social policy closer than it does today to global issues. When modern European social policies once took shape, in the wake of the World War II, social policy was part of a wider, international reconstruction of peace and development. I would argue that European social policy in the twenty-first century could similarly respond not only to domestic demands for improved competitiveness, quality of life and social cohesion but also to the challenges that people on this planet face together. Population growth, migration, pandemics, environmental degradation and climate change are processes of global significance that will shape the future of Europe. In this context, the social investment perspective has an important part to play.

References

Ackerman, F. (2008) 'Climate economics in four easy pieces', *Society for International Development*, 51, 325–31.

Andersson, J. (2007) *Between Growth and Security: Swedish Social Democracy from a Strong Society to a Third Way*. Manchester: Manchester University Press.

Baker, S. (2006) *Sustainable Development*. London and New York: Routledge.

Baker, S. (2007) 'Sustainable development as symbolic commitment: declaratory politics and the seductive appeal of ecological modernisation in the European Union', *Environmental Politics*, 16 (2), 297–317.

Barbier, E.B. (2010) *A Global Green New Deal. Rethinking the Economic Recovery*. Cambridge: Cambridge University Press and the United Nations Environment Programme.

Bartle, I. (2009) 'A strategy for better climate change regulation: towards a public interest orientated regulatory regime', *Environmental Politics*, 18 (5), 689–706.

Bertoldi, P. and Huld, T. (2006) 'Tradable certificates for renewable electricity and energy savings', *Energy Policy*, 34 (2), 212–22.

Bloom, D.E. and Canning, D. (2000) 'The health and wealth of nations', *Science*, 288, 1207–09.

Bloom, D.E. and Williamson, J.G. (1998) 'Demographic transitions and economic miracles in emerging Asia', *World Bank Economic Review*, 12 (3), 419–55.

Bloom, D.E., Canning, D. and Sevilla, J. (2003) *The Demographic Dividend: A New Perspective on the Economic Consequences of Population Change*. Santa Monica, CA: Rand.

Brodén, A and Werner, S. (2003) Heat poverty – affordable district heating in cold and poor urban regions, Report 2003:7. Gothenburg: Department of Energy, Conversion Energy Systems Technology, Chalmers University of Technology.

Christiansen, A.C. and Wettestad, J. (2003) 'The EU as a frontrunner on greenhouse gas emissions trading: how did it happen and will the EU succeed?', *Climate Policy*, 3, 3–18.

Climate Change and Employment (2007), by the European Trade Union Confederation (ETUC), Sindical de Trabajo, Ambinte y Salud (ISTAS), Social Development Agency (SDA), Syndax and Wuppertal Institute.

Compston, H. and Bailey, I. (eds) (2008) *Turning Down the Heat. The Politics of Climate Policy in Affluent Democracies*. Hampshire: Palgrave Macmillan.

Cooper, R.N. (2010) *Europe's Emissions Trading System, Harvard Project on International Climate Agreements*. Belfer Center for Science and International Affairs, Harvard Kennedy School of Government, Harvard University.

Damro, C. and MacKenzie, D. (2008) 'The European Union and the politics of multi-level climate governance', in H. Compston and I. Bailey (eds) *Turning Down the Heat. The Politics of Climate Policy in Affluent Democracies*. Hampshire: Palgrave Macmillan.

Damro, C. and Méndez, P.L. (2003) 'Emissions trading at Kyoto: from EU resistance to Union innovation', *Environmental Politics*, 12 (2), 71–94.

Defra (2009) *The UK Fuel Poverty Strategy. 7th Annual Progress Report*. London: Defra.

Eckerberg, K. (2000) 'Progression without recession', in W. Lafferty and J. Meadowcroft, (eds) *Implementing Sustainable Development. Strategies and Incentives in High Consumption Societies*. Oxford: Oxford University Press.

EEA (2004) *Energy Subsidies in the European Union. A Brief Overview*. Copenhagen.

Ellerman, A.D. and Joskow, P.L. (2008) *The European Union's Emissions Trading System in Perspective*. Washington, DC: Pew Center on Global Climate Change (May).

Engfeldt, L.-G. (2009) *From Stockholm to Johannesburg and Beyond*. Stockholm: Ministry of Foreign Affairs.

Esping-Andersen, G. (1992) 'The making of a social-democratic welfare state', in K. Misgeld et al. (eds) *Creating Social Democracy: A Century of the Social Democratic Labor Party in Sweden*. State University Park: The Pennsylvania State University Press, pp. 35–66.

Esping-Andersen, G., Gallie, D., Hemerijck, A. and Myles, J. (2002) *Why We Need a New Welfare State*. Oxford: Oxford University Press.

Euroheatcool (2006) Brussels: Euroheat and Power.

Folke, C., Hahn, T., Olsson, P. and Norberg, J. (2005) 'Adaptive governance of social-ecological systems', *Annual Review of Environment and Resources*, 30, 441–73.

Friberg, L. (2008) 'Conflict and consensus: The Swedish model of climate politics', in H. Compston and I. Bailey (eds) *Turning Down the Heat. The Politics of Climate Policy in Affluent Democracies*. Hampshire: Palgrave Macmillan.

Giddens, A. (2009) *The Politics of Climate Change*. Cambridge: Polity Press.

Hale, S. (2010) 'The new politics of climate change: Why we are failing and how we will succeed', *Environmental Politics*, 19 (2), 255–75.

Hall, P. A. (1993) 'Policy paradigms, social learning, and the state: The case of economic policymaking in Britain', *Comparative Politics*, 25 (3), 275–96.

Henning, D. and Mårdsjö, O. (2009) Fjärrvärme i Europa. Hinder att övervinna för svensk export (Executive Summary: District Heating in Europe. Barriers to Swedish District Heating Exports). Stockholm: Svensk Fjärrvärme.

IEA (1999) *World Energy Outlook. Looking at Energy Subsidies: Getting the Prices Right*. Paris: IEA.

IEA (2009) The impact of the financial and economic crisis on global energy investment. Background paper for the G8 Energy Ministers meeting 24–25 May 2009. Paris: IEA.

Jacobs, M. (1991) *The Green Economy*. London: Pluto Press.

Jenson, J. (2010) *Defining and Measuring Social Cohesion*. London: Commonwealth Secretariat and United Nations Research Institute for Social Development.

Jones, B. and Keen, M. (2009) 'Climate policy in hard times', *Finance and Development*, 46 (4).

Jones, V. (2009) *The Green Economy. How One Solution can Fix our Two Biggest Problems*. London: HarperCollins Publishers.

Kåberger, T. and Jürgensen, A. (2006) *LIP from a Socio-Economic Perspective*. Stockholm: Swedish Environmental Protection Agency.

Kap, H. and Palme, J. (2009) Analysis of the economic and social situation in Europe – challenges for social inclusion ahead, *8th European Roundtable on Poverty and Social Exclusion*, Stockholm: Swedish Presidency of the European Union.

Kjellén, B. (2008) *A New Diplomacy for Sustainable Development. The Challenge of Global Change*. New York: Routledge.

Lindh, T. and Malmberg, B. (1999) 'Age structure effects and growth in the OECD, 1950–90', *Journal of Population Economics*, 12 (3), 431–49.

Lindh, T. and Malmberg, B. (2007) 'Demographically based global income forecasts up to the year 2050', *International Journal of Forecasting*, 23 (4), 553–67.

Lorenzoni, I., O'Riordan, T. and Pidgeon, N. (2008) 'Hot air and cold feet: The UK response to climate change', in H. Compston, and I. Bailey (eds) *Turning Down the Heat. The Politics of Climate Policy in Affluent Democracies*. Hampshire: Palgrave Macmillan.

Lutz, W., Cuaresma, J.C. and Sanderson, W. (2008) 'The demography of educational attainment and economic growth', *Science*, 319 (5866), 1047–48.

Metcalf, G.E., (1999) 'A distributional analysis of green tax reforms', *National Tax Journal*, 52, 655–81.

Mkandawire, T. (2001) *Social Policy in a Development Context*. Geneva: UNRISD.

Newbery, D. (2010) *Written Evidence in the Role of Carbon Markets in Preventing Dangerous Climate Change*, the fourth report of the 2009–2010 session. UK Parliament website.

OECD (2002) *Governance for Sustainable Development. Five OECD Case Studies*. Paris: OECD.

OECD (2006) *The Political Economy of Environmentally Related Taxes*. Paris: OECD.

Ostrom, E. (1990) *Governing the Commons: The Evolution of Institutions for Collective Action*. Cambridge: Cambridge University Press.

Pye, S., Skinner, I., Meyer-Ohlendorf, N., Leipprand, A., Lucas, K. and Salmons, R. (2008) *Addressing the Social Dimensions of Environmental Policy*. Brussels: European Commission, Employment, Social Affairs and Equal Opportunities.

Raskin, P., Banuri, T., Gallopín, G., Gutman, P., Hammond, A., Kates, R. and Swart, R. (2002) *Great Transition. The Promise and Lure of the Times Ahead*. Boston: Stockholm Environment Institute.

Sommestad, L. (1997) 'Welfare state attitudes to the male breadwinning system: the United States and Sweden in comparative perspective', *International Review of Social History*, 42, Supplement 5.

Sommestad, L. (2010) 'Economics of sustainable development – a progressive alternative to neoliberalism in the 21st Century', in A. Hassel and C. Pohlmann (eds) *Market and State in European Social Democracy. Progressive Perspectives on Developing a Social and Sustainable Market Model*. Berlin: Friedrich-Ebert-Stiftung.

Stern, N. (2008) 'The economics of climate change', Richard T. Ely Lecture, *American Economic Review: Papers and Proceedings*, 98 (2), 1–37.

Stiglitz, J., Sen, A. and Fitoussi, J.-P. (2009) Report by the commission on the measurement of economic performance and social progress, available at www.stiglitz-sen-fitoussi.fr.

Touffut, J.-P. (ed.) (2009), *Changing Climate, Changing Economy*. Cheltenham: Edward Elgar.

UNECE (2008) *Measuring Sustainable Development*. Report of the joint UNECE/OECD/Eurostat working group on statistics for sustainable development, New York and Geneva.

UNEP (2008) *Green Jobs: Towards Decent Work in a Sustainable, Low-Carbon World*. Report from UNEP within the joint UNEP, ILO, IOE, ITUC Green Jobs Initiative, Nairobi.

UNFCC (2010) *GHGs without LULUCF,* www.unfcc.int.

UNIDO (2008) *Energy Development and Security. Energy Issues in the Current Macroeconomic Context.* Vienna: UNIDO.

WHO (2001) Macroeconomics and health: investing in health for economic development, Report of the Commission on Macroeconomics and Health, chaired by Jeffrey D. Sachs. Geneva: WHO.

Wilkinson, R. and Pickett, K. (2009) *Spirit Level. Why More Equal Societies Almost Always do Better.* London: Allen Lane.

THIRTEEN

From the Lisbon Strategy to EUROPE 2020

Bengt-Åke Lundvall and Edward Lorenz

The institutions of the highly organized welfare state gives an indication of how many national ties need to be complemented by corresponding international ties in order to approach international integration. The welfare idea is so deeply rooted that its manifestations within the national framework can be superseded only by corresponding institutions of an international welfare community. How this can be made is an important subject for investigation. (Svennilson, 1960: 9–10)

Introduction

In March 2010 the Commission published the new ten-year strategy for Europe, named 'EU2020'.[1] In this chapter we compare the new strategy, 'EU2020', with the Lisbon Strategy that was agreed upon in 2000 in connection with the Portuguese Presidency. We also take into account the mid-term evaluation of the Lisbon Strategy as well as the Commission's own final evaluation of the Lisbon Agenda.[2] The historical record of the Lisbon Strategy and the adequacy of the new strategy cannot be assessed without taking into account the current crisis of the European project: a crisis that involves not only high unemployment and public finance problems everywhere in Europe but also acute risks for bankruptcy in member states belonging to the euro-area currency union. The form and depth of this crisis reveal fundamental weaknesses of the Lisbon Strategy and at the same time it indicates how radical the shift in strategy needs to be.

In the first two sections we first compare the two strategies in terms of context and content and then discuss the consequences of the mid-term revision of the original Lisbon Strategy. In the fourth section we analyse how the Lisbon Strategy contributed to different objectives with special attention to respectively employment, social cohesion and knowledge-based economic growth. In the fifth section we discuss to what degree the Lisbon Strategy has succeeded to serve as scaffolding for the Economic and Monetary Union. Finally, we conclude and discuss why Europe needs a new vision as well as a more ambitious strategy than the one offered in EU2020.

Different origins, contexts and contents

While the Lisbon Strategy came out of a process where the national government in Portugal was initiator and driver (with Antonio Gutierrez as Prime Minister and with Maria Rodrigues as Sherpa), the new 'EU2020' strategy has been designed 'in-house' by the Commission. The Lisbon Strategy was prepared over a longer period, during which the Portuguese government consulted national governments and involved international experts. A preliminary version of the EU2020 strategy was presented for the European parliament in the autumn of 2009 and subsequently the Commission invited the public to give comments and come up with proposals via the internet. The final version took into account some of the comments and was presented in March 2010.

The global context was also quite different. One major factor underlying the Lisbon Strategy was unsatisfactory economic performance. During the 1990s, both employment and growth rates were higher in the USA and this was generally assumed to reflect that 'the new economy' was flourishing in the USA because of more unregulated markets, more entrepreneurial activities and higher rates of investment in knowledge capital, while it was assumed that the growth in Europe was hampered by 'rigidities' and underinvestment in research. The EU2020 strategy is introduced in a very different context where both the USA and Europe suffer from the consequences of the financial crisis, where the ecological crisis is high on the agenda and where the major competitiveness challenge comes from China and India rather than from the USA.

These differences in process and context are to some degree reflected in the content of the new strategy. The Lisbon Strategy meant that the EU set itself *a new strategic goal*: 'to become the most competitive and dynamic knowledge-based economy in the world capable of sustainable economic growth with more and better jobs and greater social cohesion'. Achieving this goal required an overall strategy aimed at 'preparing the transition to a knowledge-based economy and society by better policies for the information society and research and development (R&D), as well as by stepping up the process of structural reform for competitiveness and innovation and by completing the internal market; modernising the European social model, investing in people and combating social exclusion; sustaining the healthy economic outlook and favourable growth prospects by applying an appropriate macro-economic policy mix'. The EU2020 strategy puts forward three *priorities*: 'smart growth' – developing an economy based on knowledge and innovation; 'sustainable growth' – promoting a more resource-efficient, greener and more competitive economy; and 'inclusive growth' – fostering a high-employment economy delivering social and territorial cohesion. It also puts forward five headline targets and seven flagship initiatives (see Box 12.1).

Box 13.1: EU2020

The strategy EU2020 puts forward three (mutually reinforcing?) *priorities:*

- Smart growth: developing an economy based on knowledge and innovation.
- Sustainable growth: promoting a more resource efficient, greener and more competitive economy.
- Inclusive growth: fostering a high-employment economy delivering social and territorial cohesion.

Five headline targets are defined:

- Raise the employment rate of the population aged 20–64 from the current 69% to at least 75%.
- Achieve the target of investing 3% of GDP in R&D in particular by improving the conditions for R&D investment by the private sector, and develop a new indicator to track innovation.
- Reduce greenhouse gas emissions by at least 20% compared to 1990 levels or by 30% if the conditions are right, increase the share of renewable energy in our final energy consumption to 20%, and achieve a 20% increase in energy efficiency.
- Reduce the share of early school leavers to 10% from the current 15% and increase the share of the population aged 30–34 having completed tertiary education from 31% to at least 40%.
- Reduce the number of Europeans living below national poverty lines by 25%, lifting 20 million people out of poverty.

The Commission puts forward *seven flagship initiatives* to realise the targets:

- 'Innovation Union', to improve framework conditions and access to finance for research and innovation so as to ensure that innovative ideas can be turned into products and services that create growth and jobs.

- 'Youth on the move', to enhance the performance of education systems and to facilitate the entry of young people to the labour market.
- 'A digital agenda for Europe', to speed up the roll-out of high-speed internet and reap the benefits of a digital single market for households and firms.
- 'Resource efficient Europe', to help decouple economic growth from the use of resources, support the shift towards a low-carbon economy, increase the use of renewable energy sources, modernise our transport sector and promote energy efficiency.
- 'An industrial policy for the globalisation era', to improve the business environment, notably for SMEs, and to support the development of a strong and sustainable industrial base able to compete globally.
- 'An agenda for new skills and jobs', to modernise labour markets and empower people by developing their of skills throughout the life cycle with a view to increase labour participation and better match labour supply and demand, including through labour mobility.
- 'European platform against poverty', to ensure social and territorial cohesion such that the benefits of growth and jobs are widely shared and people experiencing poverty and social exclusion are enabled to live in dignity and take an active part in society.

Two differences deserve to be pointed out. First, the ambitions have become more modest. In EU2020 there is no promise that Europe will become the most competitive region of the world and it is realised that the economic crisis has had a major negative impact upon employment and income. Second, while the Lisbon Strategy aimed at 'knowledge-based growth with social cohesion', the new strategy adds as a new major priority the dimension of sustainable growth. But it should be noted that the EU's sustainable development strategy is actually older than the Lisbon Strategy, but to begin with operated as a parallel but separate strategy (see Chapter Twelve).

The mid-term review and the shift in political priorities and in governance

There is, however, a certain continuity in the general orientation of the two strategies. The reference to 'smart growth' may be seen as a follow-up to the concept 'the knowledge-based economy' and the reference to 'inclusive growth' as a follow-up to the 'increased social cohesion'. Does this imply that the political priorities in the European Council and/or the European Commission are the same today as they were ten years ago?

Actually, we see a shift in priorities already a few years into the Lisbon Strategy period with a weakening of the social dimension of the strategy and a stronger focus upon growth and employment. This is reflected in the debate taking place in connection with the mid-term review. Halfway through the Lisbon Strategy period, the new commission under Barroso initiated a shift in emphasis, giving more attention to economic growth and job creation and less to social cohesion. This shift was prepared by an evaluation report worked out under the leadership of the Dutch former Prime Minister Wim Kok (2004), where major complaints regarding the Lisbon Strategy were that it was weak on implementation and was unfocused and complex, with too many objectives. The resulting 'simplification' in the relaunched Lisbon Strategy reflected a change in political priorities where the objectives related to social cohesion were given second place to jobs and growth. The more or less explicit assumption was that more economic growth would by itself be transformed into social cohesion (Daly, 2008).

This change reflected a combination of factors such as the new composition of the Commission, including the role of the new president Barroso, and the intake of new member states. Most of the new members were countries that had been through a recent transition from planned to market economies. Their recent (mainly negative) experience of centralised planning changed the political balance in the EU, giving more room for pro-market ideas. But most important was perhaps the shift in the political colour of several national governments in the old membership states where right-wing governments took over after social democratic ones. The more specific priorities or objectives and targets of EU2020 are with few exceptions more in line with this 'Lisbon Strategy Mark II' than with the priorities in the original version of the Lisbon Strategy.

The change in governance

The mid-term review also involved changes in governance. The Lisbon Strategy launched the Open Method of Coordination (OMC) as a major innovation in the European integration process to be applied in policy areas where national governments retain sovereignty. In such areas the open method of coordination was expected to be helpful in realising the objectives set in the Lisbon Strategy. The idea was to develop a methodology based on common guidelines, review and deliberation.

Until 2005 the national plans were presented for discussion among representatives from the other countries for peer review. After 2005 the process engaged member states individually in a dialogue with the European Commission. The basic mechanism of the open method of coordination is that member states agree on a set of non-binding common objectives, and prepare on a regular basis national action plans which set out their policy plan to meet the common objectives, while the Commission then evaluates these and publishes them in Joint Commission/Council reports. A set of indicators is developed to allow for performance monitoring and, ideally, the process should result in convergence towards some 'best practice'.

The OMC has attracted a lot of attention among political scientists who emphasise the potential for policy learning. The development of common discourses, key concepts, policy principles and shared understandings of causal linkages have been seen as instrumental in the development of public policy in member states (Borràs and Jacobsson, 2004: 196). Some scholars expressed great scepticism early on, warning against perverse effects and inefficiency. They also pointed out that the overall process from the very beginning was characterised by 'an organisational structure with a relatively incoherent set of welfare targets and a strong neo-liberal agenda' (Chalmers and Lodge, 2003: 11). This bias was, as mentioned, actually reinforced in connection with the mid-term review.

As we shall see, the method has turned out to be very weak when it comes to realising some of the most explicit targets set in the Lisbon Strategy such as the 3% target for R&D. De la Porte and Jacobsson (Chapter Five in this volume), in their analysis of the European Employment Strategy, show that while the OMC has a certain impact upon the national discourse, the impact upon actual employment policy seems to be limited to the exceptional circumstances where active 'policy entrepreneurs' are strong enough to push for policy change in line with the EU recommendations. A similar conclusion is reached by Daly (2008) when it comes to social policy.

The EU2020 recognises this problem and refers to the future need for stronger governance:

> To achieve transformational change, the Europe 2020 strategy will need more focus, clear goals and transparent benchmarks for assessing progress. This will require a strong governance framework that harnesses the instruments at its disposal to ensure timely and effective implementation. (European Commission, 2010b: 25)

But in the text that follows there are no clear indications of changes in the distribution of power. There is strong emphasis upon the role of the European Council as being in charge of and responsible for implementing the new strategy. But the Council had this role already during the Lisbon Strategy and the result was a tendency towards de facto delegation of the management to the European Commission (Chalmers and Lodge, 2003). Neither is there anything indicating that the policy coordination will succeed in overcoming the problem that on the national scene only a handful of public servants are engaged in the communication with the Commission.

In EU2020 the fact that in the future the country reporting should cover simultaneously Europe 2020 and the Stability and Growth Pact is presented as a new idea. But, actually, this kind of coordination was established already in 2005. Since then both the Stability and Growth Pact and the OMC were supposed to be discussed jointly at the annual 'spring summit'. This simultaneity does not make it easier to reach EU2020 targets that are rooted in a social investment perspective. The procedure gives those in charge of public finance a strong say when it comes to veto public expenditure on social issues and innovation.

The new strategy's promotion of the Open Method of Coordination appears all too often to be premised on a naïve understanding of 'benchmarking'. It is assumed that there exist 'best practices' in public policy and institutional settings that can and should be spread within Europe, while there is insufficient attention to the fact that systemic features imply that the same practice will produce different outcomes depending upon the context (Lundvall and Tomlinson, 2002). For instance, in the document spelling out the flagship initiative in relation to innovation, there is a major contradiction between its idea of searching for and diffusing international best practice and its reference to *national innovation systems* (Innovation Union, 2010). The concept national innovation system rests on a notion of institutional complementarities that implies that you cannot expect a component that works well in one country to necessarily have the same kind of outcome in another (Lundvall, 2010).

Three key relationships in the Lisbon Strategy

Both the Lisbon Strategy and the new EU2020 strategy are extremely complex and in a brief account it is necessary to focus upon some key relationships. In the next section we will focus upon three themes central in the Lisbon Strategy: the creation of more and better jobs, competitiveness with more social cohesion, and the transformation to a knowledge-based economy. In these areas we try to assess the success of the Lisbon Strategy to reach its targets.

More and better jobs? Or just more jobs?

The Lisbon Strategy may in several respects be seen as a follow-up as well as a broadening and revitalisation of the European Employment Strategy (EES) that was established in 1996. A new element was the increased emphasis upon the role of knowledge and innovation. But increasing the employment rate through labour market reform has remained a central objective over the period 2000–10 and the widespread use of the OMC was inspired by the procedures already practised within the EES.[3]

The employment strategy was in its turn inspired by the OECD Jobs Study that emphasised the lack of flexibility in Europe's labour markets as the major reason for unsatisfactory job creation and economic growth. The specific design of the strategy reflected a mixture of neoliberal and social democratic ideas. The Commissioner in charge, Allan Larson, former Finance Minister of Sweden, played an important role in designing and implementing the EES.

Perhaps the most consistent aim of the Lisbon Strategy has been to increase the employment rate in member countries. This objective has wide support across the political spectrum. This reflects that high employment rates can be the outcome both of a Nordic welfare strategy and of a neoliberal strategy. This is also an area where there has been some positive development in terms of approaching the target of an average employment rate of 70%. The EU-employment rate was thus increased from 62% in 2000 to 66% in 2008 before it dropped back again to less than 65% as a result of the crisis. The new strategy sets the target for 2020 at 75%.

In the Lisbon Strategy the general formulation of the objective was originally 'to create more and better' jobs. But while the quantitative dimension was easy to measure it was not possible to agree upon an indicator of better jobs (Raveaud, 2007). One alternative option that was considered but rejected was to define good jobs as 'standard jobs' and bad jobs as part-time or 'fixed-term' jobs. This proposal was vetoed by the UK and the Netherlands on the grounds that non-standard jobs should be seen as stepping stones to standard jobs.

We propose that the international comparisons of the frequency of jobs offering employees access to organisational learning that we presented in Chapter Nine may be regarded as a more adequate indicator of quality of jobs. A major advantage of this indicator is that it links quality of jobs to the knowledge-based economy perspective. Taking this indicator as reference it is possible to see if there is a tradeoff between the quantity and the quality of jobs. Our data do not indicate any tradeoff. Rather, they indicate that high employment rates go hand in hand with a high proportion of high-quality jobs. Only the Netherlands, Denmark, Sweden, Austria and Germany have reached the target rate of employment (70%). It is interesting to note that these are also the economies where the share of jobs offering workers organisational learning is highest (see Chapter Nine).

The low priority given to the quality of jobs in the Lisbon Strategy is reflected in the profile of active labour market policies of member countries. As demonstrated by de la Porte and Jacobsson (Chapter Five) as well as by Bonoli (Chapter Seven), the active labour market policies after 2000 took an activation turn and actually gave less emphasis to upgrading skills than the policies during the 1950s and 1960s. The chapter by Nikolai (Chapter Four) confirms that while social expenditure has grown as a share of GDP in most European countries 2000–7, the share allocated to education has stagnated or diminished in most of the EU countries. The Commission's own 'evaluation' makes similar observations (European Commission, 2010a: 17). This neglect of investment in skill upgrading is especially problematic, when we take into account that in the countries with more ambitious social investment strategies that produce both more and better jobs the crucial mediating level is the competence of the workers (see Chapter Eight).

Flexicurity with little security

The Lisbon Strategy documents have increasingly made references to the concept of 'flexicurity' as an objective for the labour market institutional setup. In the Commission documents this concept has increasingly substituted unpopular requests for 'more flexibility' in labour markets. This seems to go against the tendency to narrow down the agenda towards a more neoliberal strategy. But a closer look at the use of the concept indicates a change in the definition from its original.

Flexicurity has been associated especially with the Danish labour market institutional setup. It combines few restrictions on employers' hiring and firing of workers with (until recently) tax-financed unemployment insurance that is quite generous both in terms of replacement rate and especially in terms of the length of the period of support for the unemployed. But recently the maximum period was shortened from four to two years and a series of initiatives of the activation type has put increasing pressure upon the unemployed to take a job – for instance, they are expected to write several applications per week in order to retain their right to unemployment support. The result is thus that even in the 'model country' the security dimension has been so seriously undermined that it has become dubious to refer to what is left as a flexicurity system.

The Commission's evaluation document (European Commission, 2010a: 16) refers to the endorsement of the principles of flexicurity by the European Council in December 2007 and argues that this is an area where progress has been made in several member states. There is no concrete reference to success in terms of increased security for workers and definitely none to increased income security for unemployed workers. This should be seen in the light that some of the new member countries offer almost no security for those ending in unemployment. This gradual erosion of the concept of flexicurity is problematic since in its original form it seems to bolster the learning economy (see Chapter Nine).

Weak competitiveness with less social cohesion

The analysis and prescription in the Lisbon Agenda referring to 'structural reform' was not new as compared to the strategies dominating economic policy before 2000 in Europe. It was rather a follow-up of neoliberal ideas regarding the fundamental importance of flexible labour markets supported by the OECD and other international organisations. What was new with the Lisbon Strategy was to combine this approach with the EU's historical commitment to 'social cohesion' and with a new strong emphasis upon the importance of innovation and the 'knowledge base'. Competitiveness was linked to investments in knowledge and to the upgrading of competencies.

The Lisbon Strategy recognised that the legitimacy of social policy and active state intervention in social affairs is different in Europe than in the USA. The two key concepts in the Lisbon Strategy were competitiveness *and* social cohesion. While 'structural reforms' should 'modernise' the European welfare states and make them more competitive, this should be combined with 'more social cohesion'.[4]

But there was little agreement on how to see the relationship between the two concepts. For neoliberals social expenditure and redistribution of incomes through taxes were seen as extra burdens that Europe should minimise and carry mainly for historical reasons. Among Christian Democrats as well as among French politicians brought up in the Gaullist tradition the state has a certain responsibility for 'social cohesion', irrespective of economic consequences. Many left-wing politicians saw the defence of workers' incomes and rights as an objective in itself. The basic idea behind the social investment perspective – that social cohesion could contribute to competitiveness rather than undermine it – was not widely shared. This may explain why the commitment to social cohesion was weak and unstable.

Jenson (2010) points out that social cohesion has two dimensions: one relates to inequality while the other refers to social capital. In this section we will discuss mainly the first dimension. Social cohesion and inequality may in the context of the Lisbon Strategy be analysed at least at three different levels. First, it signals a historical commitment to promote economic growth in the least developed regions of Europe; second, it refers to personal income distribution within nations; and third, it may refer to the reduction of poverty at the regional, national or European level.

The patterns of 'social cohesion' have certainly changed within the EU over the last decade and to some degree this has been influenced by politics. More than a third of the EU-budget is allocated to the regional funds. And there has actually been some convergence of GNP/capita across nation states and regions within Europe. Most studies of the impact from the use of structural funds indicate that they contribute to a reduction in interregional inequality (see, for instance, Bouvet, 2010).

But within most EU countries and for the EU as a whole the individual income distribution has become more unequal and actually public policies have contributed to this weakening of social cohesion.[5] It reflects that over the last few decades there has been a competition among EU member states to make the income tax system less burdensome for those with the highest incomes and for business enterprises.

The argument for these changes has been that the member state that offers the lowest taxes will attract skilled workers and the location of business. As a result the effective corporate tax rate for major European countries was reduced from 29% to 21% between 1987 and 2005. The marginal tax rate was reduced from 48.4% to 42.1% between 2000 and 2008. The single country going furthest in this direction is Ireland, offering a corporate tax only half of the average in the EU (12.5%) (Fitoussi and Saraceno, 2010). The financial sustainability of this competition towards the bottom has not been seriously addressed in connection with the Commission's evaluation of the Lisbon Strategy nor is it addressed in the EU2020.

One reason why the EC has not restricted the room for tax competition among member states may be that it is regarded as a positive development by the Commission. Reading carefully the document that evaluates the Lisbon Strategy gives the impression that the Commission assumes that 'what makes life easier for business is always good for competitiveness and economic growth'. For instance, there are several references to a few problematic countries where real wages have increased more rapidly than productivity, while there is *no* reference to countries where wages have fallen behind increases in productivity (European Commission, 2010a). This is remarkable since the wage share of GNP for EU-15 has fallen from 70% in 1975 to less than 60% in 2006 (Fitoussi and Laurent, 2009: 9).

The idea that wage restraint at the national level is always for the better that dominates the evaluation report is especially contestable in the current situation where the uneven levels of 'competitiveness' both at the global and at the European level are increasingly recognised as an obstacle to re-establishing economic growth. To rebalance the uneven competitiveness between, for instance, Germany and the peripheral countries through reducing wages in the weaker economies will result in more inequality, adding to the numbers of the working poor, and thus be at odds with the EU2020 goal of reducing poverty in these nations and increasing regional cohesion.

The current implementation of austerity programmes in the peripheral economies will bring the process of convergence of national income per capita within the union to an end and for the first time in the history of the European project the gap between rich and poor countries will increase. In the EU2020 there is an explicit target aimed at reducing poverty: 'Reduce the number of Europeans living below national poverty lines by 25%, lifting 20 million people out of poverty.' This may be seen as a response to the criticism that targets on social cohesion have remained vague. But at the same time it implies a narrowing down of the concept of social cohesion that is consistent with a conservative and neoliberal agenda where welfare states should have as their only major obligation keeping people out of poverty.

The knowledge-based economy – a blatant failure to reach the wrong target

The second major addition to the traditional agenda for 'structural reform' was the emphasis upon the knowledge-based economy. It was introduced with reference to the fact that the USA and Japan were investing more in science and education and that they were more successful in introducing new products especially in high-technology industries.

At the Barcelona meeting in 2002 this perspective was transformed into a quantitative target of R&D investments at 3% of GDP. It is not always made clear if this target should be aimed at every single country or if it should be seen as the target for the EU as a whole. Van Pottelsberghe (2008: 221) shows that the very uneven distribution of R&D effort in Europe – with Romania at 0.5% and Sweden at 3.8% – has its correspondence in the USA (where the distribution is even more uneven than in the EU!) – with Wyoming at 0.4% and New Mexico at 8%.

R&D intensity is a crude and lopsided indicator of 'the knowledge-based economy'. At the national level the size of this indicator will depend mainly upon industrial structure. Having a strong presence of electronics and pharmaceutical firms or firms operating in other high-technology areas will be reflected in high numbers. In order to reach the target at the national level a very rapid and radical change in the industrial structure would have been necessary. Therefore, it is not surprising that there was only marginal change over the planning period. As a matter of fact for the period 2000–6 R&D intensity stagnates in Europe (1.7%) and in the USA (2.5%), while it grows from 2.5% to 3% in Japan. China's expenditure on R&D is growing with an impressive 20% per annum and it is expected to move from the current 1.5% to reach 2.5% in 2020 (Veugelers, 2008).

The lack of commitment to the target is reflected in the fact that in 2006 none of the member countries had yet increased the share of publicly funded research to the 1% target (van Pottelsberghe, 2008). As an average for the EU the share of total R&D was actually only increased from 1.85% to 1.90% between 2000 and 2008. In EU2020 the 3% target is maintained, but now together with an additional target that measures the frequency of high-growth, knowledge-intensive enterprises.

While the incapacity to increase R&D intensity to the targets set is embarrassing for the European Union, not least when compared to the massive investments taking place in research in emerging economies such as China and India, the narrow understanding of the knowledge-based economy in the Lisbon Strategy as well as in the new EU2020 strategy is even more of a problem. There is no understanding of the implications of the learning economy for a wider set of policies.

In the era of the Lisbon Strategy policy makers in charge of social policy, labour market policy, education policy and industrial policy in Brussels and in national governments pursued business as usual and adjusted neither their discourse nor their practice to the reality of a learning economy. The idea that the new context where the most important resource is knowledge and the most important process is learning required new principles, for a wider set of policies was taken up neither by the Commission itself nor by national governments. One minor exception was the new direction of the regional funds, which became more oriented towards supporting competence building, knowledge-intensive activities and infrastructural investments with relevance for the knowledge-based economy.

The Lisbon Strategy as a scaffolding for the EMU

Already when the European Employment Strategy was designed, the strategy was presented by one of its architects, Allan Larsson (1998), as a necessary complement to the EMU and later on scholars have analysed the Lisbon Strategy in this light (Begg, 2003). This perspective is especially pertinent in the current situation where there is a substantial risk of a breakdown of the EMU. Could and should the Lisbon Strategy have helped to avoid the current crisis where several peripheral countries are at the brink of state bankruptcies?

When the EMU was established, bringing together countries at very different levels of economic development, there were warning voices that a monetary union without a common fiscal policy would be vulnerable to external shocks. In the USA, member states receive compensation through the federal budget in periods of slowdown and unemployment and this works as an important automatic stabiliser. The total budget of the EU is only a few percent of GNP and it cannot play this role. The Lisbon Strategy may be seen as an attempt to compensate for this flaw. There are two possible interpretations of what the Lisbon Strategy could have done to do so.

The first, referred to by Begg (2003), is the neoliberal strategy of 'structural reform' that can introduce more flexibility in the labour markets of the peripheral countries through, for instance, non-standard labour contracts, less protection and increased wage flexibility based upon a weakening of trade unions. With very high degrees of wage flexibility, external shocks could be absorbed by changes in the labour market. The current austerity programmes in Ireland, Greece and Portugal may be seen as short-term versions of such a programme.

A very different possible interpretation would be that the Lisbon Strategy should have reduced regional inequality by upgrading the knowledge base and the industrial structure in the peripheral countries – aiming at better jobs less exposed to global competition. It is no accident that the countries now most exposed to financial speculation are the ones that have the weakest industrial structure with the biggest proportion of workplaces exposed to direct competition with emerging economies (see Chapter Nine). This would have implied a much stronger focus upon regional and social cohesion, reforms of labour markets and education systems as well as massive investment in knowledge and learning. As we have demonstrated, the Lisbon Strategy became increasingly oriented towards the first strategy and it may therefore be argued that the current situation demonstrates that it was not the right thing to do.[6]

But the EU2020 indicates neither insight in the limitations of the first nor in the potential of the second strategy. It is interesting that the important Lisbon sentence 'more and better jobs' now appears in the introduction to the EU2020 as the somewhat vague 'more jobs and better lives' (European Commission, 2010b: 1).

From the Lisbon Strategy to EU2020 – and beyond

Our conclusion is that while the general direction of the Lisbon Strategy, and especially the focus upon social cohesion and the knowledge-based society, pointed in the right direction, those in charge of implementing the policy saw 'social cohesion' as a burden for Europe rather than as the necessary foundation for the learning economy. Therefore, the implementation became increasingly lopsided and dominated by the traditional economic focus upon 'structural reform' and flexibilisation. As a result, as demonstrated by de la Porte and Jacobsson (Chapter Five), we got a focus upon more jobs but not better jobs, upon flexicurity with little security and upon competitiveness with less, rather than more, social cohesion (as reflected in increased income inequality within many of the member countries).

Second, we conclude that, even with a more balanced political approach, the combination of a hardcore monetary union and soft coordination of the policies aimed at social cohesion and innovation was preparing the ground for the current crisis. The EU2020 reproduces these problems and we are therefore not optimistic about the future of the project of European integration. The EU2020 puts forward important objectives for economic growth as well as for social and environmental sustainability. But the social dimension that was 'social cohesion' has been reduced to 'poverty reduction', that is, narrowed down into what is typical of a (neo-)liberal view of the welfare state, and there are no indications in the new strategy of an understanding of the wider policy implications of the learning economy perspective.

Third, we point to the need for a broad understanding of social investment that transcends standard economics of rational choice and aims at the formation of the kind of 'social capital' crucial for nation building. Nothing less than a transnational welfare state of the kind alluded to in the introductory quotation should be the shared objective for such a renewed European project.

The Lisbon Strategy may be seen as an attempt to establish regional and political convergence in Europe with the ultimate aim to build a strong and cohesive union. But the Lisbon Strategy approach, with its emphasis on 'best practice' and benchmarking in specific policy areas, was technocratic and there are few signs that the strategy has been successful in stimulating popular participation in the project. It might have been easier to go forward with an idea of what could constitute the basis for forming a European identity corresponding to what historically constituted the basis for nation building. In a seminal paper written at the occasion of the conference on 'The European Identity in a Global Economy' in preparation of the Lisbon Summit under the Portuguese Presidency, Manuel Castells argued that there is a need for 'a common European identity on whose behalf citizens around Europe could be ready to share problems and build common solutions' (Castells, 2002: 234). After rejecting common religion and culture he pointed to a constellation of values that relate to welfare state and social protection as a promising candidate. It consists of 'shared feelings concerning the need for universal social protection of living conditions, social solidarity, stable employment, workers rights, universal human rights, concern about poor people around the world, extension of democracy to regional and local levels'. He proposed that if European institutions promoted these values probably the 'project identity' would grow (Castells, 2002: 234–35).

Most of the priorities set in EU2020 are relevant responses to the challenges facing Europe today. But as demonstrated by the experience from the Lisbon Strategy, setting priorities is not enough. To realise them requires committed leadership and radical reforms signalling that Europe is entering a new era. One way forward that keeps us within the existing framework would be to redefine the use of the Structural Funds and vastly increase the amounts explicitly targeted to modernising education and labour markets and with the objective to further develop the organisational and technological capabilities of the weaker member states.

A more radical reform would be the redefinition of the Economic and Monetary Union (EMU) so that it recognises the 'social dimension'; transforming it into an Economic and Social Union (ESU). This should be linked to reforms of the decision making process that combine democratic participation with efficiency in new ways.

There is hence a need for a paradigmatic shift where the fear of state intervention and the belief in markets is changed into a pragmatic perspective where governments are allowed to take on the tasks necessary to promote stable economic growth. This includes establishing a much stricter regulation of financial markets. But most importantly it involves a redesign of all institutions and sector policies so that they take seriously that we are in a new phase where knowledge is the most important resource and learning the most important process.

For Europe to reach the ambitious set of objectives outlined in the EU2020 the current mix of hard and soft instruments is not sufficient. Success would actually require a radical step ahead in the process of European integration. An obvious step now debated among macroeconomists would be to move towards a fiscal policy as a necessary complement to the monetary union. But even that might not be enough. There is a need to develop common policies at the European level that contribute to the kind of solidarity that was the historical foundation for the building of the nation states and this includes social policy and education policy as well as industrial policy. Such a radical shift might look unrealistic today. But without it the EU2020 risks becoming another example of European wishful thinking.

Notes

[1] Communication from the Commission, 'EUROPE 2020 A strategy for smart, sustainable and inclusive growth', COM(2010) 2020, 3 March 2010.

[2] See Commission Staff Working Document, Lisbon Strategy evaluation document, SEC(2010) 114 final, 2 February 2010.

[3] Maria Rodrigues, who played the role of Sherpa in the formation of the Lisbon Strategy, served as Portuguese Minister of Labour and was as such heavily involved in the EES.

[4] It is one of the main objectives of the European Union (EU) to enhance economic and social cohesion both between and within member countries (Article 2 of the Treaty on European Union).

[5] According to the figures produced by Eurostat on the basis of the EU Survey of Income and Living Conditions (EU-SILC) between 2000 and 2008 the Gini coefficient for disposable income increased or remained roughly unchanged in all EU-15 member nations with the exception of Portugal, the Netherlands and Belgium.

[6] For an interesting and original analysis of the negative impact of inequality and flexibilisation strategies upon economic growth in Europe see Galbraith (2006).

References

Begg, I. (2003) 'Complementing EMU: Rethinking cohesion policy', *Oxford Review of Economic Policy*, 19 (1), 161–79.

Borràs, S. and Jacobsson, K. (2004) 'The open method of co-ordination and new governance patterns in the EU', *Journal of European Public Policy*, 11 (2), 185–208.

Bouvet, F. (2010) 'EMU and the dynamics of regional per capita income inequality', Working paper, Department of Economics, Sonoma State University.

Castells, M. (2002) 'The construction of European identity', in M. J. Rodrigues (ed.) *The Knowledge Economy in Europe*. Cheltenham: Elgar, pp. 232–41.

Chalmers, D. and Lodge, M. (2003) 'The open method of Co-ordination and the European welfare state', ESRC Working Paper No. 11, June, London School of Economics.

Daly, M. (2008) 'Whither EU social policy? An account and assessment of developments in the Lisbon social inclusion process', *Journal of Social Policy*, 37 (1), 1–19.

European Commission (2010a) Commission Staff Working Document, Lisbon Strategy Evaluation Document, SEC (2010) 114 final, Brussels, 2 February 2010.

European Commission (2010b) Communication from the Commission, EUROPE 2020 a strategy for smart, sustainable and inclusive growth, COM(2010) 2020, Brussels, 3 March 2010.

Fitoussi, J.-P. and Laurent, E. (2009) 'Europe in 2040 : Three scenarios', OFCE/ANR Working Paper No. 10. Paris: Sciences Po.

Fitoussi, J.-P. and Saraceno, F. (2010) 'Inequality and macroeconomic performance', OFCE/ANR Working Paper No. 13. Paris: Sciences Po.

Galbraith, J.K. (2006) 'Maastricht 2042 and the fate of Europe, toward convergence and full employment', UTIP Working Paper No. 39, University of Texas.

Innovation Union (2010), Innovation Union: Europe 2020, Flagship initiative COM(2010) 546. Communication from the Commission, SEC(2010) 1161, Bruxelles.

Jenson, J. (2010) *Defining and Measuring Social Cohesion*. London: Commonwealth Secretariat and United Nations Research Institute for Social Development.

Kok, W. (2004) Report from the High Level Group: Facing the Challenge – The Lisbon Strategy for Growth and Employment. Brussels: European Communities.

Larsson, A. (1998) 'The European employment strategy and the EMU:You must invest to be able to save',The 1998 Meidner lecture presented at Swedish IRRA Association and the Working Life Institute, 18 March 1998.

Lundvall, B.-Å. (2010) *National Systems of Innovation:Toward a Theory of Innovation and Interactive Learning.* London,Anthem Press.

Lundvall, B.-Å. andTomlinson, M. (2002) 'International benchmarking as a policy learning tool', in M.J. Rodrigues (ed.) *The New Knowledge Economy in Europe:A Strategy for International Competitiveness and Social Cohesion.* Cheltenham: Elgar, pp. 120–36.

Raveaud, G. (2007) 'The European employment strategy: Towards more and better jobs?', *JCMS: Journal of Common Market Studies*, 45 (2), 411–34.

Svennilson, I. (1960) 'The Concept of the Nation and its Relevance to Economics', in E.A.G. Robinson (ed.) *Economic Consequences of the Size of Nations*, Proceedings of a Conference held by the International Economic Association. London: Macmillan.

van Pottelsberghe, B. (2008) 'Europe's R&D: Missing the wrong targets?', *Bruegel Policy Brief 2008/03.*

Veugelers, R. (2008) 'Towards a multipolar science world', Working paper for EC-BEPA, University of Leuven.

FOURTEEN

Social investment: a paradigm in search of a new economic model and political mobilisation

Nathalie Morel, Bruno Palier and Joakim Palme

We set out this book by asking a number of questions about the concept of social investment: What is it? Which policies can be associated with it? How does it perform? Is it relevant for the current and future challenges of modern welfare states? Behind these questions, there is of course a larger enterprise of searching for a strategy that would be able to regenerate the welfare state, promote social inclusion, create more and better jobs, and help address the challenges posed by the economic crisis, globalisation, population ageing and climate change. There is an underlying notion that the social investment strategy carries such potential. However, the aim of the book is also to critically assess the social investment approach in terms of the content and coherence of the ideas and policies put forward, its actual implementation and achievements, as well as its shortcomings. The book can hence be seen as an attempt to contribute to the discussion on the relevance of the social investment perspective for the new challenges that Europe and other continents are facing and, moreover, to base this discussion on a realistic view of how the world is working.

In this concluding chapter we organise the examination of what we have learnt from the contributions to the book around a number of subthemes. We start out by discussing how far the social investment approach has come in terms of an emerging paradigm by mapping out its contours both at the ideational level and in terms of the policies implemented, and ask questions around its achievements. This, in turn, raises a number of critical issues around the design and implementation of social investment policies that are elaborated on in the second section of this chapter. In the third section, we put forward some ideas for a new form of economic thinking to underpin the social investment approach, and examine the politics of the approach in order to identify what could be the driving forces behind it. Finally, we look at some of the challenges ahead and discuss possible constraints for future reforms.

The social investment perspective as an 'emerging paradigm'

The ideas

From an ideational point of view, the clear message is that a new and coherent set of ideas is emerging, even if there is some degree of ambiguity around some of the ideas (see Chapters One and Three).

From the ideational standpoint, the social investment perspective was developed with the dual ambition to modernise the welfare state so as to better address the new social risks and needs structure of contemporary societies and ensure the financial and political sustainability of the welfare state, and to sustain a different economy – the knowledge-based economy. Central to the social investment perspective is the attempt to reconcile social and economic goals.

The focus is on public policies that 'prepare' individuals, families and societies to adapt to various transformations, such as changing career patterns and working conditions, the development of new social risks, population ageing and climate change, instead of simply generating responses to 'repair' damages after markets fail or existing policies prove inadequate. By addressing problems in their infancy, the social investment paradigm stands to reduce human suffering, environmental degradation and government debt.

With regards to the modernising of the welfare state, the contention of the social investment perspective is that the sustainability of the welfare state hinges on the number and productivity of future tax payers (Esping-Andersen et al., 2002; Lindh and Palme, 2006; see also Chapter Three). This calls for policies that broaden the tax-base (by raising employment levels) and which also increase the productivity and quality of work (and therefore increase wages). A clear element of the social investment perspective is that investing in human capital should enable the creation of more and better jobs.

With respect to the economic goals, social investments are expected to generate returns in the form of economic growth. As Lundvall and Lorenz underline, 'social investments may be defined as public expenditure that combines the solution of social problems with enhancing economic performance' (Chapter Nine).

The policies

What kind of policies, then, can be said to underpin the social investment perspective? As Hemerijck underlines, three areas of public policy stand out as particularly central: human capital improvement; the relation between the productive sphere of the economy and the reproductive sphere of the family; and employment relations. In all these areas, *capacitating* public services stand out as crucial components of a strategy that aims at preparing the population to the particular social risks caused by life course contingencies.

The focus on investing in human capital is perhaps the policy domain which gathers the greatest consensus amongst social investment proponents, the idea receiving support from neoclassical economists such as Gary Becker and James Heckman as well as from more heterodox economists such as Amartya Sen. The policy recommendation to invest heavily in human capital is also based on the observation of a causal structure where education has been shown to be the central driving variable for GDP growth in Europe (Lindh and Palme, 2006).

Following Nelson and Stephens, and in light of the demonstrated benefits to high employment levels, it is clear that policies that invest in human capital are of crucial importance. Education and training policies constitute the most obvious method of improving skills – particularly cognitive and social skills – relevant to the service-based, knowledge economy. Skill acquisition in formal institutions begins in early childhood education and care, and continues in the primary, secondary and tertiary stages of education. Skill acquisition during these stages of education is realised through policies that promote high enrolment and quality instruction.

Other types of public policies, though, such as sick pay or generous unemployment benefits, along with adequate rehabilitation programmes and active labour market policies, can also protect the value of individuals' skills. Human capital policies that foster the expansion of high-quality jobs therefore include those that aid in both the acquisition of skills and the protection of the value of the skills already acquired. Well-designed unemployment insurance benefits carry the potential of also improving matching process on the labour market by working as search subsidies (Sjöberg et al., 2010).

The focus on the relation between the productive and the reproductive spheres hinges on policies that help parents combine work and family life. Here the aim is both to increase labour supply by supporting mothers' employment in order to foster economic growth and to ensure the long-term fiscal sustainability of welfare systems, but also to make families less exposed to the risk of poverty. An underlying aim is also to enable families to realise their desired fertility. Policies put forward typically include child care services and parental leave schemes. Of crucial importance here is the quality of the child care services and the design and generosity of the parental leave schemes, both for providing children with equal opportunities at the earliest age and for their cognitive development, and to promote gender equality (see Chapter Six).

The third area of focus, that of employment relations, seeks to address the issue of the increasingly differentiated employment patterns over the life course in order to reduce the probability of individuals being trapped into inactivity and welfare dependency. Here Hemerijck reminds us that 'the issue is not maximum labour market flexibility or the neoliberal mantra of "making work pay". Instead, the policy imperative is for "making transitions pay" over the life cycle through the provision of "active securities" or "social bridges", ensuring that non-standardised employment relations become stepping stones to sustainable careers.'

While a fairly broad consensus prevails concerning the policies needed to promote the development of human capital, this is less true with respect to policies to address work–family life balance, or policies to accompany life-course transitions. If there is general agreement across Europe that the state should provide publicly funded primary and secondary education, there is less advancement in terms of reaching consensus, even amongst social investment proponents regarding the desirability, type and extent of public support, to enable families to reconcile work and family life. Likewise, while there is strong agreement on the necessity to raise employment levels, there is some ambiguity regarding the means for 'activating' people and for promoting more flexibility on the labour market.

The ambiguity that characterises the social investment perspective comes out clearly when one assesses the policies that have effectively been implemented across Europe.

Assessing the policy implementation

Any attempt to assess the outcomes of social investment policies has to face the fact that only a few countries can be said to have implemented such policies in a comprehensive fashion. A second issue is that there has been no general increase in public expenditure on social investment-type policies. Another complication is that some countries have implemented social investment programmes with a restricted focus on human capital but without maintaining adequate compensatory policies. Before addressing these issues, we start with summarising our main findings concerning the development of social investment policies in Europe.

Contrary to those who claim that the developments of employment and social policies during the last two decades represent a turn towards a social investment approach, the chapters in this volume show that in reality, only a few countries have implemented a social investment approach. Most chapters confirm that neither southern European countries (Italy, Spain, Greece and Portugal) nor Eastern European countries have really entered the social investment era. Globally, the continental European countries remain traditional 'compensatory welfare systems' with few attempts to shift towards social investment, even if some countries (France, Belgium, and increasingly Germany and the Netherlands) display some orientation towards social investment in the field of family policy. The countries that display the strongest social investment profile are the Nordic countries. We can also see changes towards a more 'active' welfare state in the Netherlands as well as in the UK.

Thanks to the distinction she draws between compensatory and social investment-related expenditure, Nikolai helps us to broadly characterise the different welfare state configurations as they appear in the early twenty-first century. Contrary to the idea of a shift from passive to active social expenditure, the first main evidence is that while there has been an increase in public social expenditure as a percentage of GDP across countries, this increase has not translated into an increase in expenditure on social investment-type policies (see also Hudson and Kühner, 2009). On the contrary, old age expenditure has increased everywhere, while the typical social investment expenditure, education, has decreased in most countries. This decrease is partly explainable by the diminishing size of student cohorts due to demographic changes, but it does show that there has been no emphasis on increasing investments in education, not least when one considers that the number of years in education has tended to increase. Only in the field of family policy has social expenditure increased. Beyond these common trends, Nikolai identifies four worlds of spending profiles that we have summarised in Table 14.1.

As underlined by Nikolai, the English-speaking and the Nordic countries are the only countries that can be said to have developed more social investment types of policies but represent remarkably different examples of social investment in action. The Nordic version of the social investment approach spends much on investment-related social policies as well as on old age and passive labour market policies, while the British case shows a reorientation of public social expenditure

Table 14.1: Four worlds of social expenditure

		Social investment-related expenditure	
		−	+
Compensatory expenditure	+	Traditional compensatory welfare systems Southern Europe	Social investment with double liability: protection and promotion Nordic countries
	−	Hidden welfare state USA	Investing in human capital and low protection UK

away from compensatory social policies towards more social investment-oriented policy domains (education and family policy but not active labour market policy).

These findings, based on the analysis of expenditure data, are confirmed by the other chapters that provide a more detailed and qualitative analysis of recent policy developments. De la Porte and Jacobsson (Chapter Five) thus show that what has been implemented in the EU member states is 'recommodification' more than social investment as far as employment policies are concerned. Conditionality in unemployment insurance has been increased in most member states, replacement rates have been retrenched, and the duration of benefit periods shortened. Activation schemes are far from comprehensive, workfarist rather than individualised, and come in the form of counselling rather than comprehensive training. The quality of activation services does not live up to the social investment ideal that was supposed to be inherent in the European Employment Strategy (EES). The reform of education, activation and training institutions has in most member states not been deep enough to be labelled social investment. Bonoli (Chapter Seven) further underlines that there was more social investment content in labour market policies during the 1950s and 1960s than nowadays.

But one also sees some successes for the social investment approach. The experience of the Nordic countries suggests that social investment policies can be used to successfully combine social and economic goals. As many of the chapters have shown, these countries display high and broad-based education levels, which appear to translate into high levels of social capital and social cohesion, greater learning and innovation capacity at work (making these countries amongst the most competitive economies in the world), more flexibility on the labour market, and good economic growth including the creation of more and better jobs.

These countries also display higher female employment rates, lower poverty rates, including lower transmission of intergenerational poverty, and have been dealing successfully with demographic issues, both in terms of providing care for elderly people and in maintaining fertility levels. These countries are also the most successful when it comes to implementing climate mitigation policies. The key to this success seems to be the fact that the Nordic countries have not pursued a simple reorientation strategy with their welfare systems towards more activation, but have instead combined strong protection with heavy social investment, with the aim to promote social equality as well as gender equality.

Still, despite these examples of 'good practice', the general picture is that the social investment glass is almost empty. At best, the social investment paradigm is emerging to eventually fill the glass but then a number of issues need to be addressed. On the ideational level there is too much ambiguity and this will not be resolved until the quality of investment is given due attention. Without that, social investment cannot be properly differentiated from the neoliberal paradigm. The overriding focus on activation without proper attention to quality and to adequate protection in most countries has opened the door for the critique that the social investment approach forgets about social inclusion and poverty alleviation, and – worse – that it has in fact reinforced poverty and social exclusion (Cantillon, 2010).

It thus appears warranted to elaborate on what we see as the crucial elements of a successful social investment approach, and this is what we turn to in the following section.

Outlining the core features of a successful social investment approach

To begin with, it is necessary to clearly distinguish the social investment perspective from neoliberalism. This means that not only the tools put forward but also the very diagnosis of the problems at hand need to be clearly differentiated. Furthermore, the lesson to be drawn from the different chapters is that the social investment approach is a 'package deal' and partial implementation may at best deliver a partial success. Equality is a crucial element, and the quality of programmes is of critical importance. Equally important is the understanding that 'protection' must remain an important function of the welfare state that works as a necessary complement to activation and which can not be substituted by activation. Furthermore, the life course perspective suggests that policies can be effective only if the whole chain is maintained, and if it is aimed at the whole population and not reserved for the select few.

Distinguishing the social investment approach from neoliberalism

Based on the contributions to this book we argue that there are – or should be – some fundamental differences between the social investment perspective and neoliberalism that need to be spelt out clearly in order for the social investment perspective to avoid being considered as some form of 'neoliberalism in disguise' and in order to not only become effective but also to emerge as a coherent paradigm.

Part of the confusion, as we discussed in Chapter One, arises from the fact there is some degree of ambiguity at the ideational level within the social investment perspective, which stems in part from the different intellectual and ideological sources behind it, gathering together a more 'social democratic' approach inspired by the example of the Nordic countries and a 'Third Way' approach based on a more 'anglo-liberal' perspective on social policy.

Based on the analyses of several chapters in this volume, it seems that the Third Way approach, with its strong emphasis on activation, has had more influence on the policy orientation and developments in Europe than the social-democratic variant. This, we argue, is problematic in that the Third Way approach does not represent enough of a clear break from neoliberalism. Indeed, while Giddens and other Third Way proponents do argue – against neoliberals – for a new, more active and enabling role for the state, and seek to promote a more inclusive society with greater 'social justice' not least through schemes aimed at minimising poverty risks, they nonetheless share with neoliberals a very similar diagnosis of the failures of the traditional post-war welfare state but also a similar diagnosis of the causes of unemployment. This shared diagnosis makes it difficult to propose radically different tools for dealing with these issues (cf. Jobert, 2002). The focus on 'activating' people, at least in the way it has been pursued in the UK and across Europe over the past two decades, has thus borne too much resemblance to the kind of activation strategy promoted by neoliberals (cf. Chapters Five and Seven).

For neoliberals, unemployment is due to a problem of supply and incentives, with overly generous social benefits acting as a disincentive to work, and too much labour market protection hampering the needed flexibility in the new economy. The reforms put forward have thus aimed at deregulating the labour market, lowering payroll taxes, reducing labour costs and increasing incentives to accept jobs by reducing the level of unemployment and social assistance benefits (to 'make work pay').

Such a strategy appears wrong-headed on several accounts. These reforms have not created 'more and better jobs' but rather jobs which do not allow people to live decently (giving rise to the 'working poor' phenomenon) and which do not generate the tax revenues needed to sustain and improve the social protection model of ageing European societies. Second, such a strategy fails to recognise an increasingly important dimension to be associated with unemployment, that is, the lack of adequate qualifications. Indeed, unemployment risks and rates are much higher for the unskilled than they were a couple of decades ago, and much higher than for those with tertiary education. As the European Commission's 'New skills for new jobs' report underlines, employment rates vary greatly according to qualification levels. The employment rates across Europe as a whole in 2008 for those with high skills was 83.9%, that for medium skill levels was 70.6%, and that for low skill levels was only 48.1%. Not only this, but the wages of the low skilled have also fallen relative to more skilled individuals despite falling numbers of low-skilled individuals in the labour forces of most advanced economies, which suggests that there has been a fall in the demand for low-skilled labour (McIntosh, 2004). In fact, between 2007 and 2010, the number of jobs employing people with high skills has increased in Europe, while the number of low-skill jobs has decreased (European Commission, 2009, 2010). The effect of skills on unemployment risks is particularly pronounced in the UK and Ireland, where the unemployment rate for those with lower secondary or below education levels is about twice that for those with upper secondary education, and about four times that of those with tertiary education (McIntosh, 2004). This goes to show that in today's economy, qualifications are more important than ever, especially in view of the increasing needs in new sectors of employment, such as 'green jobs', advanced technologies and the digital economy which lie at the core of the new economy.

The fact that the unemployed are predominantly unskilled and that vacant jobs require high skills suggests that, in these times of 'aftershock', we need to complement demand-oriented Keynesian measures with supply side-oriented instruments that go beyond the neoliberal deregulation of labour markets, lowering of labour costs and provision of incentives for the unemployed to take poorly paid jobs, and instead upskill the unemployed by providing them with the necessary learning capacities. We need here to emphasise again the importance of education, training, skill formation, maintenance and updating of skills as policies preparing individuals for the current and future economy. In this context, the obvious fact that there is a large variation among countries particularly when it comes to the skill levels of the 'low skilled' (Nelson and Stephens) needs to be borne in mind. Likewise, employees in many European countries experience a large gap between their qualifications and the job demands (Lindh and Palme, 2006).

While Nelson and Stephens (Chapter Eight) as well as Lundvall and Lorenz (Chapter Nine) provide us with evidence showing the positive effects of increasing education and skill levels on employment – both in terms of increasing employment levels and in terms of creating 'good jobs' – it is evident from the chapters by de la Porte and Jacobsson (Chapter Five) and by Bonoli (Chapter Seven) that in most European countries this strategy has not been followed yet. Partly, as de la Porte and Jacobsson have argued with respect to the implementation of the European Employment Strategy (EES), this is due to the ambiguity that characterises the understanding of social investment on which the EES is supposed to rest: 'due to its political and malleable form, the EES can be used either as a comprehensive social investment strategy focusing on the development of human resources for the needs of the labour market, or alternatively, as a liberalization strategy with little or no social investment'.

Yet the implementation of neoliberal forms of activation rather than investing in quality education and skill formation has shown to carry negative consequences for poverty and social cohesion. In Germany, activation policies in the form of recommodification and lowering of wages have led to an increase in the number of 'working poor', who are now up to 11 million (see Chapter Eleven). Furthermore, as McIntosh discusses, in those countries (such as the UK, USA, Canada and Germany) where wages for the low-skilled have been allowed to deteriorate, this has increased wage inequalities and labour market polarisation between the low-skilled and the high-skilled, but with no positive effect on the employment levels of the low-skilled (McIntosh, 2004).

Thus, as Lundvall and Lorenz argue, if we want to not only reduce unemployment but also promote employment growth (especially in 'good jobs'), while also promoting social cohesion rather than polarisation, it is important to go beyond neoliberal labour market policies and consider seriously the need to invest in skills that enhance the capacity to learn. This, as they as well as Nelson and Stephens (Chapter Eight) show, is best done through policies that are broad-based, egalitarian and of high quality, and that follow the whole life course, starting with early childhood education and care.

While specific policies are needed to support the least skilled who are presently on the labour market, a true social investment strategy should not exclusively be based on programmes targeted only at 'the unskilled' or other disadvantaged groups, but should in the first place be based on the provision of universal, quality education and training programmes throughout the life course. What the contributions to the book suggest is that equality and quality must be at the centre of the social investment approach.

Social investment and equality

The relationship between social investment and equality appears vital to address on several accounts. Indeed, it is a desirable outcome of social policy if one takes seriously the wish expressed by social investment proponents to address the new social risks structure of contemporary societies, to reduce intergenerational poverty and provide individuals and families with more equal capacities to invest in their own human capital and that of their children so that they can maintain responsibility for their wellbeing via market income. It also appears to be a necessary precondition for promoting growth and employment, especially in good-quality jobs.

At stake here is both equality of access (to quality child care, to education, to lifelong training, to quality health and care services) and income equality. Indeed, it is clear from several chapters in this book that egalitarian societies are more successful in implementing social investment policies and in achieving many of the desired outcomes linked to this strategy, including in terms of climate change mitigation policies (see Chapters Eight, Nine and Twelve; see also Wilkinson and Pickett, 2009). Thus it is not just equality of opportunity ('social justice') but also equality of outcomes that matters. The fact that equality appears to be a precondition for a successful social investment strategy urges us to remember the merits of traditional social protection and antipoverty programmes, and suggests that reduction of income inequality should remain high on the social investment agenda.

Another element that needs to be made more central on the social investment agenda is that of gender equality. While gender awareness is at the very heart of the social investment perspective, focusing as it is on women's economic contributions and reproductive role and care work, Jenson has forcefully demonstrated the extent to which equality of condition or even equal opportunities for women and men have been sidetracked as policy goals in their own right within this perspective (Jenson, 2009).Thus, while many countries have successfully managed to achieve high female employment rates, and some have even managed to combine these high employment rates with moderate to high fertility rates, none has thus far managed to – or sought to – effectively address certain persistent gender inequalities such as the division of unpaid care and household labour, the gender wage gap, labour market segregation and the 'glass ceiling effect' for women.This is just as true for the more liberal countries as it is for the Nordic countries, even if inequalities take different forms in different welfare regimes. Addressing this issue means that special attention must be paid to the specific design of policies that seek to promote women's employment and to policies for reconciling work and family life (cf. Chapter Six).

Likewise, more attention needs to be devoted to the structural and political factors that contribute to the kind of ethnic inequalities that characterise European societies today and which are likely to be of increasing importance in the future if not properly addressed (Emmeneger and Cajera, 2011).This is in fact an area where the Nordic countries do not perform very well. While they do better than other European countries in terms of fostering equality in the educational system (for instance, only in Sweden does the second generation of migrants enjoy the same educational opportunities for their children as the native community – cf. Chapter Eleven), integration of immigrants and ethnic minorities on the labour market is quite poor, and unemployment rates for these groups consequently high.

This can be explained in part by the structure of the labour market in the Nordic countries which, as Lundvall and Lorenz (Chapter Nine) show, is predominantly biased towards skilled labour, with few workplaces based on aTaylorist and traditional work organisation which elsewhere often function as 'entrance points' for immigrants with low skills since they offer jobs where workers with limited communication skills can operate efficiently (see also McIntosh, 2004).This, as Lundvall and Lorenz argue, means that the integration efforts in these countries need to be even greater and focused upon upgrading the skills, including the communication skills of immigrants.

However, if the skill gap is too big, as suggested by Bonoli, there may be good reasons for also developing subsidised jobs for the least skilled – although such subsidies should be made conditional on the quality of the jobs thus subsidised, that is, such subsidies should not simply allow employers to take advantage of 'cheap labour'.

Social investment and quality

'Quality' should be another crucial component of a true social investment strategy. This relates both to the quality of jobs but also to the quality of services. Morgan (Chapter Six) emphasises that only high-quality child care can foster good cognitive skill acquisition amongst all children and help reduce social inequalities. Likewise, Nelson and Stephens (Chapter Eight) underline how participation in a course of education does not directly translate into high achievement, arguing that the quality of education matters more than simple participation for skill accumulation, particularly at the low end of the capability distribution.

When it comes to active labour market policies, Bonoli (Chapter Seven) shows how policies directed only towards 'activation' in the sense of pushing people back onto the labour market to take up 'any job', as in the neoliberal strategy, have not produced good results. While employment rates have generally increased over the 2000s, the quality of the jobs created has very often been of low quality (Guillen and Dahl, 2009), taking the shape of atypical jobs, short-term contracts, interim work, short part-time, and so on, which has resulted in increased in-work poverty (Eichhorst and Marx, 2011). Thus active labour market policy can be considered as part of a social investment strategy only if conceived as an instrument of social promotion, and not only as a way to increase employment rates at any cost. Amongst the various active labour market measures, only the 'upskilling' ones seem to fit the social investment approach. Activation is not enough.

This is all the more important since if the quality of jobs is forgotten, activation only leads to shifting people from inactivity into in-work poverty, which does not reach the economic goal of increasing employment rates in order to increase the tax base and support future pensions and health care costs. Furthermore, as Lundvall and Lorenz show, given the challenges of economic globalisation, one way to remain competitive on the world market is through innovation, and the production of goods and services of high quality.

Investing in quality means that substantial investment must be made to improve education, training and upskilling schemes, as well as to improve working conditions. This in turn means that more, rather than less, social spending or, rather, *investment* is needed. The fact that an effective social investment strategy in the short run entails increasing social expenditure cannot be ignored, all the more so as it appears clearly from the different chapters that it cannot be enough to reorient social expenditure towards 'activation' programmes, it is equally important that the welfare state also retains its traditional protection functions.

Promotion and protection

In this respect, it is important to recognise that compensation and activation may affect social inclusion in different directions. By providing adequate compensation, social benefits protect persons from poverty and the negative effects that low income has on social inclusion. On the other hand, in the absence of measures aimed at fostering employability, social protection may have unintended effects and increase benefit dependency and thus social exclusion in the sphere of employment. There is therefore a fine balance to be held between protection and activation programmes in the form of retraining and/or rehabilitation in order to promote employment, without increasing poverty and social exclusion (Palme et al., 2009).

'Flexicurity', as it has developed in the Nordic countries and in the Netherlands, appears as a useful way to reconcile protection and activation as Lorenz and Lundvall (Chapter Nine) have highlighted, although that depends on the precise design of flexicurity schemes (Chapter Five). As is now widely acknowledged, 'high unemployment benefits of short duration, coupled to strong activation incentives and obligations, supported by active labour market servicing policy, are most successful in lowering unemployment and raising labour productivity' (Chapter Two).

This means that the recasting of the welfare state should not be reduced to 'transform[ing] the safety net of entitlements into a springboard to personal responsibility' (Blair and Schröder, 1999) but rather about forming social policies so that they act as a 'bridge of change', resting on several pillars: investment in human capital *and* social protection *and* activation.

Of course, as mentioned, such a strategy requires that more rather than fewer resources be devoted to social policy. This may well appear problematic in the aftermath of the 2008 financial crisis and in a time viewed as a period of financial austerity. Yet there are good reasons for changing the way such expenditure is considered, and to take seriously the idea that these social expenditures are in fact *investments*, from which productive and economic benefits can be derived. This therefore calls for a new economic thinking and accounting to underpin the social investment perspective. In fact, the absence so far of such new economic thinking can be said to be one reason why the social investment perspective has not yet developed into a fully fledged paradigm like Keynesianism and neoliberalism.

A paradigm in search of a new economic model and political mobilisation

In this section, we discuss what seem to be the missing links for the social investment perspective to establish itself more strongly, namely the lack of a clear macroeconomic model and the lack of political coalitions to back it up.

The need for a new economic turn and thinking

The social investment approach also warrants an analysis of its own political economy, including both a theoretical and a collective action dimension. In the following we will primarily deal with the economic thinking.

As shown by Hemerijck and Jenson (Chapters Two and Three), past social policy approaches were integrated with economic theories of different kinds. This suggests that we need to go beyond Keynesian and neoclassical economic theories and anchor the social investment approach in a new economic model. Here it is obvious that the social investment approach is so far not on a par with either Keynesianism or neoliberalism, which suggests that the most evident need is to fill the macroeconomic gap. It also means that the success of a new social investment agenda depends on it being broad enough not only to match but also to supersede past approaches.

As argued earlier, the social investment approach partly rests on a different understanding of causes and solutions to unemployment. The way unemployment is understood is a defining element of past policy paradigms and is also likely to be a defining element for the social investment perspective.

However, it should be remembered that the social investment approach, while it addresses core economic issues, is not merely an economic but also a social strategy. This goes back to its intellectual origins in the world of welfare state experts. The notion of 'productive social policy' recognises the macro- and microdynamics of social policy that carries the potential of delivering economic benefits to both individuals and society: investing in good jobs will curb the rising cost of unhealthy and unsafe workplaces and benefit the health of individual workers. Investing in environments that enable learning activities promotes longer working lives as well as adding more health years to individuals. Ultimately, this is about reconciling growth and equality.

Where are the elements for the 'new' economic thinking? One important element is to be found in our accounting methods. If we take seriously the idea that social outlays can yield long-run dividends for both individuals and society as a whole, then there is a good case to be made for counting such outlays as productive investments rather than as consumption. This in turn means that we need to develop a new National Accounts System (Esping-Andersen, 2005; see also Chapter Ten).

There are also new forms of economic activity that urge us to rethink our ways of measuring productivity, not least since these activities are of growing importance. This applies to personal services and to Information and Communication Technology (ICT)-related production, as well as to green technologies.

Likewise, the rationale behind the 'Beyond GDP' agenda as formulated in the Stiglitz –Sen –Fitoussi Report (2009) is that current developmental challenges demand new and improved socioeconomic indicators to guide policy makers. As the authors remind us, what we measure affects our view of the world and in the end what we do. If our measurements are flawed, decisions may be distorted. Thus, for instance, conflict regarding choices between promoting growth and protecting the environment may be dissolved once environmental degradation is appropriately included in our measurement of economic performance.

Among other things the report points out that it is often unclear how current indicators relate to each other and that social dimensions tend to be missing. The concept of sustainable development is useful in this context with its future oriented and intergenerational focus: 'development that meets the needs of the present without compromising the ability of future generations to meet their own needs' (Brundtland Commission, 1987).

There is hence a need to work out indicators that can inform us about the sustainability of social wellbeing. The Stiglitz–Sen–Fitoussi Report describes sustainable development as 'well-being over time particularly in its economic, environmental and social dimensions' (p. 8). Other interpretations of the concept use the metaphor of the three pillars but in comparison to the economic and environmental aspects of sustainable development, social aspects tend to be neglected. This one-sided emphasis on the environmental dimension of sustainable development will not promote an efficient response to major long-term challenges such as climate change or reproduction of human capital. The Stiglitz–Sen–Fitoussi Report explicitly paves the way for a comprehensive approach in line with the social investment perspective. Their idea of measuring sustainability both in terms of flows and stocks is as important as their idea of social sustainability as an integrated part of sustainable development (and not just a 'pillar'). If sustainable development is the aim, and if sustainability is to be measured in terms of both flows and stocks, then perhaps what is needed from a macroeconomic perspective are policies that are flexible and adaptive rather than permanent and prescriptive.

As discussed by Sommestad, models including human capital accumulation (such as endogenous growth) could be seen as one source of inspiration for a new economic model, as could the concept of sustainable growth. But a new economic model also demands a deeper understanding of the transformation of capitalism, an improved vision of what the 'new' economy is, that goes beyond the concept of just being 'post-industrial'. Lundvall and Lorenz's reformulation of the 'knowledge-based economy' as the 'learning economy' is one fruitful conceptual contribution. The 'green economy' is another potentially useful metaphor.

The lack of a fully fledged economic theory or model is only one reason why the social investment approach has not gained more ground despite the widespread ideas. Another reason seems to be the lack of clear political coalitions and entrepreneurship to back it up. In the following section we reflect on the kind of political alliances that could carry this perspective.

The politics of social investment policies

What are the political motivations for implementing social investment programmes? On the ideational level, the model is overdetermined. In the real world, it appears that motives are not as elaborated as one would have thought, and have a shorter time horizon than expected.

The analysis of the underlying ideas suggests a rather complex agenda with a number of specific motives for the social investment approach: the demographic motive of increasing fertility in societies that are increasingly burdened by ageing populations; the social motive of supporting groups with social risks neglected by the traditional welfare state programmes; the economic motive of preparing workers for the new economy; the political motive of formulating a third way, different from the old paradigms and able to create new political coalitions.

Is the social investment left wing or right wing? Historically, there are obvious social democratic roots. We see this with the Myrdal agenda formulated in the 1930s in Sweden and we see the social democratic inspiration when we look at more recent formulations of it, for example, by Esping-Andersen et al. (2002). The story of the Lisbon agenda is another example. The 2000 proposal was decided when left governments were predominant across the EU. Giddens' writings were part of the New Labour mobilisation. The different chapters in this book also show that there are some clear cross-national correlations in the sense that countries with a stronger political representation of social democracy have been more inclined to implement such policies.

The fact that since the social investment ideas have been elaborated and promoted, few countries have known either left governments or encompassing party coalitions working hand in hand with encompassing unions may partly explain the lack of implementation of social investment policies beyond traditionally social democratic countries.

Another reason is that the social investment approach is naturally targeting children, youth, women, migrants and the unemployed, which do not constitute any clear or coherent political constituency, making it difficult to see which political coalitions would support it.

This is not to suggest that there is only one political path to social investment. Quite the contrary, the ambiguities of the perspective open up for a broader set of political actors, and in so far as there are achievements of the social investment approach that are attractive, why should it not be possible to learn from 'best practice'? In fact, different chapters point to the fact that the political triggers for the promotion of social investment-type programmes have often been of a substantive rather than ideological nature. In this respect, demographic arguments seem to have mattered a lot (see Chapters Six and Ten).

If Morgan (Chapter Six) is right about the changing electoral base for political parties and the growing competition for the female votes, this may bring social investment-related issues on the agenda, particularly around the care and education of young children. Here, the ambiguity that characterises the social investment perspective also carries some potential by offering an opportunity to build policy coalitions between partners who have very different world views. This suggests that social investment-type programmes could be put forward or agreed upon by very different actors not only in the individual member states but also at the EU level. It might not be necessary for everyone to recognise the failure of neoliberalism as a paradigm in order to support policies or programmes that are clearly outside the neoliberal box. The problem is that such an approach risks remaining partial and lacking in the kind of synergies suggested by our 'package' argument.

Meeting the challenges ahead: what future for the social investment welfare state?

When we discuss the social investment approach in paradigmatic terms on the ideational level a few words of caution are motivated. The approach as such has gained steam primarily out of disenchantment with neoliberal policies. The birth of the emerging paradigm is thus not associated with a crisis and an established and broadly acknowledged failure of the interpretation and solutions of the past. We would argue that it is only if the financial crisis that started in 2008 is perceived as the crisis and end of the past neoliberal economic and social paradigm that the social investment perspective may have a chance to become the new paradigm.

Yet at this stage it remains an open question whether the global financial crisis of the late 2000s will be the trigger that brings about the social investment paradigm, or whether it will, on the contrary, be its deathblow by starving the quality of social investment programmes due to large deficits in the public finances.

The first big challenge for the social investment perspective is to become a coherent and convincing economic and social policy paradigm for the years to come. The relevance of the social investment approach in the post-financial crisis context hinges not only on whether it can be reformulated in the new general context but also on whether it can be adapted to the country specific problems and potentials. There are obviously some general issues that call for commonality. Social inclusion of the young, migrants and single mothers are clear and uncontested examples. This needs to be addressed simultaneously with problems of political cohesion, demographic ageing and environmental sustainability. As the various chapters in the final part of this book underline, this is quite feasible but not certain, many things again depending on the specific design of the policies as much as on the political coalitions susceptible of sustaining such comprehensive policies.

At the EU level, even though the Lisbon Strategy has been associated with the social investment approach, the EU has often played against the development of proper social investment policies. Lundvall and Lorenz (Chapter Thirteen) emphasise the tensions embedded in the Lisbon Strategy, which was a compromise between neoliberal and social investment ideas. In this context, De la Porte and Jacobsson (Chapter Five) point to the specific negative context created by the single market and the single currency for many countries, preventing them from implementing a proper social investment approach:

the ambiguity of the Lisbon Strategy has allowed policy-makers a selective use of and reference to the message of the EES, and a bias in favour of commodification and flexibility rather than social investment and security. It is notable that despite higher employment rates, there has not been a decline in people living at risk of poverty in the Union as a whole since 2000. On the contrary, income inequalities and in-work poverty has increased in many places.

And while the new EU2020 Agenda emphasises the importance of research and higher education as well as combating school dropout, and focuses on reducing poverty, the macroeconomic focus is on controlling public expenditures rather than on increasing the revenue for investing in the future. As Hemerijck (Chapter Two) underlines: 'the role of the state as a necessary social investor is confronted with the overriding public finance constraint, anchored in the Maastricht criteria and the Stability and Growth Pact'.

The 2008 global financial crisis does not yet seem to have been interpreted as a crisis of neoliberalism: bonuses are back in banks, retrenchment is promoted to deal with deficits in the public finances, activation is back on the employment policy agenda, cuts seem to start targeting the social investment fields as well as other social benefits. Implementing neoliberal recipes to cure a crisis of neoliberalism is probably an expected phase on the way to the exhaustion of neoliberalism. According to Hall's (1993) approach to changes in policy paradigms, it corresponds to the last stage of the crisis of a policy paradigm. The bad news is that we may therefore be facing an even deeper crisis since neoliberal solutions cannot solve our current problems but will, on the contrary, lead to more difficulties.

This in turn may trigger a deep political crisis, leading to a paradigmatic shift away from neoliberalism. The outcome of a political crisis cannot, however, be predicted with any certainty. While such a crisis could pave the way towards a social investment paradigm, it might alternatively trigger a turn to protectionism and nationalist xenophobic policies. Wide public unrest and riots are other possible scenarios.

In the past few years, Germany has also provided an alternative socioeconomic model to social investment, in which increasing competitiveness by reducing the cost and social protection of labour and fiscal discipline are core components. Such a strategy also finds its expression in the Pact for the Euro and now the Euro Plus Pact (formerly Competitiveness Pact). Germany's success in considerably reducing unemployment levels, and the country's position as the main engine of growth in the eurozone, make the German model a credible competitor to the social investment perspective. Yet this economic success hides growing inequalities and a dualisation process between protected insiders in 'good jobs' and an increasing mass of outsiders in atypical jobs with low incomes and poor social protection (Palier and Thelen, 2010). This, we argue, cannot be a winning strategy in the long run, with too many negative externalities involved in terms of increased in-work poverty, social and economic dualisms, and an orientation towards low-skilled, low-quality jobs which cannot remain competitive in the long run in the global economy.

A more optimistic view on the likelihood of the social investment paradigm 'winning the day' as a new socioeconomic paradigm is based on the contention that important changes take place incrementally rather than through a policy revolution. Against the idea that paradigmatic change is inevitably a result of a rupture in the past equilibrium, there is now ample evidence that paradigmatic shifts more often come about through an accumulation of incremental but cumulatively transformative reforms (Streeck and Thelen, 2005; Palier, 2010). From the analysis of past transformations in paradigms and policies, we know that for such structural changes to occur, some conditions need to be met: we need changes in the European context that lead to a recognition of the need for a new agenda. We may foster gradual change by the 'layering' of new social policies, at the margin of the existing system. But eventually we need metapolicy reforms to circumvent piecemeal engineering and move beyond institutional and political obstacles. We not only need to make available elements of a new social and economic policy paradigm but also to suggest how they can be fitted together. Moreover, for actually achieving policy change, we not only need a renewed political coalition involving new and old social risks bearers but also political entrepreneurs at different political levels to act as agents of change.

In other words, there are a number of requirements for the social investment approach to become the next social policy paradigm. Some of these requirements are linked to the actual content and quality of policies. Here, the association with climate change mitigation policies provides an interesting opening with the focus on sustainable growth. It appears that climate policies have many joint interests with the social investment perspective. Not only do they naturally share a strong long-term perspective which has been captured by the notion of 'sustainable development', they also cannot be addressed within a neoliberal paradigm. It might be that in this context we can find a new political coalition to carry the social investment agenda.

Is there a future for social investment? This book has explicitly questioned the notion that European welfare states have been converted into social investment welfare states. First, there appears to be no universal trend towards a social investment welfare state in terms of ongoing reform work. Second, the different contributions to this book have highlighted that while comprehensive and well-designed social investment policies do perform well in terms of achieving 'economic growth with more and better jobs and greater social cohesion, and respect for the environment', the notion of social investment has been used misleadingly to label policies that have no or too little social investment content and therefore much more limited positive impact.

However, even if we take the social investment approach seriously and engage in the kind of massive implementation of investment policies such a strategy calls for, a number of policy dilemmas might still appear in front of us. If not properly designed and packaged, social investment policies might threaten to crowd out redistributive antipoverty policies of different kinds, might withdraw vital demand for consumption in the post-crisis, and might threaten the restoration of a balance in the public finances. Here, it is important to emphasise that the notion of social investment warrants us to think beyond the traditional human capital framework when it comes to both policy instruments and goals. This also requires us to rethink the usual time horizon for policy making as this is a precondition for sustainable development. At the same time, the role of the state as social investor is confronted with the process of globalisation, both in terms of its capacity to raise resources and in terms of opening up its welfare system to immigrants. This requires more, not less, European cooperation and global governance, and eventually the development of truly transnational protection systems. At any rate, properly designed social investment policies have the potential to promote social inclusion and social capital as well as social cohesion. These are assets modern societies have good reasons to nurture in order to promote societal progress that is sustainable, recognising the interdependencies of the economic, environmental, political and social aspects of it.

References

Blair, T. and Schröder, G. (2000) 'Europe: the third way/die NeueMitte', in B. Hombach (ed.) *The Politics of the New Centre.* Oxford: Blackwell, pp. 157–77.

Brundtland Commission (1987) *Our Common Future*. Oxford: Oxford University Press.

Cantillon, B. (2010) 'Disambiguating Lisbon. Growth, employment and social inclusion in the Investment State', CSB Working Paper No. 10/07.

Eichhorst, W. and Marx, P. (forthcoming) 'Whatever Works: Dualization and the Service Economy in Bismarckian Welfare States', in P. Emmeneger, S. Haüsermann, B. Palier and M. Seeleib-Kaiser (eds) *The Age of Dualization. Structures, Policies, Politics.* Oxford: Oxford University Press.

Emmeneger, P. and Cajera, R. (forthcoming) 'From Dilemma to Dualization: Social and Migration Policies in the Reluctant Countries of Immigration', in P. Emmeneger, S. Haüsermann, B. Palier and M. Seeleib-Kaiser (eds) *The Age of Dualization. Structures, Policies, Politics.* Oxford: Oxford University Press.

Esping-Andersen, G. (2005) 'Indicators and social accounting for 21st century social policy', in OECD, *Statistics, Knowledge and Policy. Key Indicators to Inform Decision Making*. Paris: OECD, pp. 176–85.

Esping-Andersen, G., Gallie, D., Hemerijck, A. and Myles, J. (2002) *Why We Need a New Welfare State*. Oxford: Oxford University Press.

European Commission (2009) *New Skills for New Jobs. Anticipating and Matching Labour Market and Skills Needs.* Luxembourg: Office for Official Publications of the European Communities.

European Commission (2010) 'New skills for new jobs: action now', a report by the Expert Group on New skills for new jobs prepared for the European Commission.

Guillen, A. and Dahl, S.-A. (2009) *Quality of Work in the European Union, Concept, Data and Debates in a Transnational Perspective*. Brussels: Peter Lang.

Hudson, J. and Kühner, S. (2009) 'Towards productive welfare? A comparative analysis of 23 OECD countries', *Journal of European Social Policy*, 19 (1), 34–46.

Jenson, J. (2009) 'Lost in translation: The social investment perspective and gender equality', *Social Politics*, 16 (4), 446–83.

Jobert, B. (2002) 'Une troisième voie très britannique. Giddens et l'Etat-providence', *Revue Française de Sociologie*, 43 (2), 407–22.

Lindh, T. and Palme, J. (eds) (2006) *Sustainable Policies in an Ageing Europe*. Stockholm: Institute for Futures Studies, Research Report Series, Society and the Future No. 3.

McIntosh, S. (2004) 'Skills and unemployment', in D. Gallie (ed.) *Resisting Marginalization: Unemployment Experience and Social Policy in the European Union*. Oxford: Oxford University Press, pp. 140–68.

Palier, B. (ed.) (2010) *A Long Goodbye to Bismarck. The Politics of Welfare Reformers in Continental Europe.* Amsterdam: Amsterdam University Press.

Palier, B. and Thelen, K. (2010) 'Institutionalizing dualism: complementarities and change in France and Germany', *Politics & Society*, 38 (1), 119–48.

Palme, J., Nelson, K., Sjöberg, O. and Minas, R. (2009) *European Social Models, Protection and Inclusion.* Stockholm: Institute for Futures Studies, Research Report 2009/1.

Sjöberg, O., Palme, J. and Carroll, E. (2010) 'Unemployment insurance', in F. Castles, S. Leibfried, J. Lewis, H. Obinger and C. Pierson (eds) *Oxford Handbook of Comparative Welfare States.* Oxford: Oxford University Press, pp. 420–34.

Stiglitz, J., Sen, A. and Fitoussi, J.-P. (2009) *Report by the Commission on the Measurement of Economic Performance and Social Progress.* www.stiglitz-sen-fitoussi.fr

Streeck, W. and Thelen, K. (eds) (2005) *Beyond Continuity. Institutional Change in Advanced Political Economies.* Oxford: Oxford University Press.

Wilkinson, R. and Pickett, K. (2009) *The Spirit Level: Why More Equal Societies Almost Always Do Better.* London: Allen Lane.

Index